Robert Henryson

THE COMPLETE WORKS

MIDDLE ENGLISH TEXTS SERIES

The Middle English Texts Series is designed for classroom use. Its goal is to make available to teachers, scholars, and students texts that occupy an important place in the literary and cultural canon but have not been readily available in student editions. The series does not include those authors, such as Chaucer, Langland, or Malory, whose English works are normally in print in good student editions. The focus is, instead, upon Middle English literature adjacent to those authors that teachers need in compiling the syllabuses they wish to teach. The editions maintain the linguistic integrity of the original work but within the parameters of modern reading conventions. The texts are printed in the modern alphabet and follow the practices of modern capitalization, word formation, and punctuation. Manuscript abbreviations are silently expanded, and *u/v* and *j/i* spellings are regularized according to modern orthography. Yogh (ȝ) is transcribed as *g*, *gh*, *y*, or *s*, according to the sound in Modern English spelling to which it corresponds; thorn (þ) and eth (ð) are transcribed as *th*. Distinction between the second person pronoun and the definite article is made by spelling the one *thee* and the other *the*, and final *-e* that receives full syllabic value is accented (e.g., *charité*). Hard words, difficult phrases, and unusual idioms are glossed either in the right margin or at the foot of the page. Explanatory and textual notes appear at the end of the text, often along with a glossary. The editions include short introductions on the history of the work, its merits and points of topical interest, and brief working bibliographies.

This series is published in association with the University of Rochester.

Medieval Institute Publications is a program of
The Medieval Institute, College of Arts and Sciences

 WESTERN MICHIGAN UNIVERSITY

Robert Henryson

THE COMPLETE WORKS

Edited by
David J. Parkinson

TEAMS • Middle English Texts Series

MEDIEVAL INSTITUTE PUBLICATIONS
Western Michigan University
Kalamazoo

Library of Congress Cataloging-in-Publication Data

Henryson, Robert, 1430?-1506?
[Poems]
The complete works / Robert Henryson ; edited by David J. Parkinson.
p. cm. -- (Middle English texts series)
Includes bibliographical references.
ISBN 978-1-58044-139-1 (paperbound : alk. paper)
1. Aesop's fables--Adaptations. 2. Cressida (Fictitious character)--Poetry. 3. Eurydice
(Greek mythology)--Poetry. 4. Orpheus (Greek mythology)--Poetry. 5. English
poetry--Middle English, 1100-1500. I. Parkinson, David John, 1956- II. Title.
PR1990.H4A17 2011
821'.2--dc22
2008012762

ISBN 978-1-58044-139-1

P 5 4 3 2 1

CONTENTS

PREFACE

Mindful of the authority of Fox's standard edition and the availability of Kindrick and Bixby's students' edition, an editor of Henryson in the early twenty-first century can justify taking up the project anew by noting the progress made during recent decades in scholarship on these poems: for example, Wheatley's study of Henryson's *Fables* in the light of medieval commentaries on Aesop, Kelly's discussion of *The Testament of Cresseid* as a medieval tragedy, or Riddy's trenchant rereading of Cresseid and her poet. Such is the excellence of much that has been written recently about the text and interpretation of these poems that it has seemed worthwhile to take stock afresh of Henryson studies. Though this edition does not contribute many new readings to the texts of Henryson's poems, it nevertheless reflects and often embodies the findings of the past three decades. As a result, its text of the *Fables* gives new prominence to the variant readings in the Bannatyne Manuscript; its *Testament of Cresseid* stays closer to the text of the Charteris print than Fox's; in perhaps its most obvious innovation, this edition of *Orpheus and Eurydice* is based throughout on the most complete text, that of the Bannatyne Manuscript. To summarize the editorial principles that emerge cumulatively through what follows, the harder readings in Thynne's text of the *Testament* represent an early sixteenth-century English poetic diction that is unlikely to reflect Henryson's fifteenth-century Scots usages; and in a greater number of instances than Fox allowed, the modernizing tendency in the clear, consistent Bassandyne print of the *Fables* has been set aside in favor of the more error-prone but conservative Bannatyne Manuscript. Overall, the introduction, text, and notes that follow are designed to reflect significant recent developments, but necessarily they are founded on older work: without the precedent of Kindrick's edition, this one would have been much harder to envision; without Fox's edition, it would have been vastly poorer.

In many respects, this edition embodies the practices of METS, the series to which it is a contribution. An introduction provides a discussion of the author and the texts; a bibliography identifies the standard and recent publications on the texts, biography, sources, and criticism of Henryson. One element of the introduction may seem anomalous in its length and detail: given the need to identify the particular features of Middle Scots as distinct from Middle English, more attention, if still necessarily preliminary, is paid to language than is the practice elsewhere in this series; a select glossary of recurrent terms also appears at the end of the volume. To reinforce the information provided in that glossary and to assist the reader with unique occurrences of potentially difficult words, each of the poems in this edition is equipped with abundant marginal glosses. Though the reader well-versed in Middle Scots may find these glosses excessive and redundant, each poem has been treated as if it is the one with which the reader is commencing.

The Textual Notes are selective, with emphasis on the key witnesses and the places at which it has been considered necessary to adopt a reading from a witness other than the base text. Some attention is given to those places where the reading of selected recent editors (notably Fox but also Burrow and Bawcutt and Riddy) differs from the one selected here, but the discussion of specific problems is perforce concisely exemplary rather than exhaustive.

Some of the prominent literary and historical contexts for the poems are identified in the Explanatory Notes. Thus Henryson's legal and educational concerns are foregrounded, with emphasis, for example, on the relation between the law and literature in fifteenth-century Scotland. Attention is also paid to the vernacular traditions of which Henryson is mindful: earlier Scots literature, including Barbour's *Bruce*, the Scots *Legends of the Saints*, and Sir Gilbert Hay's writings; the alliterative tradition continuing to flourish in fifteenth-century Scotland with Richard Holland's *The Buke of the Howlat* as well as the anonymous *Rauf Coilyear* and *Golagros and Gawane*; and the prestigious example of Chaucer and other Middle English poets, Gower and Lydgate among them. Discussion of later Scots poets' allusions to specific passages in Henryson's poems is, necessarily, selectively representative; much work remains to be done on the sixteenth-century reception of Henryson in Scotland and England. Finally, some passages scrutinized in the recent critical discourse on Henryson receive comment upon their key interpretations.

In the course of this project, debts have been incurred that cannot adequately be acknowledged here. The editor thanks Joseph Marshall, senior curator of the Rare Book Collections of the National Library of Scotland, for providing a photofacsimile reproduction of the Bassandyne print and offering advice about its fair use. Also to be thanked are the assistant editor of METS, John H. Chandler, and the managing editor of Medieval Institute Publications, Patricia Hollahan, who expertly readied the text of the edition for publication and in the process caught many an error. I am also grateful to my colleague Len Findlay, who has supported this project with unfailing enthusiasm. Three people have done much to make this book helpful, clear, and informative. Russell Peck, the general editor of the series in which this volume appears, has provided a calming voice of wise advice and encouragement at moments of perplexity; his expeditious, substantial, deeply perceptive comments have led to significant improvements at every turn. Without the support of Alasdair MacDonald (Rijksuniversiteit Groningen), this project would never have been undertaken; without his alert, deeply learned, refreshingly witty comments on every page, the outcome would have been much the poorer. My wife Heather has read, reread, and discussed every line that follows, and has saved every reader of this book from countless blurs and infelicities. The mistakes that remain are entirely due to the editor's inattention and stubbornness. It is to be hoped that this edition will contribute to its readers' delight in and illumination by the poems herein; for the editor, the shared, intense experience of these poems has been an extraordinary privilege.

 **INTRODUCTION**

"MASTER ROBERT HENRYSON"

Writing in or shortly after 1505, the Scottish poet William Dunbar surveyed the
depredations of Death among all classes of mortals, not least among poets, *makaris*, in
Scotland. Near the end of the roll call of the poets Death has taken appears the following
couplet:

> In Dunfermelyne he has done roune   *has finished whispering*
> With maister Robert Henrisoun.
> (*Timor mortis conturbat me*, lines 81–82)

Henryson dies from having been whispered to; it is as if Death has appeared to him in the
temptingly conspiratorial guise of the fox in more than one fable (e.g., line 3021); or else
like the lepers gossiping in undertones while they watch Troilus give gold and jewels to
Cresseid (*Testament*, line 521); or like one of the importunate tale-bearers who swarm around
"ane nobill lord" in *Against Hasty Credence* (line 17). The author of vivid exemplary tales about
such whispering, Henryson is now depicted by his poetic successor William Dunbar, a no-
less-spirited author of tales about secret confabulations; and Dunbar depicts Henryson,
allusively, as a protagonist in the tiny fable of his demise. Dunbar briefly portrays the figure
of the older poet's death in terms of the far more valuable kernel of the works — and thus
acknowledges Henryson's main mode of signification in the *Fables*.

Henryson's vision in the *Fables* of "maister Esope, poet lawriate" (line 1337), gracious,
moral, and wise, possibly represents his ideal of the poet in the work; but depictions of both
Aesop and Henryson were to decline from such ideals in ensuing generations.[1] It is the role
of the rough-tongued debunker of women's lore that Henryson plays in the "merry, though
somewhat unsavory" anecdote the seventeenth-century Latin translator of *The Testament of
Cresseid* preserves about the poet's death. Sir Francis Kynaston's tale about the aged, sick
poet's rebuffing an old woman's proffered remedy for diarrhea renders Henryson comparable
to other wise fools featured in sixteenth-century "merry tales," among them "Esope the
Phrygian," the "dyfformed and euylle shapen . . . dombe" churl who "had a grete wytte."[2]
The sixteenth-century prints, it might be recalled, give Henryson's *Fables* the title *Morall
Fabillis of Esope the Phrygian*.

Dunbar's lines provide the earliest basis for an association between Henryson and
Dunfermline. The later sixteenth-century prints of the *Fables* amplify Dunbar in styling the

---

[1] See Patterson, *Fables of Power*, p. 32.

[2] Fox, *Poems*, p. xiv; Lenaghan, *Caxton's Aesop*, p. 27. For Kynaston's tale, see the Appendix.

1

author "schoolmaster of Dunfermline." To judge from the slender evidence, Henryson was a "maister" in two senses: a schoolmaster and a Master of Arts, and therefore a clerk of some standing. Another Scottish poet of the early sixteenth century, Gavin Douglas, refers to "Mastir Robert Hendirson" and his "New Orpheus" (*Eneados* 1.19, note 13). In his manuscript anthology of poems (discussed below), George Bannatyne regularly precedes "Robert Henrysone" with the title *magister*. A few generations after Henryson's death, the appellation has become integral to his authorship.

Henryson's first modern editor, David Laing, noted that in 1462 a Robert Henryson graduated as Master of Arts and Bachelor of canon law at the newly-founded (1451) University of Glasgow.[3] Glasgow had important connections to European centers for legal study, specifically Bologna, Ravenna, and Louvain. As a student in Louvain in the 1430s, William Elphinstone senior (the first dean of the Glasgow Faculty of Arts) had studied civil (Roman) law and its best current scholastic commentaries.[4] In the list of those graduating from Elphinstone's faculty, Henryson was called "venerabilis vir" ("a man of age" is the poet's wording — see *Fables*, line 1013n; *Testament*, line 29n), a conventional phrase indicating seniority. To have been "venerabilis" in 1462, Henryson would certainly have reached seventy by the end of the century — ripe for a quiet confabulation or perhaps a deathbed jest.

Documentary evidence places a Master Robert Henryson as a notary and teacher at Dunfermline in 1477–78: three legal deeds include that name in the list of witnesses.[5] In Scotland, the notary public was a figure of some importance in the local administration of the church, one who recorded transactions "in various fields of law," including resignations, leases, marriages, bonds of alliance, and even "many civil actions."[6] The connection between notary public and "Scolemaister," as the sixteenth-century prints of the *Fables* term Henryson, was not unusual in late medieval Scotland.[7] Though efforts continue to be made to enlarge the biographical scope by means of extrapolation and surmise, the firmer details remain as Laing presented them in 1865. Relying heavily on the consistencies between the few documentary scraps that may pertain to the poet who wrote the *Fables* and *The Testament of Cresseid* and whose death Dunbar lamented, one is left with the faint traces of a biography. Following them, one glimpses a Henryson born about 1430 and dead by about 1500 who was a scholar in the arts and law, who worked as a notary public and schoolmaster in late fifteenth-century Dunfermline, a royal burgh on the north shore of the Firth of Forth. His home was a Scottish town of no great size but nevertheless distinguished by its Benedictine abbey, a resting place of kings and queens, among them Robert the Bruce and St. Margaret of Scotland.

To turn to the poems themselves is to perceive clearer, fuller indications of persistent values and concerns. Consider, for example, the evidence therein of the circulation and study of books, of which a partial list would include the following: the law (Gratian, *Regiam Majestatem*); the curriculum of a "song school" offering training in church music and an introduction to the medieval curriculum, principally in grammar and rhetoric (*Disticha Catonis*; *Disciplina clericalis*; Aesop, latterly in print; *Graecismus*); more advanced authors and

---

[3] Laing, *Poems and Fables*, p. xii; Fox, *Poems*, p. xiii.

[4] Walker, *Legal History*, pp. 281, 283.

[5] Laing, *Poems and Fables*, pp. xiii–xiv; Fox, *Poems*, p. xiii.

[6] Walker, *Legal History*, p. 276.

[7] Durkan, "Education in the Century of the Reformation," p. 157; Lyall, "Structure," p. 91.

their commentators (Boethius and Nicholas Trivet); Chaucer and Chaucerians (manuscript transmission of whose works in fifteenth-century Scotland is exemplified by the *Kingis Quair* manuscript, Bodley Arch. Selden. B. 24);[8] alliterative verse; religious and moral lyric along the lines of the Vernon Manuscript. The poems ascribed to Henryson consistently uphold a rhetorical ideal of brevity replete with significance. This ideal is epitomized by the literary excellence ascribed to the eloquent god Mercury in *The Testament of Cresseid*, who could "In breif sermone ane pregnant sentence wryte" (line 270). Further, his verse consistently maintains a clear metrical regularity with subtly meaningful gradations of stress, the stresses often strengthened with regular, at times almost structural, alliteration. Henryson's poems involve an ongoing concern with the function of poetry itself as a blend of truth and fiction in a world in which falsehood is the wellspring of corruption; in operation, the figure of the poet may be analogous to the foxes he repeatedly places at the center of his narratives. Hence arises an abiding concern about the abuses of the natural capacity for playful imitation, for selfish ends.

Necessary, delightful, troubling mixtures pervade these poems: the one to which Henryson returns repeatedly is the fundamental connection between body and soul and the conflict between them. Here is the connection that ensures Henryson's abiding interest in allegory — he is less a humanist "of the philological 'new learning' which was beginning to flourish in Italy in his day" than a poet who, "like Chaucer, belongs to an older and wider tradition of 'medieval humanism,' which prizes the works of the ancient writers and delights in their *sentence* and *humanitas*."[9] But there is something adventurously original about the energy with which allegory is explored in his poems.[10] Indeed, the first of the *Fables* in the earliest extant Scottish prints, *The Cock and the Jasp*, offers what A. C. Spearing has called an "allegory of allegorical interpretation," and the phrase, with its indications of parallels expanding out into existence and down into the parts of the literary work, reverberates.[11] From this perspective, Dunbar's miniature fable about Death and the allegorical fabulist takes on the strikingly apposite extended perspective, frame within frame, of a *mise en abyme*.

TEXTS

1. The Principal Witnesses

Before a preliminary description of each of the main early manuscripts and prints of poems ascribed to Robert Henryson, a few comments may be helpful regarding the presentation of the titles and indications of authorship, as well as the editions and facsimiles on which the present text is based. For the titles as also through the text of the poems, the capitalization is adjusted towards present-day practice, and a consistently light punctuation is provided. The list of manuscripts and prints is arranged chronologically. Though each transcription has been checked against more recent facsimiles and transcriptions, this edition, like Fox's, is "heavily indebted" to G. Gregory Smith's standard parallel-text edition,

---

[8] Edwards and Boffey, "Introduction," pp. 18–21.

[9] Gray, *Selected Poems of Henryson and Dunbar*, p. 365.

[10] Rutledge, "Henryson's *Orpheus*," p. 407.

[11] Spearing, *Medieval to Renaissance*, p. 194.

on which most of the following texts are based;[12] a partial exception to this line of descent involves the readings from the Asloan Manuscript, which Smith was not able to consult directly and for which William A. Craigie's diplomatic edition, cited below, has been the principal source. An important textual witness not represented in Smith's edition is the Bassandyne print of the *Fables*, the source of the form of the text in which the edition of the *Fables* is presented here.

a. The Chepman and Myllar Prints (Cm)

The so-called Chepman and Myllar Prints comprise the earliest extant products of the Scottish press, following James IV's charter (1507) granting Walter Chepman and Andro Myllar exclusive rights to print books in his realm. Their earliest extant books are the so-called Chepman and Myllar Prints (1508; Mapstone, ed.). Each of the nine prints is small, barely six inches tall; the longest is no more than twenty-three leaves long. The editors of the National Library of Scotland's online facsimile of these prints note that "The printing of vernacular texts does not come early in most countries' printing"; giving priority to relatively short pieces of literature provided the opportunity to rehearse procedures before tackling weightier projects but also anticipated a demand for copies of just such pieces.

i. *Heire begynnis the traitie of Orpheus kyng and how he yeid to hewyn and to hel to seik his quene And ane othir ballad in the lattir end.* [Edinburgh:] *Walterus Chepman* [and Andro Myllar, April, 1508.]

Below the title proper is inscribed in a sixteenth-century cursive hand, "Memento homo quod cinis es et in cinerem Reverter*is*" ("Remember, O man, that thou art ash and into ash shall return"),[13] the opening line of a moral ballade by William Dunbar; on the verso of the title leaf, in a more formal hand, appears the single word "Orpheus." *Orpheus* (collation: [a6]b6) lacks refinements of presentation: stanzas tend to run across page breaks; no indication of authorship is provided; apart from the indication of the beginning of the *Moralitas*, no headings are provided; no colophon appears. The "othir ballad" mentioned in the title is "Want of Wise Men" (*NIMEV* 2139; also in the Bannatyne Manuscript, folio 78r), which some editors ascribe to Henryson by virtue of its inclusion in the *Orpheus* tract; given the printers' practice of adding makeweight lyrics at the end of longer works regardless of authorship, this inclusion does not guarantee Henryson's authorship of "Want of Wise Men." Accordingly, this "othir ballad" is excluded from this edition.

ii. ["Praise of Age," beginning thus:] "Wythin a garth, under a rede rosere."

This is the second item in the fragmentary print of *The Flyting of Dunbar and Kennedie* [Edinburgh: Chepman and Myllar, 1508]. Chepman and Myllar provide no indication of authorship.

b. The Makculloch Manuscript, Edinburgh University Library, MS. Laing III.149 (Mk)

Texts by Henryson occupy previously empty space in this late fifteenth-century manuscript, which mainly consists of notes in Latin on the subject of logic, by Magnus Makculloch, a Scots student at Louvain in 1477 who subsequently undertook scribal duties.[14]

---

[12] Fox, *Poems*, p. xxvii.

[13] For comment, see Bawcutt, *Poems of William Dunbar*, 2:360.

[14] Stevenson, *Pieces from the Makculloch and the Gray MSS*, pp. xiv–xv; Borland, *Descriptive Catalogue*, pp. 291–96; Edwards and Boffey,"Introduction," p. 9n15.

Some time after these notes were inscribed, the *Prologue* to the *Fables* and *The Cock and the Jasp* were written on the front flyleaves; less marginal, *The Praise of Age* appears (fol. 87r) in a small sequence of moral and religious lyrics. The poems are written in a different hand, possibly that of John Purde, a priest whose signature in the manuscript indicates that he was an early owner; a conjectural date for these Henryson texts is "early sixteenth century."[15]

c. The Gray Manuscript, National Library of Scotland, Advocates' MS 34.7.3 (G)

James Gray (d. 1505), secretary to William Schevez (archbishop of St. Andrews; died 1497) was one of the scribes involved in the compilation of this manuscript, which contains the unique copy of *The Annunciation*, ascribed "quod R. Henrisoun" (fols. 70r–71v). A notary public and Master of Arts, Gray is comparable to Henryson; Edwards and Boffey review his scribal activities.[16] Though much of this compilation is in Latin, six poems in Scots and English appear at various points in the sequence;[17] with its long stanza, demandingly constrained rhyme, and pervasive alliteration, *The Annunciation* typifies a stylistic tendency in these vernacular poems.[18] Though attempts have been made to narrow the date of this text of *The Annunciation*, it is probably safest to follow Fox with the approximation 1503–32.[19]

d. The Asloan Manuscript, National Library of Scotland, MS 16500 (A)

John Asloan was a notary public active in Edinburgh 1499–1530; his scribal activity has been identified in other manuscripts, e.g., Bodleian Library, MS Douce 148, and National Library of Scotland Advocates' MS 19.2.3. The manuscript bearing his name can be dated 1515–25, though its manner of construction out of more or less independent booklets, or "fascicles," leaves open the possibility that parts were composed earlier.[20] Now consisting of 300 leaves, the Asloan Manuscript is a fraction of its original size, with many leaves lost; the scribe's Table of Contents lists 71 items, of which 34 no longer exist.[21] Among the lost are *The Testament of Cresseid*, "Master Robert Hendersonnis Dreme On Fut by Forth" (of which no copy survives), and six of the *Fables*, in the following order: *The Paddock and the Mouse, The Preaching of the Swallow, The Lion and the Mouse, The Cock and the Fox, The Fox and the Wolf*, and *The Trial of the Fox*. The one fable that survives in the depleted Asloan Manuscript, *The Two Mice*, was inscribed five poems after *The Trial of the Fox*, a fact which suggests that at this stage in the compilation, the scribe was simply adding items as they became available.[22] Since Asloan does not usually give authors' names in this table, it is possible that other poems by Henryson are included among the other lost items. In addition to "The Tale of the Uplandis Mous and the Borowstoun Mous" (*The Two Mice*; fols. 236r–240r), the Asloan Manuscript contains "The Buke of Schir Orpheus and Erudices" (*Orpheus*; fols. 247–256). Working in part with the relation between the Chepman and Myllar and Asloan texts of

---

[15] Fox, *Poems*, p. xli.

[16] Edwards and Boffey, "Introduction," p. 9.

[17] Stevenson, *Pieces from the Makculloch and the Gray MSS*, pp. xvi–xvii, 39–56.

[18] Fein, "Twelve-Line Stanza Forms," p. 388.

[19] Fox, *Poems*, p. 427.

[20] Cunningham, "Asloan Manuscript," pp. 129–31; Bawcutt, *Poems of William Dunbar*, 1:5–6.

[21] Cunningham, "Asloan Manuscript," pp. 108–16.

[22] Greentree, *Reader*, p. 99.

Orpheus, Fox argues that Asloan often copied his texts from printed editions; Chepman and Myllar may conceivably have published editions of the *Testament* and the *Fables*.[23]

e. *The Testament of Creseyde. The Workes of Geffray Chaucer Newly Printed With Dyvers Workes Whiche Were Never in Print Before, as in the table more playnly dothe appere.* Fols. 219r–222v. Ed. William Thynne. London: Godfray, 1532. (T)

Thynne's is the earliest text of the *Testament* and thus fundamental to an edition of the poem. In this large, important collection, *The Testament of Creseyde* follows *Troilus and Criseyde*, at the end of which appears the following note: "Thus endeth the fyfth and laste booke of Troylus, and here foloweth the pyteful and dolorous testament of fayre Creseyde" (fol. 219r). Thynne's inclusion of the *Testament* in his collection of Chaucer seems to have been an afterthought, with the four leaves on which the poem appears having been inserted in place of a cancelled leaf containing on the recto side the last stanzas and colophon of *Troilus* and on the verso the title of *The Legend of Good Women*, the work that follows.[24] To enhance the smoothness of this cancellation, the text of the *Testament* has been translated from Scots into English. However, Thynne's editing is not entirely successful: most glaringly, the stanzas of the "Complaynt of Creseyde" are irregular; the first two stanzas contain nine lines, the third eight, the fourth five, the fifth six, and the sixth and seventh eight. With increasing frequency of error, subsequent English editions of Chaucer's *Works* include the *Testament*; this descent ensures that a distinctively English tradition of reading the *Testament* as if it were Chaucer's continues through the sixteenth and seventeenth centuries.

f. The Bannatyne Manuscript, National Library of Scotland Advocates' 1.1.6 (Bd and B)

This manuscript, the most celebrated Scottish literary anthology manuscript, was compiled by an amateur scribe, the young George Bannatyne, an Edinburgh merchant in his early twenties. Bannatyne indicates that he wrote the manuscript "in tyme of pest," 1568; traces of the date "1566" can be detected in the heading to the final section of his vast compilation. The Bannatyne Manuscript in fact consists of two collections. The so-called Draft Manuscript (Bd) of 29 leaves (numbered as 58 pages) includes five shorter poems later editors have attributed to Henryson: *The Abbey Walk, The Praise of Age, Ane Prayer for the Pest, The Ressoning betwix Aige and Yowth*, and *The Ressoning betwix Deth and Man*; of these five, only *The Praise of Age* and *The Ressoning betwix Aige and Yowth* are explicitly identified as the poet's. The manuscript proper, a substantial 375 leaves, is organized into five parts, each with its distinct theme: (1) "Godis gloir and ouir salvatioun" (including *Ane Prayer for the Pest*); (2) "ballatis full of wisdom and moralitie" (including *The Abbey Walk, Against Hasty Credence, The Ressoning betwix Aige and Yowth, The Ressoning betwix Deth and Man, The Praise of Age*, and — ascribed to Patrick Johnston — *The Thre Deid Pollis*); (3) "ballettis mirry" (including *Sum Practysis of Medecyne*); (4) "ballatis of luve" (including *The Garmont of Gud Ladeis*).[25]

Bannatyne commences the fifth part of his anthology with the following heading: "Heir follows the fyift pairt of this buik contenyng the Fabillis of Esop with divers uthir fabillis and poeticall workis, maid and compyld be divers lernit men, 156[6]8" (fol. 298r), and diversity is indeed key to the sequence of verse tales following: *The Preaching of the Swallow*, Sir Richard

---

[23] Fox, *Poems*, p. xxxix; Cunningham, "Asloan Manuscript," p. 111.

[24] Fox, *Poems*, p. xcv.

[25] Fox, *Poems*, p. xxxvi.

Holland's *The Buke of the Howlat*, *The Cock and the Fox*, *The Fox and the Wolf*, *The Trial of the Fox*, *Orpheus*, *The Bludy Serk*, the *Prologue* to the *Fables*, *The Cock and the Jasp*, *The Paddock and the Mouse*, *The Two Mice*, *The Sheep and the Dog*, *The Wolf and the Lamb*, *The Lion and the Mouse*, and William Dunbar's *The Thistle and the Rose* and *The Golden Targe*.[26] Apart from its inclusion of poems by Henryson and others that are not part of the *Fables*, this sequence is notable for its omission of three fables that feature consistently in the early prints of the work: *The Fox, the Wolf, and the Cadger*; *The Fox, the Wolf, and the Husbandman*; and *The Wolf and the Wether*. Bannatyne's sequence of the ten fables most firmly associated with Henryson's work diverges from the order in which they are presented in the early prints and in which they also appear in this edition. Subject to ongoing debate as Bannatyne's selection and sequence are, the importance of this manuscript as a witness to readings and whole poems nowhere else attested is undeniable. Despite a generally high rate of substitutions — typically synonyms for functional adverbs, prepositions, and determiners — Bannatyne preserves readings that can often be explained as having been less affected by the pressures that the printers complied with, to modernize archaic language and provide Protestant revisions for allusions to religious beliefs and practices discredited by the Reformation.[27] One of Bannatyne's most significant contributions to Henryson's poems is his preservation of the sole extant texts of several of the shorter poems, *Robene and Makyne* among them; as well, Bannatyne provides the fullest version of the *Moralitas* to *Orpheus*.

g. The Maitland Folio, Cambridge, Pepys Library, Magdalene College, MS 2553 (Mf)

The Maitland Folio Manuscript is a literary anthology, comprising 366 pages (numbered thus), compiled by various scribes 1570–86 in and for the household of the prominent courtier and writer Sir Richard Maitland of Lethington.[28] Featuring many poems by Sir Richard himself, the Maitland Folio also includes Henryson's *The Abbey Walk*, *Against Hasty Credence*, *The Ressoning betwix Aige and Yowth*, and (ascribed here to the poet) *The Thre Deid Pollis*.

h. *The Morall Fabillis of Esope the Phrygian, Compylit in Eloquent, and Ornate Scottis Meter, be Maister Robert Henrisone, Scholemaister of Dunfermeling. . . . Newlie Imprentit at Edinburgh, be Robert Lekprevik, at the Expensis of Henrie Charteris: and ar to be sauld in his Buith, on the North syde of the gait, abone the Throne. Anno Domini MDLXX.* [STC 185]. (C)

This is a small quarto edition (A–N4), 52 leaves long (without pagination); the only extant copy is in the British Library. At the end of this volume appears the following colophon, which dates the publication of the book a year earlier: *Imprentit at Edinburgh be Robert Lekprevik, at the Expensis of Henrie Charteris, the xvi. day of December, the yeir of God ane thousand, fyve hundreth, thre scoir, nyne yeiris.* Lekprevik and Charteris published Henryson's *Fables* during a period of civil war in Scotland, the supporters of the exiled former queen Mary Stewart against the Protestants upholding the sovereignty of her young son James. At about the same time, Lekprevik printed Hary's *Wallace* (STC 13149), John Barbour's *Bruce* (STC 1377.5), and the rowdy romance *Rauf Coilyear* (STC 5487); with another printer, Charteris reprinted the works of an important early sixteenth-century Scottish poet, Sir David

[26] Ritchie, *Bannatyne Manuscript*, 4:116–261.

[27] Bawcutt, *Poems of William Dunbar*, 1:14; Drexler, "Henryson's 'Ane Prayer for the Pest,'" p. 370n8.

[28] Knighton, *Catalogue of the Pepys Library*, pp. xi–xiii; Boffey, "Maitland."

Lyndsay (STC 15659). Civil conflict appears to have stimulated interest in asserting a canon of Scottish literature with a new ideal, evident in the title to this edition, of "textual fixity."[29]

i. *The Morall Fabillis of Esope the Phrygian, Compylit in Eloquent, and Ornate Scottis Meter, be M. Robert Henrisone, Scolmaister of Dunfermling. Newlie corectit, and Vendicat, fra mony Errouris, whilkis war oversene in the last prenting, quhair baith lynes, and haill Versis war left owt. . . . Edinburgh. Inprinted att Edinburgh be me Thomas Bassandyne, dwelland at the Nether Bow Anno 1571.* [STC 185.5]. (Bs)

This is an octavo print (A–G8, H4) of 60 leaves. The unique copy is in the National Library of Scotland; previously it was in the library at York Minster, where it eluded the attention of editors of Henryson before H. Harvey Wood. Two typefaces appear in this edition: roman for the preliminaries and *Moralitates*; and for the fables proper, an unusual facsimile of cursive handwriting called *civilité*, designed in 1557 by Robert Granjon, a printer in Lyon, France; the *civilité* type was associated "with a homely kind of religious and moral instruction, with folk tales, and with books for the young."[30] Bassandyne's edition includes two illustrations, both derived from Johann Zainer's widely influential set of wood-cuts for Aesop (Ulm, 1476–77):[31] one, the representation of a churlish, ugly Aesop that became iconic in the sixteenth-century prints of the *Fables*; the other, as in the Harleian Manuscript, of what Fox calls "a cock clawing unenthusiastically a very large jewel."[32] As in most editions since Wood's, the present text of the *Fables* is based on the form of the Bassandyne print.

j. The Harleian *Fables*, British Library, Harleian MS 3865 (H)

The title page to this manuscript reads "The Morall Fabillis of Esope Compylit be Maister Robert Henrisoun Scolmaister of Dunfermling; 1571"; this phrasing already indicates the dependence of the ensuing text of the *Fables* on the Scottish prints of that work, and Fox argues that the Bassandyne print is in fact the source;[33] occasionally, however, the Harleian Manuscript provides a reading superior to those attested elsewhere in the print tradition. The text is written in green ink. Two colored illustrations are included, on fol. 3v a drawing of a rooster that resembles the woodcut illustration to *The Cock and the Jasp* in the Bassandyne print, and on fol. 43v a more original drawing of a preacher, a tree with birds, and a hand holding a bird (the first and third of these motifs resemble ones included in the woodcut on the title page of the Bassandyne print).

k. The Ruthven Manuscript, Edinburgh University Library, MS Dc. 1. 43 (R)

In a text dated 1520–30, Gavin Douglas' *Eneados*, his Scots translation of Virgil's *Aeneid*, takes up most of this manuscript; following the *Eneados* is a text of the first three stanzas of *The Testament of Cresseid*, which Fox considers to be in the hand of Patrick, third Lord

---

[29] Lynch, *Scotland*, p. 260; Machan, *Textual Criticism*, p. 176.

[30] Carter and Vervliet, *Civilité Types*, p. 34; qtd. in Fox, *Poems*, p. li.

[31] Davies, "Tale of Two Aesops," pp. 260, 267.

[32] Fox, *Poems*, p. lii.

[33] Fox, *Poems*, pp. liii–liv.

Drummond (c. 1550–c. 1602) and which is dateable before 1581.[34] This text contributes one reading, *gart*, to line 6 of the edition.

l. *The Testament of Cresseid, Compylit be M. Robert Henrysone, Sculemaister in Dunfermeling.* . . . *Imprentit at Edinburgh be Henrie Charteris. M.D.XCIII.* [STC 13165]. (Ch)

This quarto (A–B4, C2), ten leaves long, presents the earliest extant complete Scottish text of *The Testament*, printed at least a century after Henryson wrote the poem. The only copy of this edition is in the British Library. The text proper is set almost entirely in blackletter type. No prefatory or concluding comment is provided. Beside each of the stanzas introducing the planetary gods, an early seventeenth-century reader has written the name of the appropriate god, with "Phebus" crossed out and "Sol" written above it, and Cynthia named "Luna." With the sorts of editorial interference that one might expect of a late sixteenth-century edition of a fifteenth-century poem, the Charteris print is nevertheless the best witness available for the text of *The Testament of Cresseid*; it provides the form on which the present edition of that work is based.

m. *The Morall Fab[illis] of Esope, the Phrygian. Compyled into Eloquent and or* [. . .] *Meeter, by Robert Henr*[. . .] *Schoole-*[. . .] *of Dumfermeline.* . . . *Newlie Revised and Corrected.* . . . *Edinb*[urgh: Andrew Hart, 1621; STC 186]. (Ht)

In this damaged octavo edition (A–F8) of 48 leaves, the Prologues and *Moralitates* are set in roman type, while the fables proper are set in black letter. No illustrations are included.

n. *The Testament of Cresseid. Compiled by Master Robert Henrison, Schoolemaster of Dumfermeling. Printed in the Year, 1663.* [Glasgow: Andrew Anderson, 1663; Wing H1476A]. (An)

Only a single copy of this octavo edition (A8, B4; twelve leaves) survives, in the library of Trinity College, Cambridge. It was probably by means of the square of ornaments on the title page that David Laing was able to identify Anderson as the (unnamed) printer.[35] The misplacement of four stanzas (lines 302–29) suggested to Fox that Anderson derived his text from an edition in which each page held 28 lines; the Charteris print usually has 33 lines. Heavily anglicized as it is, Anderson's text thus provides a late witness to readings not present in the Charteris print of the *Testament*. Most of the text of this print is set in blackletter type, with roman used for the titles and proper names.

2. Other Texts of Henryson's Poems

The following texts do not contribute readings to the present edition and thus do not feature in its textual notes.

a. The Book of the Dean of Lismore, National Library of Scotland, Advocates' MS 72.1.37 (dated 1512–29)

On a leaf inserted into this important anthology of Gaelic poetry appears a stanza from *The Testament of Cresseid* (lines 561–67) ascribed to "Bochas that wes full gud," evidently a mistaken ascription to the English version of Giovanni Boccaccio's *De casibus virorum illustrium*, John Lydgate's *Fall of Princes*. The same stanza appeared in another, closely related manu-

---

[34] Fox, *Poems*, p. xcvii.

[35] Laing, *Poems and Fables*, p. 259; Fox, *Poems*, p. xcv.

script, now lost.[36] Like those of Lydgate or Chaucer, the more widely distributed poems of Henryson were evidently regarded as a quarry for wise and witty pronouncements on topics of interest to special groups of readers.

b. *The Fabulous Tales of Esope the Phrygian, Every tale Moralized most Aptly to this Present Time, Worthy to be Read. . . Compiled Most Eloquently in Scottish Metre by Master Robert Henryson, and Now Lately Englished. . .* (London: Richard Smith, 1577; STC 186.5)[37]

In his introduction to this translation, Richard Smith describes the circumstances in which he discovered Henryson's *Fables*:

> There came unto my hande a Scottishe Pamphlet, of the Fabulous Tales of Esope, a worke, sir as I thinke, in that language wherin it was written, verie eloquent and full of great invention. And no doubt you shall finde some smatch thereof, although very rudely I have obscured the Authour, and having two yeres since turned it into Englishe, I have kept it unpublished, hoping som els of greater skill would not have let it lyen dead. But whether most men have that nation in derision for their hollowe hearts and ungratefull mindes to this countrey always had (a people verie subject to that infection) or thinking scorne of the Authour or first inventer, let it passe, as frivolous and vaine matter: yet in my conceite there is learning for all sorts of people worthy the memorie. (pp. ii–iii)

c. St. John's College, Cambridge, MS L.1

This manuscript is distinguished by an early fifteenth-century text of *Troilus and Criseyde*. The early seventeenth-century text of *The Testament of Cresseid* inscribed into this manuscript is derived from Speght's edition of Chaucer's *Works* (1602).[38]

d. Bodleian Library MS Add. C.287 (1639), pp. 475–509

Sir Francis Kynaston's Latin translation of *The Testament of Cresseid*, included stanza by stanza with a transcript of the English text of the poem from Speght's Chaucer (1598).[39] See the Appendix for an edition of Kynaston's introduction to his translation of the *Testament*.

3. Selected Editions, 1724–1987

This section has been restricted to those editions of particular historical significance which have contributed substantially to the text, reception, and interpretation of Henryson's poems.

a. Ramsay, Allan, ed. *The Ever Green: A Collection of Scots Poems Wrote by the Ingenious before 1600*. Edinburgh: Ruddiman, 1724

To Ramsay goes the credit for first reprinting a variety of poems from the Bannatyne Manuscript, including *Robene and Makyne*, *The Garmont of Gud Ladeis*, *The Two Mice*, and *The Lion and the Mouse*. As his version of the first stanza of *The Two Mice*, which he followed

---

[36] Mapstone, "*Testament*," p. 308.

[37] Fox, *Poems*, pp. lv–lvi.

[38] Fox, *Poems*, p. xcviii.

[39] Fox, *Poems*, p. xcviii.

Bannatyne in entitling *The Borrowstoun Mous, and the Landwart Mous*, Ramsay emended with an ear for the Scots of his own day and an eye to current political debates:

> Easop relates a Tale weil worth Renown,
> Of twa wie Myce, and they war Sisters deir,   *wee; were; dear*
> Of quhom the Elder dwelt in Borrowstoun,   *whom; burgh town*
> The Yunger scho wond upon Land weil neir,   *lived in the country very nearby*
> Richt solitair beneth the Buss and Breir,   *bush; brier*
> Quhyle on the Corns and Wraith of labouring Men,   *Sometimes; grain; anger(?)*
> As Outlaws do, scho maid an easy Fen. (1.144)   *made; living*

It should be noted that Ramsay's vision had less to do with textual authenticity than with recapturing an ethos: "The Spirit of Freedom that shines throw both the serious and comick Performances of our old Poets, appears of a Piece with that Love of Liberty that our antient Heroes contended for, and maintained Sword in Hand" (1.iv).

b. Dalrymple, David, Lord Hailes, ed. *Ancient Scottish Poems Published from the MS. of George Bannatyne, MDLXVIII*. Edinburgh: Murray and Cochran for Balfour, 1770. Pp.124–79

Lord Hailes turned to the Bannatyne Manuscript for his texts of Henryson: *Robene and Makyne, The Garmont of Gud Ladeis, The Abbey Walk, The Praise of Age, The Ressoning betwix Deth and Man, Against Hasty Credence*, and *The Thre Deid Pollis* (attributed to Patrick Johnston), *The Sheep and the Dog*, and *The Wolf and the Lamb*, and the *Moralitates* of four more fables. This editor disapproved of Ramsay's editorial license: "they who look in the *Evergreen* for the state of language and poetry among us during the sixteenth century, will be misled, or disappointed"; in contrast, in Hailes' edition, he declared, "no liberties in amending or interpolating have been taken" (p. viii).

c. Laing, David. *The Poems and Fables of Robert Henryson*. Edinburgh: William Patterson, 1865

Laing's is the first complete edition and represents an important advance in the modern understanding of the texts, authorship, language, and contexts of Henryson's poems. Laing achieves an unprecedented command of the documentary sources for the biography of the poet and the text of his works. Towards his edition of *The Abbey Walk*, for example, Laing includes a transcript of the first stanza of a now-lost print of the poem (Aberdeen: John Forbes, 1686); in the apparatus to his edition of the poem, Fox collates the readings from this transcript, none of which materially affect the text.[40]

d. Smith, G. Gregory, ed. *The Poems of Robert Henryson*. 3 vols. STS first series 55, 58, 64. Edinburgh: William Blackwood and Sons, 1906–14

Until Fox, Smith set the standard in scholarship for Henryson studies. Smith presents the texts of each of the principal witnesses: e.g., for *Orpheus* he gives the Cm and A texts in parallel, followed by the B text. The accuracy of these individual texts has ensured that this edition remains a convenient introduction to the textual analysis of Henryson's poems.

e. Wood, H. Harvey, ed. *The Poems and Fables of Robert Henryson*. 1933. Second ed. Edinburgh: Oliver and Boyd, 1958

---

[40] Fox, *Poems*, pp. 156–58, 434.

For decades the standard introduction to Henryson's poems, Wood's edition was the first to make use of the newly rediscovered Bassandyne print of the *Fables* (1.i, above).

f. Burrow, J. A., ed. *English Verse 1300–1500*. London: Longman, 1977. (Bu)

In this students' anthology, Burrow reconsiders Bannatyne's texts of Henryson's *Preaching of the Swallow* and *The Two Mice* and restores several readings from them, with illuminating comment.

g. Fox, Denton, ed. *The Poems of Robert Henryson*. Oxford: Clarendon, 1981. (F)

This is the standard modern edition, in which the textual evidence is subjected to an exemplary clarity and thoroughness of analysis. Largely conservative in the readings presented in the text proper, this edition features a commentary that provides subsequent editors with a wealth of evidence for further emendation. Fox's strategy in editing Henryson was to balance alert caution, comprehensive knowledge of the sources and language of the poems, and acumen of emendation.

h. Bawcutt, Priscilla, and Felicity Riddy, eds. *Longer Scottish Poems*. Vol. 1: *1375–1650*. Edinburgh: Scottish Academic Press, 1987. (Br)

The texts provided here of Henryson's *The Two Mice, The Lion and the Mouse, The Fox, the Wolf, and the Cadger*, and *The Testament of Cresseid* deserve careful study as judicious revaluations of several of the readings in Fox's edition.

HENRYSON'S LANGUAGE

1. Introduction

Henryson wrote in Scots — not Scots Gaelic, the language of western Scotland, especially north of the geographical divide marked by the estuaries of the rivers Forth and Clyde, but the variety of English emerging in the burghs of eastern and southern Scotland that became, in the fifteenth century, the official language of the realm. The language of Henryson's poems — and the theme of language in those poems — can reveal much about Scots at an important juncture in its history.

In its chronology, Scots does not coincide with English. "Middle English" refers to the phase in the history of the language from the twelfth to the fifteenth century, attested by an increasing wealth of documentary evidence and characterized by dialectalization, reduction of inflections, and a rise in borrowings, especially from French. "Middle Scots," in contrast, refers to a phase in which Scots, for which the recorded evidence before 1375 is fragmentary, comes into its own as a national standard for public discourse, increasingly consistent in its phonetic, grammatical, and lexical contrasts to English and upheld by a distinct literary canon. The Middle Scots period, for its part, thus coincides historically more with Early Modern than with Middle English. The umbrella term "Older Scots" covers linguistic developments 1375–1700; though "Middle Scots" refers to the last two-and-a-half centuries of this period, it pertains especially to the period of greatest distinctiveness and consistency, 1450–1550.[41]

---

[41] Aitken and Macafee, "History of Scots to 1700," §1.1.3 (p. xxxiv).

A continuous history of the Scots language begins with literature, specifically the *Brus*, a long historical poem about the deeds of Robert the Bruce and his lieutenants, especially Sir James Douglas, in the climactic phase of the wars against English suzerainty; this initiatory work was written in 1375 by John Barbour, archdeacon of Aberdeen and royal clerk. Barbour's Early Scots is not as distinct from northern Middle English as Henryson's Middle Scots. Decisive in the development of Early into Middle Scots is its selection as the language of the statutes of the Scottish Parliament, beginning 1424. Henryson's poetry thus coincides with and participates in the consolidation of Middle Scots as the official language of the realm of Scotland.

Though Gaelic was the dominant vernacular language throughout much of medieval Scotland, Scots arose along with the royal initiatives in the establishment of monasteries and especially towns. The long reign (1124–53) of David I began to turn the linguistic tide: son of the devout English princess Margaret (later canonized) and Malcolm III (victor over Macbeth), David founded burghs and monasteries (including, in 1128, Dunfermline Abbey),[42] invited noble and bourgeois immigrants from England, France, and Flanders, and introduced feudalism to Scotland. In the southeast, the new royal burghs came to include Roxburgh, Berwick, Haddington, Edinburgh, Linlithgow, Stirling, and in 1322, by a charter of Robert the Bruce, the burgh of Dunfermline on the north shore of the Firth of Forth. Small trading colonies at strategic locations, the burghs were defined by their boundaries and trading rights, but also by the blend of immigrants they attracted.

The burghs played a decisive role in the development of Scotland and the Scots language in particular. The dominant influence upon the urban lingua franca came, with many of the new merchants, from northeastern England. The product of generations of overlay between English and Old Norse, their language had arisen from a long coexistence between Viking settlers and the Northumbrian English. Other immigrants from the Low Countries and northern France brought their languages into the mix; with the number of burghs expanding, internal migration enhanced "the homogeneity of the dialect that spread as a result."[43] Given the polyglot, urban, mercantile origin and development of his language, it is all the more striking that Henryson depicts it as a "mother toung," "hamelie" and "rude" (*Fables*, lines 31, 36) — and that in the *Fables* he depicts the courtly aspirations of Middle Scots as delusory and corruptive.

2. Henryson's Vocabulary

The Middle Scots word-stock which Henryson worked, expanded, and refined had several distinct sources. To survey these offers a practical starting place for the study of Henryson's language.

a. Northumbrian Old English and northern Middle English

At this level, Henryson's Scots has much in common with the language of northern Middle English works such as *Cursor Mundi* or *The Awntyrs off Arthure*. Examples of this common northern word-stock include *barne* (*child*), *bud* (*bribe*), *daft* (*foolish*), *doolie* (*gloomy*), *dyke* (*embankment* or *ditch*), *greit* (*weep*), *hals* (*neck*), *kyith* (*exhibit*), *lowe* (*flame*), *lug* (*ear*), *rax* (*stretch*; *DOST rax* v.5; *OED rax* v.), *runkillit* (*wrinkled*), *thraf caikkis* ("tharf-cakes"), *thoill, thole*

---

[42] Whyte, *Scotland before the Industrial Revolution*, pp. 34–35.

[43] Aitken and Macafee, "History of Scots to 1700," §2.3.2 (p. xliv).

(*endure*), and *truker* (*trickster*). Predictably, the root vowels in Scots words of Old English origin differ from those in English, at times confusingly: thus the noun *bair* is not "bear" but "boar"; *bewis* is the plural form of *beuch*, "bough." In its pattern of retentiveness of words of Old English origin, Scots differs from English: *abone* (*above*), *lesum* (*proper*), *paynchis* (*entrails* as food; compare English *paunch*), *syis* (*times*; the fossilized plural form of *sithe*), *thig* (*beg*), *thrawin* (*twisted*); the limits of such retentiveness can be seen in *erdfast* ("securely founded"), Henryson's adjective for the country mouse's home (*Fables*, line 199), for which the six-teenth-century printers substituted the more common synonym *steidfast*.

b. Old Norse

So closely interrelated are Old Norse and Northumbrian Old English in the background to Older Scots that it is extremely difficult to apportion many words between these two principal sources. Words of Norse origin are deep-seated in the core vocabulary of Scots, as they are in northern English: ordinal numerals; common adverbs such as *thyne* (*thence*) and *syne* (*then, afterwards*); the adjectives *awin* (*own*), *donk* (*damp*, "dank"), *hair* (*hoary*), *na* (*no*, as in *Fables*, line 50 "Na mervell is"), *tait* (*energetic*), and *trig* (*nimble*); verbs such as *gar* (*command*; *compel*), possibly *glar* (*befoul*), *graith* (Henryson's *grathit* is the past participle: "arrayed"), *ken* (*know, recognize*), and *louk* (again, Henryson uses the past participle as an adjective, *lukkin*, "webbed"); nouns such as *bir* (*rush*; compare Middle English *bere*), *draf* (*dregs*), possibly *dub* (*puddle*), *flet* (the interior of a house), *campis* (Old Norse *kampr*, "beard, moustache"), *kirk* (compare "church"), *mail* (*rent*), *sark* (*shirt*), *stottis* (*young oxen*), and *withgang* (*free access*). Given the proliferation of cognate pairs of virtual synonyms in the overlay of Old Norse upon Old English (the classic example is *shirt/skirt*), one might suppose that Scots thereby inherits a tendency towards doublets of closely related terms, a tendency frequently apparent in Henryson's style. In Scots, the word of Old Norse origin sometimes prevails over its Old English cognate: thus *stra* rather than *straw*, *carl* instead of *churl*, *birk* for *birch*, and in verse *boun* rather than *bound* (*ready*), as well as *raik* (*wander*).

c. French

One of the principal means by which Scots achieved distinctiveness was through its borrowings from French. Much of this borrowing draws on the phenomenal influx of French words into English generally in the fourteenth century, but, given the history of feudal and burghal development in Scotland, areas of difference in form or meaning were bound to arise early on: *renye* (*arraign*), *eschaip* (*escape*), *gin* (*craft, trick*; compare "engine"), *noter* (*notary*), *pley* (*plea*), *sonyeis* (*excuses*). The law is one area where Scots drew distinctively on French: *air* (*circuit court*), *breif* (*writ*), *civile* (compare *civil law*), *compeir* (*appear in court*), *porteous* (*list of persons indicted*). Borrowings from Norman and Central French can enter both Scots and English, but be preserved in different forms and with distinct meanings: *abasitlie* (*abashedly*), *busteous* (compare *boisterous*), *contrufit* (compare *contrived*), *corbie* (compare *corbin*, "raven"), *demand* (*ask*), *dyte* (*text*; compare "ditty"), *dour, effeir* (*business*; compare "affair"), *flour* (*flower*), *hurcheon* (*hedgehog*; compare "urchin"), *intermell* (compare "intermeddle"), *leill* (*loyal*), *lever* ("louver"), *lyart* (*dappled gray*), *miching* (*loitering*; compare "mooching"), *oblis* (compare "oblige"), *oursyle* (compare Shakespeare's *seel*, "to close"), *parabole* (compare the commoner English form *parable*), *remord* (*examine*; compare "remorse"), *weir* (*war*). French idioms take hold in Henryson's Scots: "makis mentioun" (*Fables*, line 162), "it cryis ane vengeance" (*Fables*, line 2761). A distinctive group of French borrowings with eloquent associations come to Henryson via English, often with Chaucerian associations: e.g., *dedene* (deign), *lawriate* (laureate), *poetre* (poetry), *polite* (polished, refined, "polite"), *preclair* (bright, magnificent), *rhetore* (rhetoric).

d. Latin

As in Middle English, Latin borrowings enter Middle Scots largely by way of French; e.g., Henryson's important words *figurall* and *inventioun*, as well as legal terms such as *apparitor* ("summoner"), *declyne* ("reject jurisdiction"), *indorsat* ("cognate with endorsed"). By the mid-fifteenth century, however, Scots is adopting increasing numbers of words directly from Latin; in fact, several latinisms make their earliest appearance in Henryson's poems: directly from Latin are legalisms such as *feriate* ("out of session"), *fulminait* ("censure," "censured"), *instante* ("immediately"), *propone* ("state a plea"), and *repudie* ("divorce"); latinisms are also associated with praise and other contexts for eloquence: *fontall* ("original"), *progenitrys* ("female progenitor"), and, in a pejorative direction, *maculait* ("stained"), *pungitive* ("stinging"), *rusticate* ("boorish"), *toxicate* ("poisonous"), and *vilipend* ("belittle"). In his borrowings from Latin as in other aspects of learned or courtly style, however, Henryson is more restrained than his younger compatriot William Dunbar. It is worth noting that while the past participle of the Latin verb is often the form on which the Scots borrowing is based (*fulminait*), the form of the present tense may also serve as the source (*propone*).

e. Middle Dutch

The Scottish economy depended greatly on trade with the Low Countries, which were also an important source for migration into the late medieval burghs. Therefore, Dutch contributed various sorts of words to Scots: pejorative terms (*loun*, "rogue"; *lour*, "skulk" — compare Middle English *lour*, "scowl"), names for coins (including *plank*; see the Explanatory Note to *Fables*, line 2270), apparent colloquialisms (*nekhering*, "blow to the neck"; *smoirand*, "smothering"), onomatopoeic verbs (*swak*), and common everyday terms (*crag*, "neck"; *crous* "bold"; *ming* "mix"; *pad*, "frog"; Henryson's *paddock* includes the diminutive suffix *-ock*).

f. Gaelic

Very few words of Gaelic origin occur in Henryson's poems, the most memorable being Cresseid's *ochane* (*Testament*, line 541; Gaelic *ochan*, *ochoin*, a lamenting interjection); another Gaelic word long established in Scots is *peit* (Irish *pit*), which Henryson uses in the topographical term *peitpoit* ("peat pot"; *Fables*, line 828). A less familiar Gaelic borrowing may be detected in *crufe* (*Fables*, line 2738; Gaelic *cró*, a sheepfold or hut). Given the development of Older Scots in the late medieval burghs and the related tendency to characterize Gaelic and its speakers as rural, and therefore fixed in distinctive traditions and hence resistant to "improvement," this topical range, lack of prominence, and paucity of actual items are understandable. For a reading of *Lowrence*, the name of the fox in the *Fables*, as a Brythonic Celtic survival, see the Explanatory Note to line 429.

3. Pronouncing Henryson's Middle Scots

Urban, middle-class, and diverse in its antecedents, Scots emerges as distinctive but never separate from English. The contrasts and continuities are to be noted at every level. For example, the Great Vowel Shift, the development in pronunciation that contributed a new set of diphthongs to fifteenth- and sixteenth-century English, also affects Scots, though to a more limited extent and with different outcomes. The sounds of Middle Scots are thus fundamental indices of the distinctiveness and contingency of Henryson's language; understanding them helps one to identify the particular achievements of Henryson's versification. In surveying these sounds and reviewing some important elements of grammar and vocabulary, the following examples are drawn from Henryson's lexicon as represented in this edition, and especially from the oldest texts with strong evidence for authorship.

The richest and surest evidence for the pronunciation of Scots vowels is to be found in Henryson's rhymes, alliteration, and other prosodic elements. However, the earliest manuscripts and prints containing his poems date well after his lifetime; in the case of the *Fables* and *The Testament of Cresseid*, the distance in time expands. During the intervening years, the pronunciation of Scots vowels was changing. As well, the rise of print, the increased prominence of Scots as an official language, and perhaps a rise in literacy were tending to make spellings somewhat more regular than they had been in the fifteenth century. To assist the reader who is beginning to learn Scots, therefore, the following brief, pragmatic, simplified introduction to pronunciation reflects the state of Scots in the later sixteenth century; the ideal is the pronunciation of a reader and copyist of these poems — someone like George Bannatyne in the 1560s — if not quite Henryson himself in the 1480s. For a closely reasoned array of models for various kinds of recitation, see Aitken, "How to Pronounce Older Scots."

a. Long vowels and diphthongs

Arranged in rhyming pairs, most of the following examples are monosyllabic; where a word of two syllables is given, it is the vowel in the stressed syllable that is being signified.

i. *syne / nyne*; *ire / fyre*; *child / fyld*; *write / dite*

Considered simply, the sound here is equivalent to the diphthong in the modern *nine*, *ire*, *child*. Length is indicated by a silent *e* after the subsequent consonant or by a subsequent consonant pair such as *ld*. Note the variation in spelling, either *i* or *y*.

ii. *quene / grene*; *heir / speir*; *greit / weit*; *kepe / depe*; *he / me*; *frie / hie*

Pronounced like the long vowel in the modern *queen*, *spear*, *greet*, *free*. The length of this vowel can be indicated by a final silent *e* or by the pair *ei*. In *wepit*, the long *e* is shown by the suffix *-it* following a single consonant. In a final syllable, the long *e* can appear alone: *the* ("thee"), *poetre* ("poetry"). Note that words like *hie* and *die* are pronounced with this vowel: not "high" and "die" but "he" and "dee." Henryson's verse provides evidence for the merging in Scots of the long *e* sounding "ay" as in Chaucer and the long *i* sounding "ee"; to this change can be adduced some of the so-called bad rhymes that occur occasionally in each of his major poems.[44]

iii. *trace / face*; *name / schame*; *hair / bair / sair*

In Scots, this vowel is moving from *a* as in *father* to *a* as in *radio*. Length can be indicated, as in vowel ii above, with a silent *e* after the subsequent consonant or with an *i* immediately following the vowel. The last two words cited show the Scots and northern Middle English fronting of the Old English / Old Norse back vowel *ā* (compare southern Middle English *bore*, *soor*; present-day *boar*, *sore*).

---

[44] Fox, *Poems*, pp. 492–94.

iv. *stone / anone*; *wo / go*; *dote / note*; *mold / gold*

The long *o*, equivalent to the English *gold*, *stone*, *woe*, *note*. Length can be indicated by the same means as with vowels ii and iv; note *purpois* in line 14 of the *Prologue* to the *Fables*.

v. *laboure / doloure*; *ground / sound*; *swoun / boune*

In English, *ou*, *ow* tends to become a diphthong (*ground*, *powder*, *down*), but in Middle Scots it remains a long vowel, sounding like the vowel in *loose*, *noon*.

vi. *flude / stude*; *rude / understude*; *sollicitude / gud(e)*

Closer to French *lune* than to the *u* in modern English *June*. Length can be indicated, as above, by means of an *i* or a silent *e*: thus *gud* can also be spelled *guid* or *gude*. This vowel shows the Scots fronting of the Old English / Old Norse back vowel ō; compare southern Middle English *stode*, *gode* (present-day *stood*, *good*).

vii. The dipthong *oi* is equivalent to that in the modern *noise*.

viii. *tauld / wald*; *snawe / saw*

Pronounced similar to modern *law*, this long vowel is frequently represented in *-al-* and *-aw-* contexts. Occasionally in Henryson, the so-called vocalization of the consonant *l* after this vowel, more commonly reflected in later Middle Scots spellings, can be traced: *gaw* for *gall* (*Sum Practysis of Medecyne*, line 43).

ix. *how / argow*; *soucht / broucht*

In essence, this is a dipthong produced by the combination of vowel v, above, with *w* or *u*. The spellings for this diphthong are also used for the long *u* (vi above), which can produce ambiguity.

x. *teuch* [modern English *tough*] / *aneuch*; *drewe / grewe*; *hew / vertewe*

Spelling (*ew* or *eu*) indicates the pronunciation of this dipthong.

b. Short vowels

The first four of the short vowels are effectively identical with their modern equivalents: *i* as in *bid*, *e* as in *elf*, *a* as in *fast*, *o* as in *sob*. The fifth short vowel, *u*, is consistently pronounced as in present-day *put*. Of particular significance in comparison to the vowels and hence the meter of Chaucer's verse (see below), the final *-e* is generally silent in Middle Scots. Henryson has recourse to a different optional syllable, however: the *-is* suffix may be pronounced as an unstressed syllable or may simply contribute a final *-s*, depending on the metrical constraints — whether an unstressed syllable is required or not.

c. Consonants

In this edition, two of the distinctive features of Middle Scots consonants — the use of yogh (ȝ) for consonantal *y* as well as the interchange of *u*, *v*, and *w* — are normalized in accordance with METS editorial practice. Other consonantal features of Henryson's Middle Scots have been preserved, a few of which should be noted.

i. *thocht, nocht, rycht, teuch*

In positions of equivalence to modern English *gh* (*though, nought, right, tough*), Middle Scots *ch* is a fricative pronounced (depending on whether a front vowel like *i* or a back vowel like *o* precedes it) as in *Bach* or, appropriately enough, *loch*.

ii. *schell, schort, scho*

The *sch* spelling is pronounced equivalent to modern *sh*, as in *shell, short*, or *she*. See, for example, *schulderis* (*Fables*, line 1355; English *shoulders*).

iii. *quhy, quha, quhome, quhilk*

The *quh* spelling may appear the most troublesome element of Middle Scots spelling, and its capacity to distract readers is increased by its appearance in several common words. Related to Old English *hw* (*Hwæt!*) and pronounced accordingly, it is equivalent to modern *wh*, as in *why, who, whom*, and *which*. For an introduction to the grammatical functions of some important words beginning with these sounds, see pages 21–22, below; for a fuller discussion of the pronunciation of *quh*, see Aitken and Macafee ("History of Scots to 1700," §6.31.1).

iv. *sik, mikill; fedder, wedder, slidder, togidder*

In common with northern Middle English, Scots typically gives *k* and *d* where one would expect *ch* and *th* in standard southern English. For example, the voiced fricative *th* in most medial contexts (as in English *feather*; Old English *feðer*) has a regular contrast in the Scots voiced plosive *d* (*feddir, weddir*); however, the *th* appears sporadically, as in *father, mother* — elsewhere, *fadir, modir*.

v. *sall, suld*

In contrast to the *sh* in present-day English *shall* and *should*, the *s* (pronounced thus) features in Henryson's Scots (compare *OED shall*, v.).

vi. *knew, gnaw, wryte*

The consonant clusters *kn, gn*, and *wr* are pronounced with both consonants sounded, as in Middle English — not with the initial letter silent and only the *n* or *r* sounded, as in modern English.

4. Distinctive Elements in the Grammar of Middle Scots

In general, the grammar of Middle Scots corresponds to that of northern late Middle English, a brief introduction to which is provided in Burrow and Turville-Petre's *Book of Middle English* (pp. 6, 272). In the Explanatory Notes of this edition, some of Henryson's rarer constructions are discussed. For the present, however, it might be useful to consider some examples of a few distinctive features.

a. Concord

Concord refers to the system of agreement, principally by means of inflection, between subjects and verbs. Some examples follow in which the person and number of the subject varies. (1) "clerkis sayis" (*Fables*, line 19): the plural subject *clerkis* governs the verb in present tense; that is, they both have *-is* suffixes indicating the third person plural; contrast present-day English "clerks say." (2) "The cat cummis" (*Fables*, line 384; "The cat approaches"): the verb takes the *-is* suffix to agree with the singular third person subject; the *-s* suffix has become standard in this context in modern English. (3) "thow ganis not for me" (*Fables*, line 112): here the *-is* suffix of the verb indicates agreement with the second person singular pronoun that is the subject; compare early modern English "thou gainest." Some verbs agree only inconsistently with second person singular subjects: for example, *hes* (*has*; early modern English *hast*) in "Thow hes na corne" (*Fables*, line 99).

Conserving a practice falling out of currency in Middle Scots, Henryson occasionally uses the *-is* suffix with an imperative verb to indicate that more than one person is being addressed: "Exempill takis be thir jolie flouris" (*Fables*, line 1653), "Take an example from these pretty flowers."

b. The past tense
i. *-it*
Equivalent to *-ed* in present-day English, the suffix commonly marking the past tense in Middle Scots is *-it*. For example, "The uther answerit" (*Fables*, line 318). However, the so-called strong verbs (a larger group than in present-day English) indicate the past tense by a change to the root vowel: "he fand ane jolie jasp" (*Fables*, line 69; "he found a lovely jasper"); "'Knew ye my father?' quod the cok and leuch" (*Fables*, line 446: "'Did you know my father?' said the rooster and laughed"); "So hie scho clam" (*Fables*, line 338; "So high she climbed").

ii. *can, couth*
Henryson also forms the past tense by means of auxiliary verbs, especially *can* (compare Chaucer's *gan*) and its past tense *couth*: "Apon the burges mous loud can scho cry" (*Fables*, line 342; "Against the town mouse loudly did she cry"); "Under covert full prevelie couth thay creip" (*Fables*, line 254: "Under cover very stealthily did they creep"). As in "starklie can reprufe" (*Testament*, line 280: "[she] brazenly denounces"), the verb *can* occasionally serves as a metrical filler without indicating the past tense.

c. Verbs of motion
Like other Middle English and Middle Scots writers, Henryson tends to be most idiomatic in handling verbs of motion in the past tense: "Rampand he said, 'Ga furth, ye brybouris baith!' / And thay to ga withowtin tarying" (*Fables*, lines 999–1000; "Rearing up he said, 'Get going, you two rascals!' and they set off without delay." See also line 2158). Likewise, the omission of the verb of motion where the adverb (e.g., *up*) makes it implicit, is common in vivid, colloquial narrative (*DOST up* adv. 3; *OED up* adv. 31): "The burges up with that" (*Fables*, line 327; "With that, the burgher leapt up").

d. Past and present participles
i. *-it* and *-in*
As well as marking the past tense of many Scots verbs (as *-ed* does for most English verbs), the *-it* suffix and its reduced *-t* equivalent also feature in the past participle of many Scots verbs: "Jowellis are tint . . . and swopit furth" (*Fables*, lines 75–76; "Jewels are lost and swept out"). However, the past participles of strong verbs are formed differently: "The wolff wes neir weill dungin to the deid" (*Fables*, line 2196: "The wolf was almost beaten to death"); compare *ding*, "beat").

ii. *-and* and *-ing*

The suffix *-and* usually indicates the present participle used to modify a noun or as part of a progressive verb phrase: "ane cok . . . Seikand his meit" (*Fables*, line 63: "a cock seeking his food"); "scho wes full sair dredand" (*Fables*, line 310; "she was very keenly dreading"). The *-ing* suffix, by contrast, indicates the gerund, a part of the verb functioning as a noun: "in sweeping of the hous" (*Fables*, line 70: "during [the] sweeping of the house"); "Quhilk wan hir fude off spinning on hir rok" (*Fables*, line 412: "Who earned her sustenance from spinning on her distaff").

e. Pronouns and articles

Only those elements that distinguish Henryson's Scots from more general Middle English usage are discussed here.

i. *thow* and *ye*

The subtlety of Henryson's treatment of second person pronouns calls for particular attention. In various passages, gradations of respect are made apparent by means of alternation between the familiar *thow* and the polite plural *ye*. In the negotiations between the fox, the wolf, and the husbandman, for example (*Fables*, lines 2301–70), "the wolf uses the familiar *thou* in speaking to both the fox and the husbandman; the husbandman uses the respectful *ye* to both the wolf and the fox; the fox uses *ye* to the wolf, but *thou* to the husbandman."[45] Discussing *The Paddock and the Mouse* as the final part of the *Fables*, Edward Wheatley notes the attenuation of the audience to a single person, *thow*; previously, the audience has tended to be addressed as a group, formally (e.g., lines 40, 63, 190, 365, 571, 588, 1208, 1594, 2210).[46] This tendency is by no means uniform in the *Fables*, the reader being occasionally addressed in the familiar singular: for instance, in a rhetorical evocation of a particular social occasion, as if the speaker is an intimate friend (lines 389–91) or a preacher (lines 1115, 1126, 1129; see also 2726, 2735–40, 2763.). Although the last fable, *The Paddock and the Mouse*, ends with a passing reversion to the formal *ye* in an imperative construction ("Gif this be trew, speir ye at thame that saw," "Ask those who witnessed it if this is true," line 2909), the intimate singular mode becomes dominant in the final *Moralitas*, addressed to "My brother" (lines 2910, 2930); the last stanza addresses first "my freind," "Say *thow* I left the laif unto the freiris" (line 2971) and then the prayerful "Now Christ . . . as thow art salviour" (lines 2973–74).

ii. *thay, thair, thame*

In Scots as in northern Middle English, the third person plural forms of the personal pronouns derive from Old Norse forms with *th* rather than Old English–derived forms with *h*; contrast southern Middle English *hir*, *hem*.

iii. *thir*

As a demonstrative pronoun equivalent to *these*, *thir* also occurs in some northern Middle English texts (*OED*, *thir*).

---

[45] Fox, *Poems*, p. 303n2316.

[46] Wheatley, *Mastering Aesop*, p. 187.

iv. *ane*

In Middle Scots, the indefinite article ("a") appears as *ane* before consonants as well as vowels; "there is no evidence (for instance, from modern dialect speech) that the /n/ was pronounced in this position."[47]

f. *Quha, quhair*, etc.

Once one gets beyond the apparent oddness of the *quh* for *wh*, it is possible to trace Henryson's extension and refinement of these valuably functional words.

i. *Quha*

The usual modern use of *who*, the cognate of *quha*, is as a relative pronoun, as in "The messenger who brought me the news has returned home." Henryson treats such constructions rather freely: note the looseness of the antecedent in "Schir Corbie Ravin wes maid apparitour / Quha pykit had full mony scheipis ee" ("Sir Carrion Raven was appointed summoner, / Who had plucked out very many a sheep's eye"; *Fables*, lines 1160–61). Henryson is much more comfortable with *quha* as an interrogative, as in "Quha may be hardie, riche, and gratious?" ("Who can be brave, rich, and gracious?"; *Fables*, line 134). He also often uses this pronoun indefinitely, as one would use "whoever" or "anyone who": "Quha hes this stane sall have gude hap to speid" ("Whoever has this stone shall have good fortune to succeed"; *Fables*, line 125).

ii. *Quhair*

Henryson uses this word adeptly and frequently as an indefinite indicator of place, as in "Than Lourence luikit up quhair he couth ly" ("Then Lawrence looked up from the place where he lay"; *Fables*, line 625). Shortly after this line, the pronoun reappears used relatively: "Out of the wod unto ane hill he went / Quhair he micht se the twinkling sternis cleir" ("He went out of the forest to a hill / Where he could see the brightly twinkling stars," *Fables*, lines 628–29). Finally, the interrogative function is apparent in lines like "Quhair is thy respite?" ("Where is your document of permission?"; *Fables*, line 1017).

iii. *Quhais*

Quhais is rare in Henryson's language, appearing only twice in the *Fables* and once in the *Testament*. It functions as an indefinite indicator, as in the rather elliptical "Full lytill worschip have ye wyn thairfoir / To quhais strenth is na comparisoun" ("Very little honor have you won thereby, / Since to your strength [there] is no comparison"; *Fables*, lines 1484–85).

iv. *Quhat*

As an equivalent to *what* ("They don't care what we do"), *quhat* appears in passages like "thay tak na tent / Quhat be thairin swa that the flure be clene" ("they pay no attention / To whatever might be in [the sweepings] so long as the floor [should] be clean"; *Fables*, lines 73–74). Straightforward for a present-day reader is the interrogative usage in "Quhat plesans is in festis delicate?" ("What pleasure is there in fancy feasts?"; *Fables*, line 232).

---

[47] Aitken and Macafee, "History of Scots to 1700," §7.5.1 (p. cvii).

v. *Quhen*

Like *quhair*, this word functions smoothly in Henryson's language as an adverb, in lines like "Quhen rigour sittis in the tribunall, / The equitie of law quha may sustene?" ("When severity sits in the judgement seat, / Who can uphold the equity of law?"; *Fables*, lines 1472–73).

vi. *Quhy*

In Henryson's Scots, idiomatic compounds are emerging to represent abstract relations. Take for example the following: "I may not droun for quhy my oppin gill / Devoidis ay the watter I resaif" ("I cannot drown, because my open gill regularly / Expels the water I take in"; *Fables*, lines 2816–17). *Quhy* regularly functions to signal causal relations, as in "the caus quhy that thay first began / Wes to repreif thee of thi misleving" ("The reason why they [the ancient fables] were originally instituted / Was to rebuke thee for thy wickedness"; *Fables*, lines 5–6).

vii. *Quhilk, quhilkis*

One of Henryson's especially useful words, *quhilk* is cognate with *which*, and functions in many of the same ways. For instance, "His wyfe it span and twynit it into threid / Of quhilk the fowlar nettis maid indeid" ("His wife spun it [the flax] and twisted it into thread, / From which the birdcatcher did indeed make nets"; *Fables*, lines 1830–31). For the *-is* form, the following provides an example: "mychtie men haifand aneuch plentie / Quhilkis ar sa gredie and sa covetous / Thay will not thoill in peax ane pureman be" ("powerful men possessing ample wealth / Who are so greedy and covetous / That they will not allow a poor man to exist in peace"; *Fables*, lines 2729–31).

5. Versification

If his own versification is anything to go by, Henryson is the most perceptive of fifteenth-century readers of Chaucer's meter, but Chaucer is not his only model. Perhaps the first poet in English or Scots to adapt the iambic pentameter line for use consistently without the pronunciation of final *-e*, Henryson has occasional recourse to the lyric caesura, the pause after the inversion of the second foot ("Than *of jas*pis | ane mekill multitude"; *Fables*, line 96), a feature of late medieval French verse.[48] He also tends to employ the suffix *-is* with flexibility and sensitivity, using it as an unstressed syllable when metrically expedient; likewise, he makes subtle, telling use of contracted forms (e.g. *dude* for *do it*; *Fables*, line 676) to signal a lowering of style into colloquialism. The foremost Scots poem of the late fourteenth century, John Barbour's *Brus*, may well have helped to train Henryson's ear toward such practices. Whatever the antecedents for Henryson's pentameter, his handling of various line-lengths need not have derived its expressive flexibility solely from the Chaucerian tradition of late medieval verse-making. Henryson knows "the right places" to depart from the regular alternation of stressed and unstressed syllables in order to achieve "poetic foregrounding."[49] For any consideration of possible emendations, this poet's prosodic skill is important to bear in mind.

---

[48] Duffell, "Italian Line," p. 296.

[49] J. Smith, "Language of Older Scots Poetry," p. 200.

Alliteration is never far away in Henryson's verse, whatever the genre or form. In passages of complaint, for example, it amplifies key stresses as a prime technique of foregrounding. Henryson's penchant for alliteration is rooted in Middle English verse, with the lyrics of British Library MS Harley 2253 indicating that "lyric verse of a high technical standard was being composed in many regions of England in the late thirteenth and early fourteenth centuries."[50] The interplay of the pentameter line and extended alliteration can generate considerable force. A decisive element in Henryson's prosodic technique, alliteration distinguishes his verse from Chaucer's usual practice and becomes key to his own stylistic legacy for subsequent Scots poets, Dunbar and Douglas prominent among them.

In his handling of stanza forms, Henryson is more of an innovator than has often been recognized. It is much more common to note that he proclaims his affiliation to Chaucer by means of his staple stanza form, rhyme royal, the seven-line stanza rhyming *ababbcc* that comprises the bulk of the *Fables*, the *Testament*, and the narrative proper of *Orpheus*. An earlier Scottish poet, James I, had already used this Chaucerian stanza, in *The Kingis Quair*;[51] Henryson's advance is to transform the rhyme royal into a versatile frame for all registers of Middle Scots discourse, from the gnomic to the colloquial to the exclamatory, and from rich description to rapid narration to philosophical exposition. To distinguish inset passages of complaint or moralization, Henryson uses longer stanzas, sometimes with refrainlike last lines: the inset Complaints of Orpheus and Cresseid, the former in what George Saintsbury long ago called "quite an extraordinary" ten-line stanza,[52] the latter in the nine-line stanza Chaucer used in *Anelida and Arcite*; the moralizing conclusions to *The Two Mice* and *The Paddock and the Mouse*, in the eight-line ballade. But it is in the balance of rich rhetorical potential and tight form of the rhyme royal that Henryson has his greatest prosodic achievements, "a really wonderful sureness" and an "astonishing variety of colour and tone":[53] one stanza can proceed fluently into the next (e.g., *Testament*, lines 119–20), or a single stanza can stand out as a frame for an inset central line (e.g., *Fables*, lines 1461–67). Henryson assures the continued centrality of rhyme royal in the Middle Scots poetic tradition.

6. Style

A consideration of Henryson's style should begin with three points. First, as in the work of other skilled writers, the mode of discourse governs the style, so that narrative of violent action contrasts with ceremonious praise, pithy moralizing, elaborate description, lapidary brevity, plangent lament, or the exposition of abstract ideas. Second, rapid and extreme changes of style typify Henryson's verse, though style-switching has not yet settled into a mannerism; indeed, this quality can with propriety be seen to correlate with a strong thematic emphasis on the intermingling of joy and sorrow, morality and comedy (e.g., Explanatory Notes to line 26), so much so that this technique may be described as one of Henryson's particular contributions to the hallmarks of early modern Scottish verse style. Third, the individual poems ascribed to Henryson differ stylistically from each other, to a degree that confounds most attempts to adduce a consistent manner as a hallmark of authorship.

---

[50] Fein, "Twelve-Line Stanza Forms," p. 368.

[51] Mooney and Arn, *Kingis Quair and Other Prison Poems*, pp. 17–18, 22.

[52] *aabaabbcbC*; Saintsbury, *History of English Prosody*, 1:272.

[53] Saintsbury, *History of English Prosody*, 1:271.

Henryson is expert at briefly indicating colloquial speech: he can underscore or deflate exalted language with a well-chosen idiom or term: "I do it on them" (e.g., *Fables*, line 1229); the onomatopoeic, almost flippant *clink* of Orpheus' harp (*Orpheus*, line 288). As a formal occasion unwinds into hilarity, the increasing raciness of style is borne out by the rapid exchange of voices in dialogue (e.g., *Fables*, lines 278–80) — the line between dialogue and narrative comment, it must be noted, is not always distinct (e.g., *Fables*, lines 1031, 1298). Henryson also has the knack of repeating words and phrases to indicate changed circumstances: for instance, *subcharge* (*Fables*, lines 281, 346). An example of this technique is the recurrence of *rax and rin(g)* ("expand and rule"), a usually pejorative expression for the wrongful extension of power (e.g., *Fables*, lines 539, 820, 1108), which unexpectedly reappears positively — "Than sall ressoun ryse, rax, and ring" (*Fables*, line 1116).

Conciseness has been justly called a hallmark of Henryson's style;[54] copiousness, a profusion of apt terms, has been recognized less often. Admittedly, the display of learned, courtly, or moral terms can be rendered ironic by the hypocrisy, deceit, or incomprehension of the speaker: one thinks of the mouth-filling speeches of Lowrence the fox, the fulminations of Chantecleir's wives, or the tragedy-queen aria of Cresseid in the lepers' lodge. Still, Henryson does not tend to indulge in combinations of native, French, and Latinate words for the sheer love of copiousness: as well as providing a wealth of synonyms, latinisms "increase semantic range," introducing new concepts to Scots.[55] Henryson's neologisms are durably packed with significance: *figurall, inventioun, radicate, tribunall*. Likewise, he has a compendious store of proverbs from scriptural, literary, and popular sources,[56] for pithy gravity, ironic characterization, or mock-heroic description. In each of these techniques, Chaucer offers valuable precedents, but Henryson selects and modifies these; to call his style "Chaucerian" is to distort his influences and diminish his achievement. Douglas Gray nicely sums up these aspects: "The concision of Henryson's style is made possible by the copiousness of his vocabulary, which ranges from the local and humble (*slonkis, bollis, fowmart*, etc., etc.) to the clerkly (*vilipend, contumax*, etc.)."[57]

7. Structure

The question continues to be debated whether the *Fables* is a structurally and integrated whole, as epitomized in the print tradition,[58] or whether that tradition merely bears witness to an editorial digest of groups of fables left discrete by the author. The very richness of Henryson's inventiveness has been seen as an impediment to structural integration: "each one of the *Fables* gives the impression of a fresh start, not a repeat performance."[59] Proponents of the latter position see the print tradition as an early modern editor's tidying of what had come to seem a late medieval mess. Those arguing for the authenticity of the integral *Fables* point to the tendency among scribes like Asloan and Bannatyne to abridge and select from their sources. Present-day readers also continue to debate the relation

---

[54] Spearing, *Medieval to Renaissance*, pp. 170–71; Gray, *Robert Henryson*, p. 83n13.

[55] Corbett, "Aureation Revisited," p. 190; J. Smith, "Language of Older Scots Poetry," pp. 205–06.

[56] Gopen, *Moral Fables of Aesop*, pp. 218–24.

[57] Gray, *Robert Henryson*, p. 83n13.

[58] E.g., Fox, *Poems*, pp. lxxv–lxxxi.

[59] Mehl, "Robert Henryson's *Moral Fables*," p. 88.

between narratives and the morals apparently arbitrarily applied to them, in the *Fables* but also in *Orpheus*. Similarly, not all readers have been impressed by the integration of the set-piece description of the planetary gods into the narrative of *The Testament of Cresseid*.[60] So fundamental and far-reaching are these questions that they deserve the consideration of every careful reader of Henryson.

THIS EDITION

1. The Problems

Richly celebratory but often also irresolvably ironic, Henryson's depictions of eloquent, learned poets such as Mercury, Aesop, Orpheus, or Chaucer should convey a special lesson for the prospective editor of the *Fables*, *The Testament of Cresseid*, *Orpheus and Eurydice*, and the shorter poems: the recovery of the author's intention may be an impossible ideal to realize. Of prime significance for any edition of Henryson is the gap in time between the date of their composition and the date of their earliest extant texts. This gap is multiply significant. If the Chepman and Myllar prints are anything to go by, vernacular poems were printed in early sixteenth-century Scotland in small, frail editions, not designed for prestige or permanence: in a short poem introducing his manuscript, Bannatyne refers to working from "copeis awld, mankit, and mutillait" (old, maimed, and mutilated; "The Wryttar to the Reidaris," line 7). Further, the later copyists were themselves aware of the cultural and linguistic distance at which they stood from the poems they wished to preserve and circulate. A present-day editor may thus serve Henryson's readers best by providing a clear, consistent representation of an integral text, even when that text is a century later than the poem it conveys.

Such a representation ought to take into account the discrepancies within textual traditions: for the *Fables*, the manuscripts versus the prints; for the *Testament*, Thynne's English text versus the much later Scots text of Charteris; for *Orpheus and Eurydice*, the incompleteness of the two earliest witnesses. Such discrepancies take various forms. Between the late fifteenth century and the 1570s, the decade of the earliest complete prints of the *Fables*, the Reformation intervenes in Scotland, with the result that in the printed text, many overt references to late medieval religion are revised away. The late sixteenth-century witnesses — prints and manuscripts — present Henryson's language in a standardized, modernized garb: spellings follow contemporary practice; obsolete words are often replaced with familiar alternatives.[61] Meanwhile, the earlier texts, including those in the Makculloch and Asloan Manuscripts and the Chepman and Myllar Prints, are fragmentary and display a high incidence of variation; it is worth emphasizing that even in these sources, the texts have been produced a few decades later than the composition of the poems — enough time for linguistic changes and textual variation to occur. The gaps between the textual traditions, therefore, produce ample variation line by line.

2. Editorial Practice

In the present edition, each of Henryson's poems appears in the form of a manuscript or print that has been selected for the completeness and consistency of its text and the clarity

---

[60] E.g., Heaney, *Testament*, p. 9.

[61] Bawcutt, *Poems of William Dunbar*, 1:12, 25n42.

of its representation of Middle Scots. This principle results in the selection of late witnesses as base texts: thus the *Fables* is based on the text of the Bassandyne print (Bs), *The Testament of Cresseid* on the text of the Charteris print (Ch), *Orpheus and Eurydice* on the Bannatyne Manuscript's text, and the shorter poems on the most complete witnesses, with particular reliance perforce on Bannatyne again. An important difference between this edition and many earlier ones is that at times a later witness will be preferred over an earlier one in order to produce edited texts that consistently reflect the language of their bases. Emendations are adopted into this edition when the usual source is demonstrably in error: the meter falters unaccountably;[62] a familiar word has been substituted for an unfamiliar one; printers have substituted euphemisms for references to discredited beliefs and practices; or one of various kinds of error in transcription or typesetting has occurred. Of these kinds of error, the first and second are recorded in the Textual Notes, but usually (given the sheer bulk of the potential evidence) only when an emendation is being adopted. An important exception to this practice is to be found in the Textual Notes to *Orpheus*: since this edition departs from previous ones in using the Bannatyne Manuscript for its base text, the variants are recorded quite fully, though still selectively.

Some adjustments and alterations have been made as consistently as possible with regard to the spelling and punctuation of this edition:

a. The letter *i* consistently represents a vowel, with *j* substituted for the consonant; thus *iustice* is spelled *justice*.

b. The letter *u* represents a vowel, and *v* a consonant; thus *vse* is spelled *use*, and *ouer* is spelled *over*.

c. Where the letter *u* appears where *w* would be expected in the modern English equivalent, *w* has been substituted: *jowell*, *betwix*, *saw*, *swete*, etc.

d. When appropriate, the initial *v* has been substituted with *w* according to modern practice: thus *vont* has become *wont*. The reverse substitution has also been normalized: thus *wyle* has become *vyle*.

e. The scribe often writes "off" for the preposition *of*, and "of" for the adverb or preposition *off*, though not always. I have normalized the spelling to reflect modern usage.

f. The letter form ß appearing in the manuscripts is given as *s* unless the grammatical and metrical context makes clear that it indicates the *-is* suffix: *myß* becomes *mys*; *courß* becomes *coursis*.

g. In Middle Scots the yogh (ȝ) appears in contexts equivalent to those filled by consonantal *y* in present-day English; in the later prints, this character begins to appear as *z*. In such contexts, *y* appears here: *yit* instead of *ȝit*.

h. The thorn (þ), which appears sporadically in the manuscripts, is replaced with *th*.

i. Proper nouns are capitalized according to modern conventions. Where, however, a noun is not explicitly a name, it has tended not to be capitalized.

j. Corresponding to the practice in the principal manuscript and print witnesses, major sections in the poems are marked by a bold initial letter. Such letters indicate the beginning and ending of inset passages, such as Cresseid's complaint (*Testament*, lines 407, 470); in the case of the acrostic *O FICTIO* (*Testament*, lines 57–63), each line involved is thus marked.

k. This edition is punctuated more lightly than were its recent predecessors. The guiding principle of punctuation has been that Henryson's sentences tend to involve coordination

---

[62] Compare Mann, *Geoffrey Chaucer*, p. lxv–lxvi; Machan, *Textual Criticism*, p. 63.

rather than subordination. As an emphasis, greater flexibility of grammatical relationships has been preferred to more explicit hierarchies of meaning, even if some of the sentences begin to look somewhat "run-on" as a result. Dozens of opportunities for colons and semi-colons have thus produced commas instead; and many of the commas articulating the text of previous editions have vanished.

Prologue

	Thocht feinyeit fabils of ald poetre	*Though fictitious tales of old poetry*
	Be not al grunded upon truth, yit than	*completely; but even so*
	Thair polite termes of sweit rhetore	*polished; sweet rhetoric*
	Richt plesand ar unto the eir of man	*Very pleasing are; ear*
5	And als the caus quhy that thay first began	*also; why*
	Wes to repreif thee of thi misleving,	*reprove; your evil way of life*
	O man, be figure of ane uther thing,	*by [the] representation of a different*
	In lyke maner as throw a bustious eird,	*similar; through; intractable soil*
	Swa it be laubourit with grit diligence,	*If; cultivated; great effort*
10	Springis the flouris and the corne abreird	*The flowers shoot up; wheat in early growth*
	Hailsum and gude to mannis sustenence,	*Healthy and good for man's sustenance*
	Sa springis thar a morall sweit sentence	*In this way there grows; meaning*
	Oute of the subtell dyte of poetry	*subtle artifice*
	To gude purpois, quha culd it weill apply.	*good purpose, if one could interpret it well*
15	The nuttis schell thocht it be hard and teuch	*nut's shell though; tough*
	Haldis the kirnell sweit and delectabill,	*Contains; sweet; delectable*
	Sa lyis thair ane doctrine wyse aneuch	*And thus there lies a; wise enough*
	And full of frute under ane fenyeit fabill,	*fruitful implication beneath a fictitious story*
	And clerkis sayis it is richt profitabill	*scholars say; most advantageous*
20	Amangis ernist to ming ane merie sport	*serious matters to mix some amusing fun*
	To blyth the spreit and gar the tyme be schort.	*delight the spirit; make; short*
	For as we se, ane bow that ay is bent	*see; is always bent*
	Worthis unsmart and dullis on the string	*Becomes weak; slackens*
	Sa dois the mynd that ay is diligent	*As does; always*
25	In ernistfull thochtis and in studying.	*toilsome thoughts*
	With sad materis sum merines to ming	*serious matters some merriment to mix*
	Accordis weill; thus Esope said iwis,	*well; Aesop; indeed*
	Dulcius arrident seria picta iocis.[1]	

---

[1] *Serious matters please more sweetly when mixed with entertainment*

29

Of this authour, my maisteris, with your leif, — *leave*
30 Submitting me to your correctioun, — *myself*
In mother toung, of Latyng, I wald preif — *tongue; out of Latin; want to try*
To mak ane maner of translatioun, — *make a kind*
Nocht of myself for vane presumptioun — *of my own will; vain arrogance*
Bot be requeist and precept of ane lord — *But by request*
35 Of quhome the name it neidis not record. — *whom; is not necessary [to]*

In hamelie language and in termes rude — *homely; plain words*
Me neidis wryte for quhy of eloquence — *It is necessary for me to write because*
Nor rethorike I never understude, — *rhetoric I never did understand*
Thairfoir meiklie I pray your reverence — *meekly I request of your worships*
40 Gif ye find ocht that throw my negligence — *If; anything; through*
Be deminute or yit superfluous, — *diminished or else*
Correct it at your willis gratious. — *according to your gracious wishes*

My author in his fabillis tellis how
That brutal beistis spak and understude — *irrational beasts spoke; understood*
45 And to gude purpois dispute and argow, — *good purpose [did]; argue*
Ane sillogisme propone and eik conclude, — *Advance a hypothetical argument; also*
Puttyng exempill and similitude — *Providing [an] example; likeness*
How mony men in operatioun — *How [it is that] many; manner of action*
Ar like to beistis in conditioun. — *Are in a condition like that of the beasts*

50 Na mervell is ane man be lyke ane beist — *[It] is no surprise; likened to a beast*
Quhilk lufis ay carnall and foull delyte — *Who constantly loves; foul delight*
That schame cannot him renye nor arreist — *Whom shame cannot challenge or restrain*
Bot takis all the lust and appetyte — *But indulges*
Quhilk throw custum and the daylie ryte — *Which through; daily routine*
55 Syne in the mynd sa fast is radicate — *Subsequently; so firmly is rooted*
That he in brutal beist is transformate. — *into an irrational beast is turned*

This nobill clerk Esope, as I haif tauld, — *scholar; have told*
In gay metir and facound purpurat — *fine meter and purpled eloquence*
Be figure wrait his buke for he nocht wald — *Figuratively wrote; wish*
60 Tak the disdane off hie nor low estate, — *To suffer scorn from high; social class*
And to begin, first of ane cok he wrate, — *about a rooster; wrote*
Seikand his meit, quhilk fand ane jolie stone, — *Seeking; food, who found*
Of quhome the fabill ye sall heir anone. — *About whom; you shall hear forthwith*

The Cock and the Jasp — *Rooster; Jasper*

Ane cok sumtyme with feddram fresch and gay, — *plumage*
65 Richt cant and crous albeit he was bot pure, — *Very lively; bold; poor*
Flew furth upon ane dunghill sone be day. — *just at daybreak*
To get his dennar set was al his cure. — *all his effort was committed*
Scraipand amang the as be aventure — *Scraping among the ashes, by chance*

He fand ane jolie jasp richt precious   *found a brilliant piece of chalcedony very*
70   Wes castin furth in sweping of the hous.   *[That] had been cast out during the sweeping*

As damisellis wantoun and insolent   *As when irresponsible and rebellious maidservants*
That fane wald play and on the streit be sene,   *Who would rather; be seen in the street*
To swoping of the hous thay tak na tent   *About the sweeping; take no care*
Quhat be thairin swa that the flure be clene,[1]
75   Jowellis ar tint as oftymis hes bene sene   *Jewels; lost; often has been seen*
Upon the flure and swopit furth anone.   *swept out at once*
Peradventure sa wes the samin stone.   *By accident; same*

Sa mervelland upon the stane, quod he,   *marveling at the stone, he said*
"O gentill jasp, O riche and nobill thing,   *excellent jasper*
80   Thocht I thee find, thow ganis not for me.   *Though; are of no use*
Thow art ane jowell for ane lord or king.   *Thou; jewel*
It wer pietie thow suld in this mydding   *It would be a pity should you; dung heap*
Be buryit thus amang this muke and mold   *buried; among this dung and dirt*
And thow so fair and worth sa mekill gold.   *When you; beautiful; so much*

85   "It is pietie I suld thee find for quhy   *because*
Thy grit vertew nor yit thy cullour cleir   *great power; bright color*
I may nouther extoll nor magnify,   *exalt; glorify*
And thow to me may mak bot lyttill cheir,   *can; hardly any feast*
To grit lordis thocht thow be leif and deir.   *By great; precious and dear*
90   I lufe fer better thing of les availl   *love far; something of less value*
As draf or corne to fill my tume intraill.   *Such as malt; grain; empty guts*

"I had lever ga skraip heir with my naillis   *rather go scrape here; claws*
Amangis this mow and luke my lifys fude   *dust; seek the sustenance needed for my life*
As draf or corne, small wormis or snaillis,   *Such as*
95   Or ony meit wald do my stomok gude   *any food [that] would; stomach good*
Than of jaspis ane mekill multitude,   *a great*
And thow agane upon the samin wyis   *in the same way*
May me as now for thin availl dispyis.   *despise me now in terms of your wellbeing*

"Thow hes na corne and thairof I had neid.   *[if] I had need thereof*
100   Thy cullour dois bot confort to the sicht   *color provides comfort only to the sight*
And that is not aneuch my wame to feid   *enough to feed my belly*
For wyfis sayis that lukand werk is licht.   *wives say; the act of looking; unsustaining*
I wald sum meit have, get it geve I micht,   *would have some food, if I might get it*
For houngrie men may not weil leif on lukis.   *hungry; live adequately on looks*
105   Had I dry breid, I compt not for na cukis.   *If I had; bread, I would not care; any chefs*

---

[1] *What [may] be therein just as long as the floor is clean*

Why can't the jewel talk if the chicken talks? (handwritten)

"Quhar suld thow mak thy habitatioun, — *Where should*
Quhar suld thow dwell bot in ane royall tour, — *except; tower*
Quhar suld thow sit bot on ane kingis croun, —
Exaltit in worship and in grit honour? — *Exalted in glory; great*

110   Rise, gentill jasp, of all stanis the flour, — *stones; flower*
Out of this fen and pas quhar thow suld be. — *filth; go*
Thow ganis not for me nor I for thee." — *Thou art of no use to me*

Later (handwritten)

Levand this jowell law upon the ground — *Leaving; low*
To seik his meit this cok his wayis went; — *seek his food; went on his way*

115   Bot quhen or how or quhome be it wes found — *when; by whom it was*
As now I set to hald na argument, — *intend; carry on no debate*
Bot of the inward sentence and intent — *meaning*
Of this fabill as myne author dois write
I sall reheirs in rude and hamelie dite. — *give an account; rough; homely style*

Moralitas — *Moralization*

120   This jolie jasp hes properteis sevin. — *has seven attributes*
The first, of cullour it is mervelous,
Part lyke the fyre and part is lyke the hevin.
It makis ane man stark and victorious, — *mighty*
Preservis als fra cacis perrillous. — *also; dangerous situations*

125   Quha hes this stane sall have gude hap to speid. — *good luck; succeed*
Of fyre nor fallis him neidis not to dreid.[1]

This gentill jasp richt different of hew — *highly variegated of hue*
Betakinnis perfite prudence and cunning — *Signifies perfect; intelligence*
Ornate with mony deidis of vertew — *deeds of virtue*

130   Mair excellent than ony eirthly thing, — *earthly*
Quhilk makis men in honour ay to ring, — *always to reign*
Happie and stark to haif the victorie — *Fortunate; capable; have*
Of all vicis and spirituall enemie. — *Over all vices and [the] devil*

Quha may be hardie, riche, and gratious? — *Who is able to be courageous; benevolent*

135   Quha can eschew perrell and aventure? — *avoid peril and jeopardy*
Quha can governe ane realme, cietie, or hous? — *city*
Without science, no man, I yow assure. — *knowledge*
It is riches that ever sall indure
Quhilk maith nor moist nor uther rust can freit. — *maggots; damp; consume*

140   To mannis saull it is eternall meit.

This cok, desyrand mair the sempill corne — *desiring more; mere*
Than ony jasp, may till ane fule be peir — *to a fool be equivalent*
Makand at science bot ane knak and scorne — *Making of; merely a mockery*

Why? (handwritten)

---

[1] *About mishaps there's no need for him to fear*

And na gude can, als lytill will he leir. — *can do no good, and as little; learn*
145 His hart wammillis wyse argumentis to heir — *heart shudders; hear*
As dois ane sow to quhome men for the nanis — *does; for whom; for example*
In hir draf troich wald saw the precious stanis. — *swill trough might strew; stones*

Quha is enemie to science and cunning — *learning and wisdom*
Bot ignorants that understandis nocht — *ignorant people who do not understand*
150 Quhilk is sa nobill, precious, and ding — *[Something] that; exalted*
That it may with na eirdlie thing be bocht. — *earthly; bought*
Weill wer that man over all uther that mocht — *Favored would be; others who could*
All his lyfe dayis in perfite studie wair — *expend*
To get science for him neidit na mair. — *nothing more was needful*

155 Bot now allace this jasp is tynt and hid. — *alas; lost; hidden*
We seik it nocht nor preis it for to find. — *hasten not to find it*
Haif we richis, na better lyfe we bid, — *If we have; we aspire to*
Of science thocht the saull be bair and blind. — *though; soul; destitute*
Of this mater to speik, it wair bot wind, — *About; matter; speak, it only wastes breath*
160 Thairfore I ceis and will na forther say. — *cease; say no more*
Ga seik the jasp quha will for thair it lay. — *Go seek; whoever wants*

The Two Mice

Esope myne authour makis mentioun
Of twa myis and thay wer sisteris deir — *dear*
Of quham the eldest in ane borous toun, — *whom; borough town*
165 The yungir wynnit uponland weill neir — *dwelt up-country very nearby*
Richt soliter, quhyle under busk and breir, — *alone, sometimes; bush; briar*
Quhilis in the corne in uther mennis skaith — *Sometimes; to other men's loss*
As owtlawis dois and levit on hir waith. — *live; gleanings*

This rurall mous into the wynter tyde — *time*
170 Had hunger, cauld, and tholit grit distres. — *cold; suffered great*
The tother mous that in the burgh couth byde, — *other; who dwelt in the town*
Was gild brother and made ane fre burges, — *Was a guild member; citizen*
Toll-fre alswa but custum mair or les — *also without the greater tax*
And fredome had to ga quhairever scho list — *wherever she wished*
175 Amang the cheis and meill in ark and kist. — *cheese; milled grain; coffer; chest*

Ane tyme quhen scho wes full and unfutesair, — *Once when; comfortable*
Scho tuke in mynd hir sister uponland — *She remembered*
And langit for to heir of hir weilfair — *longed to hear; prosperity*
To se quhat lyfe scho led under the wand. — *"out in the sticks"*
180 Bairfute, allone, with pykestaf in hir hand — *Barefoot; walking stick*
As pure pylgryme scho passit owt off town — *Like a poor; went out from*
To seik hir sister baith oure daill and down. — *over hill and dale*

	Throw mony wilsum wayis can scho walk,	*Along; lonely paths did*
	Throw mure and mosse, throw bankis, busk, and breir,[1]	
185	Fra fur to fur, cryand fra balk to balk,	*From furrow; crying; ridge*
	"Cum furth to me, my awin sweit sister deir,	*own*
	Cry peip anis!" With that the mous couth heir	*Just cry "peep"!; did hear*
	And knew hir voce as kinnismen will do	*recognized her voice; kinfolk*
	Be verray kynd and furth scho come hir to.	*By sheer instinct; came to her*
190	The hartlie cheir, lord God geve ye had sene	*heartfelt show of affection; if you*
	Beis kythit quhen thir sisteris twa war met,	*Was displayed when these*
	Quhilk that oft syis wes schawin thame betwene!	*many times; displayed between them*
	For quhylis thay leuch and quhylis for joy thay gret,	*sometimes; laughed; wept*
	Quhyle kissit sweit and quhilis in armis plet	*embraced*
195	And thus thay fure quhill soberit wes their mude,	*carried on until; mood*
	Syne fute for fute unto the chalmer yude.	*Then with joint step; room [they] went*
	As I hard say, it was ane semple wane	*heard; humble dwelling*
	Of fog and farne full misterlyk wes maid,	*Of winter grass; fern; poorly was built*
	Ane sillie scheill under ane erdfast stane	*mere hut; firmly fixed stone*
200	Of quhilk the entres wes not hie nor braid	*entry; high or broad*
	And in the samin thay went but mair abaid	*the same; without more delay*
	Withoutin fyre or candill birnand bricht	*burning bright*
	For comonly sic pykeris luffis not lycht.	*such pilferers love not the light*
	Quhen thay wer lugit thus, thir sely myse, hie	*lodged; these poor little mice*
205	The youngest sister into hir butterie hyid	*hastened into the pantry*
	And brocht furth nuttis and peis insteid of spyce.	*brought; peas instead*
	Giff thair wes weilfair, I do it on thame besyde.	*If; abundance; leave it to*
	The burges mous prompit forth in pryde	*started*
	And said, "Sister, is this your dayly fude?"	
210	"Quhy not?" quod scho, "Think ye this meis nocht gude?"	*nourishment not good*
	"Na be my saull I think it bot ane scorne."	*by; soul; only an insult*
	"Madame," quod scho, "ye be the mair to blame.	
	My mother sayd, efter that we wer borne,	
	That I and ye lay baith within ane wame.	*both inside the same womb*
215	I keip the ryte and custome of my dame	*routine; mother*
	And of my syre, levand in povertie,	*father, living*
	For landis hald we nane in propertie."	
	"My fair sister," quod scho, "hald me excusit.	*said; consider me excused*
	This rude dyat and I can not accord.	*coarse diet*
220	To tender meit my stomok is ay usit	*delicate food; is invariably accustomed*
	For quhy I fair alsweill as ony lord.	*Because; live as well*

---

[1] *Across moor and bog, through banks, thicket, and thornbush*

Thir wydderit peis and nuttis or thay be bord *These withered; before; gnawed into*
Wil brek my teith and mak my wame ful sklender *stomach very slender*
Quhilk usit wes before to meitis tender." *accustomed; to*

225 "Weil, weil, sister," quod the rurall mous, *Well; said*
"Geve it yow pleis, sic thing as ye se heir, *If it please you, such; here*
Baith meit and dreink, harberie and hous *shelter*
Sal be your awin will ye remane al yeir. *even should you stay*
Ye sall it have wyth blyith and hartlie cheir *in a joyous and sincere spirit*
230 And that suld mak the maissis that ar rude *servings; crude*
Amang freindis richt tender, sweit, and gude. *both*

"Quhat plesans is in festis delicate *pleasure is there; feasts*
The quhilkis ar gevin with ane glowmand brow? *which; given; scowling*
Ane gentill hart is better recreate *delighted*
235 With blyith visage than seith to him ane kow; *joyful face; cook up a cow for him*
Ane modicum is mair for till allow *of much more account*
Swa that Gude Will be kerver at the dais, *As long as; carver*
Than thrawin vult with mony spycit mais." *frowning face; spiced dishes*

For all this mery exhortatioun *Despite; cheerful encouragement*
240 This burges mous had littill will to sing *little inclination to sing along*
Bot hevilie scho kest hir browis doun *gloomily; cast*
For all the daynteis that scho culd hir bring, *Despite; dainties; could bring her*
Yit at the last scho said halff in hething, *derision*
"Sister, this victuall and your royall feist *victuals; feast*
245 May weill suffice for sic ane rurall beist. *such*

"Lat be this hole and cum unto my place, *Give up; come*
I sall yow schaw be trewe experience *shall show you by actual*
My Gude Friday is better nor your Pace, *Good Friday fast; than your Easter feast*
My dische likingis is worth your haill expence. *lickings; whole outlay*
250 I have housis anew of grit defence. *aplenty; great security*
Of cat, na fall, na trap I have na dreid." *nor; box-trap(?); dread*
"I grant," quod scho, and on togidder yeid. *accept; went ahead together*

In skugry ay throw rankest gers and corne *Under cover always; thickest grass*
Under covert full prevelie couth thay creip. *secretly did they creep*
255 The eldest was the gyde and went beforne, *guide; ahead*
The younger to hir wayis tuke gude keip. *paid good attention*
On nicht thay ran and on the day can sleip *At night; went ahead; slept*
Quhill in the morning or the laverok sang *Until; before the lark*
Thay fand the town and in blythlie couth gang. *found; joyously did walk in*

260 Not fer fra thyne unto ane worthie wane *from thence; fine building*
This burges brocht thame sone quhare thay suld be. *brought; soon where; should*
Withowt godspeid thair herberie wes tane *Without any word of blessing; shelter; taken*

Into ane spence with vittell grit plentie,   *pantry; most abundant foodstuffs*
Baith cheis and butter upon skelfis hie,   *shelves*
265   Flesche and fische aneuch, baith fresche and salt,   *aplenty*
And sekkis full of grotis, meile, and malt.   *sacks; groats, meal*

Efter quhen thay disposit wer to dyne,   *Afterwards when; were ready to eat*
Withowtin grace thay wesche and went to meit,   *Without prayer; washed; feast*
With all coursis that cukis culd devyne,   *cooks could dream up*
270   Muttoun and beif strikin in tailyeis greit.   *cut; great slices*
Ane lordis fair thus couth thay counterfeit   *lord's style of dining*
Except ane thing, thay drank the watter cleir
Insteid of wyne bot yit thay maid gude cheir.   *but nevertheless*

With blyith upcast and merie countenance,   *demeanor; merry*
275   The eldest sister sperit at hir gest   *asked her guest*
Giff that scho thocht be ressoun difference   *If; noticed by her judgment [there was any]*
Betwix that chalmer and hir sarie nest.   *Between; room; miserable*
"Ye, dame!" quod scho. "bot how lang will this lest?"   *Yes; long; last*
"For evermair, I wait, and langer to."   *Forever after; suppose; longer too*
280   "Gif it be swa, ye ar at eis," quod scho.   *If it is so, you; ease*

Till eik thair cheir ane subcharge furth scho brocht,   *To increase; side dish; brought*
Ane plait of grottis and ane disch full of meill.   *plate; groats; more fine-ground grain*
Thraf caikkis als I trow scho spairit nocht   *flat oatcakes; believe; did not neglect*
Aboundantlie about hir for to deill   *to serve out around her*
285   And mane full fyne scho brocht insteid of geill   *fine bread; meat jelly*
And ane quhyte candill owt of ane coffer stall   *white; out from a stand of boxes*
Insteid of spyce to gust thair mouth withall.   *Instead; flavor their mouth[s] as well*

Thus maid thay merie quhill thay micht na mair   *until they could*
And "Haill, Yule, haill!" thay cryit upon hie,   *at the top of their voices*
290   Yit efter joy oftymes cummis cair   *often comes care*
And troubill efter grit prosperitie.
Thus as thay sat in all thair jolitie,
The spenser come with keyis in his hand,   *steward approached*
Oppinnit the dure, and thame at denner fand.   *found them at dinner*

295   They taryit not to wesche as I suppose   *tarried; wash*
Bot on to ga quha micht formest win.   *go, whoever could take the lead*
The burges had ane hole and in scho gois.   *goes*
Hir sister had na hole to hyde hir in.   *hide herself in*
To se that selie mous it wes grit sin,
300   So desolate and will off all gude reid.   *deprived of; good advice*
For verray dreid scho fell in swoun neir deid.   *dread; swoon; dead*

Bot as God wald, it fell ane happie cace.   *wished; turned out in a happy way*
The spenser had na laser for to byde,   *no extra time to stay around*

305	Nowther to seik nor serche, to char nor chace,	*Neither; seek; knock aside*

Nowther to seik nor serche, to char nor chace, — *Neither; seek; knock aside*
305 Bot on he went and left the dure up wyde. — *door open*
This bald burges his passage weill hes spyde. — *bold citizen [the elder mouse]*
Out of hir hole scho come and cryit on hie, — *came*
"How, fair sister! Cry peip, quhairever ye be!" — *Ho; wherever*

This rurall mous lay flatlingis on the ground — *outstretched*
310 And for the deith scho wes full sair dredand — *death; dreading very grievously*
For till hir hart straik mony wofull stound, — *struck; grievous pang*
As in ane fever trimbillit fute and hand. — *foot*
And quhan hir sister in sic ply hir fand, — *found her in such a plight*
For verray pietie scho began to greit, — *weep*
315 Syne confort hir with wordis hunny sweit. — *words sweet as honey*

"Quhy ly ye thus? Ryse up, my sister deir, — *are you lying [there] like that*
Cum to your meit, this perrell is overpast." — *peril has been overcome*
The uther answerit with a hevie cheir, — *gloomy expression*
"I may not eit, sa sair I am agast. — *severely upset*
320 I had lever thir fourty dayis fast — *rather have fasted these forty days*
With watter caill and gnaw benis or peis — *watery cabbage soup*
Than all your feist in this dreid and diseis." — *unease*

With fair tretie yit scho gart hir upryse. — *entreaty; she made her get up*
To burde thay went and on togidder sat — *table; again sat together*
325 And scantlie had thay drunkin anis or twyse — *scarcely; once*
Quhen in come Gib Hunter our jolie cat — *When; came "Gilbert"; fine*
And bad godspeid. The burges up with that. — *welcome; [got] up*
And till hir hole scho fled as fyre of flint. — *like fire from a flint*
Bawdronis the uther be the bak hes hint. — *"Baldwin" [the cat] the other [mouse] by; seized*

330 Fra fute to fute he kest hir to and fra, — *tossed*
Quhylis up, quhylis doun, als tait as ony kid. — *Sometimes; nimble; any*
Quhylis wald he lat hir rin under the stra, — *let her run under the straw*
Quhylis wald he wink and play with hir buk-heid. — *hide and seek*
Thus to the selie mous grit pane he did — *great pain to the poor mouse he caused*
335 Quhill at the last throw fair fortune and hap — *through good fortune and luck*
Betwix the dosor and the wall scho crap, — *Between; curtain; crept*

Syne up in haist behind the parraling — *Then; haste; wall hanging*
So hie scho clam that Gilbert micht not get hir — *climbed; could*
And be the clukis craftelie can hing — *claws; did hang*
340 Till he wes gane. Hir cheir wes all the better, — *gone. Her mood*
Syne doun scho lap quhen thair wes nane to let hir. — *came; no one; prevent*
Apon the burges mous loud can scho cry, — *Against; loudly did she*
"Fairweill, sister, thy feist heir I defy. — *renounce*

"Thy mangerie is mingit all with cair,   *banquet is mixed*
345 Thy guse is gude, thy gansell sour as gall.   *sauce*
The subcharge of thy service is bot sair,   *second course; utter pain*
Sa sall thow find heir-efterwart ma fall.   *shall; hereafter may come to pass*
I thank yone courtyne and yone perpall wall   *that curtain; partition*
Of my defence now fra yone crewell beist.   *For; cruel beast*
350 Almichtie God keip me fra sic ane feist!   *protect; from such a feast*

"Wer I into the kith that I come fra   *native district*
For weill nor wo I suld never cum agane."   *woe*
With that scho tuke hir leif and furth can ga   *took her leave*
Quhylis throw the corne and quhylis throw the plane.   *open country*
355 Quhen scho wes furth and fre, scho wes full fane   *out; eager*
And merilie scho markit unto the mure.   *merrily; headed to; moor*
I can not tell how eftirwart scho fure   *how she fared afterwards*

Bot I hard say scho passit to hir den   *heard; went*
Als warme as woll suppose it wes not greit,   *[Which was] as; wool although*
360 Full beinly stuffit baith but and ben   *amply; outer; inner [rooms of the house]*
Of beinis and nuttis, peis, ry, and quheit.   *rye; wheat*
Quhenever scho list, scho had aneuch to eit   *was inclined; enough*
In quyet and eis withoutin ony dreid   *ease*
Bot to hir sisteris feist na mair scho yeid.   *went*

Moralitas   *Moralization*
365 Freindis, heir may ye find, will ye tak heid,   *if you choose to pay attention*
In this fabill ane gude moralitie.
As fitchis myngit ar with nobill seid   *vetches are mixed*
Swa intermellit is adversitie   *intermingled*
With eirdlie joy swa that na state is frie   *unencumbered*
370 Without trubill or sum vexatioun   *some distress*
And namelie thay quhilk clymmis up maist hie   *they who climb most high*
And not content with small possessioun.

Blissed be sempill lyfe withoutin dreid,   *simple*
Blissed be sober feist in quietie.   *moderate meal in quietude*
375 Quha hes aneuch, of na mair hes he neid   *Whoever*
Thocht it be littill into quantatie.   *Though; small in amount*
Grit aboundance and blind prosperitie
Oftymes makis ane evill conclusioun.   *Often bring about; unhappy end*
The sweitest lyfe thairfoir in this cuntrie   *country*
380 Is sickernes with small possessioun.   *security; few belongings*

O wantoun man that usis for to feid   *who is accustomed to feed*
Thy wambe and makis it a god to be,   *belly; turn it into a god*
Luke to thyself, I warne thee weill ondeid.   *Look; indeed*
The cat cummis and to the mous hes ee.   *has an eye*

385 Quhat is avale than thy feist and royaltie   *What is then the use [of]*
With dreidfull hart and tribulatioun?   *fearful*
Thairfoir best thing in eird, I say for me,   *as far as I am concerned*
Is merry hart with small possessioun.   *heart*

Thy awin fyre, freind, thocht it be bot ane gleid,   *ember*
390 It warmis weill and is worth gold to thee.
As Solomon sayis, gif that thow will reid,   *if; read*
"Under the hevin I can not better se   *I can see nothing better*
Than ay be blyith and leif in honestie,"   *always to be carefree; live*
Quhairfoir I may conclude be this ressoun,   *with this thought*
395 Of eirthly joy it beiris maist degree,   *bears highest rank*
Blyithnes in hart with small possessioun.

The Cock and the Fox   *Rooster*

Thocht brutall beistis be irrationall,   *Although brute beasts*
That is to say, wantand discretioun,   *lacking the ability to discern*
Yit ilkane in thair kyndis naturall   *each one; their species*
400 Hes mony divers inclinatioun: *different tendencies*
The bair busteous, the wolf, the wylde lyoun,   *the violent boar*
The fox fenyeit, craftie, and cautelows,   *deceptive; devious*
The dog to bark on nicht and keip the hows.   *at night and guard*

Sa different thay ar in properteis   *in [their respective] traits*
405 Unknawin unto man and infinite,   *Undiscovered by*
In kynd havand sa fell diversiteis,   *By nature having so many*
My cunning it excedis for to dyte.   *understanding; transcends to write*
Forthy as now I purpose for to wryte   *Therefore; intend*
Ane cais I fand quhilk fell this ather yeir   *event I learned; befell; other*
410 Betwix ane foxe and gentill Chantecleir.   *Between; noble Chantecleer [the rooster]*

Ane wedow dwelt intill ane drop thay dayis   *widow; in a hamlet [in] those*
Quhilk wan hir fude off spinning on hir rok   *Who earned; from; distaff*
And na mair had forsuth as the fabill sayis   *no more; indeed*
Except of hennis scho had ane lyttill flok   *hens*
415 And thame to keip scho had ane jolie cok   *to guard them*
Richt curageous that to this wedow ay   *Very spirited; for; regularly*
Devydit nicht and crew befoir the day.   *Measured; crowed*

Ane lyttill fra this foirsaid wedowis hows,   *little way; foresaid*
Ane thornie schaw thair wes, of grit defence,   *thicket there was, of great security*
420 Quhairin ane foxe, craftie and cautelous,   *In which; devious*
Maid his repair and daylie residence   *Made; residence; daily lodging*
Quhilk to this wedow did grit violence   *Who*
In pyking off hir pultrie day and nicht   *snatching away her poultry*
And na way be revengit on him scho micht.   *by no means; she could*

425	This wylie tod, quhen that the lark couth sing,	*wily fox; did sing*
	Full sair hungrie unto the toun him drest	*sorely; farm betook himself*
	Quhair Chantecleir into the gray dawing,	*Where; in the gray dawn*
	Werie for-nicht, wes flowen fra his nest.	*Weary from staying up; had flown from*
	Lowrence this saw and in his mynd he kest	*[the fox]; considered*
430	The juparteis, the wayis, and the wyle,	*risks; subterfuges; cunning*
	Be quhat menis he micht this cok begyle.	*what means he might*
	Dissimuland into countenance and cheir,	*Feigning; look; manner*
	On kneis fell and simuland thus he said,	*knees; pretending*
	"Gude morne, my maister, gentill Chantecleir."	*Good morning; master*
435	With that the cok start bakwart in ane braid.	*recoiled with a jump*
	"Schir, be my saull, ye neid not be effraid	*Sir, by; soul; need; afraid*
	Nor yit for me to start nor fle abak;	*on my account; recoil*
	I come bot heir yow service for to mak.	*come here only to do you service*
	"Wald I not serve to yow, it wer bot blame	*Did I not wish; [nothing] but*
440	As I have done to yowr progenitouris.	*ancestors*
	Your father oft fulfillit hes my wame	*often has filled up; belly*
	And send me meit fra midding to the muris	*sent; food; midden; moors*
	And at his end I did my besie curis	*devoted my full energies*
	To hald his heid and gif him drinkis warme,	*hold; head; give*
445	Syne at the last the sweit swelt in my arme."	*Until; darling passed away*
	"Knew ye my father?" quod the cok and leuch.	*laughed*
	"Yea my fair sone, forsuth I held his heid	*son, indeed*
	Quhen that he deit under ane birkin beuch,	*died; the bough of a birch*
	Syne said the dirigie quhen that he wes deid.	*Then; dirge when; dead*
450	Betwix us twa how suld thair be ane feid?	*Between; two; could; feud*
	Quhame suld ye traist bot me your servitour	*trust but; servant*
	That to your father did sa grit honour?	*paid such great respect*
	"Quhen I behald your fedderis fair and gent,	*feathers; noble*
	Your beik, your breist, your hekill, and your kame,	*beak; breast; neck-feathers; comb*
455	Schir, be my saull and the blissit Sacrament,	*by; holy Mass*
	My hart warmys, me think I am at hame.	*grows warm; it seems to me*
	Yow for to serve I wald creip on my wame	*To serve you; creep*
	In froist and snaw, in wedder wan and weit,	*gloomy and wet weather*
	And lay my lyart loikkis under your feit."	*gray hair*
460	This fenyeit foxe fals and dissimulate	*insincere; hypocritical*
	Maid to this cok ane cavillatioun.	*groundless objection*
	"Me think yow changit and degenerate	*You seem to me changed*
	Fra your father and his conditioun.	*From; character*
	Of craftie crawing he micht beir the croun	*crowing; could take; crown*
465	For he wald on his tais stand and craw.	*toes; crow*
	This is na le, I stude beside and saw."	*no lie; stood*

	With that the cok upon his tais hie	*tiptoes*
	Kest up his beik and sang with all his micht.	*Raised*
	Quod schir Lowrence, "Weill said, sa mot I the!	*Well tried, so may I prosper*
470	Ye ar your fatheris sone and air upricht	*son and rightful heir*
	Bot of his cunning yit ye want ane slicht —	*technique you lack a special touch*
	"Quhat!" quod the cok — "he wald, and haif na dout,	*have no doubt*
	Baith wink and craw and turne him thryis about."	*himself thrice*

	The cok inflate with wind and fals vanegloir	*puffed up*
475	That mony puttis unto confusioun,	*bring many to perdition*
	Traisting to win ane grit worschip thairfoir,	*Trusting; great accolade*
	Unwarlie winkand, walkit up and doun,	*Heedlessly closing his eyes*
	And syne to chant and craw he maid him boun	*made himself ready*
	And suddandlie be he had crawin ane note,	*suddenly by the time that; crowed*
480	The foxe wes war and hint him be the throte,	*alert; grabbed; by the throat*

	Syne to the woid but tarie with him hyit,	*forest without delay; rushed*
	Of countermaund haifand bot lytill dout.	*forbiddance having; fear*
	With that Pertok, Sprutok, and Toppok cryit.	*that [outcome]; cried out*
	The wedow hard and with ane cry come out.	*widow heard; came*
485	Seand the cace, scho sichit and gaif ane schout,	*Seeing; situation; sighed*
	"How! murther! reylok!" with ane hiddeous beir,	*Ho!; robbery; yell*
	"Allace, now lost is gentill Chantecleir!"	*noble*

	As scho wer woid, with mony yell and cry,	*As if; insane*
	Ryvand hir hair, upon hir breist can beit,	*Tearing at; did beat*
490	Syne paill of hew, half in ane extasy,	*pale; complexion; trance*
	Fell doun for cair in swoning and in sweit.	*grief; fainting; a sweat*
	With that the selie hennis left thair meit	*poor; food*
	And quhill this wyfe wes lyand thus in swoun	*while; was lying*
	Fell of that cace in disputatioun.	*about that situation; debate*

	"Allace," quod Pertok, makand sair murning	*making heavy mourning*
495	With teiris grit attour hir cheikis fell,	*great tears over; cheeks*
	"Yone wes our drowrie and our dayis darling,	*amour*
	Our nichtingall and als our orlege bell,	*also; clock tower*
	Our walkryfe watche us for to warne and tell	*wakeful lookout*
500	Quhen that Aurora with hir curcheis gray	*kerchiefs*
	Put up hir heid betwix the nicht and day.	*Raised up her head between*

	"Quha sall our lemman be, quha sall us leid,	*lover; who shall lead us*
	Quhen we ar sad quha sall unto us sing?	*When; who shall*
	With his sweit bill he wald brek us the breid —	*would break; bread*
505	In all this warld wes thair ane kynder thing? —	
	In paramouris he wald do us plesing	*During sex; give us pleasure*
	At his power as nature did him geif.	*nature endowed him*
	Now efter him allace how sall we leif?"	*live*

	Quod Sprutok than, "Ceis, sister, of your sorrow.	*Cease*
510	Ye be to mad, for him sic murning mais.	*too; [who] make such mourning*
	We sall fair weill, I find, Sanct Johne to borrow.	*do fine, I expect, trust me*
	The proverb sayis, 'Als gude lufe cummis as gais.'	*As good love comes; goes*
	I will put on my halydais clais	*holiday clothes*
	And mak me fresch agane this jolie May,	*make myself over in time for*
515	Syne chant this sang, 'Wes never wedow sa gay!'	*Then sing*
	"He wes angry and held us ay in aw	*restrained; always; fear*
	And woundit with the speir of jelowsy.	*wounded; spear*
	Of chalmer glew, Pertok, full weill ye knaw	*bedroom pleasure; you know very well*
	Waistit he wes, of nature cauld and dry.	*Exhausted; by nature cold*
520	Sen he is gone thairfoir sister, say I,	*Since*
	Be blyith in baill for that is best remeid.	*glad in misfortune; remedy*
	Let quik to quik and deid ga to the deid."	*the living; the dead go*
	Than Pertok spak that feinyeit faith befoir,	*spoke who pretended loyalty earlier*
	In lust but lufe that set all hir delyte.	*without love*
525	"Sister, ye wait of sic as him ane scoir	*know [that] of such; score*
	Wald not suffice to slaik our appetyte.	*Would not be enough; satisfy*
	I hecht yow be my hand sen ye ar quyte,	*promise; by; since; free*
	Within ane oulk, for schame and I durst speik,	*week; if I dare speak*
	To get ane berne suld better claw oure breik."	*man; tickle; crotch*
530	Than Toppok lyke ane curate spak full crous,	*like; priest; boldly*
	"Yone wes ane verray vengeance from the hevin.	*That; true*
	He wes sa lous and sa lecherous,	*so promiscuous*
	Seis coud he nocht with kittokis ma than sevin	*Cease; wenches more*
	Bot rychteous God haldand the balandis evin,	*holding; scales [of justice]*
535	Smytis rycht sair, thocht he be patient,	*Smites very painfully though*
	Adulteraris that list thame not repent.	*Adulterers who prefer not to*
	"Prydefull he wes and joyit of his sin	*delighted in*
	And comptit not for Goddis favour nor feid	*took no account; enmity*
	Bot traistit ay to rax and sa to rin,	*expected; gain power; reign*
540	Quhill at the last his sinnis can him leid	*sins led him*
	To schamefull end and to yone suddand deid.	*that sudden death*
	Thairfoir it is the verray hand of God	*veritable*
	That causit him be werryit with the tod."	*snatched by the fox*
	Quhen this wes said, this wedow fra hir swoun	*When; out of her swoon*
545	Start up on fute and on hir kennettis cryde,	*Jumped; called to her dogs*
	"How! Birkye, Berrie, Bell, Bawsie Broun,	*Ho! Birchy; Clumsy Brown*
	Rype-schaw, Rin-weil, Curtes, Nuttieclyde,	*Tear-thicket, Run-well, Bobtail*
	Togidder all but grunching furth ye glyde,	*without complaining; hasten*
	Reskew my nobill cok or he be slane	*before*
550	Or ellis to me se ye cum never agane."	*else; see that; never return*

With that but baid thay braidet over the bent,   *delay; raced; ground*
As fyre off flint thay over the feildis flaw,   *flew across the fields*
Full wichtlie thay throw wood and wateris went   *energetically; through*
And ceissit not schir Lourence quhill thay saw;   *did not stop; while*
555   Bot quhen he saw the raches cum on raw   *hounds; in a row*
Unto the cok in mynd he said, "God sen   *in his mind; God grant*
That I and thow wer fairlie in my den."   *were actually*

Then spak the cok with sum gude spirit inspyrit,   *spoke; by some; inspired*
"Do my counsall and I sall warrand thee.   *shall protect*
560   Hungrie thow art and for grit travell tyrit,   *and tired after great effort*
Richt faint of force and may not ferther fle.   *low in energy; flee further*
Swyith turne agane and say that I and ye   *Turn back at once*
Freindis ar maid and fellowis for ane yeir.   *Have made friends; year*
Than will thay stint, I stand for it, and not steir."   *Then; quit; promise it; move*

565   This tod, thocht he wes fals and frivolus   *deceptive*
And had fraudis his querrell to defend,   *to cover up his scheme*
Desavit wes be menis richt mervelous   *Deceived; means; amazing*
For falset failyeis ay at the latter end.   *falsehood fails always*
He start about and cryit as he wes kend.   *called out; taught*
570   With that the cok he braid unto a bewch.   *shot up onto a bough*
Now juge ye all quhairat schir Lowrence lewch.   *judge; at what sir; laughed*

Begylit thus, the tod under the tre   *Tricked*
On kneis fell and said, "Gude Chantecleir,   *Fell to [his] knees*
Cum doun agane and I but meit or fe   *without food or wages*
575   Sal be your man and servand for ane yeir."   *Shall*
"Na, murther, theif, and revar, stand on reir.   *murderer; rustler, stand back*
My bludy hekill and my nek sa bla   *so lividly bruised*
Hes partit love for ever betwene us twa.   *broken affection; two*

"I wes unwyse that winkit at thy will,   *closed my eyes; wish*
580   Quhairthrow almaist I loissit had my heid."   *Because of which; lost*
"I wes mair fule," quod he, "coud nocht be still   *the bigger fool; [who] could*
But spake to put my pray into pleid."   *make my prey a matter for legal negotiation*
"Fair on, fals theif, God keip me fra thy feid."   *Go your way; from; enmity*
With that the cok over the feildis tuke his flicht.   *took his flight*
585   In at the wedowis lever couth he licht.   *louver he landed*

Moralitas   *Moralization*
Now worthie folk, suppose this be ane fabill   *granted [that]*
And overheillit wyth typis figurall,   *covered over; figurative images*
Yit may ye find ane sentence richt agreabill   *a very suitable lesson*
Under thir fenyeit termis textuall.   *fictional language of the text*
590   To our purpose this cok weill may we call   *For; we may well term*

Nyse proud men, woid and vaneglorious *Conceited; crazy; vain*
Of kin and blude, quhilk ar presumpteous. *About family; lineage, who; arrogant*

Fy, puft up pryde, thow is full poysonabill. *puffed-up; very poisonous*
Quha favoris thee on force man haif ane fall. *Whoever; needs must have*
595 Thy strenth is nocht, thy stule standis unstabill. *nothing; stool*
Tak witnes of the feyndis infernall *Take as an example the devils of hell*
Quhilk houndit doun wes fra that hevinlie hall *Who were hounded down*
To hellis hole and to that hiddeous hous
Because in pryde thay wer presumpteous.

600 This fenyeit foxe may weill be figurate *compared*
To flatteraris with plesand wordis quhyte, *pleasant, shining words*
With fals mening and mynd maist toxicate *meaning; most toxic*
To loif and le that settis thair haill delyte. *flatter; lie; commit; whole*
All worthie folk at sic suld haif despyte *for such [people]; contempt*
605 For quhair is thair mair perrellous pestilence *a more dangerous plague*
Nor gif to learis haistelie credence? *Than [to] give; liars hastily*

The wickit mynd and adullatioun, *flattery*
Of sucker sweit haifand the similitude, *sweet sugar having; likeness*
Bitter as gall and full of fell poysoun *deadly poison*
610 To taist it is, quha cleirlie understude. *whoever clearly*
Forthy as now, schortlie to conclude, *Therefore for now, briefly*
Thir twa sinnis, flatterie and vaneglore, *These two*
Ar vennomous. Gude folk, fle thame thairfoir. *flee them*

The Fox and the Wolf

Leif we this wedow glaid, I yow assure, *Let us leave; glad widow*
615 Of Chantecleir mair blyith than I can tell, *About; more blithe* [glad]
And speik we of the fatal aventure *occurrence*
And destenie that to this foxe befell
Quhilk durst na mair with miching intermell *dared not get more mixed up in pilfering*
Als lang as leme or licht wes of the day *brightness; from*
620 Bot bydand nicht full styll lurkand he lay *awaiting night very; hiding*

Quhill that Thetes the goddes of the flude *Until Thetis; goddess; sea*
Phebus had callit to the harbery *Had called Phoebus home*
And Hesperous put off his cluddie hude *took off his cloudy hood*
Schawand his lustie visage in the sky, *Showing; handsome face*
625 Than Lourence luikit up quhair he couth ly *looked; from the place where*
And kest his hand upon his ee on hicht, *placed; over his upturned eyes*
Merie and glade that cummit wes the nicht. *the night had come*

Out of the wod unto ane hill he went
Quhair he micht se the twinkling sternis cleir *stars*

630   And all the planetis of the firmament,
       Thair cours and eik thair moving in the spheir,   *orbits and also; celestial hemisphere*
       Sum retrograde and sum stationeir   *Some moving backward; stationary*
       And off the zodiak in quhat degree   *what*
       Thay wer ilkane as Lowrence leirnit me: *They each were; taught*

635   Than Saturne auld wes enterit in Capricorne
       And Juppiter movit in Sagittarie   *moved forward in Sagittarius*
       And Mars up in the Rammis heid wes borne   *was ascendent in the Ram's head (Aries)*
       And Phebus in the Lyoun furth can carie,   *hastened ahead in Leo*
       Venus the Crab, the Mone wes in Aquarie,   *in Cancer; Moon; Aquarius*
640   Mercurius the god of eloquence
       Into the Virgyn maid his residence.   *Resided in Virgo*

       But astrolab, quadrant, or almanak,   *Without; astronomical calendar*
       Teichit of nature be instructioun,   *Taught by the instruction of nature*
       The moving of the hevin this tod can tak   *fox did perceive*
645   Quhat influence and constellatioun   *What; stellar power*
       Wes lyke to fall upon the eirth adoun   *likely; descend down to earth*
       And to himself he said withoutin mair,   *without hesitation*
       "Weill worth thee, father, that send me to the lair. *May good befall; who sent; school*

       "My destenie and eik my weird I wait,   *also my fate I know*
650   My aventure is cleirlie to me kend.   *risk; known*
       With mischeif myngit is my mortall fait,   *misadventure mixed; fate*
       My misleving the soner bot I mend.   *sinful life; sooner unless*
       Deid is reward of sin, and schamefull end.   *Death; and a shameful end*
       Thairfoir I will ga seik sum confessour   *go seek some confessor*
655   And schryiff me clene of all sinnis to this hour." *purge myself*

       "Allace," quod he, "richt waryit ar we thevis.   *utterly accursed; thieves*
       Our lyif is set ilk nicht in aventure.   *placed each night at risk*
       Our cursit craft full mony man mischevis   *brings very many a man to grief*
       For ever we steill and ever alyk ar pure.   *steal; always are just as poor*
660   In dreid and schame our dayis we indure,
       Syne 'Widdinek' and 'Crakraip' callit als   *Noose-neck; Crack-rope; too*
       And till our hyre ar hangit be the hals."   *for our reward; throat*

       Accusand thus his cankerit conscience,   *Blaming; cankered*
       Into ane craig he kest about his ee,   *Upon; crag; directed; eyesight*
665   So saw he cummand ane lyttill than frome thence   *coming; a little way from there*
       Ane worthie doctour of divinitie,   *doctor; theology*
       Freir Wolff Waitskaith, in science wonder sle,   *Friar Do-harm; learning most expert*
       To preiche and pray wes new cum fra the closter   *newly arrived; cloister*
       With beidis in hand, sayand his Pater Noster.   *prayer beads; saying*

670	Seand this wolff, this wylie tratour tod	*wily traitor fox*
	On kneis fell with hude into his nek.	*knees; hood [down] around*
	"Welcome, my gostlie father under God,"	*spiritual father*
	Quod he with mony binge and mony bek.	*many a servile bow; nod*
	"Ha," quod the wolff, "schir tod, for quhat effek	*reason*
675	Mak ye sic feir? Ryse up, put on your hude!"	*[Do] you put on such an act*
	"Father," quod he, "I haif grit cause to dude:	*do it*
	"Ye ar the lanterne and the sicker way	*dependable path*
	Suld gyde sic sempill folk as me to grace.	*[That] should guide such*
	Your bair feit and your russet coull of gray,	*homespun, undyed cowl*
680	Your lene cheik, your paill and pietious face,	*lean; pale; compassionate*
	Schawis to me your perfite halines	*perfect holiness*
	For weill wer him that anis in his lyve	*[it] were well for him [who]*
	Had hap to yow his sinnis for to schryve."	*opportunity; you; confess*
	"Na, selie Lowrence," quod the wolf and leuch,	*O, poor; said; laughed*
685	"It plesis me that ye ar penitent."	*pleases*
	"Of reif and stouth, schir, I can tell aneuch	*plunder; pilfering, sir; plenty*
	That causis me full sair for to repent.	*sorely*
	Bot father, byde still heir upon the bent,	*stay; here in the open*
	I yow beseik, and heir me to declair	*beseech; hear*
690	My conscience that prikkis me sa sair."	*pricks*
	"Weill," quod the wolff, "sit doun upon thy kne."	*get down on thy knees*
	And he doun bairheid sat full humilly	*bareheaded; humbly*
	And syne began with "Benedicitie."	*"Give blessing"*
	Quhen I this saw, I drew ane lytill by,	*withdrew a little away*
695	For it effeiris nouther to heir nor spy	*is fitting neither; listen*
	Nor to reveill thing said under that seill	*reveal; vow of secrecy*
	But to the tod thisgait the wolf couth mele,	*in this way; did speak*
	"Art thow contrite and sorie in thy spreit	*spirit*
	For thy trespas?" "Na, schir, I can not duid.	*sin?" "O, sir; do it*
700	Me think that hennis ar sa honie sweit	*hens; so honey-sweet*
	And lambes flesche that new ar lettin bluid,	*freshly bled*
	For to repent my mynd can not concluid	*resolve*
	Bot of this thing that I haif slane sa few."	*Except for; have slain*
	"Weill," quod the wolf, "in faith thow art ane schrew.	*a villain*
705	"Sen thow can not forthink thy wickitnes,	*Since; feel regret [for]*
	Will thow forbeir in tyme to cum and mend?"	*refrain; reform*
	"And I forbeir, how sall I leif allace,	*If; shall I live*
	Haifand nane uther craft me to defend?	*to support myself*
	Neid causis me to steill quhairever I wend.	*Necessity; steal wherever; go*
710	I eschame to thig, I can not wirk ye wait,	*am ashamed; beg; work; know*
	Yit wald I fane pretend to gentill stait."	*gladly lay claim; rank*

"Weill," quod the wolf, "thow wantis pointis twa   *lack two elements*
Belangand to perfyte confessioun.   *Pertaining*
To the thrid part of pennance let us ga.   *third; proceed*
715   Will thow tak pane for thy transgressioun?"   *submit to a penalty*
"A, schir, considder my complexioun,   *my physical constitution*
Seikly and waik and of my nature tender;   *Sickly and weak*
Lo, will ye se, I am baith lene and sklender.   *both lean*

"Yit nevertheles I wald, swa it wer licht,   *would, if; easy*
720   Schort, and not grevand to my tendernes,   *painful*
Tak part of pane, fulfill it gif I micht,   *if I could carry it out*
To set my selie saull in way of grace."   *poor soul*
"Thow sall," quod he, "forbeir flesch hyne to Pasche   *refrain; meat from now; Easter*
To tame this corps, that cursit carioun,   *body; accursed carrion*
725   And heir I reik thee full remissioun."   *here; offer*

"I grant thairto swa ye will giff me leif   *as long as you give me leave*
To eit puddingis or laip ane lyttill blude   *eat sausage; sip a little blood*
Or heid or feit or paynchis let me preif   *head; feet; entrails; taste*
In cace I faut of flesch unto my fude."   *case I lack flesh in my diet*
730   "For grit mister I gif thee leif to dude   *In sore necessity; leave to do it*
Twyse in the oulk, for neid may haif na law."   *Twice; week; need; have*
"God yeild yow schir, for that text weill I knaw."   *reward; I know well*

Quhen this wes said, the wolf his wayis went.   *went on his way*
The foxe on fute he fure unto the flude.   *proceeded towards the water*
735   To fang him fisch haillelie wes his intent   *get himself [some]; wholly was*
Bot quhen he saw the walterand wallis woude,   *wild, heaving waves*
All stonist still into ane stair he stude   *discouraged motionless; horror; stood*
And said, "Better that I had biddin at hame   *stayed at home*
Nor bene ane fischar in the devillis name.   *Than [to have] been a fisher*

740   "Now man I scraip my meit out of the sand   *must I scrape my food*
For I haif nouther boittis, net, nor bait."   *neither boats*
As he wes thus for falt of meit murnand,   *While; lack; grumbling*
Lukand about his leving for to lait,   *Seeking around to find his sustenance*
Under ane tre he saw ane trip of gait.   *a herd of goats*
745   Than wes he blyith and in ane hewch him hid,   *happy; hid himself in a ravine*
And fra the gait he stall ane lytill kid,   *from the goats; stole*

Syne over the heuch unto the see he hyis   *Then; sea; hastens*
And tuke the kid be the hornis twane   *took; by; two horns*
And in the watter outher twyis or thryis   *either twice or thrice*
750   He dowkit him and till him can he sayne,   *dunked; to him did he say*
"Ga doun schir kid, cum up schir salmond agane,"   *sir; salmon*
Quhill he wes deid, syne to the land him drewch   *Until; dead; then; dragged*
And of that new-maid salmond eit anewch.   *ate plenty*

Thus fynelie fillit with young tender meit, — *nicely stuffed; meat*

755 Unto ane derne for dreid he him addrest — *secret spot; made his way*

Under ane busk quhair that the sone can beit — *bush; the sun shone brightly*

To beik his breist and bellie he thocht best — *warm; thought*

And rekleslie he said quhair he did rest, — *recklessly; where*

Straikand his wame aganis the sonis heit, — *Outstretching; belly in*

760 "Upon this wame set wer ane bolt full meit." — *it would be very fitting to place an arrow*

Quhen this wes said, the keipar of the gait, — *keeper; goats*

Cairfull in hart his kid wes stollen away, — *Aggrieved at heart*

On everilk syde full warlie couth he wait — *every; carefully did he peer*

Quhill at the last he saw quhair Lowrence lay. — *Until; where*

765 Ane bow he bent, ane flane with fedderis gray — *arrow; feathers*

He haillit to the heid, and or he steird — *drew; before he moved*

The foxe he prikkit fast unto the eird. — *skewered; earth*

"Now," quod the foxe, "allace and wellaway. — *woe is me*

Gorrit I am and may na forther gane. — *Punctured; can no further go*

770 Methink na man may speik ane word in play — *It seems to me; say; in jest*

Bot now on dayis in ernist it is tane." — *nowadays; taken*

The hird him hynt and out he drew his flane — *goatherd seized him; pulled his arrow*

And for his kid and uther violence — *other violent offenses*

He tuke his skyn and maid ane recompence.

Moralitas

775 **T**his suddand deith and unprovysit end — *Moralization*

Of this fals tod without contritioun — *unprepared-for*

Exempill is exhortand folk to mend — *exhorting; reform*

For dreid of sic ane lyke conclusioun — *such a similar*

For mony gois now to confessioun — *many now go*

780 Cannot repent nor for thair sinnis greit — *lament*

Because thay think thair lustie lyfe sa sweit.

Sum bene also throw consuetude and ryte — *Some [there] are; custom and habit*

Vincust with carnall sensualitie. — *Vanquished*

Suppose thay be as for the tym contryte, — *Although; for a while*

785 Cannot forbeir nor fra thair sinnis fle. — *[They] cannot forbear; flee from their sins*

Use drawis nature swa in propertie — *Habit pulls; in such a way*

Of beist and man that neidlingis thay man do — *necessarily; must*

As thay of lang tyme hes bene hantit to. — *have been accustomed*

Bewar, gude folke, and feir this suddane schoit — *fear; shot*

790 Quhilk smytis sair withoutin resistence. — *That smites hard; opposition*

Attend wyislie and in your hartis noit, — *Pay attention; take note*

Aganis deith may na man mak defence. — *no one can mount a defense*

Ceis of your sin, remord your conscience, — *Desist from; penitently examine*

	Do wilfull pennance here and ye sall wend	*willing; shall go*
795	Efter your deith to blis withouttin end.	

The Trial of the Fox

	This foirsaid foxe that deit for his misdeid	*died; misdeeds*
	Had not ane barne wes gottin richteouslie	*child [who]; legally sired*
	That to his airschip micht of law succeid	*estate*
	Except ane sone the quhilk in lemanrie	*a son; which in illicit love*
800	He gottin had in purches privelie	*begotten in clandestine appropriation*
	And till his name wes callit Father-war	*Who for; Father-worse*
	That luifit weill with pultrie tig and tar.	*loved; poultry tussle; tease*

	It followis weill be ressoun naturall	*according to natural reason*
	And gre be gre of richt comparisoun,	*step by; by proper analogy*
805	Of evill cummis war, of war cummis werst of all,	*From; worse*
	Of wrangus get cummis wrang successioun.	*From illegitimate offspring*
	This foxe, bastard of generatioun,	*parentage*
	Of verray kynde behuifit to be fals.	*By true nature had to be*
	Swa wes his father and his grandschir als.	*grandfather too*

810	As nature will, seikand his meit be sent,	*demands; seeking; food by scent*
	Off cace he fand his fatheris carioun,	*By chance; found; corpse*
	Nakit, new slane and till him is he went,	*Flayed; freshly slain; to him has he gone*
	Tuke up his heid and on his kne fell doun	*Lifted; head*
	Thankand grit God of that conclusioun	*Thanking; outcome*
815	And said,"Now sall I bruke, sen I am air,	*possess, since; heir*
	The boundis quhair thow wes wont for to repair."	*territories where thou; resort*

	Fy covetice, unkynd and venemous.	*Shame on covetousness, unnatural*
	The sone wes fane he fand his father deid	*pleased; found; dead*
	Be suddand schot for deidis odious	*By sudden; hateful deeds*
820	That he micht ringe and raxe intill his steid,	*reign; grow strong in; stead*
	Dreidand nathing the samin lyfe to leid	*Fearing; to lead the same life*
	In stouth and reif as he had done befoir	*filching; plunder as his [father]*
	Bot to the end attent he tuke no moir.	*he paid no further heed*

	Yit nevertheles throw naturall pietie	*sentiment*
825	The carioun upon his bak he tais.	*takes*
	"Now find I weill this proverb trew," quod he,	*I certainly find; true*
	"Ay rinnis the foxe, als lang as he fute hais,"	*The fox keeps going; has*
	Syne with the corps unto ane peitpoit gais	*goes to a pool in the peat bog*
	Of watter full and kest him in the deip	*threw; deep*
830	And to the Devill he gaif his banis to keip.	*bones; keep*

	O fulische man plungit in wardlynes	*immersed; worldliness*
	To conqueis wrangwis guidis, gold and rent,	*amass wrongful possessions*

	To put thy saull in pane or hevines,	*subject; soul; pain; anguish*
	To riche thy air quhilk efter thow art went,	*enrich; heir; have deceased*
835	Have he thy gude, he takis bot small tent	*When he has; small pains*
	To sing or say for thy salvatioun.	*recite [a dirge]*
	Fra thow be dede, done is thy devotioun.	*Once; dead; finished*
	This tod to rest he carit to ane craig	*In order to rest, this fox went to a crag*
	And thair he hard ane buisteous bugill blaw	*heard; blaring bugle blow*
840	Quhilk as him thocht maid all the warld to waig,	*[it] seemed to him; rock*
	Than start he up quhen he this hard and saw	*Then he leapt*
	Ane unicorne come lansand over ane law,	*bounding; hill*
	With horne in hand, ane bill in breist he bure,	*document; carried*
	Ane pursephant semelie, I yow assure.	*proper pursuivant [herald of junior rank]*
845	Unto ane bank quhair he micht se about	*could look around*
	On everilk syde, in haist he culd him hy,	*every; did betake himself*
	Schot out his voce full schyll, and gaif ane schout	*Projected; voice out high; gave*
	And "Oyas, oyas" twyse or thryse did cry.	*"Hear ye, hear ye" twice*
	With that the beistis in the feild thairby,	*At that [sign]; nearby*
850	All mervelland quhat sic ane thing suld mene,	*wondering what such*
	Govand agast, thay gaderit on ane grene.	*Staring; gathered; field*
	Out of his buste ane bill sone can he braid	*box; quickly did; pull*
	And red the text withoutin tarying.	*read; without hesitation*
	Commandand silence, sadlie thus he said:	*solemnly*
855	"'We, nobill Lyoun, of all beistis the king,	*[the "royal We"]; the king of all the beasts*
	Greting to God ay lestand but ending,	*Greetings; everlasting without*
	To brutall beistis and irrationall	*[And] to brute; unreasoning*
	I send as to my subjectis grit and small.	*great*
	"'My celsitude and hie magnificence	*eminence; high*
860	Lattis yow to wit that evin incontinent	*Permits; know; exactly now*
	Thinkis the morne with royall deligence	*Intends tomorrow*
	Upon this hill to hald ane parliament.	*convene*
	Straitlie thairfoir I gif commandement	*Strictly; give*
	For to compeir befoir my tribunall	*meet*
865	Under all pane and perrell that may fall.'"	*Subject to; befall*
	The morrow come, and Phebus with his bemis	*came; sunbeams*
	Consumit had the mistie cluddis gray.	*Dissolved*
	The ground wes grene and as the gold it glemis	*gleams*
	With gresis growand gudelie, grit, and gay.	*grasses growing; tall*
870	The spyce thay spred to spring on everilk spray.	*spices spread; bud; each twig*
	The lark, the maveis, and the merll full hie	*thrush; blackbird; loud*
	Sweitlie can sing, trippand fra tre to tre.	*hopping*

	Thre leopardis come, a croun of massie gold	*came; solid*
	Beirand thay brocht unto that hillis hicht	*Carrying; brought; summit*
875	With jaspis jonit and royall rubeis rold	*jasper stones attached; adorned*
	And mony diveris dyamontis dicht.	*diverse; decked out*
	With pollis proud ane palyeoun doun thay picht	*poles; pavilion; pitched*
	And in that throne thair sat ane wild lyoun	
	In rob royall with sceptour, swerd, and croun.	*robe*

880	Efter the tennour off the cry befoir	*Following; proclamation*
	That gais on fut all beistis in the eird	*All beasts that go on foot*
	As thay commandit wer withoutin moir	*without delay*
	Befoir thair lord the lyoun thay appeird	*appeared*
	And quhat thay wer, to me as Lowrence leird,	*what; as Lowrence the fox taught me*
885	I sall reheirs ane part of everilk kynd	*recite a sample of each*
	Als fer as now occurris to my mynd.	*As much*

	The minotaur, ane monster mervelous,	
	Bellerophont, that beist of bastardrie,	*Chimera; beast; illegitimate birth*
	The warwolf and the pegase perillous	*werewolf; dangerous flying horse*
890	Transformit be assent of sorcerie,	*Transformed; means*
	The linx, the tiger full of tiranie,	*lynx; of cruelty*
	The elephant and eik the dromedarie,	*also the dromedary*
	The cameill with his cran-nek furth can carie,	*neck like a crane's; hurried on*

[handwritten annotation: Starts ul mythical]

	The leopard as I haif tauld beforne,	*have mentioned before*
895	The anteloip the sparth furth couth speid,	*antelope hastened forth the ax(?)*
	The peyntit pantheir and the unicorne,	*colorfully marked panther*
	The rayndeir ran throw reveir, rone, and reid,	*river, thicket; reeds*
	The jolie jonet and the gentill steid,	*small Spanish horse; noble stallion*
	The asse, the mule, the hors of everilk kynd,	*every*
900	The da, the ra, the hornit hart, the hynd,	*doe; roe-deer; antlered male red deer*

[handwritten annotation: alt & assor]

	The bull, the beir, the bugill, and the bair,	*bear; wild ox; wild boar*
	The wodwys, wildcat, and the wild wolfyne,	*wild man; she-wolf*
	The hardbakkit hurcheoun and the hirpland hair,	*hedgehog; limping hare*
	Baith otter and aip and pennit porcupyne,	*Both; ape; spiny*
905	The gukit gait, the selie scheip, the swyne,	*foolish goat; harmless sheep*
	The baver, bakon, and the balterand brok,	*bison(?); tumbling badger*
	The fowmart with the fibert furth can flok,	*polecat; otter(?)*

	The gray grewhound with slewthound furth can slyde	*bloodhound; did lope forth*
	With doggis all divers and different,	
910	The rattoun ran, the globard furth can glyde,	*rat; dormouse*
	The quhrynand quhitret with the quhasill went,	*squeaking stoat; weasel*
	The feitho that hes furrit mony fent,	*ferret; furred; gown*
	The mertrik with the cunning and the con,	*marten; rabbit; squirrel*
	The bowranbane and eik the lerion,	*[unidentified animal]; also the garden dormouse*

915	The marmisset the mowdewart couth leid	*did guide the mole*
	Because that nature denyit had hir sicht.	*not given her sight*
	Thus dressit thay all furth for dreid of deid.	*proceeded; fear of death*
	The musk — the lytill mous with all hir micht	*civet*
	In haist haikit unto that hillis hicht —	*she trudged towards that hilltop*
920	And mony kynd of beistis I couth not knaw	*did not know*
	Befoir thair lord the lyoun thay loutit law.	*bowed low*
	Seing thir beistis all at his bidding boun,	*these; ready at his command*
	He gaif ane braid and blenkit him about,	*sudden movement; glanced around him*
	Than flatlingis to his feit thay fell all doun.	*stretched out flat; feet*
925	For dreid of deith, thay droupit all in dout.	*all sank in fear*
	The lyoun lukit quhen he saw thame lout	*noticed; bow*
	And bad thame with ane countenance full sweit,	*commanded them; gentle*
	"Be not efferit bot stand up on your feit.	*afraid*
	"I lat yow wit my micht is merciabill	*know [that] my power; merciful*
930	And steiris nane that ar to me prostrait,	*troubles none who; prostrate*
	Angrie, austerne, and als unamyabill	*severe, and also unloving*
	To all that standfray ar to myne estait.	*who are in opposition to my exalted rank*
	I rug, I reif all beistys that makis debait	*tug, I rend*
	Aganis the micht of my magnyficence.	*Against; authority; grandeur*
935	Se nane pretend to pryde in my presence.	*See [that]; lay claim to status*
	"My celsitude and my hie majestie	*eminence; high*
	With micht and mercie myngit sall be ay.	*shall be conjoined always*
	The lawest heir I can full sone uphie	*lowest; very quickly exalt*
	And mak him maister over yow all I may.	*I have the power*
940	The dromedarie giff he will mak deray,	*if he wants to make trouble*
	The grit camell thocht he wer never sa crous,	*though; bold*
	I can him law als lytill as ane mous.	*debase him*
	"Se neir be twentie mylis quhair I am	*Ensure; within; miles where*
	The kid ga saiflie be the gaittis syde,	*walks safely alongside the goat*
945	Se tod Lowrie luke not upoun the lam	*not look; lamb*
	Na revand beistis nouther ryn nor ryde."	*Nor [any] predatory; neither run nor go raiding*
	Thay couchit all efter that this wes cryde.	*lay down; announced*
	The justice bad the court for to gar fence,	*judge; to prepare to begin*
	The sutis call, and foirfalt all absence.	*call the suits; condemn*
950	The panther with his payntit coit-armour	*painted coat of arms*
	Fensit the court as of the law effeird.	*Constituted; by law was proper*
	Tod Lowrie lukit up quhair he couth lour	*Lowrie the fox looked; was skulking*
	And start on fute all stonist and all steird.	*leapt; astonished; upset*
	Ryifand his hair, he rarit with ane reird,	*Tearing; howled; loud voice*
955	Quaikand for dreid and sichand couth he say,	*Quaking; groaning*
	"Allace this hour, allace this dulefull day.	*doleful*

"I wait this suddand semblie that I se   *know; assembly; see*
Haifand the pointis of ane parliament   *Having; qualities*
Is maid to mar sic misdoars as me.   *made to harm such evildoers*
960   Thairfoir geve I me schaw, I will be schent,   *if; show myself; punished*
I will be socht and I be red absent,   *looked for if; declared*
To byde or fle it makis no remeid,   *stay or flee; provides; solution*
All is alyke, thair followis not bot deid."   *there; nothing but death*

Perplexit thus in his hart can he mene   *did he consider*
965   Throw falset how he micht himself defend.   *falsehood; could*
His hude he drew far doun attoure his ene   *hood; over his eyes*
And winkand with the ane eye furth he wend.   *with the one eye shut; went*
Clinscheand he come that he micht not be kend   *Limping; came; recognized*
And for dreddour that he suld thoill arreist   *terror; suffer detention*
970   He playit bukhude behind fra beist to beist.   *blindman's buff; [moving] from beast*

O fylit spreit and cankerit conscience   *defiled spirit; cankered*
Befoir ane roy renyeit with richteousnes,   *Summoned with justice before a king*
Blakinnit cheikis and schamefull countenance,   *Pale cheeks; ashamed face*
Fairweill thy fame, now gone is all thy grace!   *Goodbye to your good reputation*
975   The phisnomie, the favour of thy face   *expression, appearance*
For thy defence is foull and disfigurate,   *In; repulsive and disfigured*
Brocht to the licht basit, blunt, and blait.   *cowed, dull-witted; oafish*

Be thow atteichit with thift or with tressoun   *If you are accused of*
For thy misdeid wrangous and wickit fay,   *criminal misdeed; bad faith*
980   Thy cheir changis, Lowrence, thow man luke doun.   *expression; must look*
Thy worschip of this warld is went away.   *status in this world is gone*
Luke to this tod how he wes in effray   *Consider this fox; terror*
And fle the filth of falset, I thee reid,   *flee; falsehood; counsel you*
Quhairthrow thair fallowis syn and schamefull deid.   *Through which there*

985   Compeirand thus befoir thair lord and king   *Assembling*
In ordour set as to thair stait effeird,   *Placed as befit their rank*
Of everilk kynd he gart ane part furth bring   *each; had; brought forth*
And awfullie he spak and at thame speird   *awe-inspiringly; spoke; asked*
Geve there wes ony beist into this eird   *If; any beast in this world*
990   Absent and thairto gart thame deiplie sweir   *made them solemnly swear to that*
And thay said nane except ane gray stude meir.   *breeding mare*

"Ga make ane message sone unto that stude."   *at once*
The court than cryit, "My lord, quha sall it be?"   *who shall [the messenger] be*
"Cum furth, Lowrie, lurkand under thy hude."   *skulking*
995   "Aa, schir, mercie, lo I have bot ane ee,   *only one eye*
Hurt in the hoche and cruikit as ye may se.   *leg-joint; lame*
The wolff is better in ambassatry   *diplomacy*
And mair cunning in clergie fer than I."   *far more learned in the clerkly disciplines*

Rampand he said, "Ga furth, ye brybouris baith!"   *Rearing up [the lion] said; wretches*
1000 And thay to ga withowtin tarying.   *they [proceeded] to go; delay*
Over ron and rute thay ran togidder raith   *thicket; root; quickly*
And fand the meir at hir meit in the morning.   *food*
"Now," quod the tod, "Madame, cum to the king.   *come*
The court is callit, and ye ar *contumax*."   *called; in contempt*
1005 "Let be, Lowrence," quod scho, "your cowrtlie knax."   *Cease; legal jargon*

"Maistres," quod he, "cum to the court ye mon.   *Mistress; you must*
The lyoun hes commandit so indeid."   *has indeed commanded this*
"Schir tod, tak ye the flyrdome and the fon.   *you undergo; mockery; folly*
I have respite ane yeir and ye will reid."   *letter permitting absence; if*
1010 "I can not spell," quod he, "sa God me speid.   *said; so God help me*
Heir is the wolff, ane nobill clerk at all   *Here; scholar in every way*
And of this message is maid principall.   *designated chief*

"He is autentik and ane man of age   *duly qualified; maturity*
And hes grit practik of the chancellary.   *experience; chancellor's office*
1015 Let him ga luke and reid your privilage
And I sall stand and beir witnes yow by."   *serve as a witness here with you*
"Quhair is thy respite?" quod the wolff in hy.   *document; in haste*
"Schir, it is heir under my hufe, weill hid."   *here; hoof*
"Hald up thy heill," quod he, and so scho did.   *heel*

1020 Thocht he wes blindit with pryde, yit he presumis   *Though; undertakes*
To luke doun law quhair that hir letter lay.   *look; where*
With that the meir gird him upon the gumis   *struck; gums*
And straik the hattrell of his heid away.   *struck; the top of his skull right off his head*
Halff out of lyif, thair lenand doun he lay.   *life; there he lay crumpled over*
1025 "Allace," quod Lowrence, "Lupus, thow art loist."   *Wolf; defeated*
"His cunning," quod the meir, "wes worth sum coist.   *learning; deserved; payment*

"Lowrence," quod scho,"will thow luke on my letter   *look at*
Sen that the wolff nathing thairoff can wyn?"   *gain nothing from that [letter]*
"Na, be Sanct Bryde," quod he. "me think it better   *by Saint Bridget; it seems to me*
1030 To sleip in haill nor in ane hurt skyn.   *sleep in an undamaged rather than a*
Ane skrow I fand and this wes writtin in   *scroll; found; written in [it]*
(For fyve schillingis I wald not anis forfaut him),   *shillings; once disobey it*
Felix quem faciunt aliena pericula cautum."[1]

With brokin skap and bludie cheikis reid,   *scalp; red*
1035 This wretchit wolff weipand on his wayis went   *weeping*
Of his menye markand to get remeid —   *Aiming to get some remedy from his folk*
To tell the king the cace wes his intent.   *the situation was*

---

[1] *Happy are those who take warning from the perils of others*

"Schir," quod the tod, "byde still upon this bent   *stay in this place*
          And fra your browis wesche away the blude   *from; wash; blood*
1040   And tak ane drink for it will do yow gude."

          To fetche watter this fraudfull foxe furth fure.   *went forth*
          Sydelingis a bank he socht unto ane syke.   *Along; searched for; stream*
          On cace he meittis, cummand fra the mure,   *By chance; coming; moor*
          Ane trip of lambis dansand on ane dyke.   *flock; dancing; embankment*
1045   This tratour tod, this tirrant and this tyke,   *bully; cur*
          The fattest of this flock he fellit hais   *has struck down*
          And eit his fill, syne to the wolff he gais.   *ate; then; goes*

          Thay drank togidder and syne thair journey takis   *then make their way*
          Befoir the king, syne kneillit on thair kne.
1050   "Quhair is yone meir, schir tod, wes *contumax*?"   *that mare; in contempt*
          Than Lowrence said, "My lord, speir not at me.   *do not ask me*
          This new-maid doctour of divinitie   *newly-made; theology*
          With his reid cap can tell yow weill aneuch."   *red; well enough*
          With that the lyoun and all the laif thay leuch.   *rest; laughed*

1055   "Tell on the cais now, Lowrence, let us heir."   *situation; hear*
          "This wittie wolf," quod he, "this clerk of age,   *clever; scholar of mature age*
          On your behalff he bad the meir compeir   *ordered; mare appear*
          And scho allegit to ane privilage: *cited a special right*
          'Cum neir and se, and ye sall haiff your wage.'   *near; shall have*
1060   Because he red hir rispite plane and weill,   *read her letter of permission*
          Yone reid bonat scho raucht him with hir heill."   *bonnet; gave*

          The lyoun said, "Be yone reid cap I ken   *that; know*
          This taill is trew, quha tent unto it takis.   *true, whoever pays heed to it*
          The greitest clerkis ar not the wysest men,   *greatest scholars*
1065   The hurt of ane happie the uther makis."   *of one makes the other lucky*
          As thay wer carpand in this cais with knakis   *chatting; witty comments*
          And all the court in garray and in gam,   *uproar; playfulness*
          Swa come the yow, the mother of the lam,   *Just then came; ewe*

          Befoir the justice on hir kneis fell,   *judge*
1070   Put out hir playnt on this wyis wofully,   *in this way*
          "This harlet huresone and this hound of hell,   *rascal son of a whore*
          He werryit hes my lamb full doggitly   *has dismembered; doggishly*
          Within ane myle in contrair to your cry.   *proclamation*
          For Goddis lufe my lord, gif me the law   *love; enact for my sake*
1075   Of this lurker." With that Lowrence let draw.   *Upon; drew back*

          "Byde!" quod the lyoun, "Lymmer, let us se   *Wait; Villain*
          Giff it be suthe the selie yow hes said."   *If; truth; poor ewe*
          "Aa soverane lord, saif your mercie," quod he,   *Ah; preserve*

1080   "My purpois wes with him for to haif plaid,   *to have played with him*
Causles he fled as he had bene effraid,   *Without cause; afraid*
For dreid of deith he duschit over ane dyke   *plunged; embankment*
And brak his nek." "Thow leis," quod scho, "fals tyke."   *broke; You lie; cur*

"His deith be practik may be previt eith: *by observation; proven easily*
Thy gorrie gumis and thy bludie snout,   *gory gums*
1085   The woll, the flesche yit stikkis on thy teith   *are still sticking; teeth*
And that is evidence aneuch but dout."   *enough, without doubt*
The justice bad ga cheis ane sis about   *choose; jury*
And so thay did and fand that he wes fals   *found; guilty*
Of murther, thift, and party tressoun als.   *partly treason as well*

1090   Thay band him fast, the justice bad belyif   *bound; tight; ordered promptly*
To gif the dome and tak off all his clais,   *The sentence to be pronounced; clothes*
The wolf that new-maid doctour couth him schrif,   *did give him confession*
Syne furth him led and to the gallows gais   *led him forth; goes*
And at the ledder fute his leif he tais.   *foot of the ladder; says farewell*
1095   The aip wes basare and bad him sone ascend   *ape; executioner; at once*
And hangit him and thus he maid his end.

Moralitas   *Moralization*
Richt as the mynour in his minorall   *miner; metallurgy*
Fair gold with fyre may fra the leid weill wyn,   *from; lead; extract*
Richt so under ane fabill figurall   *figurative fable*
1100   Sad sentence men may seik and efter fyne   *Serious meaning; seek; refine*
As daylie dois the doctouris of devyne   *teachers of theology*
Apertly be oure leving can apply   *Explicitly according to our lives; apply a moralization*
And preve thare preching be a poesye.   *demonstrate their; by means of a poetical composition*

The lyoun is the warld be liklynace   *likeness*
1105   To quhome loutis baith empriour and king   *whom bow both emperors and kings*
And thinkis of this warld to get mare grace   *expect from; more favor*
And gapis daylie to get mair leving,   *desire daily; more livelihood*
Sum for to reull and sum to raxe and ring,   *Some govern; prevail; reign*
Sum gadderis geir, sum gold, sum uther gude,   *gather possessions; goods*
1110   To wyn this warld, sum wirkis as thay wer wod.   *gain; work as if; insane*

This wolf I likkin to sensualitie   *liken*
As quhen lyke brutall beistis we accord   *brute beasts; reconcile*
Our mynd all to this warldis vanitie,   *completely*
Lyking to tak and loif him as our lord.   *Wishing; extol [the world]*
1115   Fle fast thairfra gif thow will richt remord,   *Flee; from that; rightly repent*
Than sall ressoun ryse, rax, and ring   *gain power, and reign*
And for thy saull thair is na better thing.   *soul*

	The meir is men of contemplatioun	*mare; people of the contemplative life*
	Of pennance walkand in this wildernes	*For; walking*
1120	As monkis and othir men of religioun	*Such as*
	That presis God to pleis in everilk place,	*Who seek to please God; every*
	Abstractit from this warldis wretchitnes	*Withdrawn; wretchedness*
	In wilfull povertee fra pomp and pryde,	*willing; away from vainglory*
	And fra this warld in mynd ar mortyfyde.	*are made as if dead*

1125	Hir hufe I likkin to the thocht of deid.	*hoof; thought; death*
	Will thow remember, man, that thow man de,	*thou must die*
	Thow may brek sensualiteis heid	*break; head*
	And fleschlie lust away fra thee sall fle.	*shall flee away from you*
	Wis Salomon sais — will thow nocht see —	*Wise; says*
1130	"For as thow may thy sely saull now wyn,	*So that; can save thy sorry soul*
	Think on thy end — thow sall not glaidlie sin."	*Consider thy death; willingly*

	This tod I likkin to temptationis	*liken*
	Beirand to mynd mony thochtis vane	*Bringing; vain thoughts*
	That daylie sagis men of religounis,	*daily besieges members of religious orders*
1135	Cryand to thame, "Cum to the warld agane!"	*Come back to the world*
	Yit gif thay se sensualitie neir slane	*see; nearly killed*
	And suddand deith with ithand panis sore,	*incessant, grievous pains*
	Thay go abak and temptis thame no more.	*pull back; tempt themselves*

	O Mary myld mediatour of mercy meik	*kindly intermediary of gentle mercy*
1140	Sitt doun before thy sone celestiall,	*in front of thy heavenly son*
	For us synnars his celsitude beseke	*beseech his highness*
	Us to defend fra pane and perrellis all	*To defend us*
	And help us up unto that hevinlie hall	
	In gloir quhair we may se the face of God	*glory; see*
1145	And thus endis the talking of the tod.	*story*

The Sheep and the Dog

	Esope ane taill puttis in memorie	*tale*
	How that ane doig because that he wes pure	*poor*
	Callit ane scheip unto the consistorie	*bishop's court*
	Ane certane breid fra him for to recure.	*loaf of bread; recover*
1150	Ane fraudfull wolff wes juge that tyme and bure	*judge; wielded*
	Authoritie and jurisdictioun	
	And on the scheip send furth ane strait summoun,	*strict summons*

	For by the use and cours and commoun style	*procedure*
	On this maner maid his citatioun,	*summons*
1155	"I, Maister Wolff, partles of fraud and gyle,	*devoid; guile*
	Under the panis of hie suspensioun,	*penalties of; deprival of rights*
	Of grit cursing and interdictioun,	*excommunication; exclusion*

Schir Scheip, I charge thee straitly to compeir   *Sir Sheep; strictly; appear in court*
And answer to ane doig befoir me heir."   *before; here*

1160   Schir Corbie Ravin wes maid apparitour   *designated summoner*
       Quha pykit had full mony scheipis ee,   *had pecked out; eye*
       The charge hes tane and on the letteris bure,   *[he] has taken; forth; carried*
       Summonit the scheip befoir the wolff that he
       "Peremptourlie within the dayis thre   *Without delay; three*
1165   Compeir under the panis in this bill   *subject to the penalties*
       To heir quhat Perrie doig will say thee till."   *hear what; wishes to say to you*

       This summondis maid befoir witnes anew,   *before sufficient witnesses*
       The ravin, as to his office weill effeird,   *well pertained*
       Indorsat hes the write and on he flew.   *Endorsed; writ*
1170   The selie scheip durst lay na mouth on eird   *poor; did not dare; earth*
       Till he befoir the awfull juge appeird   *awe-inspiring judge*
       Be oure off cause quhilk that court usit than — [1]
       Quhen Hesperus to schaw his face began.   *When the Evening Star; show*

       The foxe wes clerk and noter in the cause,   *notary; case*
1175   The gled, the graip up at the bar couth stand   *kite; vulture; did stand*
       As advocatis expert into the lawis,   *lawyers*
       The doggis pley togidder tuke on hand   *plea together [they]*
       Quhilk wer confidderit straitlie in ane band   *Who; allied strictly; pact*
       Aganis the scheip to procure the sentence.
1180   Thocht it wes fals thay had na conscience.   *Though; remorse*

       The clerk callit the scheip, and he wes thair.   *present*
       The advocatis on this wyse couth propone: *in this style did state the plea*
       "Ane certane breid worth fyve schilling or mair   *shillings; more*
       Thow aw the doig of quhilk the terme is gone."   *owe; of which [debt]; expired*
1185   Of his awin heid, but advocate, allone,   *On his own behalf, without*
       Avysitlie gaif answer in the cace: *Judiciously [the sheep]*
       "Heir I declyne the juge, the tyme, the place.   *object to*

       "This is my cause in motive and effect: *case; purpose; intent*
       The law sayis it is richt perrillous   *very dangerous*
1190   Till enter pley befoir ane juge suspect   *plea; biased judge*
       And ye, schir wolff, hes bene richt odious   *have been very hateful*
       To me for with your tuskis ravenous   *fangs*
       Hes slane full mony kinnismen of myne,   *Have slain; kinsmen*
       Thairfoir as juge suspect I yow declyne.   *biased judge; reject you*

---

[1] *By the assigned time of sitting that court used then*

1195	"And schortlie, of this court ye memberis all,	*in short, all you members of this court*
	Baith assessouris, clerk, and advocate,	*judicial advisors*
	To me and myne ar ennemies mortall	*my [friends and kin]*
	And ay hes bene as mony scheipheird wate.	*always; been; many a shepherd knows*
	The place is fer, the tyme is feriate	*remote; out of session*
1200	In quhilk no jugeis suld sit in consistory	*During which; judges; court*
	Sa lait at evin. I yow accuse for-thy."	*late in the evening; therefore*
	Quhen that the juge in this wyse wes accusit,	*in this way*
	He bad the parteis cheis with ane assent	*commanded; parties choose*
	Twa arbeteris as in the law is usit	*arbitrators; customarily done*
1205	For to declair and gif arbitriment	*give [an] arbitration*
	Quhidder the scheip suld answer in jugement	*Whether; had to*
	Befoir the wolff and so thay did but weir,	*without doubt*
	Of quhome the namis eftir ye sall heir.	*whom; you shall hear now*
	The beir, the brok, the mater tuke on hand	*bear; badger; matter; in*
1210	For to discyde gif this exceptioun	*decide whether; objection*
	Wes of na strenth or lauchfully mycht stand,	*lawfully*
	And thairupon as jugis thay sat doun	
	And held ane lang quhyle disputatioun,	*a debate [for] a long while*
	Seikand full mony decreitis of the law	*Researching; decrees of canon law*
1215	And glosis als, the veritie to knaw.	*commentaries too*
	Of civile mony volum thay revolve,	*Very many volumes of civil law; study*
	The codies and digestis new and ald,	*codes [of Justinian]; digests*
	Pro and contra, strait argumentis resolve,	*For and against, precise*
	Sum a doctryne and sum anothir hald.	*one opinion*
1220	For prayer nor price, trow ye, thay wald fald	*entreaty; bribe; compromise*
	Bot held the glose and text of the decreis	*gloss; decrees*
	As trew jugis. I schrew thame ay that leis.	*curse; lie*
	Schortlie to mak ane end of this debait,	*Quickly; bring this dispute to a conclusion*
	The arbiteris than summar and plane	*summarily; plainly*
1225	The sentence gave and proces fulminait:	*issued the summons*
	The scheip suld pas befoir the wolff agane	*had to go before*
	And end his pley. Than wes he nathing fane	*cease his plea; in no way pleased*
	For fra thair sentence couth he not appeill.	*from; he could not appeal*
	On clerkis I do it gif this sentence wes leill.	*leave it [to prove] if; legal*
1230	The scheip agane befoir the wolff derenyeit,	*arraigned*
	But advocate, abasitlie couth stand.	*Without; dejectedly*
	Up rais the doig and on the scheip thus plenyeit,	*The dog got up; against; complained*
	"Ane soume I payit have befoir the hand	*A sum; in advance*
	For certane breid." Thairto ane borrow he fand	*witness' statement; produced*
1235	That wrangouslie the scheip did hald the breid,	*wrongfully; keep*
	Quhilk he denyit, and thair began the pleid.	*dispute*

	And quhen the scheip this stryif had contestait,	*had contested this lawsuit*
	The justice in the cause furth can proceid.	*judge; case*
	Lowrence the actis and the proces wrait	*[The fox]; record; proceedings wrote*
1240	And thus the pley unto the end thay speid.	*they progress to the outcome*
	This cursit court, corruptit all for meid,	*bribery*
	Aganis gude faith, gude law, and conscience,	
	For this fals doig pronuncit the sentence.	*In favor of*
	And it till put to executioun,	*to put it into*
1245	The wolff chargit the scheip without delay	*commanded*
	Under the panis of interdictioun	*Subject to the penalty of a prohibition*
	The soume of silver or the breid to pay.	*sum of money*
	Of this sentence allace quhat sall I say,	*About; alas what*
	Quhilk dampnit hes the selie innocent	*has condemned*
1250	And justifyit the wrangous jugement?	*wrongful*
	The scheip, dreidand mair persecutioun,	*fearing more*
	Obeyand to the sentence and couth tak	*Submitting; did take*
	His way unto ane merchand of the toun	*merchant*
	And sauld the woll that he bure on his bak	*sold; wool; bore*
1255	Syne bocht the breid and to the doig couth mak	*Then bought; did make*
	Reddie payment as he forjugeit was,	*as he was legally required*
	Naikit and bair syne to the feild couth pas.	*Naked; bare; did go*

Moralitas — *Moralization*

	This selie scheip may present the figure	*likeness*
	Of pure commounis that daylie ar opprest	*poor commoners; oppressed*
1260	Be tirrane men quhilkis settis all thair cure	*cruel; who exert; their effort*
	Be fals meinis to mak ane wrang conquest	*evil methods; unjust*
	In hope this present lyfe suld ever lest;	*belief; last forever*
	Bot all begylit thay will in schort tyme end	*utterly mistaken; die*
	And efter deith to lestand panis wend.	*go to everlasting torments*
1265	This wolf I likkin to ane schiref stout	*liken; oppressive sheriff*
	Quhilk byis ane forfalt at the kingis hand	*buys; power of forfeiture*
	And hes with him ane cursit assyis about,	*accursed judicial panel convened*
	And dytis all the pure men uponland.	*indicts; poor; in the outlying countryside*
	Fra the crownar haif laid on him his wand,	*Once; coroner; laid on [a poor man]*
1270	Suppois he be als trew as wes Sanct Johine,	*Even if he [the poor man]; honest*
	Slain sall he be or with the juge compone.	*make payment to the judge*
	This ravin I likkin to ane fals crownair	*coroner*
	Quhilk hes ane porteous of the inditement	*Who; a list of those named in*
	And passis furth befoir the justice air	*goes; sitting of circuit court*
1275	All misdoaris to bring to jugement;	*felons*
	Bot luke gif he be of ane trew intent	*consider whether*

To scraip out "Johne" and wryte in "Will" or "Wat"   *scrape; "Walt"*
And swa ane bud at boith the parteis skat.   *thus exacts a bribe from both sides*

1280
Of this fals tod of quhilk I spak befoir   *fox of whom; spoke*
And of this gled, quhat thay micht signify,   *kite*
Of thair nature, as now I speik no moir,   *According to their; say; more*
Bot of this scheip and of his cairfull cry   *sorrowful complaint*
I sall reheirs for as I passit by   *speak; passed*
1285
Quhair that he lay, on cais I lukit doun   *Where; by chance; looked*
And hard him mak sair lamentatioun.   *heard him make [a] bitter lament*

"Allace," quod he, "this cursit consistorie   *bishop's court*
In middis of the winter now is maid   *[the] midst; held*
Quhen Boreas with blastis bitterlie   *the north wind; gusts*
And frawart froistes thir flouris doun can faid.   *harsh frosts these; wither*
1290
On bankis bair now may I mak na baid,"   *bare; can; delay*
And with that word into ane coif he crap   *cave he crept*
Fra hair wedder and froistis him to hap.   *icy weather; to protect himself*

Quaikand for cauld, sair murnand ay amang,   *Shivering; mourning all along*
Kest up his ee unto the hevinnis hicht   *Raised; eyes; height*
1295
And said, "O lord, quhy sleipis thow sa lang?   *why do you sleep*
Walk and discerne my cause groundit on richt,   *Wake; perceive; based; justice*
Se how I am be fraud, maistrie, and slicht   *See; by; oppression; trickery*
Peillit full bair and so is mony one   *Stripped utterly bare*
Now in this warld richt wonder wobegone.   *very shockingly miserable*

1300
"Se how this cursit syn of covetice   *accursed sin; covetousness*
Exylit hes baith lufe, lawtie, and law.   *Has exiled; loyalty*
Now few or nane will execute justice,   *none; carry out*
In falt of quhome the pure man is overthraw.   *lack; whom; overthrown*
The veritie suppois the jugis knaw,   *Even if the judges were to know the truth*
1305
Thay ar so blindit with affectioun   *blinded; selfishness*
But dreid for meid thay thoill the richt go doun.[1]

"Seis thow not, lord, this warld overturnit is   *Do you not see; is turned upside-down*
As quha wald change gude gold in leid or tyn.   *As [if] one; into lead; tin*
The pure is peillit, the lord may do na mis,   *fleeced; can do no wrong*
1310
And simonie is haldin for na syn.   *considered to be no sin*
Now is he blyith with okker maist may wyn.   *happy [who] can profit most from usury*
Gentrice is slane and pietie is ago.   *Gentility; slain; pity; gone*
Allace gude lord, quhy tholis thow it so?   *why endure*

Fable contures into moral- crossing genres boundaries?

---

[1] *Without fear for bribes they allow the right to fail*

	"Thow tholis this evin for our grit offence.	*tolerate even this [injustice] because of*
1315	Thow sendis us troubill and plaigis soir	*grievous plagues*
	As hunger, derth, grit weir, or pestilence	*famine; war*
	Bot few amendis now thair lyfe thairfoir.	*their lives for this reason*
	We pure pepill as now may do no moir	*at this time can do no more*
	Bot pray to thee: sen that we ar opprest	*since; oppressed*
1320	Into this eirth, grant us in hevin gude rest."	*Upon; earth; good*

The Lion and the Mouse

Prologue

	In middis of June that joly sweit seasoun	*midst; sweet time of year*
	Quhen that fair Phebus with his bemis bricht	*Phoebus; bright sunbeams*
	Had dryit up the dew fra daill and doun	*dried; valley and hill*
	And all the land maid with his lemis licht,	*made light with his rays*
1325	In ane mornyng betwix midday and nicht	*On a; between noon; nightfall*
	I rais and put all sleuth and sleip asyde	*arose; set aside all sloth and sleep*
	And to ane wod I went allone but gyde.	*forest; without a guide*

	Sweit wes the smell of flouris quhyte and reid,	*Sweet; flowers white; red*
	The noyes of birdis richt delitious,	*noise; utterly delightful*
1330	The bewis braid blomit abone my heid,	*broad branches bloomed above*
	The ground growand with gresis gratious.	*flourishing; pleasant grasses*
	Of all plesance that place wes plenteous,	*Of; pleasure; was plentiful*
	With sweit odouris and birdis harmony,	*sweet fragrances; birdsong*
	The morning myld, my mirth wes mair forthy.	*joy was greater therefore*

1335	The rosis reid arrayit rone and ryce,	*red roses; bush; stem*
	The prymeros and the purpour viola.	*primrose; purple violet*
	To heir it wes ane poynt of paradice	*hear; a foretaste of*
	Sic mirth the mavis and the merle couth ma.	*Such; thrush; blackbird did make*
	The blossummis blythe brak upon bank and bra,	*merrily opened; hillside*
1340	The smell of herbis and the fowlis cry	*plants; song*
	Contending quha suld have the victory.	*Competing [to see] who*

	Me to conserve than fra the sonis heit,	*To protect myself; from; sun's heat*
	Under the schaddow of ane hawthorne grene	*green*
	I lenit doun amang the flouris sweit	*lay down among*
1345	Syne maid a cors and closit baith my ene.	*Then; sign of the cross; closed both; eyes*
	On sleip I fell amang thir bewis bene	*these fine boughs*
	And in my dreme methocht come throw the schaw	*through; wood*
	The fairest man that ever befoir I saw.	

	His gowne wes of ane claith als quhyte as milk,	*[made] of; cloth; white*
1350	His chymmeris wes of chambelate purpour broun,	*robe; deep purple camel's hair*
	His hude of scarlet bordowrit weill with silk	*hood; edged well*
	On hekillit wyis untill his girdill doun,	*In a fringed style down to his waist*

His bonat round and of the auld fassoun,   *cap [was] round and in the old style*
His beird wes quhyte, his ene wes grit and gray   *eyes were large*
1355 With lokker hair quhilk over his schulderis lay.   *curling; which; shoulders*

Ane roll of paper in his hand he bair,   *carried*
Ane swannis pen stikand under his eir,   *swan's quill sticking*
Ane inkhorne with ane prettie gilt pennair,   *inkwell; an artfully gilded pen-case*
Ane bag of silk all at his belt he weir,   *ready at; wore*
1360 Thus wes he gudelie grathit in his geir.   *finely dressed; apparel*
Of stature large and with ane feirfull face,   *an awe-inspiring face*
Evin quhair I lay he come ane sturdie pace   *Up to where; [at] a brisk pace*

And said, "God speid, my sone," and I wes fane   *save [you]; son; gladdened*
Of that couth word and of his cumpany.   *By; familiar; by*
1365 With reverence I salusit him agane,   *greeted him in return*
"Welcome, father," and he sat doun me by.   *down beside me*
"Displeis yow not my gude maister thocht I   *Do not be displeased; though*
Demand your birth, your facultye, and name,   *Ask about; profession (learning)*
Quhy ye come heir or quhair ye dwell at hame."   *Why; here; where; home*

1370 "My sone," said he, "I am of gentill blude.   *noble lineage*
My natall land is Rome withoutin nay   *native; without doubt*
And in that towne first to the sculis I yude,   *I went to the schools*
In civile law studyit full mony ane day   *[I] studied Roman law very many*
And now my winning is in hevin for ay.   *dwelling; heaven for always*
1375 Esope I hecht. My writing and my werk   *am named; work*
Is couth and kend to mony cunning clerk."   *known and familiar; learned scholar*

"O maister Esope, poet lawriate,
God wait ye ar full deir welcum to me.   *knows; most dearly welcome*
Ar ye not he that all thir fabillis wrate   *who wrote all these fables*
1380 Quhilk in effect suppois thay fenyeit be,   *Which; even if they are fictional*
Ar full of prudence and moralitie?"   *wisdom*
"Fair sone," said he, "I am the samin man."   *same*
God wait gif that my hert wes merie than.   *knows if; then*

I said, "Esope, my maister venerabill,   *honored master*
1385 I yow beseik hartlie for cheritie   *beseech sincerely; good will*
Ye wald dedene to tell ane prettie fabill   *would deign*
Concludand with ane gude moralitie."   *Concluding; moral*
Schaikand his heid, he said, "My sone, lat be   *Shaking; let [it] be*
For quhat is it worth to tell ane fenyeit taill   *what; made-up story*
1390 Quhen haly preiching may nathing availl?   *When holy preaching*

"Now in this warld me think richt few or nane   *very; none*
To Goddis word that hes devotioun.   *who have reverence*
The eir is deif, the hart is hard as stane,   *ear; deaf; heart; stone*

Asop was actually a slave!!

	Now oppin sin without correctioun,	*Now [there is] blatant sin*
1395	The e inclynand to the eirth ay doun,	*eye directed; always down*
	Sa roustit is the warld with canker blak	*So rotten; black*
	That now my taillis may lytill succour mak."	*tales can bring little help*

	"Yit, gentill schir," said I, "For my requeist,	*noble sir; request*
	Not to displeis your fatherheid I pray,	*offend; fatherhood*
1400	Under the figure off ane brutall beist	*likeness of a brute beast*
	Ane morall fabill ye wald denye to say.	*you would deign*
	Quha wait nor I may leir and beir away	*Who knows if; learn; carry*
	Sumthing thairby heirefter may availl?'	*thereby [that] hereafter*
	"I grant," quod he, and thus begouth ane taill.	*agree; began; tale*

The Fable

1405	**A**ne lyoun, at his pray wery foirrun,	*prey; exhausted by running*
	To recreat his limmis and to rest,	*relax his limbs*
	Beikand his breist and belly at the sun,	*Warming; breast; in*
	Under ane tre lay in the fair forest.	*Lay under a tree*
	Swa come ane trip of myis out off thair nest	*Just then; troupe of mice; their*
1410	Richt tait and trig, all dansand in ane gyis	*Very glad; nimble; dancing; masquerade*
	And over the lyoun lansit twyis or thryis.	*hopped twice; thrice*

	He lay so still, the myis wes not effeird	*were not afraid*
	Bot to and fro out over him tuke thair trace.	*across; took; dance-steps*
	Sum tirlit at the campis of his beird,	*plucked; whiskers; beard*
1415	Sum spairit not to claw him on the face.	*did not refrain from clawing*
	Merie and glaid thus dansit thay ane space	*awhile*
	Till at the last the nobill lyoun woke	
	And with his pow the maister mous he tuke.	*paw; master; grabbed*

	Scho gave ane cry and all the laif, agast,	*She; all the rest, terrified*
1420	Thair dansing left and hid thame sone alquhair.	*themselves soon everywhere*
	Scho that wes tane cryit and weipit fast	*who was captured; wept incessantly*
	And said allace oftymes that scho come thair.	*alas often; she [had]; there*
	"Now am I tane ane wofull presonair	*taken; woeful prisoner*
	And for my gilt traistis incontinent	*guilt expects at once*
1425	Of lyfe and deith to thoill the jugement."	*suffer*

	Than spak the lyoun to that cairfull mous,	*spoke; sorrowful*
	"Thow cative wretche and vile unworthie thing,	*Thou miserable*
	Over malapart and eik presumpteous	*Overly rude; also*
	Thow wes to mak out over me thy tripping.	*make across; dancing*
1430	Knew thow not weill I wes baith lord and king	*well; was both*
	Of beistis all?" "Yes," quod the mous, "I knaw,	*Of all beasts; know*
	Bot I misknew because ye lay so law.	*was fooled; low*

"Lord, I beseik thy kinglie royaltie   *beseech*
Heir quhat I say and tak in patience.   *Hear what; receive [it]*
1435 Considder first my simple povertie
And syne thy mychtie hie magnyfycence.   *then; mighty high*
Se als how thingis done of neglygence,   *See also; through*
Nouther of malice nor of prodissioun,   *Neither from; treason*
Erer suld have grace and remissioun.   *Sooner; receive; forgiveness*

1440 "We wer repleit and had grit aboundance   *full of food; great*
Off alkin thingis sic as to us effeird.   *all sorts of; such; suited*
The sweit sesoun provokit us to dance   *inspired*
And mak sic mirth as nature to us leird.   *as nature taught us*
Ye lay so still and law upon the eird   *low; earth*
1445 That be my saull we weind ye had bene deid, *by; soul; thought; been dead*
Elles wald we not have dancit over your heid." *Otherwise we would; head*

"Thy fals excuse," the lyoun said agane,   *in reply*
"Sall not availl ane myte, I underta.   *help [even] a little; assert*
I put the cace I had bene deid or slane   *pose; hypothesis; slain*
1450 And syne my skyn bene stoppit full of stra,   *then; stuffed; straw*
Thocht thow had found my figure lyand swa, *Even though; lying thus*
Because it bare the prent of my persoun,   *bore the image*
Thow suld for feir on kneis have fallin doun.   *ought; fear; knees*

"For thy trespas thow can mak na defence   *offense; make no*
1455 My nobill persoun thus to vilipend.   *treat with contempt*
Of thy feiris nor thy awin negligence   *your companions; own*
For to excuse thow can na cause pretend.   *you can offer no defense*
Thairfoir thow suffer sall ane schamefull end   *shall*
And deith sic as to tressoun is decreit,   *death such; decreed*
1460 Onto the gallous harlit be the feit."   *gallows dragged; feet*

"A, mercie, lord, at thy gentrice I ase   *Ah; from; noble mercy; ask*
As thow art king of beistis coronate,   *Since; crowned*
Sober thy wraith and let thi yre overpas   *Calm; wrath; ire pass away*
And mak thy mynd to mercy inclynate.   *make; inclined*
1465 I grant offence is done to thyne estate,   *your rank*
Quhairfoir I worthie am to suffer deid   *Because of which; death*
Bot gif thy kinglie mercie reik remeid.   *Unless your; offer help*

"In everie juge mercy and reuth suld be   *judge; pity should exist*
As assessouris and collaterall.   *advisors; colleagues*
1470 Without mercie, justice is crueltie
As said is in the lawis spirituall.   *the canon laws*
Quhen rigour sittis in the tribunall,   *When severity*
The equitie of law quha may sustene?   *who can uphold*
Richt few or nane but mercie gang betwene. *Very; unless mercy intervene*

1475 "Alswa ye knaw the honour triumphall — *Also; know*
Of all victour upon the strenth dependis — *depends on the strength*
Of his conqueist quhilk manlie in battell — *captives who*
Throw jeopardie of weir lang defendis. — *Through the peril of war maintain a long defense*
Quhat pryce or loving quhen the battell endis — *prize; praise when the battle is over*
1480 Is said off him that overcummis ane man — *who overcomes*
Him to defend quhilk nouther may nor can? — *Who neither may nor can defend himself?*

"Ane thowsand myis to kill and eik devoir — *mice; also devour*
Is lytill manheid to ane strang lyoun, — *paltry prowess for; strong*
Full lytill worschip have ye wyn thairfoir, — *Very little honor; won*
1485 To quhais strenth is na comparisoun. — *Since to your strength [there]*
It will degraid sum part of your renoun — *degrade; renown*
To sla ane mous quhilk may mak na defence — *slay; who can*
Bot askand mercie at your excellence. — *Except for begging; from*

"Also it semis not your celsitude — *is not fitting to your majesty*
1490 Quhilk usis daylie meittis delitious — *consumes; delicious foods*
To fyle your teith or lippis with my blude — *defile; blood*
Quhilk to your stomok is contagious. — *stomach; infectious*
Unhailsum meit is of ane sarie mous — *Unwholesome food; from; vile*
And that namelie untill ane strang lyoun — *especially for*
1495 Wont till be fed with gentill vennesoun. — *Accustomed to; noble venison*

"My lyfe is lytill worth, my deith is les, — *death; less*
Yit and I leif I may peradventure — *Yet if I live; perhaps*
Supplie your hienes beand in distres — *Assist; highness being*
For oft is sene ane man of small stature — *it is often seen; low rank*
1500 Reskewit hes ane lord of hie honour — *Has rescued*
Keipit that wes in poynt to be overthrawin — *Imprisoned who was about*
Throw misfortoun. Sic cace may be your awin." — *Through; Such a situation; own*

Quhen this wes said, the lyoun his langage — *When; way of speaking*
Paissit and thocht according to ressoun — *Calmed; thought; reason*
1505 And gart mercie his cruell ire asswage — *made; assuage his cruel ire*
And to the mous grantit remissioun, — *granted forgiveness*
Oppinnit his pow and scho on kneis fell doun — *Opened; paw*
And baith hir handis unto the hevin upheild, — *both; raised up*
Cryand, "Almichty God mot yow foryeild!" — *Crying, "May Almighty God reward you!"*

1510 Quhen scho wes gone, the lyoun held to hunt — *continued*
For he had nocht bot levit on his pray — *owned nothing but lived; prey*
And slew baith tayme and wyld as he wes wont — *both tame; accustomed*
And in the cuntrie maid ane grit deray — *made; great disturbance*
Till at the last the pepill fand the way — *people found*
1515 This cruell lyoun how that thay mycht tak. — *could capture*
Of hempyn cordis strang nettis couth thay mak — *Out of hemp; strong; did*

And in ane rod quhair he wes wont to ryn — *path; run*
With raipis rude fra tre to tre it band, — *strong ropes from tree; bound it*
Syne kest ane range on raw the wod within, — *sent; line [of beaters]; row in the forest*
1520 With hornis blast and kennettis fast calland. — *fanfare; hounds eagerly calling*
The lyoun fled and throw the ron rynnand — *running through the bushes*
Fell in the net and hankit fute and heid. — *entangled feet; head*
For all his strenth he couth mak na remeid. — *did not make any progress*

Welterand about with hiddeous rummissing, — *Struggling; roaring*
1525 Quhyle to, quhyle fra, quhill he mycht succour get — *Now; until he could get relief*
Bot all in vane, it vailyeit him nathing. — *vain; availed; not at all*
The mair he flang, the faster wes he knet. — *more; jerked; tighter; tied*
The raipis rude wes sa about him plet — *were so twisted around him*
On everilk syde that succour saw he nane — *every*
1530 Bot styll lyand, thus murnand maid his mane. — *lying; lamenting; complaint*

"O lamit lyoun liggand heir sa law, — *lamed; lying here; low*
Quhair is the mycht of thy magnyfycence — *Where; power*
Of quhome all brutall beist in eird stude aw — *whom; on earth stood in awe*
And dred to luke upon thy excellence? — *dreaded; look*
1535 But hoip or help, but succour or defence, — *Without hope*
In bandis strang heir man I ly allace — *bonds; here must*
Till I be slane, I se nane uther grace. — *see no other relief*

"Thair is na wy that will my harmis wreik — *no person who; avenge*
Nor creature do confort to my croun. — *offer; crown*
1540 Quha sall me bute, quha sall my bandis breik, — *Who shall help me; break*
Quha sall me put fra pane off this presoun?" — *get me out of the pain*
Be he had maid this lamentatioun, — *Once; made*
Throw aventure the lytill mous come neir — *By chance; came near*
And of the lyoun hard the pietuous beir. — *heard the sad voice of the lion*

1545 And suddanlie it come intill hir mynd — *into*
That it suld be the lyoun did hir grace — *this had to be; [that] showed*
And said, "Now wer I fals and richt unkynd — *disloyal; very wicked*
Bot gif I quit sum part thy gentilnes — *Unless; repaid part of*
Thow did to me," and on with that scho gais — *goes*
1550 To hir fellowis and on thame fast can cry, — *eagerly did call*
"Cum help, cum help!" and thay come all in hy. — *in haste*

"Lo," quod the mous, "this is the same lyoun — *same*
That grantit grace to me quhen I wes tane — *when; captured*
And now is fast heir bundin in presoun, — *here tied up tightly; prison*
1555 Brekand his hart with sair murning and mane. — *Breaking; bitter; lament*
Bot we him help, of souccour wait he nane. — *Unless; he expects none*
Cum help to quyte ane gude turne for ane uther, — *pay; another*
Go lous him sone"; and thay said, "Ye, gude brother." — *loose; at once; Yes*

	Thay tuke na knyfe, thair teith wes scharpe aneuch.	*brought; sharp enough*
1560	To se that sicht forsuith it wes grit wounder	*see; indeed; great wonder*
	How that thay ran amang the rapis tewch,	*among; tough ropes*
	Befoir, behind, sum yeid abone, sum under	*went above*
	And schuir the raipis of the mastis in schunder,	*cut; meshes asunder*
	Syne bad him ryse and he start up anone	*Then told; got up at once*
1565	And thankit thame, syne on his way is gone.	*them*

	Now is the lyoun fre of all danger,	*free from*
	Lows and delyverit to his libertie	*Loose; rescued into*
	Be lytill beistis of ane small power	*By*
	As ye have hard because he had pietie."	*heard; showed clemency*
1570	Quod I, "Maister, is thair ane moralitie	
	In this fabill?" "Yea, sone," he said, "richt gude."	*[a] very good [one]*
	"I pray yow, schir," quod I, "Ye wald conclude."	*ask; sir; [If] you would*

Moralitas	*Moralization*

	"**As** I suppois, this mychtie gay lyoun	*suppose; powerful splendid*
	May signifie ane prince or empriour,	
1575	Ane potestate or yit ane king with croun	*ruler; or else*
	Quhilk suld be walkrife gyde and governour	*Who should; vigilant guide*
	Of his pepill and takis na labour	*exerts no effort*
	To reule and steir the land and justice keip,	*rule; direct*
	Bot lyis still in lustis, sleuth, and sleip.	*relaxes always; sloth; sleep*

1580	The fair forest with levis lowne and le,	*sheltered and restful leaves*
	With foulis sang and flouris ferlie sweit	*birds' song; wonderfully*
	Is bot the warld and his prosperitie	*only*
	As fals plesance myngit with cair repleit.	*pleasure mixed; ample grief*
	Richt as the rois with froist and wynter weit	*Just; rose; wintry storm*
1585	Faidis, swa dois the warld and thame desavis	*Fades, so; deceives those*
	Quhilk in thair lustis maist confidence havis.	*Who; pleasures; have most confidence*

	Thir lytill myis ar bot the commountie,	*mice; only; common folk*
	Wantoun, unwyse without correctioun.	*Unruly; [if] lacking*
	Thair lordis and princis quhen that thay se	*when they [the commons] see*
1590	Of justice mak nane executioun,	*exact no penalty*
	Thay dreid nathing to mak rebellioun	*They are not at all afraid*
	And disobey for quhy thay stand nane aw	*because; have no respect*
	That garris thame thair soveranis misknaw.	*causes them; to disregard*

	Be this fabill, ye lordis of prudence	*By; prudent rulers*
1595	May considder the vertew of pietie	*virtue; pity*
	And to remit sumtyme ane grit offence	*pardon occasionally*
	And mitigate with mercy crueltie.	*cruelty by means of mercy*
	Oftymis is sene ane man of small degree	*Often; seen; low rank*

1600	Hes quit ane kinbute baith for gude and ill As lord hes done rigour or grace him till.	*compensated an injury both* *shown severity; mercy to him*
1605	Quha wait how sone ane lord of grit renoun Rolland in wardlie lust and vane plesance May be overthrawin, destroyit, and put doun Throw fals fortoun quhilk of all variance Is haill maistres and leidar of the dance Till injust men and blindis thame so soir That thay na perrell can provyde befoir?	*Who knows; soon* *Abounding; vain pleasure* *overthrown* *Through; which; mutability* *complete; leader* *For unjust; them so utterly* *can prepare for no danger*
1610	Thir rurall men that stentit hes the net In quhilk the lyoun suddandlie wes tane Waittit alway amendis for to get. For hurt, men wrytis in the marbill stane. Mair till expone as now I lett allane Bot king and lord may weill wit quhat I mene. Figure heirof oftymis hes bene sene."	*have outstretched* *which; suddenly; taken* *Watched; to get restitution* *[To record] injury; write* *More; explain; I leave unsaid* *well perceive what; mean* *Examples of this often have*
1615 1620	Quhen this wes said, quod Esope, "My fair child, Persuaid the kirkmen ythandly to pray That tressoun of this cuntrie be exyld And justice regne and lordis keip thair fay Unto thair soverane lord baith nycht and day," And with that word he vanist and I woke, Syne throw the schaw my journey hamewart tuke.	*When; said* *clergy continually* *from this country* *reign; maintain their loyalty* *both night* *vanished* *Then; wood; took homeward*

The Preaching of the Swallow

1625	The hie prudence and wirking mervelous, The profound wit of God omnipotent Is sa perfyte and sa ingenious, Excellent far all mannis argument For quhy to him all thing is ay present Rycht as it is or ony tyme sall be Befoir the sicht of his divinitie,	*exalted; wonderful operation* *intellect of* *so perfect; discerning* *Exceeding; human reasoning* *Because; everything is always* *Exactly; shall* *In the perception of*
1630 1635	Thairfoir our saull with sensualitie So fetterit is in presoun corporall, We may not cleirlie understand nor se God as he is, a thing celestiall. Our mirk and deidlie corps materiale Blindis the spirituall operatioun Lyke as ane man wer bundin in presoun.	*Therefore; soul* *fettered; bodily prison* *clearly; see* *a heavenly being* *dark; mortal material body* *function* *Just as if a; confined; prison*
	In Metaphisik Aristotell sayis That mannis saull is lyke ane bakkis ee	*Metaphysics* *the eye of a bat*

Quhilk lurkis still als lang as licht of day is — *Which hides; daylight lasts*
And in the gloming cummis furth to fle. — *dusk comes out to fly*
1640 Hir ene ar waik, the sone scho may not se. — *Her eyes; weak; she cannot see the sun*
Sa is our saull with fantasie opprest — *hampered by delusion*
To knaw the thingis in nature manifest. — *From knowing; manifested*

For God is in his power infinite, — *infinite in power*
And mannis saull is febill and over small, — *feeble; too*
1645 Of understanding waik and unperfite — *weak; imperfect*
To comprehend him that contenis all; — *contains everything*
Nane suld presume be ressoun naturall — *No one should; by*
To seirche the secreitis of the Trinitie, — *penetrate*
Bot trow fermelie and lat dirk ressounis be. — *believe firmly; cease arcane speculations*

1650 Yit nevertheles we may haif knawlegeing — *have knowledge*
Of God almychtie be his creatouris, — *through his creations*
That he is gude, fair, wyis, and bening. — *good; wise; benevolent*
Exempill takis be thir jolie flouris — *Take the example of these pretty flowers*
Rycht sweit of smell and plesant of colouris, — *Very sweet of*
1655 Sum grene, sum blew, sum purpour, quhyte, and reid, — *blue; purple, white, and red*
Thus distribute be gift of his godheid. — *distributed by; from; divine being*

The firmament payntit with sternis cleir — *sphere of heaven painted; bright stars*
From eist to west rolland in cirkill round, — *east; revolving; a complete revolution*
And everilk planet in his proper spheir, — *each; own orbit*
1660 In moving makand harmonie and sound, — *motion making*
The fyre, the air, the watter, and the ground: — *earth*
Till understand it is aneuch iwis — *To; certainly enough*
That God in all his werkis wittie is. — *works is wise*

Luke we the fische that swimmis in the se, — *Let us study; sea*
1665 Luke we in eirth all kynd of bestyall, — *earth; kinds of animals*
The foulis fair sa forcelie thay fle, — *birds; vigorously; fly*
Scheddand the air with pennis grit and small; — *Cleaving; feathers large*
Syne luke to man that he maid last of all — *Then look; made*
Lyke to his image and his similitude; — *In his; resemblance*
1670 Be thir we knaw that God is fair and gude. — *By these [things]; know*

All creature he maid for the behufe — *created things; benefit*
Of man and to his supportatioun — *for his support*
Into this eirth, baith under and abufe, — *On; as well as below and above*
In number, wecht, and dew proportioun, — *weight; due*
1675 The difference of tyme and ilk seasoun — *diversity of; each*
Concorddand till our opurtunitie — *Suited to; needs*
As daylie be experience we may se. — *daily by; see*

	The somer with his jolie mantill grene	*lovely green robe*
	With flouris fair furrit on everilk fent,	*like fur on each opening in the garment*
1680	Quhilk Flora goddes of the flouris quene	*Which; goddess; flowers queen*
	Hes to that lord as for his seasoun lent	*Has*
	And Phebus with his goldin bemis gent	*lovely golden sunbeams*
	Hes purfellit and payntit plesandly	*adorned; pleasantly*
	With heit and moysture stilland from the sky.	*heat; distilled*

1685	Syne harvest hait quhen Ceres that goddes	*Then hot autumn when*
	Hir barnis benit hes with abundance	*Has blessed her children*
	And Bachus god of wyne renewit hes	*has refilled*
	Hir tume pyipis in Italie and France	*Her empty casks*
	With wynis wicht and liquour of plesance	*strong wines; pleasing liquor*
1690	And *copia temporis* to fill hir horne	*the bounty of the season*
	That never wes full of quheit nor uther corne.	*wheat nor other grain*

	Syne wynter wan quhen austerne Eolus	*dismal winter when grim Aeolus*
	God of the wynd with blastis boreall	*wind; northern gusts*
	The grene garment of somer glorious	*glorious summer*
1695	Hes all to-rent and revin in pecis small.	*Has; torn up; ripped; pieces*
	Than flouris fair faidit with froist man fall,	*flowers; faded; must*
	And birdis blyith changit thair noitis sweit	*changed their sweet tunes*
	In styll murning, neir slane with snaw and sleit.	*Into ceaseless; nearly slain; sleet*

	Thir dalis deip with dubbis drounit is,	*These valleys; puddles*
1700	Baith hill and holt heillit with frostis hair	*wood covered; hoary frosts*
	And bewis bene ar bethit bair of blis.	*fine branches; dried bare of bliss*
	Be wickit windis of the winter wair,	*By wicked; warned*
	All wyld beistis than from the bentis bair	*empty fields*
	Drawis for dreid unto thair dennis deip,	*Withdraw; fear; deep dens*
1705	Coucheand for cauld in coifis thame to keip.	*Crouching; caves themselves*

	Syne cummis ver quhen winter is away,	*Then comes spring when*
	The secretar of somer with his sell	*confidential servant; seal*
	Quhen columbie up keikis throw the clay	*the columbine peers out*
	Quhilk fleit wes befoir with froistes fell.	*was scared; by grim frosts*
1710	The mavis and the merle beginnis to mell,	*thrush; blackbird; sing*
	The lark on loft with uther birdis smale	*aloft; other little birds*
	Than drawis furth fra derne over doun and daill.	*comes out; hiding; hill; dale*

	That samin seasoun into ane soft morning,	*same; on a fine*
	Rycht blyth that bitter blastis wer ago,	*Very happy; winds were gone*
1715	Unto the wod to se the flouris spring	*wood; see; flowers bud*
	And heir the mavis sing and birdis mo,	*hear; other birds*
	I passit furth, syne lukit to and fro	*went out, then looked*
	To se the soill that wes richt sessonabill,	*was very seasonable*
	Sappie, and to resave all seidis abill.	*Moist, and ready to receive all seeds*

[handwritten annotation] A Spindler End?

1720 Moving thusgait, grit myrth I tuke in mynd | *in this way; took*
Of lauboraris to se the besines, | *laborers; see; hard work*
Sum makand dyke and sum the pleuch can wynd, | *digging ditches; guide the plow*
Sum sawand seidis fast frome place to place, | *sowing seeds*
The harrowis hoppand in the saweris trace. | *harrow hopping; track*
1725 It wes grit joy to him that luifit corne | *loved grain*
To se thame laubour baith at evin and morne, | *them; both at evening*

And as I baid under ane bank full bene, | *rested; very pleasant hillside*
In hart gritlie rejosit of that sicht, | *greatly delighted by; sight*
Unto ane hedge under ane hawthorne grene, | *Into; green hawthorn tree*
1730 Of small birdis thair come ane ferlie flicht | *came a marvelous flock*
And doun belyif can on the leifis licht | *down suddenly; did alight on the leaves*
On everilk syde about me quhair I stude, | *where I stood*
Rycht mervellous, ane mekill multitude. | *large*

Amang the quhilks ane swallow loud couth cry | *Among; which; did cry aloud*
1735 On that hawthorne hie in the croip sittand, | *high; treetop sitting*
"O ye birdis on bewis heir me by, | *branches here beside me*
Ye sall weill knaw and wyislie understand | *shall well know; wisely*
Quhair danger is or perrell appeirand | *Where; approaching*
It is grit wisedome to provyde befoir | *get ready in advance*
1740 It to devoyd for dreid it hurt yow moir." | *To avoid it; fear; you more*

"Schir swallow," quod the lark agane and leuch, | *said; in reply; laughed*
"Quhat have ye sene that causis yow to dreid?" | *What; seen; causes; dread*
"Se ye yone churll," quod scho, "beyond yone pleuch | *Do you see that; plow*
Fast sawand hemp, lo se, and linget seid, | *sowing hemp there, see; flax seed*
1745 Yone lint will grow in lytill tyme indeid | *flax; in a little while indeed*
And thairof will yone churll his nettis mak | *from it; that; make his nets*
Under the quhilk he thinkis us to tak. | *which; intends to catch us*

"Thairfoir I reid we pas quhen he is gone | *advise [that]; go when*
At evin and with our naillis scharp and small | *sharp little claws*
1750 Out of the eirth scraip we yone seid anone | *earth we scrape that; at once*
And eit it up for giff it growis we sall | *eat; if; shall*
Have cause to weip heirefter ane and all. | *reason; weep hereafter one*
Se we remeid thairfoir furthwith instante, | *We must remedy this; at once*
Nam levius laedit quicquid praevidimus ante. | *[see note]*

1755 "For clerkis sayis it is nocht sufficient | *scholars; not*
To considder that is befoir thyne ee | *think about what; before; eye*
Bot prudence is ane inwart argument | *inner mental process*
That garris ane man provyde befoir and see | *causes; get ready in advance*
Quhat gude, quhat evill, is liklie for to be | *What good; likely to emerge*
1760 Of everilk thingis at the fynall end, | *Of all things [to come to pass] at the time of death*
And swa fra perrell ethar him defend." | *thus from; more readily*

Human observing animal conversation

	The lark lauchand the swallow thus couth scorne	*laughing; did mock*
	And said scho fischit lang befoir the net.	*fished far ahead of*
	"The barne is eith to busk that is unborne.	*baby; easy; dress*
1765	All growis nocht that in the ground is set.	*Not everything grows*
	The nek to stoup quhen it the straik sall get	*bend when; blow shall*
	Is sone aneuch. Deith on the fayest fall."	*soon enough; most fated*
	Thus scornit thay the swallow ane and all.	*they mocked*
	Despysing thus hir helthsum document,	*her beneficial advice*
1770	The foulis ferslye tuke thair flicht anone,	*birds fiercely took; at once*
	Sum with ane bir thay braidit over the bent	*rush; hastened; field*
	And sum agane ar to the grene wod gone.	*again are; greenwood*
	Upon the land quhair I wes left allone,	*where*
	I tuke my club and hamewart couth I carie	*staff; homeward did; hurry*
1775	Swa ferliand as I had sene ane farie.	*Just as astonished as if; supernatural vision*
	Thus passit furth quhill June that jolie tyde	*time passed until; lovely time*
	And seidis that wer sawin of beforne	*planted before*
	Wer growin hie that hairis mycht thame hyde	*hares could hide themselves*
	And als the quailye craikand in the corne.	*also; quail clucking; grain*
1780	I movit furth betwix midday and morne	*went out between*
	Unto the hedge under the hawthorne grene	
	Quhair I befoir the said birdis had sene,	*previously mentioned*
	And as I stude be aventure and cace	*stood, by luck; chance*
	The samin birdis as I haif said yow air,	*same; have told; earlier*
1785	I hoip because it wes thair hanting place,	*suppose; their usual place to go*
	Mair of succour or yit mair solitair,	*More sheltered; quiet*
	Thay lychtit doun and quhen thay lychtit wair,	*alighted; were*
	The swallow swyth put furth ane pietuous pyme,	*promptly let out; plaintive cry*
	Said, "Wo is him can not bewar in tyme.	*Woe; look out*
1790	"O blind birdis and full of negligence,	*heedlessness*
	Unmyndfull of your awin prosperitie,	*own well-being*
	Lift up your sicht and tak gude advertence,	*sight; take good notice*
	Luke to the lint that growis on yone le.	*flax; that pasture*
	Yone is the thing I bad forsuith that we,	*commanded indeed*
1795	Quhill it wes seid, suld rute furth off the eird.	*When; uproot out; ground*
	Now is it lint, now is it hie on breird,	*high in first growth*
	"Go yit quhill it is tender, young, and small,	*yet while*
	And pull it up, let it na mair incres.	*grow no bigger*
	My flesche growis, my bodie quaikis all,	*flesh shudders; trembles*
1800	Thinkand on it I may not sleip in peis."	*about; cannot sleep in peace*
	Thay cryit all and bad the swallow ceis	*ordered; cease*
	And said, "yone lint heirefter will do gude,	*later on; good*
	For linget is to lytill birdis fude.	*food for little birds*

	"We think quhen that yone lint bollis ar ryip	*those; pods; ripe*
1805	To mak us feist and fill us of the seid	*make ourselves a feast; seed*
	Magré yone churll and on it sing and pyip."	*In spite of that; peep*
	"Weill," quod the swallow, "freindes, hardilie beid,	*friends, by all means be it so*
	Do as ye will bot certane sair I dreid	*wish; certainly I sorely dread*
	Heirefter ye sall find als sour as sweit	*What comes; just as; sweet*
1810	Quhen ye ar speldit on yone carlis speit.	*When; split open; churl's spit*

	"The awner of yone lint ane fouler is,	*owner; bird catcher*
	Richt cautelous and full off subteltie.	*Very tricky; cunning*
	His pray full sendill tymis will he mis	*prey; few times; miss*
	Bot gif we birdis all the warrer be.	*Unless; be all the warier*
1815	Full mony of our kin he hes gart de	*Very many; caused to die*
	And thocht it bot ane sport to spill thair blude.	*thought; merely a game*
	God keip me fra him, and the halie rude."	*protect; from; holy cross*

	Thir small birdis haveand bot lytill thocht	*These; having only little care*
	Of perrell that mycht fall be aventure,	*befall by chance*
1820	The counsell of the swallow set at nocht	*valued at nothing*
	Bot tuke thair flicht and furth togidder fure,	*took; went away together*
	Sum to the wode, sum markit to the mure.	*headed; moor*
	I tuke my staff quhen this wes said and done	*when*
	And walkit hame for it drew neir the none.	*near; noon*

1825	The lynt ryipit, the carll pullit the lyne,	*ripened; flax plants*
	Rippillit the bollis and in beitis set,	*Raked off; seedpods; put [the stalks] in bundles*
	It steipit in the burne and dryit syne	*Soaked it; stream; then dried*
	And with ane bittill knokkit it and bet,	*mallet pounded; beat*
	Syne swingillit it weill and hekkillit in the flet.	*scraped; combed; indoors on the floor*
1830	His wyfe it span and twynit it into threid	*spun it; twisted; thread*
	Of quhilk the fowlar nettis maid indeid.	*which; bird catcher made nets*

	The wynter come, the wickit wind can blaw,	*wicked; did blow*
	The woddis grene wer wallowit with the weit,	*withered; wet*
	Baith firth and fell with froistys wer maid faw,	*forest; hill; frosts; mottled*
1835	Slonkis and slaik maid slidderie with the sleit.	*Hollows; valleys; slippery; sleet*
	The foulis fair for falt thay fell of feit.	*fine birds; hunger; feet*
	On bewis bair it wes na bute to byde	*bare branches; use; stay*
	Bot hyit unto housis thame to hyde.	*hastened; to hide themselves*

	Sum in the barn, sum in the stak of corne	*Some; stack of grain*
1840	Thair lugeing tuke and maid thair residence.	*Took their lodging; made*
	The fowlar saw and grit aithis hes he sworne	*has sworn great oaths*
	Thay suld be tane trewlie for thair expence.	*should certainly be caught; depredations*
	His nettis hes he set with diligence	*He has laid out his nets*
	And in the snaw he schulit hes ane plane	*shoveled; flat area*
1845	And heillit it all over with calf agane.	*covered; chaff again*

Thir small birdis, seand the calff, wes glaid. *seeing the chaff, were glad*
Trowand it had bene corne, thay lychtit doun *Supposing; grain; flew down*
Bot of the nettis na presume thay had *But; no expectation*
Nor of the fowlaris fals intentioun. *bird catcher's wicked plan*
1850 To scraip and seik thair meit thay maid thame boun. *food; set themselves to work*
The swallow into a branche litill by, *in a sapling off to one side*
Dreiddand for gyle, thus loud on thame couth cry: *Fearing trickery; to them did*

"Into that calf scraip quhill your naillis bleid, *scrape until; bleed*
Thair is na corne, ye laubour all in vane, *vain*
1855 Trow ye yone churll for pietie will yow feid? *Do you believe that; pity; feed*
Na, na, he hes it lyit heir for ane trane. *laid it out here; trick*
Remove, I reid, or ellis ye will be slane; *Get away; advise; else*
His nettis he hes set full prively, *very covertly*
Reddie to draw; in tyme be war forthy. *Ready; pull; beware therefore*

1860 "Grit fule is he that puttis in dangeir *[A] great fool*
His lyfe, his honour, for ane thing of nocht. *a thing of no value*
Grit fule is he that will not glaidlie heir *willingly pay heed to*
Counsall in tyme quhill it availl him mocht. *while it might help him*
Grit fule is he that nathing hes in thocht *nothing in mind*
1865 Bot thing present and efter quhat may fall *Except; what may occur later*
Nor of the end hes na memoriall." *of the outcome; thought*

Thir small birdis, for hunger famischit neir, *almost starving*
Full besie scraipand for to seik thair fude, *Very busily; find their food*
The counsall of the swallow wald not heir, *did not want to hear*
1870 Suppois thair laubour dyd thame lytill gude. *Even though; did them*
Quhen scho thair fulische hartis understude *understood [to be]*
Sa indurate, up in ane tre scho flew. *So stubborn; into a tree*
With that, this churll over thame his nettis drew. *pulled his nets over them*

Allace it wes rycht grit hertis sair to se *Alas; great pain at heart; see*
1875 That bludie bowcheour beit thay birdis doun *bloody butcher beat those*
And for till heir quhen thay wist weill to de *they fully expected to die*
Thair cairfull sang and lamentatioun. *sorrowful song*
Sum with ane staf he straik to eirth on swoun, *Some; struck; unconscious*
Sum off the heid, off sum he brak the crag, *The heads from some; neck*
1880 Sum half on lyfe he stoppit in his bag. *alive; stuffed*

And quhen the swallow saw that thay wer deid, *when; dead*
"Lo," quod scho, "thus it happinnis mony syis *times*
On thame that will not tak counsall nor reid *To those who; advice*
Of prudent men or clerkis that ar wyis. *From; scholars; wise*
1885 This grit perrell I tauld thame mair than thryis. *told them [about] more*
Now ar thay deid, and wo is me thairfoir." *woe*
Scho tuke hir flicht, bot I hir saw no moir. *I saw her no more*

Moralitas	*Moralization*
Lo worthie folk, Esope that nobill clerk,	*noble scholar*
Ane poet worthie to be lawreate,	
1890 Quhen that he vaikit from mair autentik werk	*relaxed; valuable work*
With uther ma, this foirsaid fabill wrate	*many others; previous; wrote*
Quhilk at this tyme may weill be applicate	*Which; explained*
To gude morall edificatioun,	*instruction*
Haifand ane sentence according to ressoun.	*Having; meaning accordant*

intellectual separation

1895 This carll and bond of gentrice spoliate,	*bondman; void of gentility*
Sawand this calf thir small birdis to sla,	*Sowing; chaff these; slay*
It is the feind quhilk fra the angelike state	*devil, who from angelic rank*
Exylit is as fals apostata	*Exiled; traitorous rebel*
Quhilk day and nycht weryis not for to ga	*Who; does not weary; go*
1900 Sawand poysoun and mony wickit thocht	*poison; wicked thought*
In mannis saull quhilk Christ full deir hes bocht.	*soul; very dearly; redeemed*

And quhen the saull as seid into the eird	*when; like seed in the ground*
Gevis consent in delectatioun,	*Gives; in delight*
The wickit thocht beginnis for to breird	*sprout*
1905 In deidlie sin quhilk is dampnatioun.	*mortal; which*
Ressoun is blindit with affectioun	*Reason; willful emotion*
And carnall lust growis full grene and gay	*fleshly desire; lush*
Throw consuetude hantit from day to day.	*By habit indulged*

Proceding furth be use and consuetude,	*by; custom*
1910 The sin ryipis and schame is set on syde,	*ripens; aside*
The feynd plettis his nettis stark and rude,	*weaves his strong and rough nets*
And under plesance previlie dois hyde,	*secretly hides [them]*
Syne on the feild he sawis calf full wyde,	*Then; sows chaff very widely*
Quhilk is bot tume and verray vanitie	*Which; empty; total vanity*
1915 Of fleschlie lust and vaine prosperitie.	

Thir hungrie birdis wretchis we may call	*These; we may term wretches*
Ay scraipand in this warldis vane plesance,	*Always scraping; delight*
Greddie to gadder gudis temporall,	*Greedy; amass temporal goods*
Quhilk as the calf ar tume without substance,	*Which like; chaff; empty*
1920 Lytill of vaill and full of variance,	*Of little use; changeability*
Lyke to the mow befoir the face of wind	*dust [that]*
Quhiskis away and makis wretchis blind.	*Whirls; makes*

This swallow quhilk eschaipit thus the snair	*that has escaped*
The halie preichour weill may signifie,	*holy preacher*
1925 Exhortand folk to walk and ay bewair	*Exhorting; watch; always*
Fra nettis of our wickit enemie	*Against*
Quha sleipis not bot ever is reddie	*Who does not sleep*

Quhen wretchis in this warld calf dois scraip — *do scrape chaff*
To draw his net that thay may not eschaip. — *cannot escape*

1930 Allace, quhat cair, quhat weiping is and wo, — *Alas, what sorrow*
Quhen saull and bodie partit ar in twane: — *When soul; are parted; two*
The bodie to the wormis keitching go; — *worms' kitchen*
The saull to fyre, to everlestand pane. — *everlasting torment*
Quhat helpis than this calf, thir gudis vane, — *these worthless goods*
1935 Quhen thow art put in Luceferis bag — *When*
And brocht to hell and hangit be the crag? — *brought; hanged; neck*

Thir hid nettis for to persave and se, — *concealed; perceive; see*
This sarie calf wyislie to understand, — *miserable chaff wisely*
Best is bewar in maist prosperitie — *[It] is best [to]; greatest*
1940 For in this warld thair is na thing lestand. — *there is nothing permanent*
Is na man wait how lang his stait will stand, — *[There]; [who] knows; state*
His lyfe will lest, nor how that he sall end — *shall*
Efter his deith nor quhidder he sall wend. — *After; death; where; go*

Pray we thairfoir quhill we ar in this lyfe — *We should pray; while*
1945 For four thingis: the first, fra sin remufe, — *withdraw from sin*
The secund is to seis all weir and stryfe, — *cease; conflict and strife*
The thrid is perfite cheritie and lufe, — *perfect charity*
The feird thing is and maist for our behufe — *fourth; most for our benefit*
That is in blis with angellis to be fallow, — *bliss; angels; comrades*
1950 And thus endis the Preiching of the Swallow.

The Fox, the Wolf, and the Cadger — *Fish Peddler*

Quhylum thair wynnit in ane wildernes — *Once there dwelt*
(As myne authour expreslie can declair) — *explicitly does state*
Ane revand wolff that levit upon purches — *A thieving; lived; poaching*
On bestiall and maid him weill to fair. — *animals; himself manage well*
1955 Wes nane sa big about him he wald spair, — *[There] was no one; spare*
And he war hungrie, outher for favour or feid, — *If; were; either bribe; threat*
Bot in his breith he weryit thame to deid. — *fury; shook them to death*

Swa happinnit him in waithing as he went — *[It] so befell; poaching*
To meit ane foxe in middis of the way. — *meet; middle of the path*
1960 He him foirsaw and fenyeit to be schent — *saw first; pretended; in awe*
And with ane bek he bad the wolff gude day. — *nod; wished good*
"Welcum to me," quod he, "thow Russell gray." — *said [the wolf]*
Syne loutit doun and tuke him be the hand, — *Then leaned; took; by*
"Ryse up, Lowrence, I leif thee for to stand. — *[the fox's name]; permit*

1965 "Quhair hes thow bene this sesoun fra my sicht? — *Where hast thou; out of my sight*
Thow sall beir office and my stewart be, — *hold office; be my steward*

For thow can knap doun caponis on the nicht   *knock down capons in; night*
And lourand law thow can gar hennis de."   *crawling low; make hens die*
"Schir," said the foxe, "that ganis not for me   *Sir; that does not suit me*
1970 And I am rad gif thay me se on far   *afraid if they see me afar*
That at my figure beist and bird will skar."   *appearance; take fright*

"Na," quod the wolff, "thow can in covert creip   *under cover crawl*
Upon thy wame and hint thame be the heid   *belly; grab them by; head*
And mak ane suddand schow upon ane scheip,   *sudden sortie; sheep*
1975 Syne with thy wappinnis wirrie him to deid."   *Then; teeth and claws shake; death*
"Schir," said the foxe, "ye knaw my roib is reid   *know; robe; red*
And thairfoir thair will na beist abyde me   *wait for me*
Thocht I wald be sa fals as for to hyde me."   *Even though; hide myself*

"Yis," quod the wolff, "throw buskis and throw brais   *across thickets; hillsides*
1980 Law can thow lour to come to thy intent."   *Low; crawl; reach your goal*
"Schir," said the foxe, "ye wait weill how it gais.   *understand well; goes*
Ane lang space fra thame, thay will feill my sent,   *long distance; notice; smell*
Than will thay eschaip suppois thay suld be schent   *escape, unless; killed*
And I am schamefull for to cum behind thame   *ashamed; come up behind them*
1985 Into the feild thocht I suld sleipand find thame."   *even though; sleeping*

"Na," quod the wolff, "thow can cum on the wind.   *approach upwind*
For everie wrink forsuith thow hes ane wyle."   *precaution indeed; trick*
"Schir," said the foxe, "that beist ye mycht call blind   *animal you could*
That micht not eschaip than fra me ane myle.   *could; escape; a mile off*
1990 How micht I ane of thame that wyis begyle?   *trick one of them in that way*
My tippit twa eiris and my twa gray ene   *two [black-]tipped ears; two gray eyes*
Garris me be kend quhair I wes never sene."   *Makes; recognized where*

Than said the wolff, "Lowrence, I heir thee le   *hear; you lying*
And castys for perrellis thy ginnes to defend,   *[you] search; risks; tricks; protect*
1995 Bot all thy sonyeis sall not availl thee   *excuses shall*
About the busk with wayis thocht thow wend.   *around the bush; ruses; you beat*
Falset will failye ay at the latter end.   *Falsehood; always fail*
To bow at bidding and byde not quhill thow brest   *not wait until; break*
Thairfoir I giff thee counsall for the best."   *[that is] for*

2000 "Schir," said the foxe, "it is Lentring, ye se;   *Lent; see*
I can nocht fische, for weiting of my feit,   *not fish; getting my feet wet*
To tak ane banestikill, thocht we baith suld de.   *catch a stickleback; should both starve*
I have nane uther craft to win my meit.   *no other; get; food*
Bot wer it Pasche, that men suld pultrie eit,   *But if it were Easter, when*
2005 As kiddis, lambis, or caponis into ply,   *kids, in [fine] condition*
To beir your office than wald I not set by."   *hold; would; not refuse*

Than said the wolff in wraith, "Wenis thou with wylis — *wrath; Do you suppose*
And with thy mony mowis me to mat? — *many tricks to defeat me*
It is ane auld dog doutles that thow begylis; — *doubtless; you deceive*
2010 Thow wenis to draw the stra befoir the cat." — *expect to pull; straw*
"Schir," said the foxe, "God wait, I mene not that; — *knows; do not mean*
For and I did it wer weill worth that ye — *if I; were entirely proper*
In ane rude raip had tyit me till ane tre. — *strong rope; tied; to a tree*

"Bot now I se he is ane fule perfay — *see; he is indeed a fool*
2015 That with his maister fallis in ressoning. — *master enters into debate*
I did bot till assay quhat ye wald say. — *did [it] only to find out what*
God wait, my mynd wes on ane uther thing. — *knows; another*
I sall fulfill in all thing your bidding — *in every respect; command*
Quhat-ever ye charge on nichtis or on dayis." — *Whatever; require; nights*
2020 "Weill," quod the wolf, "I heir weill quhat thou sayis — *hear; what*

"Bot yit I will thow mak to me ane aith — *yet I want; [to] make; oath*
For to be leill attour all levand leid." — *loyal; above; living being*
"Schir," said the foxe, "that ane word maks me wraith, — *single; makes; angry*
For now I se ye have me at ane dreid; — *see; hold me in suspicion*
2025 Yit sall I sweir, suppois it be nocht neid, — *swear, even if; no need*
Be Juppiter and on pane of my heid, — *By; under penalty; head*
I sall be trew to you quhill I be deid." — *shall; true; until; dead*

With that ane cadgear with capill and with creillis — *fish peddler; horse; baskets*
Come caryand furth. Than Lowrence culd him spy; — *proceeding along; did; see*
2030 The foxe the flewer off the fresche hering feillis — *aroma; fresh herring; smells*
And to the wolff he roundis prively, — *whispers stealthily*
"Schir, yone ar hering the cadgear caryis by; — *there; is carrying along*
Thairfoir I reid that we se for sum wayis — *Therefore; advise; look*
To get sum fische aganis thir fasting dayis. — *fish in readiness for these*

2035 "Sen I am stewart, I wald we had sum stuff; — *Since; intend [that]; goods*
And ye ar silver-seik, I wait richt weill. — *sick with poverty; know very well*
Thocht we wald thig yone verray churlische chuff, — *beg; truly boorish miser*
He will not giff us ane hering off his creill, — *give; from his basket*
Befoir yone churle on kneis thocht we wald kneill. — *In front of; knees though; kneel*
2040 Bot yit I trow alsone that ye sall se — *believe that very soon you shall see*
Gif I can craft to bleir yone carlis ee. — *If; know how to pull the wool over the churl's eyes*

"Schir, ane thing is and we get of yone pelff, — *there is one thing, if; some of; prize*
Ye man tak travell and mak us sum supple — *make an effort; give; help*
For he that will not laubour and help himselff — *that does not want to work*
2045 Into thir dayis he is not worth ane fle. — *In these days; a flea*
I think to work als besie as ane be — *intend; as busily as a bee*
And ye sall follow ane lytill efterwart — *shall; a short way behind*
And gadder hering for that sall be your part." — *gather herring; shall; job*

With that he kest ane cumpas far about	took a circuitous route
2050 And straucht him doun in middis of the way.	outstretched himself; middle
As he wer deid he fenyeit him but dout	made himself seem indeed
And than upon lenth unliklie lay:	then lay in an unnatural pose
The quhyte he turnit up of his ene tway,	whites; upturned; two eyes
His toung out hang ane handbreid of his heid,	hung; hand'sbreadth; head
2055 And still he lay als straucht as he wer deid.	motionless; stiff as if; were
The cadgear fand the foxe and he wes fane	found; delighted
And till himself thus softlie can he say,	to; quietly did
"At the nixt bait, in faith, ye sall be flane,	next rest-stop; shall be flayed
And off your skyn I sall mak mittenis tway."	from; make a pair of mittens
2060 He lap full lichtlie about him quhair he lay	leapt very nimbly; where
And all the trace he trippit on his tais;	way; danced; toes
As he had hard ane pyper play he gais.	As if; heard; moves
"Heir lyis the Devyll," quod he, "deid in ane dyke;	Here; said; dead; ditch
Sic ane selcouth saw I not this sevin yeir.	Such a freak occurrence
2065 I trow ye have bene tussillit with sum tyke	suppose; attacked by; dog
That garris you ly sa still withoutin steir.	makes; lie so; without motion
Schir Foxe, in faith ye ar deir welcum heir.	indeed; warmly welcome here
It is sum wyfis malisone, I trow,	some wife's curse
For pultrie pyking, that lychtit hes on yow.	poaching poultry; has landed
2070 "Thair sall na pedder, for purs nor yit for glufis	There; peddler; purse; gloves
Nor yit for poyntis, pyke your pellet fra me.	laces; swindle; pelt from
I sall of it mak mittenis to my lufis	shall from; for my hands
Till hald my handis hait quhairever I be.	To keep; hot wherever; am
Till Flanderis sall it never saill the se."	To; sail the sea
2075 With that in hy he hint him be the heillis	in haste; grabbed; by; heels
And with ane swak he swang him on the creillis	thud; threw; baskets
Syne be the heid the hors in hy hes hint.	Then by; head; haste has seized
The fraudfull foxe thairto gude tent hes tane	has paid close attention
And with his teith the stoppell or he stint	stopper as quickly as he could
2080 Pullit out and syne the hering ane and ane	[He] pulled; one by one
Out of the creillis he swakkit doun gude wane.	flung down a good number
The wolff wes war and gadderit spedilie.	was ready; gathered [them]
The cadgear sang, "Huntis up, up," upon hie.	in a loud voice
Yit at ane burne the cadgear lukit about.	But; stream; glanced behind
2085 With that the foxe lap quyte the creillis fray.	leapt completely free from the baskets
The cadgear wald have raucht the foxe ane rout	given; punch
Bot all for nocht; he wan his hoill that day.	nothing; made it to safety
Than with ane schout thus can the cadgear say,	Then; shout; did
"Abyde, and thou ane nekhering sall haif	Wait; "neck-herring"; have
2090 Is worth my capill, creillis, and all the laif."	worth my horse; all the rest

Human + animal speak to each other

"Now," quod the foxe, "I schrew me and we meit.	*curse myself if we meet*
I hard quhat thou hecht to do with my skyn.	*heard what; promised*
Thy handis sall never in thay mittinnis tak heit	*those; take warmth*
And thou wer hangit, carll, and all thy kyn.	*Even if; hanged [for it], churl*
2095 Do furth thy mercat, at me thou sall nocht wyn	*Continue; trade; from; profit*
And sell thy hering thou hes thair till hie price,	*have left for a high*
Ellis thow sall wyn nocht on thy merchandice."	*Or else; not profit*
The cadgear trimmillit for teyne quhair that he stude.	*shook; rage where; stood*
"It is weill worthie," quod he, "I want yone tyke	*just deserts; [that] I have lost; cur*
2100 That had nocht in my hand sa mekill gude	*Who; nothing; of so much use*
As staff or sting yone truker for to stryke."	*pole; trickster*
With that lychtlie he lap out over ane dyke	*nimbly; leapt; ditch*
And hakkit doun ane staff, for he wes tene,	*cut down; infuriated*
That hevie wes and of the holyne grene.	*of green holly*
2105 With that the foxe unto the wolff could wend	*did go*
And fand him be the hering quhair he lyis.	*found; beside; where*
"Schir," said he than,"maid I not fair defend?	*did I not make a brave defense*
Ane wicht man wantit never, and he wer wyis.	*strong; never lacked, if*
Ane hardie hart is hard for to suppryis."	*brave heart; take by surprise*
2110 Than said the wolff, "Thow art ane berne full bald	*a very bold man*
And wyse at will, in gude tyme be it tald.	*when wanted; let it be said*
"Bot quhat wes yone the carll cryit on hie	*what was that; cried aloud*
And schuke his hand," quod he, "Hes thou no feill?"	*shook; fist; no idea*
"Schir," said the foxe, "that I can tell trewlie.	*Sir; accurately*
2115 He said the nekhering wes intill the creill."	*was inside*
"Kennis thou that hering?" "Ye, schir, I ken it weill	*Know; Yes*
And at the creill mouth I had it thryis but dout.	*rim; thrice without doubt*
The wecht of it neir tit my tuskis out.	*weight; nearly pulled; teeth*
"Now suithlie schir, micht we that hering fang,	*truly; if we could; grab*
2120 It wald be fische to us thir fourtie dayis."	*these forty*
Than said the wolf, "Now God nor that I hang	*God let me be hanged*
Bot to be thair I wald gif all my clays	*there; give; clothes*
To se gif that my wappinnis mycht it rais."	*if; teeth and claws could lift it*
"Schir," said the foxe, "God wait I wischit you oft	*knows; wanted; often*
2125 Quhen that my pith micht not beir it on loft.	*strength could; lift it up high*
"It is ane syde of salmond as it wair	*side of salmon as it were*
And callour, pypand lyke ane pertrik ee.	*fresh; speckled; partridge eye*
It is worth all the hering ye have thair,	*there*
Ye and we had it swa, is it worth sic thre."	*if; thus; three times as much*
2130 Than said the wolff, "Quhat counsell gevis thou me?"	
"Schir," said the foxe, "wirk efter my devyis	*proceed according to; plan*
And ye sall have it and tak you na suppryis.	*suffer no ambush*

weary journey

"First, ye man cast ane cumpas far about,   *must take a circular route*
Syne straucht you doun in middis of the way.   *Then outstretch yourself*

2135 Baith heid and feit and taill ye man streik out,   *Both; you must stretch*
Hing furth your toung, and clois weill your ene tway,[1]
Syne se your heid on ane hard place ye lay   *make sure*
And dout not for na perrell may appeir   *do not be afraid*
Bot hald you clois quhen that carll cummis neir.   *keep yourself still; comes*

2140 "And thocht ye se ane staf, have ye na dout,   *though; see; have no concern*
Bot hald you wonder still into that steid   *keep yourself utterly; place*
And luke your ene be clois as thay wer out   *make sure; tight shut as if*
And se that ye schrink nouther fute nor heid.   *twitch*
Than will the cadgear carll trow ye be deid   *believe*

2145 And intill haist will hint you be the heillis   *in haste; grab; heels*
As he did me and swak you on his creillis."   *throw; baskets*

"Now," quod the wolff, "I sweir thee be my thrift,   *swear to you by; luck*
I trow yone cadgear carll dow not me beir."   *expect; cannot lift me*
"Schir," said the foxe, "on loft he will you lift   *up high*

2150 Upon his creillis and do him lytill deir.   *cause himself little strain*
Bot ane thing dar I suithlie to you sweir.   *Only; I dare honestly*
Get ye that hering sicker in sum place,   *If you get; safe; some*
Ye sall not fair in fisching mair quhill Pasche.   *go fishing again until Easter*

"I sall say *In principio* upon yow   *"In the beginning" over you*

2155 And crose your corps from the top to tay.   *sign the cross on; body; toe*
Wend quhen ye will, I dar be warrand now   *Go when; wish; venture to be a guarantor*
That ye sall de na suddand deith this day."   *die no sudden*
With that the wolff gird up sone and to gay   *sprang; at once; left*
And caist ane cumpas about the cadgear far,   *went a circular route around*

2160 Syne raucht him in the gait or he come nar.   *stretched himself; path; before; near*

He laid his halfheid sicker, hard, and sad,   *cheek securely, firmly; heavily*
Syne straucht his four feit fra him and his heid   *feet away from; head*
And hang his toung furth as the foxe him bad.   *hung out; tongue; taught him*
Als styll he lay as he wer verray deid,   *As; were indeed dead*

2165 Rakkand nathing of the carlis favour nor feid   *Caring; kindness; enmity*
Bot ever upon the nekhering he thinkis   *But continually about*
And quyte foryettis the foxe and all his wrinkis.   *quite forgets; tricks*

With that the cadgear, als wraith as ony wind   *as furious*
Come rydand on the laid, for it wes licht,   *riding; cartload; light*

2170 Thinkand ay on the foxe that wes behind   *Thinking continually about*
Upon quhat wyse revenge him best he micht   *How to avenge himself*

---

[1] *Hang out your tongue, and close tight your two eyes*

And at the last of the wolff gat ane sicht — *caught a sight*
Quhair he in lenth lay streikit in the gait, — *Where; lay prone; path*
Bot gif he lichtit doun or nocht, God wait! — *Whether he got down; knows*

2175 Softlie he said, "I wes begylit anis; — *was fooled once*
Be I begylit twyis, I schrew us baith, — *If I am fooled twice; curse the both of us*
That evill bat it sall licht upon thy banis — *wicked blow; land; bones*
He suld have had that hes done me the skaith." — *[That]; injury*
On hicht he hovit the staf for he wes wraith — *Up high; raised; furious*
2180 And hit him with sic will upon the heid — *such purpose; head*
Quhill neir he swonit and swelt into that steid.[1]

Thre battis he bure or he his feit micht find — *blows; received before; feet*
Bot yit the wolff wes wicht and wan away. — *strong; got*
He mycht not se, he wes sa verray blind, — *could; see; truly*
2185 Nor wit reddilie quhether it wes nicht or day. — *know readily whether*
The foxe beheld that service quhair he lay — *watched; treatment from where*
And leuch on loft quhen he the wolf sa seis, — *laughed out loud; sees thus*
Baith deif and dosinnit, fall swonand on his kneis. — *Both deaf; dazed; fainting; knees*

He that of ressoun cannot be content — *according to reason*
2190 Bot covetis all, is abill all to tyne. — *covets everything; likely to lose everything*
The foxe, quhen that he saw the wolff wes schent, — *when; was beaten*
Said to himself, "Thir hering sall be myne." — *These; shall*
(I le or ellis he wes a stewart fyne — *I lie; else; a fine steward*
That fand sic wayis his maister for to greif!) — *found such; to torment*
2195 With all the fische thus Lowrence tuke his leif. — *took his leave*

The wolff wes neir weill dungin to the deid — *nearly thrashed quite to death*
That uneith with his lyfe away he wan — *hardly; he escaped*
For with the bastoun weill brokin wes his heid. — *staff his head was nearly broken*
The foxe into his den sone drew him than — *quickly withdrew himself then*
2200 That had betraisit his maister and the man. — *betrayed his master and the cadger*
The ane wantit the hering of his creillis; — *lacked; from his baskets*
The utheris blude wes rynnand over his heillis. — *other's blood; running; heels*

Moralitas — *Moralization*
This taill is myngit with moralitie — *tale is mingled*
As I sall schaw sumquhat or that I ceis. — *show in part before; cease*
2205 The foxe unto the warld may likkinnit be, — *may be likened*
The revand wolf unto ane man but leis, — *thieving; without lies*
The cadgear deith quhome under all man preis; — *under whom everyone must hasten*
That ever tuke lyfe throw cours of kynd man dee — *came to; nature's course; die*
As man and beist and fische into the see. — *in the sea*

---

[1] *Until he almost fainted and died in that place*

2210	The warld, ye wait, is stewart to the man	*you understand; steward*
	Quhilk makis man to haif na mynd of deid	*Who; pay no heed to death*
	Bot settis for winning all the craftis thay can.	*engages; profit; they know*
	The hering I likkin unto the gold sa reid,	*liken; so red [i.e., pure]*
	Quhilk gart the wolf in perrell put his heid;	*Which made*
2215	Richt swa the gold garris landis and cieteis	*Just so; makes; cities*
	With weir be waistit daylie, as men seis.	*war; devastated; men see*

	And as the foxe with dissimulance and gyle	*trickery; guile*
	Gart the wolf wene to haif worschip forever,	*Made; expect; have respect*
	Richt swa this warld with vane glore for ane quhyle	*Just so; vanity; while*
2220	Flatteris with folk as thay suld failye never;	*Fawns upon; as if they should never fail*
	Yit suddandlie men seis it oft dissever	*suddenly; see the world often part company*
	With thame that trowis oft to fill the sek.	*For those who expect; sack*
	Deith cummis behind and nippis thame be the nek.	*Death pinches them by; neck*

	The micht of gold makis mony men sa blind	*power; makes; so*
2225	That settis on avarice thair felicitie	*make greed their greatest joy*
	That thay forget the cadgear cummis behind	*So that; comes*
	To stryke thame, of quhat stait sa ever thay be.	*whatever rank they hold*
	Quhat is mair dirk than blind prosperitie?	*What; more dark*
	Quhairfoir I counsell mychtie men to haif mynd	*Wherefore; advise; have*
2230	Of the nekhering interpreit in this kynd.	*interpreted; way*

	The Fox, the Wolf, and the Husbandman	*Farmer*

	In elderis dayis, as Esope can declair,	*ancestors'; does declare*
	Thair wes ane husband quhilk had ane plewch to steir.[1]	
	His use wes ay in morning to ryse air,	*practice; always; rise early*
	Sa happinnit him in streiking tyme of yeir	*[It] so befell; plowing; of year*
2235	Airlie in the morning to follow furth his feir,	*Early; proceed according to his custom*
	Unto the pleuch bot his gadman and he,	*At the plow only; drover*
	His stottis he straucht with *Benedicité*.	*young oxen; urged; blessing*

	The caller cryit, "How! Haik!" upon hicht,	*driver; "Hey! Move!" out loud*
	"Hald draucht, my dowis," syne broddit thame full sair.	*Pull straight; doves; goaded*
2240	The oxin wes unusit, young, and licht	*inexperienced; frisky*
	And for fersnes thay couth the fur forfair.	*from exuberance they ruined the furrow*
	The husband than woxe angrie as ane hair,	*then grew; hare*
	Syne cryit and caist his patill and grit stanis:	*Then yelled; threw; spade; big rocks*
	"The wolff," quod he, "mot have you all at anis!"	*said; may take; once*

2245	Bot yit the wolff wes neirar nor he wend,	*yet; nearer than he supposed*
	For in ane busk he lay and Lowrence baith,	*thicket; [the fox] also*

---

[1] *There was a farmer who had a plow; to guide*

	In ane rouch rone wes at the furris end	*Under; gnarled rowan [that]; furrow's end*
	And hard the hecht. Than Lowrence leuch full raith,	*heard; vow; laughed; eagerly*
	"To tak yone bud," quod he, "it wer na skaith."	*that offer; were no hardship*
2250	"Weill," quod the wolff, "I hecht thee be my hand,	*promise you by*
	Yone carlis word as he wer king sall stand."	*That churl's; were king shall*

	The oxin waxit mair reulie at the last,	*became more disciplined*
	Syne efter thay lousit fra that it worthit weill lait.[1]	
	The husband hamewart with his cattell past,	*homeward; went*
2255	Than sone the wolff come hirpilland in his gait	*hobbling; in [the husbandman's] path*
	Befoir the oxin and schupe to mak debait.	*Ahead of; got ready; dispute*
	The husband saw him and worthit sumdeill agast	*grew somewhat afraid*
	And bakwart with his beistis wald haif past.	*would have gone*

	The wolff said, "Quhether dryvis thou this pray?	*Where are you driving; prey*
2260	I chalenge it for nane of thame ar thyne!"	*none of them*
	The man thairoff wes in ane felloun fray	*for that reason; great shock*
	And soberlie to the wolff answerit syne,	*gravely [he] then replied to the wolf*
	"Schir, be my saull, thir oxin ar all myne:	*Sir, by; soul, these oxen*
	Thairfoir I studdie quhy ye suld stop me,	*wonder why; should obstruct*
2265	Sen that I faltit never to you, trewlie."	*Since; never defaulted; truly*

	The wolff said, "Carll, gaif thou not me this drift	*Churl, gave; team*
	Airlie quhen thou wes eirrand on yone bank,	*Earlier when; plowing; that slope*
	And is thair ought, sayis thou, frear than gift?	*anything; more free than a*
	This tarying wyll tyne thee all thy thank:	*delay; lose; thanks*
2270	Far better is frelie for to gif ane plank	*willingly; fourpenny coin*
	Nor be compellit on force to gif ane mart.	*Than; by necessity; fat ox*
	Fy on the fredome that cummis not with hart!"	*generosity; comes; sincerity*

	"Schir," quod the husband, "ane man may say in greif	*said; annoyance*
	And syne ganesay fra he avise and se.	*then contradict once; reflect*
2275	I hecht to steill, am I thairfoir ane theif?	*vow; steal*
	God forbid, schir, all hechtis suld haldin be.	*vows should be adhered to*
	Gaif I my hand or oblissing," quod he,	*Did I give; [a] contract*
	"Or have ye witnes or writ for to schaw?	*show*
	Schir, reif me not bot go and seik the law."	*rob; take legal proceedings*

2280	"Carll," quod the wolff, "ane lord and he be leill,	*if he is loyal*
	That schrinkis for schame or doutis to be repruvit,	*shrinks from; fears; rebuked*
	His saw is ay als sickker as his seill.	*word; always as secure; seal*
	Fy on the leid that is not leill and lufit.	*Shame; man who; trustworthy; respected*
	Thy argument is fals and eik contrufit	*also fabricated*

---

[1] *Then after they were unhitched once it grew very light*

2285	For it is said in proverb, "But lawte,	*Without trustworthiness*
	All uther vertewis ar nocht worth ane fle."	*other virtues; not; a flea*
	"Schir," said the husband, "remember of this thing:	*farmer; about this*
	Ane leill man is not tane at half ane taill.	*honest; taken in; partial story*
	I may say and ganesay, I am na king.	*speak and contradict*
2290	Quhair is your witnes that hard I hecht thame haill?"	*heard; promised; entirely*
	Than said the wolff, "Thairfoir it sall nocht faill.	*For that reason; shall*
	Lowrence," quod he, "cum hidder of that schaw,	*come here from; thicket*
	And say nathing bot as thow hard and saw."	*except; heard*
	Lowrence come lourand for he lufit never licht	*crawling; loved; [the] light*
2295	And sone appeirit befoir thame in that place.	*quickly appeared*
	The man leuch na thing quhen he saw that sicht.	*did not laugh at all when*
	"Lowrence," quod the wolff, "thow man declair this cace	*must settle; case*
	Quhairof we sall schaw the suith in schort space.	*Of which; reveal; truth; time*
	I callit on thee leill witnes for to beir	*called; to bear true witness*
2300	Quhat hard thou that this man hecht me lang eir."	*heard; promised; a while ago*
	"Schir," said the tod, "I cannot hastelie	*fox*
	Swa sone as now gif sentence finall	*As soon; give final sentence*
	Bot wald ye baith submit yow heir to me	*were you both; yourselves*
	To stand at my decreit perpetuall,	*abide by my binding decree*
2305	To pleis baith I suld preif gif it may fall."	*please both; try if; it so turn out*
	"Weill," quod the wolff, "I am content for me."	*Well; for my part*
	The man said, "Swa am I, however it be."	*So*
	Than schew thay furth thair allegeance but fabill	*showed; cases without deceit*
	And baith proponit thair pley to him compleit.	*presented; entire pleas to him*
2310	Quod Lowrence, "Now I am juge amycabill;	*benevolent judge*
	Ye sall be sworne to stand at my decreit	*shall; pledged; abide by my ruling*
	Quhether heirefter ye think it soure or sweit."	*Whether afterwards; sweet*
	The wolf braid furth his fute, the man his hand	*extended out; foot*
	And on the toddis taill sworne thay ar to stand.	*they have sworn to abide*
2315	Than tuke the tod the man furth till ane syde	*took; fox; away on one side*
	And said him, "Freind, thou art in blunder brocht.	*told him; brought into trouble*
	The wolf will not forgif thee ane oxe hyde	*forgive; ox hide*
	Yit wald myself fane help thee and I mocht	*willingly; if I might*
	Bot I am laith to hurt my conscience ocht.	*loath; in any way*
2320	Tyne nocht thy querrell in thy awin defence;	*Do not lose; claim; own*
	This will not throu but grit coist and expence.	*[go] through without*
	"Seis thou not buddis beiris bernis throw	*Seest; [that] bribes carry men through*
	And giftis garris crukit materis hald full evin?	*make crooked; straight*
	Sumtymis ane hen haldis ane man in ane kow.	*a hen keeps a cow for a man*
2325	All ar not halie that heifis thair handis to hevin."	*holy; raise their*

"Schir," said the man, "ye sall have sex or sevin — *shall; six*
Richt off the fattest hennis of all the floik. — *Of the very; flock*
I compt not all the laif, leif me the coik." — *do not care [about]; rest, leave; rooster*

"I am ane juge!" quod Lowrence than and leuch, — *laughed*
2330 "Thair is na buddis suld beir me by the rycht. — *deflect me from justice*
I may tak hennis and caponis weill aneuch — *capons; enough*
For God is gane to sleip as for this nycht. — *gone; sleep; night*
Sic small thingis ar not sene into his sicht. — *Such; seen in; sight*
Thir hennis," quod he, "sall mak thy querrell sure: — *These; shall; case assured*
2335 With emptie hand na man suld halkis lure." — *will lure hawks*

Concordit thus, than Lowrence tuke his leif — *Agreed; then; took his leave*
And to the wolff he went into ane ling, — *went directly*
Syne prevelie he plukkit him be the sleiff, — *Then covertly; pulled; sleeve*
"Is this in ernist," quod he, "ye ask sic thing? — *earnest; request such*
2340 Na be my saull, I trow it be in heithing." — *believe; mockery*
Than said the wolf, "Lowrence, quhy sayis thou sa? — *why; so*
Thow hard the hecht thyself that he couth ma. — *heard; vow; did make*

"The hecht," quod he, "yone man maid at the pleuch, — *that; made; plow*
Is that the cause quhy ye the cattell craif?" — *why; demand the cattle*
2345 Half into heithing said Lowrence than and leuch, — *in mockery; then*
"Schir, be the rude, unroikit now ye raif. — *Sir, by the cross, unrocked; rave*
The devill ane stirk tail thairfoir sall ye haif. — *calf's; have*
Wald I tak it upon my conscience — *Would I wish to undertake it*
To do sa pure ane man as yone offence? — *so poor a man as that [an]*

2350 "Yit haif I commonnit with the carll," quod he, — *I have talked; churl; said*
"We ar concordit upon this cunnand: — *settled; agreement*
Quyte off all clamis swa ye will mak him fre, — *Clear; claims as long as; without condition*
Ye sall ane cabok have into your hand — *shall; cheese*
That sic ane sall not be in all this land — *such [a] one shall*
2355 For it is somer cheis baith fresche and fair, — *soft cheese*
He sayis it weyis ane stane and sumdeill mair." — *weighs; fourteen pounds; rather more*

"Is that thy counsell," quod the wolff, "I do — *[that] I make it*
That yone carll for ane cabok suld be fre?" — *that churl; should; free*
"Ye be my saull and I wer sworne yow to, — *Yes; if; bound to you by oath*
2360 Ye suld nane uther counsell have for me, — *as far as I am concerned*
For gang ye to the maist extremitie, — *if you go; furthest extreme*
It will not wyn yow worth ane widderit neip. — *the value of a withered turnip*
Schir, trow ye not I have ane saull to keip?" — *do you not suppose; keep*

"Weill," quod the wolff, "it is aganis my will — *against*
2365 That yone carll for ane cabok suld ga quyte." — *go free*
"Schir," quod the tod, "ye tak it in nane evill, — *you [should] not take it hard*

For be my saull, yourself had all the wyte."   *by my soul; blame*
Than said the wolff, "I bid na mair to flyte   *intend to quarrel no more*
Bot I wald se yone cabok of sic pryis."   *wish to see that; such esteem*
2370   "Schir," said the tod, "he tauld me quhair it lyis."   *told; where*

Than hand in hand thay held unto ane hill.   *headed toward*
The husband till his hous hes tane the way   *to; taken the path*
For he wes fane he schaippit from thair ill   *glad; escaped; their harm*
And on his feit woke the dure quhill day.   *feet [he] guarded; door until*
2375   Now will we turne unto the uther tway.   *other two*
Throw woddis waist thir freikis on fute can fair   *empty woods these men; go*
Fra busk to busk quhill neir midnycht and mair.   *From bush; until near; later*

Lowrence wes ever remembring upon wrinkis   *always thinking; wiles*
And subtelteis, the wolff for to begyle.   *stratagems; to deceive*
2380   That he had hecht ane caboik he forthinkis   *promised; cheese; regrets*
Yit at the last he findis furth ane wyle,   *comes up with a trick*
Than at himself softlie couth he smyle.   *quietly did he smile*
The wolf sayis, "Lowrence, thou playis bellie blind.[1]
We seik all nycht bot nathing can we find."   *search; night*

2385   "Schir," said the tod, "we ar at it almaist;   *we have almost reached it*
Soft yow ane lytill and ye sall se it sone."   *Quiet; shall soon see it*
Than to ane manure place thay hyit in haist.   *manor; hurried; haste*
The nycht wes lycht, and pennyfull the mone.   *round as a penny; moon*
Than till ane draw-well thir senyeours past but hone   *to; elders went without delay*
2390   Quhair that twa bukkettis severall suithlie hang. *two separate buckets did indeed hang*
As ane come up ane uther doun wald gang.   *one; another down; go*

The schadow off the mone schone in the well.   *reflection; shone*
"Schir," said Lowrence, "anis ye sall find me leill,   *for once; trustworthy*
Now se ye not the caboik weill yoursell,   *see; cheese clearly yourself*
2395   Quhyte as ane neip and round als as ane seill?   *White; turnip; also; seal*
He hang it yonder that na man suld it steill.   *hung; there so that; steal it*
Schir, traist ye weill, yone caboik ye se hing   *trust; see hanging*
Micht be ane present to ony lord or king."   *Could; for*

"Na," quod the wolff, "mycht I yone caboik haif   *If I could get that cheese*
2400   On the dry land as I it yonder se,   *I see it there*
I wald quitclame the carll of all the laif.   *declare the churl free; rest*
His dart oxin I compt thame not ane fle,   *worthless(?); value; flea*
Yone wer mair meit for sic ane man as me.   *That would be finer food; such*
Lowrence," quod he, "leip in the bukket sone   *said; leap; at once*
2405   And I sall hald the ane quhill thow have done." *hold the [other] bucket until*

---

[1] *The wolf says, "Lowrence, you are playing 'It' in blindman's buff"*

Lowrence gird doun baith sone and subtellie, *sprang down both fast; nimbly*
The uther baid abufe and held the flaill. *stayed above; crank*
"It is sa mekill," quod Lowrence, "it maisteris me. *[The cheese]; big; defeats*
On all my tais it hes not left ane naill. *toes; a single claw*

2410 Ye man mak help upwart and it haill: *must give; and haul it up*
Leip in the uther bukket haistelie *Leap; quickly*
And cum sone doun and mak me sum supple." *come down now; give; aid*

Than lychtlie in the bukket lap the loun. *promptly; leapt; fool*
His wecht but weir the uther end gart ryis. *weight without doubt; made*

2315 The tod come hailland up, the wolff yeid doun. *rising quickly; went down*
Than angerlie the wolff upon him cryis, *angrily*
"I cummand thus dounwart, quhy thow upwart hyis?" *coming down thus; hasten*
"Schir," quod the foxe, "thus fairis it of fortoun: *goes it according to fortune*
As ane cummis up, scho quheillis ane uther doun." *comes; wheels another down*

2420 Than to the ground sone yeid the wolff in haist. *well-bottom at once went*
The tod lap on land, als blyith as ony bell *leapt; blithe as any bell*
And left the wolf in watter to the waist.
Quha haillit him out I wait not, of the well. *hauled; do not know, from*
Heir endis the text, thair is na mair to tell, *Here; no more*

2425 Yyt men may find ane gude moralitie *But*
In this sentence thocht it ane fabill be. *passage; although*

Moralitas *Moralization*
This wolf I likkin to ane wickit man *liken; wicked*
Quhilk dois the pure oppres in everie place *Who oppresses the poor*
And pykis at thame all querrellis that he can *starts quarrels with them all*

2430 Be rigour, reif, and uther wickitnes. *harshness, theft*
The foxe the feind I call into this cais, *I call the devil; situation*
Arctand ilk man to ryn unrychteous rinkis, *Compelling each; follow; courses*
Thinkand thairthrow to lok him in his linkis. *by that means; lock; chains*

The husband may be callit ane godlie man *farmer; called; devout*
2435 With quhome the feynd falt findes, as clerkis reids, *whom; finds fault; scholars teach*
Besie to tempt him with all wayis that he can. *Busy; methods; knows*
The hennis ar warkis that fra ferme faith proceidis. *[good] works; from firm*
Quhair sic sproutis spreidis, the evill spreit thair not speids *grow; does not prosper*
Bot wendis unto the wickit man agane, *goes back to the wicked man*
2440 That he hes tint his travell is full unfane. *wasted; effort; displeased*

The wodds waist quhairin wes the wolf wyld *empty woods; the wolf was decieved*
Ar wickit riches, quhilk all men gaipis to get. *which; yearn*
Quha traistis in sic trusterie ar oft begyld, *Whoever trusts; trash(?)*
For mammon may be callit the devillis net *evil wealth; called*
2445 Quhilk Sathanas for all sinfull hes set. *Which Satan; all sinful people*

With proud plesour quha settis his traist thairin — *whoever places; trust*
But speciall grace, lychtlie can not outwin. — *Without exceptional; easily; get out*

The cabok may be callit covetyce — *cheese; covetousness*
Quhilk blomis braid in mony mannis ee. — *Which blooms broad; eye*
2450 Wa worth the well of that wickit vyce — *Woe betide; source; wicked vice*
For it is all bot fraud and fantasie — *all entirely; delusion*
Dryvand ilk man to leip in the buttrie — *Spurring each; jump; pantry*
That dounwart drawis unto the pane off hell. — *pulls downward; torment*
Christ keip all Christianis from that wickit well. — *preserve*

The Wolf and the Wether — *Ram*

2455 Quhylum thair wes, as Esope can report, — *Once there; does report*
Ane scheipheird dwelland be ane forrest neir — *A shepherd dwelling by; near*
Quhilk had ane hound that did him grit comfort. — *Who; gave him great service*
Full war he wes to walk his fauld but weir, — *Very diligent; guard; enclosure without doubt*
That nouther wolf nor wildcat durst appeir — *So that neither; dared*
2460 Nor foxe on feild nor yit no uther beist — *in; nor even any other animal*
Bot he thame slew or chaissit at the leist. — *Unless; killed them; least*

Sa happinnit it, as everilk beist man de, — *So; every; must die*
This hound of suddand seiknes to be deid, — *to die of a sudden sickness*
Bot than, God wait, the keipar of the fe — *then; knows; keeper; livestock*
2465 For verray wo woxe wanner nor the weid. — *utter; grew paler than; [withered] weed*
"Allace," quod he, "now se I na remeid — *Alas; I see no help*
To saif the selie beistis that I keip — *save; poor animals; keep*
For with the wolf weryit beis all my scheip." — *all my sheep are savaged*

It wald have maid ane mannis hart sair to se — *made a man's heart sore; see*
2470 The selie scheiphirdis lamentatioun. — *pitiable shepherd's lament*
"Now is my darling deid allace," quod he, — *dead*
"For now to beg my breid I may be boun, — *bread; destined*
With pyikstaff and with scrip to fair off toun — *walking stick; bag; leave the farm*
For all the beistis befoir that bandonit bene — *that were kept under control before*
2475 Will schute upon my beistis with ire and tene." — *attack my animals; anger; rage*

With that ane wedder wichtlie wan on fute. — *valiantly approached*
"Maister," quod he, "mak merie and be blyith. — *Master; make merry; blithe*
To brek your hart for baill it is na bute. — *break; sorrow; no use*
For ane deid dog ye na cair on yow kyith. — *should show no grief in your appearance*
2480 Ga fetche him hither and fla his skyn off swyth, — *Go; here; flay; at once*
Syne sew it on me and luke that it be meit, — *Then; check; well-fitting*
Baith heid and crag, bodie, taill, and feit. — *Both head and neck; feet*

"Than will the wolf trow that I am he — *Then; believe; I am the dog*
For I sall follow him fast quharever he fair. — *shall; persistently wherever he goes*

2485	All haill the cure I tak it upon me	*The complete responsibility*
	Your scheip to keip at midday, lait, and air;	*keep; noon, late, and early*
	And he persew, be God I sall not spair	*If he goes hunting, by God; cease*
	To follow him as fast as did your doig	*dog*
	Swa that I warrand ye sall not want ane hoig."	*So; pledge; lose; one young sheep*

2490	Than said the scheipheird, "This come of ane gude wit.	*came from; good mind*
	Thy counsall is baith sicker, leill, and trew.	*both reliable, loyal; trustworthy*
	Quha sayis ane scheip is daft, thay lieit of it."	*Whoever; stupid; lied about it*
	With that in hy the doggis skyn off he flew	*haste; he flayed off*
	And on the scheip rycht softlie couth it sew.	*very gently did sew it*
2495	Than worth the wedder wantoun of his weid:	*the ram grew proud; clothes*
	"Now of the wolff," quod he, "I have na dreid."	*no fear*

	In all thingis he counterfait the dog	*imitated*
	For all the nycht he stude and tuke na sleip	*stood guard; took no sleep*
	Swa that weill lang thair wantit not ane hog.	*So; for a long time; lacked; a young sheep*
2500	Swa war he wes and walkryfe thame to keip	*alert; watchful to guard them*
	That Lowrence durst not luke upon ane scheip	*[the fox] did not dare to look*
	For and he did, he followit him sa fast	*if; the wether chased him so*
	That of his lyfe he maid him all agast.	*for his life; made; afraid*

	Was nowther wolff, wildcat, nor yit tod	*neither; fox*
2505	Durst cum within thay boundis all about	*Dared enter any part of that district*
	Bot he wald chase thame baith throw rouch and snod.	*Lest; over rough; even [ground]*
	Thay bailfull beistis had of thair lyvis sic dout,	*Those miserable; for; such fear*
	For he wes mekill and semit to be stout,	*large; seemed; powerful*
	That everilk beist thay dred him as the deid,	*every; feared him like death*
2510	Within that woid that nane durst hald thair heid.	*[So that]; forest; raise*

	Yit happinnit thair ane hungrie wolff to slyde	*a hungry wolf chanced to sneak there*
	Out-throw his scheip quhair thay lay on ane le:	*Amongst; where; pasture*
	"I sall have ane," quod he, "quhatever betyde,	*shall; whatever happens*
	Thocht I be werryit, for hunger or I de."	*attacked, or else I die of hunger*
2515	With that ane lamb intill his cluke hint he.	*he seized in his claws*
	The laif start up for thay wer all agast	*rest leapt; terrified*
	Bot God wait gif the wedder followit fast.	*God knows if the ram*

	Went never hound mair haistelie fra the hand	*Never went; from being held*
	Quhen he wes rynnand maist raklie at the ra	*running; speedily; roe deer*
2520	Nor went this wedder baith over mois and strand,	*Than; bog; brook*
	And stoppit nouther at bank, busk, nor bra,	*neither; thicket, nor slope*
	Bot followit ay sa ferslie on his fa	*always; fiercely; foe*
	With sic ane drift quhill dust and dirt over-draif him,	*such a pace; spattered over*
	And maid ane vow to God that he suld have him.	*[he] made; should capture*

2525	With that the wolff let out his taill on lenth	*stretched; length*
	For he wes hungrie and it drew neir the ene	*it was getting close to evening*
	And schupe him for to ryn with all his strenth.	*gathered himself up to run*
	Fra he the wedder sa neir cummand had sene,	*Once; coming so close; seen*
	He dred his lyfe, and he overtane had bene;	*feared for; if; overtaken*
2530	Thairfoir he spairit nowther busk nor boig,	*avoided neither thicket; bog*
	For weill he kennit the kenenes of the doig.	*well; knew; fierceness*

	To mak him lycht, he kest the lamb him fra,	*unburden himself; threw*
	Syne lap over leis and draif throw dub and myre.	*leapt; fields; rushed; puddles; mire*
	"Na," quod the wedder, "in faith we part not swa.	*will not be separated thus*
2535	It is not the lamb bot thee that I desyre.	*that I am after*
	I sall cum neir for now I se thee tyre."	*get close; see you grow weak*
	The wolf ran till ane rekill stude behind him	*a pile of peats [that] lay(?)*
	Bot ay the neirar the wedder he couth bind him.	*always; closer; did stick to*

	Sone efter that, he followit him sa neir	*followed him so close*
2540	Quhill that the wolf for fleidnes fylit the feild,	*Until; terror befouled*
	Syne left the gait and ran throw busk and breir	*Then; path; bush and brier*
	And schupe him fra the schawis for to scheild.	*braced himself to ward off the thickets*
	He ran restles for he wist of na beild.	*without pause; knew of no safe haven*
	The wedder followit him baith out and in	*both in and out*
2545	Quhill that ane breir busk raif rudelie off the skyn.	*Until; tore roughly*

	The wolff wes wer and blenkit him behind	*alert; glanced behind him*
	And saw the wedder come thrawand throw the breir,	*hurtling*
	Syne saw the doggis skyn hingand on his lind.	*Then; hanging; buttocks*
	"Na!" quod he, "Is this ye that is sa neir,	*O!; Are you the one who*
2550	Richt now ane hound and now quhyte as ane freir?	*Just now; white; friar*
	I fled over fer and I had kennit the cais.	*too far if; known; situation*
	To God I vow that ye sall rew this rais.	*regret this pursuit*

	"Quhat wes the cause ye gaif me sic ane katche?"	*What; gave; such a chase*
	With that in hy he hint him be the horne.	*haste; seized; by*
2555	"For all your mowis, ye met anis with your matche,	*jests; have met finally; match*
	Suppois ye leuch me all this yeir to scorne.	*Even if; laughed; year*
	For quhat enchessoun this doggis skyn have ye borne?"	*what reason; worn*
	"Maister," quod he, "bot to have playit with yow.	*just to have played with you*
	I yow requyre that ye nane uther trow."	*ask; believe nothing else*

2560	"Is this your bourding in ernist than?" quod he,	*Is then this joke in earnest*
	"For I am verray effeirit and on flocht;	*totally terrified; in a fright*
	Cum bak agane and I sall let yow se."	*Retrace the route; shall; see*
	Than quhar the gait wes grimmit he him brocht.	*where; path; befouled; brought*
	"Quhether call ye this fair play or nocht	*Do you call; or [do you] not*
2565	To set your maister in sa fell effray,	*put; such dreadful fright*
	Quhill he for feiritnes hes fylit up the way?	*Until; fear; mucked; path*

"Thryis, be my saull, ye gart me schute behind: — *Thrice; made; defecate*
Upon my hoichis the senyeis may be sene; — *haunches; evidence; seen*
For feiritnes full oft I fylit the wind. — *fear; sullied the air*
2570 Now is this ye? Na, bot ane hound, I wene! — *is it you; without a; I think*
Me think your teith over schort to be sa kene. — *It seems; too short; fierce*
Blissit be the busk that reft yow your array, — *Blessed; bush; stripped; costume*
Ellis, fleand, bursin had I bene this day." — *Or else, fleeing, ruptured*

"Schir," quod the wedder, "suppois I ran in hy, — *granted that I ran at top speed*
2575 My mynd wes never to do your persoun ill. — *intent; do ill to your person*
Ane flear gettis ane follower commounly — *An escaper; chaser*
In play or ernist, preif quha sa ever will. — *prove it whoever wishes*
Sen I bot playit, be gracious me till — *Since; only; merciful to me*
And I sall gar my freindis blis your banis. — *make; pray for your bones*
2580 Ane full gude servand will crab his maister anis." — *wholly good; annoy; once*

"I have bene oftymis set in grit effray — *often been put; great fear*
Bot be the rude, sa rad yit wes I never — *by the cross; terrified yet*
As thow hes maid me with thy prettie play. — *made; charming game*
I schot behind quhen thow overtuke me ever — *shat; each time*
2585 Bot sikkerlie now sall we not dissever." — *truly; we shall not part*
Than be the crag bane smertlie he him tuke — *neck bone roughly he took him*
Or ever he ceissit, and it in schunder schuke. — *Before he ever stopped; apart*

Moralitas — *Moralization*
Esope that poet, first father of this fabill, — *The poet Aesop; originator*
Wrait this parabole quhilk is convenient — *Wrote; parable that; fitting*
2590 Because the sentence wes fructuous and agreabill, — *beneficial; suitable*
In moralitie exemplative prudent — *Wise in exemplary moral instruction*
Quhais problemes bene verray excellent — *Whose analogies are truly*
Throw similitude of figuris to this day, — *similarity; likenesses*
Gevis doctrine to the redaris of it ay. — *[And] give precepts; always*

2595 Heir may thow se that riches of array — *Here; see; richness; clothing*
Will cause pure men presumpteous for to be. — *poor; to be arrogant*
Thay think thay hald of nane, be thay als gay, — *owe loyalty to no one; so fine*
Bot counterfute ane lord in all degree. — *counterfeit; in every respect*
Out of thair cais in pryde thay clym sa hie — *Above their rank; climb*
2600 That thay forbeir thair better in na steid — *submit to; betters; no place*
Quhill sum man tit thair heillis over thair heid. — *Until someone tips; heels*

Richt swa in service uther sum exceidis; — *Just as; some outdo others*
And thay haif withgang, welth, and cherising — *If they; free access; encouragement*
That thay will lychtlie lordis in thair deidis — *scorn; actions*
2605 And lukis not to thair blude nor thair ofspring — *pay no heed; lineage*
Bot yit nane wait how lang that reull will ring. — *no one knows; regime; last*

Bot he was wyse that bad his sone considder, *who instructed his son to*
"Bewar in welth, for hall benkis ar rycht slidder." *hall benches are very slippery*

Thairfoir I counsell men of everilk stait *every class*
2610 To knaw thameself and quhome thay suld forbeir, *know; whom; should respect*
And fall not with thair better in debait, *their betters*
Suppois thay be als galland in thair geir. *Even if; as stylish; apparel*
It settis na servand for to uphald weir *suits; keep up a dispute*
Nor clym sa hie quhill he fall off the ledder *climb; until; ladder*
2615 Bot think upon the wolf and on the wedder. *about*

The Wolf and the Lamb

Ane cruell wolff richt ravenous and fell *very; fierce*
Upon ane tyme past to ane reveir *At one time went; a river*
Descending from ane rotche unto ane well, *cliff; pool*
To slaik his thrist drank of the watter cleir. *quench; thirst; clear*
2620 Swa upon cace ane selie lamb come neir *It so happened that a little; came*
Bot of his fa the wolff na thing he wist *foe; he knew nothing*
And in the streme laipit to cule his thrist. *sipped; cool*

Thus drank thay baith bot not of ane intent, *both; with the same idea*
The wolfis thocht wes all on wickitnes, *thought was; wickedness*
2625 The selie lamb wes meik and innocent. *poor little lamb; meek*
Upon the rever in ane uther place *At; river; another*
Beneth the wolff he drank ane lytill space *Downstream from; while*
Quhill him thocht gude, presomyng thair nane ill. *While; supposing; no harm*
The wolff this saw and rampand come him till. *saw this; raging; to him*

2630 With girnand teith and angrie, austre luke, *gnashing; fierce look*
Said to the lamb, "Thow cative, wretchit thing, *[He] said; Thou miserable, wretched*
How durst thow be sa bald to fyle this bruke *dare; so bold; defile; brook*
Quhar I suld drink with thy foull slavering! *Where; might; slobbering*
It wer almous thee for to draw and hing *would be a good deed; to drag and hang*
2635 That suld presume with thy foull lippis vyle *vile*
To glar my drink and this fair watter fyle." *beslime; defile*

The selie lamb quaikand for verray dreid *shaking; utter dread*
On kneis fell and said, "Schir, with your leif, *knees; by your leave*
Suppois I dar not say thairoff ye leid *Even if; dare; you lied about that*
2640 Bot be my saull, I wait ye can nocht preif *by; soul; know; cannot prove*
That I did ony thing that suld yow greif. *anything that should; annoy*
Ye wait alswa that your accusatioun *know as well*
Failyeis fra treuth and contrair is to ressoun. *Deviates from; contrary*

"Thocht I can nocht, nature will me defend *Though; am not able; defend me*
2645 And of the deid perfyte experience. *perfect knowledge of the fact*

All hevie thing man of the self discend   *heavy; must descend from its place*
Bot giff sumthing on force mak resistence,   *Unless something forcibly*
Than may the streme on na way mak ascence   *Thus can; in no way make an ascent*
Nor ryn bakwart. I drank beneth yow far,   *flow backwards; below you*
2650 Ergo for me your bruke wes never the war.   *Therefore; brook; worse*

"Alswa my lippis, sen that I wes ane lam,   *Also; lips, since; was; lamb*
Tuitchit na thing that wes contagious   *Touched; infectious*
Bot sowkit milk from pappis of my dam,   *sucked; teats of my mother*
Richt naturall, sweit, and als delitious."   *sweet; also delightful*
2655 "Weill," quod the wolff, "thy language rigorus   *"Well," said; strict manner of speech*
Cummis thee of kynd; swa thy father before   *Comes to you by nature; so*
Held me at bait baith with boist and schore.   *in dispute; both boast; threat*

"He wraithit me and than I culd him warne,   *annoyed; did warn him*
Within ane yeir and I brukit my heid   *if I kept my head*
2660 I suld be wrokkin on him or on his barne   *should; avenged; child*
For his exorbetant and frawart pleid.   *outrageous; perverse lawsuit*
Thow sall doutles for his deidis be deid."   *shall doubtless; actions; dead*
"Schir, it is wrang that for the fatheris gilt   *Sir; wrong; guilt*
The saikles sone suld punist be or spilt.   *innocent son; ruined*

2665 "Haiff ye not hard quhat halie scripture sayis   *Have; heard; holy*
Endytit with the mouth of God almycht,   *Dictated by*
'Of his awin deidis ilk man sall beir the pais   *own deeds each; bear; weight*
As pyne for sin, reward for werkis rycht.'   *torment; good deeds*
For my trespas quhy suld my sone have plycht?   *why should; blame*
2670 Quha did the mis, lat him sustene the pane."   *Whoever; wrong, let; suffer the pain*
"Yaa," quod the wolff, "yit pleyis thow agane?   *are you arguing a legal case yet again*

"I let thee wit quhen that the father offendis   *understand, when*
I will cheris nane of his successioun   *befriend none; descendants*
And of his barnis I may weill tak amendis   *from; children; compensation*
2675 Unto the twentie degree descending doun.   *twentieth*
Thy father thocht to mak ane strang poysoun   *intended to make a strong poison*
And with his mouth into my watter spew."   *vomit into my drinking water*
"Schir," quod the lamb, "thay twa ar nouther trew.   *those two [allegations]*

"The law sayis and ye will understand,   *if you care to*
2680 Thair suld na man for wrang nor violence   *There should; for injury*
His adversar punis at his awin hand   *Punish his adversary with*
Without proces of law and audiens   *legal proceedings; hearing*
Quhilk suld have leif to mak lawfull defence   *Which should have permission*
And thairupon summond peremtourly   *to that end [be]; promptly*
2685 For to propone, contrairie, or reply.   *To put forward a countercharge, refute, or respond*

"Set me ane lauchfull court, I sall compeir   *legitimate; appear*
Befoir the lyoun, lord and leill justice,   *lawful judge*
And be my hand I oblis me rycht heir   *by; pledge myself; here*
That I sall byde ane unsuspect assyis.   *undergo; impartial inquiry*
2690   This is the law, this is the instant wys,   *present practice*
Ye suld pretend thairfoir ane summondis mak   *undertake; to make*
Aganis that day to gif ressoun and tak."   *In readiness for; give and receive arguments*

"Ha," quod the wolff, "thou wald intruse ressoun   *intrude*
Quhair wrang and reif suld dwell in propertie.   *oppression; plunder; ownership*
2695   That is ane poynt and part of fals tressoun   *an element and aspect*
For to gar reuth remane with crueltie.   *make mercy*
Be Goddis woundis, fals tratour, thow sall de   *By God's wounds, false traitor; shall die*
For thy trespas and for thy fatheris als."   *offense; father's as well*
With that anone he hint him be the hals.   *at once; grabbed; throat*

2700   The selie lamb culd do nathing bot bleit.   *nothing but bleat*
Sone wes he heidit, the wolff wald do na grace,   *beheaded; show no mercy*
Syne drank his blude and of his flesche can eit   *Then; did eat*
Quhill he wes full, syne went his way on pace.   *Until, went swiftly on his way*
Of his murther quhat sall we say allace,   *murder; what shall*
2705   Wes not this reuth, wes not this grit pietie,   *Was this not mercy; great pity*
To gar this selie lamb but gilt thus de?   *make; poor; without guilt; die*

Moralitas   *Moralization*
The pure pepill this lamb may signifie   *poor people; can represent*
As maill men, merchandis, and all laboureris   *Like renters; laborers*
Of quhome the lyfe is half ane purgatorie   *For whom*
2710   To wyn with lautie leving as efferis.   *earn; dutifulness a living as is proper*
The wolf betakinnis fals extortioneris   *represents*
And oppressouris of pure men as we se   *poor; see*
Be violence or craft in sutelté.   *By; skill; mental subtlety*

Thre kynd of wolfis in this warld now rings.   *Three; now reign*
2715   The first ar fals perverteris of the lawis   *deceitful misinterpreters*
Quhilk under poleit termis falset mingis,   *Who; polished; mix falsehood*
Lettand that all wer gospell that he schawis,   *Pretending; alleges*
Bot for ane bud the pure man he overthrawis,   *bribe; he ruins the poor man*
Smoirand the richt, garrand the wrang proceid.   *Smothering; right, making; succeed*
2720   Of sic wolfis hellis fyre sall be thair meid.   *For such; shall; their reward*

O man of law, let be thy subteltie   *relinquish; mental dexterity*
With nice gimpis and fraudis intricait   *trivial details; tricks*
And think that God in his divinitie   *divine nature*
The wrang, the richt of all thy werkis wait.   *Knows the wrong and right of all thy deeds*
2725   For prayer, price, for hie nor law estait,   *request, reward; high or low rank*

Of fals querrellis se thow mak na defence,   *wrongful disputes see*
Hald with the richt, hurt not thy conscience.   *Remain*

Ane uther kynd of wolfis ravenous   *Another*
Ar mychtie men haifand aneuch plentie *possessing more than enough*
2730 Quhilkis ar sa gredie and sa covetous   *Who are*
Thay will not thoill in peax ane pureman be. *allow a poor man to live in peace*
Suppois he and his houshald baith suld de *Even though; family as well should die*
For falt of fude, thairof thay gif na rak   *lack of food; give no care*
Bot over his heid his mailling will thay tak. *head; leased property; seize*

2735 O man but mercie, quhat is in thy thocht, *without; what; intention*
War than ane wolf and thow culd understand! *Worse; if you could*
Thow hes aneuch, the pure husband richt nocht *poor farmer absolutely not*
Bot croip and crufe upon ane clout of land. *Except crop; hovel; scrap*
For Goddis aw, how durst thow tak on hand *fear of God; dare; undertake*
2740 And thow in barn and byre sa bene and big *cowshed so fine and solid*
To put him fra his tak and gar him thig? *evict; from; lease; make; beg*

The thrid wolf ar men of heritage   *third; with inherited property*
As lordis that hes land be Goddis lane   *by God's permission*
And settis to the mailleris ane village *leases; renters a single common pasture*
2745 And for ane tyme gressome payit and tane, *annual fee [is] paid; received*
Syne vexis him or half his terme be gane   *Then harasses; before; over*
With pykit querrellis for to mak him fane *fabricated complaints; eager*
To flit or pay his gressome new agane.   *decamp or else; over*

His hors, his meir, he man len to the laird *mare; must lend; landlord*
2750 To drug and draw in cairt and cariage,   *drag; haul*
His servand or his self may not be spaird *servant; cannot be exempted*
To swing and sweit withoutin meit or wage. *From toiling; sweating; food*
Thus how he standis in labour and bondage *In what a way does he; remains*
That scantlie may he purches by his maill *So that barely; afford after; rent*
2755 To leve upon dry breid and watter caill! *live; cabbage broth*

Hes thow not reuth to gar thy tennentis sweit *no pity; make; sweat*
Into thy laubour with faynt and hungrie wame *weak; belly*
And syne hes lytill gude to drink or eit *then has; good; eat*
With his menye at evin quhen he cummis hame? *household; evening when; home*
2760 Thow suld be rad for richteous Goddis blame *should; afraid; reproof*
For it cryis ane vengeance unto the hevinnis hie *demands*
To gar ane pure man wirk but meit or fe. *make; without food or wage*

O thow grit lord that riches hes and rent, *who has wealth; property*
Be nocht ane wolf thus to devoir the pure. *devour the poor*
2765 Think that nathing cruell nor violent
May in this warld perpetuallie indure.   *Can; last forever*

This sall thow trow and sikkerlie assure:	*must; believe; firmly expect*
For till oppres, thow sall haif als grit pane	*To engage in oppression; have as*
As thow the pure with thy awin hand had slane.	*As if; poor; slain*

2770 God keip the lamb quhilk is the innocent	*preserve; who*
From wolfis byit and men extortioneris,	*wolf's bite and human extortioners*
God grant that wrangous men of fals intent	*evildoing*
Be manifest and punischit as effeiris.	*made known; as is fitting*
And God, as thow all rychteous prayer heiris,	*since you hear all righteous prayers*
2775 Mot saif our king and gif him hart and hand	*May; determination; strength*
All sic wolfis to banes of the land.	*such wolves; banish from*

The Paddock and the Mouse   *Frog*

Upon ane tyme as Esope culd report,	*Once upon a; did record*
Ane lytill mous come till ane rever syde.	*came to the edge of a river*
Scho micht not waid, hir schankis wer sa schort,	*She could; wade; legs were so*
2780 Scho culd not swym, scho had na hors to ryde,	*could; no*
Of verray force behovit hir to byde	*utter necessity it was incumbent on her to wait*
And to and fra besyde that revir deip	*fro; deep*
Scho ran cryand with mony pietuous peip.	*crying; many a pitiful squeak*

"Help over! Help over!" this silie mous can cry,	*poor; did cry*
2785 "For Goddis lufe, sumbodie, over the brym."	*the love of God; depth*
With that ane paddok in the watter by	*nearby*
Put up hir heid and on the bank can clym	*Raised; head; did climb*
Quhilk be nature culd douk and gaylie swym.	*That by; dive; easily swim*
With voce full rauk scho said on this maneir,	*very hoarse voice; in this way*
2790 "Gude morne schir mous, quhat is your erand heir?"	*Good morning, sir; here*

"Seis thow," quod scho, "of corne yone jolie flat	*Seest thou; said; grain; fine field*
Of ryip aitis, of barlie, peis, and quheit?	*ripe oats; peas; wheat*
I am hungrie and fane wald be thair at	*eagerly want to be there*
Bot I am stoppit be this watter greit	*held back by; vast*
2795 And on this syde I get nathing till eit	*to eat*
Bot hard nuttis quhilkis with my teith I bore.	*nuts that; teeth; break open*
Wer I beyond, my feist wer fer the more.	*Were; feast would be much greater*

"I have no boit, heir is no maryner	*boat, here; sailor*
And thocht thair war, I have no fraucht to pay."	*even if there; money for fare*
2800 Quod scho, "Sister, lat be your hevie cheir,	*Said; set aside; gloomy mood*
Do my counsall and I sall find the way	*Follow my advice; shall*
Withoutin hors, brig, boit, or yit galay	*bridge, boat; even galley*
To bring yow over saiflie, be not afeird,	*safely; afraid*
And not wetand the campis of your beird."	*without wetting; whiskers; beard*

2805 "I haif mervell than," quod the lytill mous,   *am puzzled then*
      "How thow can fleit without fedder or fin.   *float; feather*
      This rever is sa deip and dangerous,   *so deep*
      Methink that thow suld drowin to wed thairin.   *It seems to me; wade*
      Tell me thairfoir quhat facultie or gin   *therefore, what ability; skill*
2810 Thow hes to bring thee over this watter wan."   *dark water*
      That to declair the paddok thus began.   *To explain that*

      "With my twa feit," quod scho, "lukkin and braid   *two feet; webbed; wide*
      Insteid off airis I row the streme full styll   *oars; continually*
      And thocht the brym be perrillous to waid   *though; depth; dangerous*
2815 Baith to and fra I swyme at my awin will.   *Both; at my own volition*
      I may not droun for quhy my oppin gill   *because my open*
      Devoidis ay the watter I resaif   *Always ejects; receive*
      Thairfoir to droun forsuith na dreid I haif."   *indeed I have no fear*

      The mous beheld unto hir fronsit face,   *looked at her crumpled*
2820 Hir runkillit cheikis and hir lippis syde,   *wrinkled; wide lips*
      Hir hingand browis and hir voce sa hace,   *overhanging; voice as hoarse*
      Hir loggerand leggis and hir harsky hyde.   *crooked; rough skin*
      Scho ran abak and on the paddok cryde,   *recoiled; to; cried*
      "Giff I can ony skill of phisnomy,   *If; know; of physiognomy*
2825 Thow hes sumpart of falset and invy.   *some amount; deceit; envy*

      "For clerkis sayis the inclinatioun   *scholars say*
      Of mannis thocht proceidis commounly   *thought proceeds usually*
      Efter the corporall complexioun   *Following; combination of bodily instincts*
      To gude or evill, as nature will apply.   *exert influence*
2830 Ane thrawart will, ane thrawin phisnomy: *perverse intention; twisted*
      The auld proverb is witnes of this lorum,   *conclusion*
      Distortum vultum sequitur distortio morum."   *(see line 2830)*

      "Na," quod the taid, "that proverb is not trew   *No; toad; true*
      For fair thingis oftymis ar fundin faikin,   *beautiful; exposed as deceitful*
2835 The blaberyis thocht thay be sad of hew   *blackberries though; dark of hue*
      Ar gadderit up quhen primeros is forsakin,   *gathered; when primroses are passed up*
      The face may faill to be the hartis takin,   *fail; sign of the heart*
      Thairfoir I find this scripture in all place,   *Wherefore; motto everywhere*
      'Thow suld not juge ane man efter his face.'   *should; judge; by*

2840 "Thocht I unhailsum be to luke upon   *Though; repulsive; look at*
      I have na wyt quhy suld I lakkit be.   *I do not understand why; blamed*
      Wer I als fair as jolie Absolon   *Were I as; handsome*
      I am no causer of that grit beutie.   *originator of; great beauty*
      This difference in forme and qualitie   *distinction*
2845 Almychtie God hes causit dame Nature   *has caused lady*
      To prent and set in everilk creature.   *imprint; fix; every*

"Of sum the face may be full flurischand | *For; at peak of perfection*
With silkin toung and cheir rycht amorous | *silken tongue; appearance; lovable*
With mynd inconstant, fals, and variand, | *perfidious; fickle*
2850 Full of desait and menis cautelous." | *deceit; wily strategems*
"Let be thy preiching," quod the hungrie mous, | *Cease thy preaching*
"And be quhat craft thow gar me understand | *by what; make me*
That thow wald gyde me to yone yonder land." | *intend to convey; that distant*

"Thow wait," quod scho, "ane bodie that hes neid | *know; she [the frog] someone; need*
2855 To help thameself suld mony wayis cast. | *consider many methods*
Thairfoir ga tak ane doubill twynit threid | *a doubly twisted thread*
And bind thy leg to myne with knottis fast: | *tight knots*
I sall thee leir to swym, be not agast, | *shall teach you; afraid*
Als weill as I." "As thow?" than quod the mous. | *As well*
2860 To preif that play, it wer rycht perrillous! | *try out that game; very*

"Suld I be bund and fast quhar I am fre | *bound; fastened where; free*
In hoip of help, na, than I schrew us baith | *On the expectation; curse*
For I mycht lois baith lyfe and libertie. | *could lose*
Gif it wer swa, quha suld amend the skaith | *If; thus, who; pay the damage*
2865 Bot gif thow sweir to me the murthour aith | *Unless; swear; murder oath*
But fraud or gyle to bring me over this flude | *Without; guile; river*
But hurt or harme." "In faith," quod scho, "I dude." | *Without; I will do it*

Scho goikit up and to the hevin can cry, | *She [the frog] gazed upward; did cry*
"O Juppiter, of nature god and king, | *god and king of nature*
2870 I mak ane aith trewlie to thee that I | *sincerely*
This lytill mous sall over this watter bring." |
This aith wes maid; the mous but persaving | *was made; without perceiving*
The fals ingyne of this foull crappald pad | *deceitful mind; toadlike frog*
Tuke threid and band hir leg as scho hir bad. | *Took; tied; directed her*

2875 Than fute for fute thay lap baith in the brym | *foot; leapt; water*
Bot in thair myndis thay wer rycht different, | *were very*
The mous thocht nathing bot to fleit and swym, | *thought of; except; float*
The paddok for to droun set hir intent. |
Quhen thay in midwart of the streme wer went, | *midst; had gone*
2880 With all hir force the paddok preissit doun | *pushed downwards*
And thocht the mous without mercie to droun. | *intended*

Persavand this, the mous on hir can cry, | *Realizing; did cry to her*
"Tratour to God, and manesworne unto me! | *perjured*
Thow swore the murthour aith richt now that I | *oath just now*
2885 But hurt or harme suld ferryit be and fre." | *Without; ferried*
And quhen scho saw thair wes bot do or de, | *was only "do or die"*
Scho bowtit up and foirsit hir to swyme, | *bobbed; forced herself; swim*
And preissit upon the taiddis bak to clym. | *struggled onto; toad's; climb*

	The dreid of deith hir strenthis gart incres	*fear; made her strength grow*
2890	And forcit hir defend with mycht and mane.	*might and main*
	The mous upwart, the paddok doun can pres.	*upward; pushes down*
	Quhyle to, quhyle fra, quhyle doukit, up agane,	*Now; submerged*
	This selie mous, this plungit in grit pane,	*thus immersed; torment*
	Gan fecht als lang as breith wes in hir breist	*Kept fighting; breath*
2895	Till at the last scho cryit for ane preist.	*she called; priest [for the last rites]*

	Fechtand thusgait, the gled sat on ane twist	*[While they were] fighting thus; kite; twig*
	And to this wretchit battell tuke gude heid	*miserable; paid close attention*
	And with ane wisk or owthir of thame wist,	*swoop before either; realized*
	He claucht his cluke betwix thame in the threid,	*clutched; talons between*
2900	Syne to the land he flew with thame gude speid,	*Then; them speedily*
	Fane of that fang, pyipand with mony "Pew!"	*Keen for; catch; whistling*
	Syne lowsit thame and baith but pietie slew,	*untied; both; without pity*

	Syne bowellit thame, that boucheour with his bill,	*disembowelled; butcher; beak*
	And bellieflaucht full fettislie thame fled	*skin over head; neatly; flayed*
2905	Bot all thair flesche wald scant be half ane fill,	*would hardly be half enough*
	And guttis als, unto that gredie gled.	*With the guts added, for that greedy kite*
	Of thair debait thus quhen I hard outred,	*when I heard settled thus*
	He tuke his flicht and over the feildis flaw.	*took; flight*
	Gif this be trew, speir ye at thame that saw.	*If; ask those who saw*

	Moralitas	*Moralization*
2910	**M**y brother, gif thow will tak advertence	*if; pay attention*
	Be this fabill thow may persave and se	*perceive; see*
	It passis far all kynd of pestilence	*far exceeds; plague*
	Ane wickit mynd with wordis fair and sle.	*An evil intent; fine and clever*
	Bewar thairfore with quhome thow fallowis thee	*whom; you associate yourself*
2915	For thow wer better beir of stane the barrow	*carry a [hand-]barrow-load of stone*
	Or sweitand dig and delf quhill thow may dre	*sweating; delve; can endure*
	Than to be matchit with ane wickit marrow.	*joined up; wicked companion*

	Ane fals intent under ane fair pretence	*malicious purpose; appearance*
	Hes causit mony innocent for to de.	*Has caused; die*
2920	Grit folie is to gif over sone credence	*folly; give credence too soon*
	To all that speiks fairlie unto thee.	*everyone who speaks*
	Ane silkin toung, ane hart of crueltie,	*silken tongue; heart*
	Smytis more sore than ony schot of arrow.	*Strikes; any shot*
	Brother, gif thow be wyse, I reid the flee	*if thou; advise you to avoid*
2925	To matche thee with ane thrawart fenyeit marrow.	*join yourself; bad, dishonest*

	I warne thee als, it is grit nekligence	*also; great carelessness*
	To bind thee fast quhair thow wes frank and free.	*thyself tight; free and clear*
	Fra thow be bund, thow may mak na defence	*Once; bound*
	To saif thy lyfe nor yit thy libertie.	*save; yet*

2930   This simpill counsall, brother, tak at me   *advice; take from*
        And it to cun perqueir see thow not tarrow: *learn by heart; delay*
        Better but stryfe to leif allane in le   *without; live alone; peace*
        Than to be matchit with ane wickit marrow.   *joined; companion*

        This hald in mynd, rycht more I sall thee tell   *held; much*
2935   Quhairby thir beistis may be figurate.   *By which these; emblematic*
        The paddok usand in the flude to dwell   *habituated to live in the water*
        Is mannis bodie swymand air and lait   *swimming early and late*
        Into this warld with cairis implicate   *entangled with troubles*
        Now hie, now law, quhylis plungit up, quhylis doun,   *high; low, sometimes*
2940   Ay in perrell and reddie for to droun,   *Always; liable to*

        Now dolorus, now blyth as bird on breir,   *sorrowful; joyous; brier*
        Now in fredome, now wardit in distres,   *at liberty; confined*
        Now haill and sound, now deid and brocht on beir,   *safe; carried on a bier*
        Now pure as Job, now rowand in riches,   *poor; rolling*
2945   Now gounis gay, now brats laid in pres,   *fine clothes; rags put; chest*
        Now full as fysche, now hungrie as ane hound,
        Now on the quheill, now wappit to the ground.   *up on the wheel [of Fortune]; thrown*

        This lytill mous heir knit thus be the schyn   *here tied; by; shin*
        The saull of man betakin may indeid,   *soul; may well signify*
2950   Bundin and fra the bodie may not twin   *Bound; from; cannot part*
        Quhill cruell deith cum brek of lyfe the threid,   *Until; come to break; thread*
        The quhilk to droun suld ever stand in dreid   *which; should; stay; fear*
        Of carnall lust be the suggestioun   *by; seduction*
        Quhilk drawis ay the saull and druggis doun.   *Which always attracts; drags*

2955   The watter is the warld ay welterand   *ceaselessly surging*
        With mony wall of tribulatioun   *wave*
        In quhilk the saull and bodye ay waverand,   *which; always drifting*
        Standis distinyt in thair opinioun,   *Remaining divided; intention*
        The spreit upwart, the body precis doun,   *pushes*
2960   The saull rycht fane wald be brocht over iwis   *very eagerly; carried; indeed*
        Out of this warld into the hevinnis blis.   *joys of heaven*

        The gled is deith that cummis suddandlie   *kite; death; comes*
        As dois ane theif and cuttis sone the batall.   *does a thief; at once cuts short*
        Be vigilant thairfoir and ay reddie   *always*
2965   For mannis lyfe is brukill and ay mortall.   *insubstantial; invariably*
        My freind, thairfoir mak thee ane strang castell   *strong*
        Of gud deidis for deith will thee assay   *good deeds; assail you*
        Thow wait not quhen, evin, morrow, or midday.   *knowest; when; evening, morning*

        Adew my freind and gif that ony speiris   *Adieu; if; anyone asks*
2970   Of this fabill sa schortlie I conclude,   *About; that I end so briefly*

Say thow I left the laif unto the freiris   *remainder for the friars*
To mak a sample or similitude.   *exemplary tale; parable*
Now Christ, for us that deit on the rude,   *who died for us on the cross*
Of saull and lyfe as thow art salviour,   *since; savior*
2975 Grant us till pas intill ane blissit hour.   *to proceed; blessed*

THE TESTAMENT OF CRESSEID

	Ane doolie sessoun to ane cairfull dyte	*A dismal season; sad poem*
	Suld correspond and be equivalent	*Should answer; concordant*
	Richt sa it wes quhen I began to wryte	*Just as; when*
	This tragedie, the wedder richt fervent	*weather very bitter*
5	Quhen Aries in middis of the Lent	*When; in the middle*
	Schouris of haill gart fra the north discend	*Made showers of hail fall from the north*
	That scantlie fra the cauld I micht defend,	*So that hardly could I shelter from the cold*
	Yit nevertheles within myne oratur	*Yet; my private chapel*
	I stude quhen Titan had his bemis bricht	*stood; Phoebus; bright sunbeams*
10	Withdrawin doun and sylit under cure	*down; retracted; cover*
	And fair Venus the bewtie of the nicht	*beauty; night*
	Uprais and set unto the west full richt	*Rose up; directed to; straight*
	Hir goldin face in oppositioun	
	Of god Phebus direct discending doun.	*To; directly; down*
15	Throwout the glas hir bemis brast sa fair	*Through; window; rays broke so clearly*
	That I micht se on everie syde me by	*could see all around me*
	The northin wind had purifyit the air	*northern; purified*
	And sched the mistie cloudis fra the sky,	*scattered; from*
	The froist freisit, the blastis bitterly	*frost froze; gusts*
20	Fra pole artick come quhisling loud and schill	*From; came whistling; shrill*
	And causit me remufe aganis my will.	*forced; step back against*
	For I traistit that Venus luifis quene	*believed; queen of love*
	To quhome sum tyme I hecht obedience	*whom for some time; vowed*
	My faidit hart of lufe scho wald mak grene,	*withered; she would make green with love*
25	And therupon with humbill reverence	*to that purpose; devout*
	I thocht to pray hir hie magnificence.	*intended; pray to her high*
	Bot for greit cald as than I lattit was	*great cold just then; prevented*
	And in my chalmer to the fyre can pas.	*to the fire in my room did go*
	Thocht lufe be hait yit in ane man of age	*hot still; an old man*
30	It kendillis nocht sa sone as in youtheid	*kindles not; soon; youth*
	Of quhome the blude is flowing in ane rage,	*In which; blood; in haste*
	And in the auld the curage doif and deid	*vigor [is] faint; dead*
	Of quhilk the fyre outward is best remeid.	*For whom; externally; remedy*

104

| | To help be phisike quhair that nature faillit | *with medicine where; failed* |
| 35 | I am expert for baith I have assaillit. | *for I have tried both* |

	I mend the fyre and beikit me about	*stoked; warmed myself all around*
	Than tuik ane drink my spreitis to comfort	*took; to soothe my spirits*
	And armit me weill fra the cauld thairout.	*protected myself well from*
	To cut the winter nicht and mak it schort	*night; make*
40	I tuik ane quair, and left all uther sport,	*book; abandoned; pastime*
	Writtin be worthie Chaucer glorious	*by great, renowned Chaucer*
	Of fair Creisseid and worthie Troylus.	*About lovely; great Troilus*

	And thair I fand efter that Diomeid	*there I discovered after*
	Ressavit had that lady bricht of hew	*Had received; lovely of hue*
45	How Troilus neir out of wit abraid	*almost went out of his mind*
	And weipit soir with visage paill of hew	*wept bitterly; a face pale*
	For quhilk wanhope his teiris can renew	*which despair; tears did revive*
	Quhill Esperus rejoisit him agane.	*Until Hesperus gladdened*
	Thus quhyle in joy he levit, quhyle in pane.	*awhile; lived; torment*

50	Of hir behest he had greit comforting,	*her vow; consolation*
	Traisting to Troy that scho suld mak retour	*Trusting; she should; return*
	Quhilk he desyrit maist of eirdly thing	*Which; wanted most [of] any earthly*
	For quhy scho was his only paramour.	*Because she; lover*
	Bot quhen he saw passit baith day and hour	*when; elapsed both the*
55	Of hir ganecome than sorrow can oppres	*coming again then; did*
	His wofull hart in cair and hevines.	*heart; care; dejection*

	Of his distres me neidis nocht reheirs	*need not be repeated by me*
	For worthie Chauceir in the samin buik	*same book*
	In gudelie termis and in joly veirs	*eloquent words; lively verse*
60	**C**ompylit hes his cairis quha will luik.	*Has compiled; whoever; look*
	To brek my sleip ane uther quair I tuik	*prevent; another book; took*
	In quhilk I fand the fatall destenie	*which; found; fated*
	Of fair Cresseid that endit wretchitlie.	*died in distress*

	Quha wait gif all that Chauceir wrait was trew?	*Who knows if; wrote; true*
65	Nor I wait nocht gif this narratioun	*Nor do I know if; narrative*
	Be authoreist or fenyeit of the new	*authoritative; devised anew*
	Be sum poeit throw his inventioun,	*By some poet through; creative skill*
	Maid to report the lamentatioun	*Devised; narrate; lament*
	And wofull end of this lustie Creisseid	*sorrowful death; beautiful*
70	And quhat distres scho thoillit and quhat deid.	*Both what; suffered; death*

	Quhen Diomeid had all his appetyte	*When*
	And mair fulfillit of this fair ladie,	*more sated by*
	Upon ane uther he set his haill delyte	*another; whole pleasure*
	And send to hir ane lybell of repudie	*sent; declaration; divorce*

75	And hir excludit fra his companie.	*banished her from*
	Than desolait scho walkit up and doun	*left alone; wandered*
	And, sum men sayis, into the court commoun.	
	O fair Creisseid the flour and A per se	*flower; first and foremost*
	Of Troy and Grece, how was thow fortunait	*did it befall you*
80	To change in filth all thy feminitie	*into; womanliness*
	And be with fleschelie lust sa maculait	*so defiled*
	And go amang the Greikis air and lait	*early and late*
	Sa giglotlike takand thy foull plesance!	*lewdly taking*
	I have pietie thee suld fall sic mischance.	*pity such misfortune should befall you*
85	Yit nevertheles, quhatever men deme or say	*whatever; [may] judge*
	In scornefull langage of thy brukkilnes,	*about your frailty*
	I sall excuse als far furth as I may	*to the utmost that I can*
	Thy womanheid, thy wisdome and fairnes,	*womanhood*
	The quhilk Fortoun hes put to sic distres	*which; has placed in such*
90	As hir pleisit, and nathing throw the gilt	*pleased her; not at all; guilt*
	Of thee — throw wickit langage to be spilt.	*to be ruined by slander*
	This fair lady, in this wyse destitute	*deprived in this way*
	Of all comfort and consolatioun,	
	Richt privelie, but fellowschip, on fute,	*Very discreetly, without; foot*
95	Disagysit passit far out of the toun	*In disguise departed; town*
	Ane myle or twa unto ane mansioun	*A mile or two*
	Beildit full gay quhair hir father Calchas	*Built very finely where*
	Quhilk than amang the Greikis dwelland was.	*Who then; was living*
	Quhen he hir saw, the caus he can inquyre	*When; saw her; did ask*
100	Of hir cumming. Scho said, siching full soir,	*visit; sighing very bitterly*
	"Fra Diomeid had gottin his desyre	*Once; taken his pleasure*
	He wox werie and wald of me no moir."	*grew weary; wanted no more of me*
	Quod Calchas, "Douchter, weip thow not thairfoir,	*Said; Daughter, weep; about that*
	Peraventure all cummis for the best.	*Perhaps everything comes*
105	Welcum, to me thow art full deir ane gest."	*a very dear guest*
	This auld Calchas efter the law was tho	*old; according to; then*
	Wes keiper of the tempill as ane preist	*keeper; priest*
	In quhilk Venus and hir sone Cupido	*which; son*
	War honourit, and his chalmer was thame neist,	*Were; chamber; nearest to them*
110	To quhilk Cresseid with baill aneuch in breist	*which; sorrow aplenty; breast*
	Usit to pas, hir prayeris for to say	*Used to go, her prayers*
	Quhill at the last upon ane solempne day,	*Until; a holy feast day*
	As custome was, the pepill far and neir	*was the custom; people; near*
	Befoir the none unto the tempill went	*Before noon*
115	With sacrifice devoit in thair maneir.	*devout; according to; custom*

Bot still Cresseid, hevie in hir intent, *gloomy; mind*
Into the kirk wald not hirself present *church would; show herself*
For giving of the pepill ony deming *To give people any inkling*
Of hir expuls fra Diomeid the king *About; expulsion from*

120 Bot past into ane secreit orature *went; a private chapel*
Quhair scho micht weip hir wofull desteny. *Where; could bemoan*
Behind hir bak scho cloisit fast the dure *she closed the door tight*
And on hir kneis bair fell doun in hy, *bare knees; down; haste*
Upon Venus and Cupide angerly *angrily*
125 Scho cryit out and said on this same wyse, *in this very way*
"Allace that ever I maid yow sacrifice! *Alas; offered sacrifice to you*

"Ye gave me anis ane devine responsaill *once a divine reply*
That I suld be the flour of luif in Troy, *would; flower; love*
Now am I maid ane unworthie outwaill *made into; outcast*
130 And all in cair translatit is my joy. *into sorrow; transferred*
Quha sall me gyde, quha sall me now convoy *Who shall guide me; convey*
Sen I fra Diomeid and nobill Troylus *Since; from*
Am clene excludit as abject odious? *utterly; as a hateful castoff*

"O fals Cupide, is nane to wyte bot thow *no one is to blame but you*
135 And thy mother of lufe the blind goddes. *the blind goddess of love*
Ye causit me alwayis understand and trow *caused; believe*
The seid of lufe was sawin in my face *seed; love; sown*
And ay grew grene throw your supplie and grace, *always; help; favor*
Bot now allace that seid with froist is slane *killed*
140 And I fra luifferis left and all forlane." *apart from lovers; utterly shunned*

Quhen this was said, doun in ane extasie, *When; trance*
Ravischit in spreit intill ane dreame scho fell *Enraptured; spirit, into a*
And be apperance hard quhair scho did ly, *in an illusion heard where*
Cupide the king ringand ane silver bell *was ringing*
145 Quhilk men micht heir fra hevin unto hell, *Which; could hear from*
At quhais sound befoir Cupide appeiris *the sound of which; [there] appear*
The sevin planetis discending fra thair spheiris *from their spheres*

Quhilk hes power of all thing generabill *have; over all created things*
To reull and steir be thair greit influence *rule; control*
150 Wedder and wind and coursis variabill, *Weather; mutable processes*
And first of all Saturne made apparence *made his appearance*
Quhilk gave to Cupide litill reverence *Who showed; scant respect*
Bot as ane busteous churle on his maneir *blustering peasant in*
Come crabitlie with auster luik and cheir. *angrily; grim; expression*

155 His face fronsit, his lyre was lyke the leid, *wrinkled; complexion; lead*
His teith chatterit and cheverit with the chin, *shivered along with*

His ene drowpit, how sonkin in his heid,   *eyes drooped, sunk deep; head*
Out of his nois the meldrop fast can rin,   *nose; thin mucus; did run*
With lippis bla and cheikis leine and thin.   *livid lips; cheeks lean*
160   The ice schoklis that fra his hair doun hang   *icicles; from; hung down*
Was wonder greit and as ane speir als lang.   *Were amazingly large; spear; long*

Atouir his belt his lyart lokkis lay   *Over; gray hair*
Felterit unfair, ovirfret with froistis hoir,   *Matted unattractively, spangled; hoarfrost*
His garmound and his gyte full gay of gray,   *robe; very attractive gown of gray*
165   His widderit weid fra him the wind out woir,   *faded clothing; stretched out*
Ane busteous bow within his hand he boir,   *powerful; in; carried*
Under his girdill ane flasche of felloun flanis   *belt; quiver; sturdy arrows*
Fedderit with ice and heidit with hailstanis.   *Feathered; tipped; hailstones*

Than Juppiter richt fair and amiabill,   *very pleasant; friendly*
170   God of the starnis in the firmament   *over; stars; heavens*
And nureis to all thing generabill,   *nurse; engendered things*
Fra his father Saturne far different   *From; very*
With burelie face and browis bricht and brent,   *noble; fine; unwrinkled*
Upon his heid ane garland wonder gay   *head; very splendid wreath*
175   Of flouris fair as it had bene in May.   *flowers; as if it; been May*

His voice was cleir, as cristall wer his ene,   *clear; crystal were his eyes*
As goldin wyre sa glitterand was his hair,   *wire; glittering*
His garmound and his gyte full gay of grene   *most attractive in green*
With goldin listis gilt on everie gair.   *edgings gilded; pleat*
180   Ane burelie brand about his middill bair,   *sturdy sword; at; waist [he] wore*
In his richt hand he had ane groundin speir   *right; held; sharpened spear*
Of his father the wraith fra us to weir.   *To avert his father's wrath from us*

Nixt efter him come Mars the god of ire,   *came; anger*
Of strife, debait, and all dissensioun,
185   To chide and fecht als feirs as ony fyre   *Keen as any fire to quarrel and fight*
In hard harnes, hewmound, and habirgeoun,   *sturdy armor, helmet; habergeon*
And on his hanche ane roustie, fell fachioun   *hip; rusty, deadly falchion*
And in his hand he had ane roustie sword.   *rusty*
Wrything his face with mony angrie word.   *Distorting*

190   Schaikand his sword, befoir Cupide he come   *Brandishing; in front of; came*
With reid visage and grislie glowrand ene   *red face; frightful staring eyes*
And at his mouth ane bullar stude of fome,   *hung a blob of spittle*
Lyke to ane bair quhetting his tuskis kene,   *boar whetting; sharp tusks*
Richt tuilyeour-lyke, but temperance in tene.   *like a brawler, without; wrath*
195   Ane horne he blew with mony bosteous brag   *many a harsh bray*
Quhilk all this warld with weir hes maid to wag.   *Which; war has made; shake*

	Than fair Phebus, lanterne and lamp of licht	*Then; light*
	Of man and beist, baith frute and flourisching,	*For; both fruit; flowers*
	Tender nureis and banischer of nicht	*nurturer; banisher; night*
200	And of the warld causing be his moving	*for; by his motion*
	And influence lyfe in all eirdlie thing,	*earthly*
	Without comfort of quhome, of force to nocht	*from whom, perforce to nothing*
	Must all ga die that in this warld is wrocht.	*go to die; created*
	As king royall he raid upon his chair	*rode; chariot*
205	The quhilk Phaeton gydit sumtyme upricht.	*which; once guided upwards*
	The brichtnes of his face quhen it was bair	*when; uncovered*
	Nane micht behald for peirsing of his sicht.	*No one could; piercing; sight*
	This goldin cart with fyrie bemis bricht	*fiery sunbeams*
	Four yokkit steidis full different of hew	*harnessed horses; altogether; color*
210	But bait or tyring throw the spheiris drew.	*Without rest or wearying*
	The first was soyr with mane als reid as rois	*sorrel; as red; rose*
	Callit Eoye, into the orient.	*at the sunrise*
	The secund steid to name hecht Ethios,	*horse; was called*
	Quhitlie and paill, and sumdeill ascendent.	*Whitish; somewhat higher*
215	The thrid, Peros, richt hait and richt fervent.	*third; very hot; burning*
	The feird was blak and callit Philogie	*fourth*
	Quhilk rollis Phebus doun into the sey.	*Which; down; sea*
	Venus was thair present, that goddes gay,	*present there; goddess*
	Hir sonnis querrell for to defend and mak	*son's accusation; to make*
220	Hir awin complaint, cled in ane nyce array,	*own; clad; showy outfit*
	The ane half grene, the uther half sabill blak,	*one; green; other; sable*
	Quhyte hair as gold kemmit and sched abak	*Blonde; combed; pulled back*
	Bot in hir face semit greit variance,	*appeared; variability*
	Quhyles perfyte treuth, and quhyles inconstance.	*Sometimes; faith; inconstancy*
225	Under smyling scho was dissimulait,	*While smiling; two-faced*
	Provocative with blenkis amorous	*Alluring; loving glances*
	And suddanely changit and alterait,	*altered*
	Angrie as ony serpent vennemous,	*any poisonous snake*
	Richt pungitive with wordis odious.	*Very caustic; offensive words*
230	Thus variant scho was, quha list tak keip,	*fickle; whoever cared to; heed*
	With ane eye lauch and with the uther weip	*one; to laugh; other to weep*
	In taikning that all fleschelie paramour	*As token; passion*
	Quhilk Venus hes in reull and governance	*Which; under control*
	Is sumtyme sweit, sumtyme bitter and sour,	*sometimes sweet*
235	Richt unstabill and full of variance	*Wholly unstable; variability*
	Mingit with cairfull joy and fals plesance,	*Mixed; anxious; delight*
	Now hait, now cauld, now blyith, now full of wo,	*hot; blithe*
	Now grene as leif, now widderit and ago.	*leaf; withered; bygone*

With buik in hand than come Mercurius,   *book; came*
240 Richt eloquent and full of rethorie,   *Very; rhetorical skill*
With polite termis and delicious,   *polished and delightful diction*
With pen and ink to report all reddie,   *to record the proceedings*
Setting sangis and singand merilie.   *Composing songs; singing*
His hude was reid, heklit atouir his croun   *hood; red, fringed over; crown*
245 Lyke to ane poeit of the auld fassoun.   *old style*

Boxis he bair with fyne electuairis   *carried; medicinal compotes*
And sugerit syropis for digestioun,   *sugared*
Spycis belangand to the pothecairis   *apothecaries*
With mony hailsum sweit confectioun —   *health-giving sweet nostrum*
250 Doctour in phisick, cled in ane skarlot goun   *of medicine, clad; scarlet*
And furrit weill as sic ane aucht to be,   *furred well; such; ought*
Honest and gude and not ane word culd lie.   *good; did lie*

Nixt efter him come lady Cynthia   *Next after; came*
The last of all and swiftest in hir spheir,   *sphere*
255 Of colour blak, buskit with hornis twa   *adorned; two horns*
And in the nicht scho listis best appeir   *night; most prefers to appear*
Haw as the leid, of colour nathing cleir,   *Livid; lead; not at all bright*
For all hir licht scho borrowis at hir brother   *from*
Titan, for of hirself scho hes nane uther.   *The sun; has no other [light]*

260 Hir gyte was gray and full of spottis blak,   *gown; black spots*
And on hir breist ane churle paintit full evin   *[was] painted very accurately*
Beirand ane bunche of thornis on his bak   *Bearing; bundle; back*
Quhilk for his thift micht clim na nar the hevin.   *Who because of; theft; could; nearer*
Thus quhen thay gadderit war, thir goddes sevin,   *when; were convened, these*
265 Mercurius thay cheisit with ane assent   *they chose unanimously*
To be foirspeikar in the parliament.   *chairman*

Quha had bene thair and liken for to heir   *been there; [had] liking; hear*
His facound toung and termis exquisite,   *eloquent tongue*
Of rethorick the prettick he micht leir   *rhetoric; art; could learn*
270 In breif sermone ane pregnant sentence wryte.[1]
Befoir Cupide veiling his cap alyte,   *tipping; a little*
Speiris the caus of that vocatioun   *[He] asks; summoning*
And he anone schew his intentioun.   *promptly revealed; purpose*

"Lo," quod Cupide, "quha will blaspheme the name   *whoever chooses to*
275 Of his awin god, outher in word or deid,   *own; either; or deed*
To all goddis he dois baith lak and schame   *does; insult; shame*
And suld have bitter panis to his meid.   *should; torments as his reward*

---

[1] *In a few words to write statements full of meaning*

I say this by yone wretchit Cresseid,   *about that wretched*
The quhilk throw me was sumtyme flour of lufe,   *She who because of; once*
280   Me and my mother starklie can reprufe,   *[who] brazenly denounces*

"Saying of hir greit infelicitie   *great misfortune*
I was the caus and my mother Venus   *cause*
Ane blind goddes hir cald that micht not se,   *called her who could not see*
With sclander and defame injurious.   *slander; harmful defamation*
285   Thus hir leving unclene and lecherous   *her way of life*
Scho wald returne on me and my mother,   *would deflect back upon*
To quhome I schew my grace abone all uther.   *whom; bestowed; above*

"And sen ye ar all sevin deificait,   *since; deified*
Participant of devyne sapience,   *Sharing in; wisdom*
290   This greit injure done to our hie estait   *high rank*
Me think with pane we suld mak recompence.   *It seems to me; torment; should make*
Was never to goddes done sic violence,   *[There] was; gods; such*
Asweill for yow as for myself I say.   *As much; speak*
Thairfoir ga help to revenge, I yow pray."   *For which reason; pray you*

295   Mercurius to Cupide gave answeir   *answer*
And said, "Schir king, my counsall is that ye   *counsel*
Refer yow to the hiest planeit heir   *Entrust yourself; highest*
And tak to him the lawest of degre   *take with him; lowest; rank*
The pane of Cresseid for to modifie,   *punishment; determine*
300   As god Saturne with him tak Cynthia."   *Namely; [and] with; select*
"I am content," quod he, "to tak thay twa."   *select those two*

Than thus proceidit Saturne and the mone   *Then; proceeded; [Cynthia] the moon*
Quhen thay the mater rypelie had degest: *thoroughly; pondered*
For the dispyte to Cupide scho had done   *injury; she [Cresseid]*
305   And to Venus, oppin and manifest,   *patient and revealed*
In all hir lyfe with pane to be opprest   *Through; pain; oppressed*
And torment sair with seiknes incurabill   *tormented; incurable sickness*
And to all lovers be abhominabill.   *detestable*

This duleful sentence Saturne tuik on hand   *grievous; took in*
310   And passit doun quhair cairfull Cresseid lay   *descended to where sad*
And on hir heid he laid ane frostie wand   *upon her head; placed*
Than lawfullie on this wyse can he say,   *according to law in; way did*
"Thy greit fairnes and all thy bewtie gay,   *great; glorious beauty*
Thy wantoun blude and eik thy goldin hair   *lustful blood; also*
315   Heir I exclude fra thee for evermair.   *Here; banish from; forever*

"I change thy mirth into melancholy   *bilious depression*
Quhilk is the mother of all pensivenes,   *Which; gloomy anxiety*
Thy moisture and thy heit in cald and dry,   *heat into cold*

	Thyne insolence, thy play and wantones	*arrogance; pleasure; lust*
320	To greit diseis, thy pomp and thy riches	*Into great distress; wealth*
	In mortall neid and greit penuritie.	*Into desperate need; poverty*
	Thow suffer sall and as ane beggar die."	*shalt suffer*
	O cruell Saturne fraward and angrie,	*spiteful*
	Hard is thy dome and to malitious!	*judgment; too*
325	On fair Cresseid quhy hes thow na mercie	*why hast thou no*
	Quhilk was sa sweit, gentill, and amorous?	*Who*
	Withdraw thy sentence and be gracious —	*Retract; merciful*
	As thow was never — sa schawis throw thy deid,	*as is plain through; deed*
	Ane wraikfull sentence gevin on fair Cresseid.	*vengeful; delivered upon*
330	Than Cynthia quhen Saturne past away	*when; went*
	Out of hir sait discendit doun belyve	*throne descended; promptly*
	And red ane bill on Cresseid quhair scho lay	*read a document over; where*
	Contening this sentence diffinityve,	*Containing; determinative sentence*
	"Fra heit of bodie I thee now depryve	*Of bodily heat*
335	And to thy seiknes sall be na recure	*for; sickness; remedy*
	Bot in dolour thy dayis to indure.	*misery; span of life*
	Thy cristall ene mingit with blude I mak,	*crystal eyes mingled; blood; cause to be*
	Thy voice sa cleir, unplesand, hoir and hace,	*clear [I cause to be]; harsh and hoarse*
	Thy lustie lyre, ovirspred with spottis blak	*lovely skin, [to be]*
340	And lumpis haw appeirand in thy face.	*purplish lumps appearing on*
	Quhair thow cummis, ilk man sall fle the place.	*you approach, each; shall flee*
	This sall thow go begging fra hous to hous	*Thus; from*
	With cop and clapper lyke ane lazarous."	*begging bowl; rattle; leper*
	This doolie dreame, this uglye visioun	*dismal*
345	Brocht to ane end, Cresseid fra it awoik,	*Brought; awoke from it*
	And, all that court and convocatioun	*assembly*
	Vanischit away, than rais scho up and tuik	*rose; took*
	Ane poleist glas and hir schaddow culd luik	*polished mirror; saw her reflection*
	And quhen scho saw hir face sa deformait,	*when; deformed*
350	Gif scho in hart was wa aneuch, God wait.	*If; woeful enough; knows*
	Weiping full sair, "Lo, quhat it is," quod sche,	*Weeping; bitterly; what; said*
	"With fraward langage for to mufe and steir	*bold; incite; provoke*
	Our craibit goddis and sa is sene on me.	*ireful gods; thus; proven*
	My blaspheming now have I bocht full deir.	*paid very dearly for*
355	All eirdlie joy and mirth I set areir.	*earthly; set behind me*
	Allace this day, allace this wofull tyde	*Alas; time*
	Quhen I began with my goddis for to chyde!"	*When; to upbraid*
	Be this was said, ane chyld, come fra the hall	*Once; boy [who had]; from*
	To warne Cresseid the supper was reddy,	

360	First knokkit at the dure and syne culd call,	*knocked; door; then did*
	"Madame, your father biddis yow cum in hy.	*commands you; haste*
	He hes merwell sa lang on grouf ye ly	*is amazed; long you lie prone*
	And sayis your beedes bene to lang sumdeill.	*prayers are too; somewhat*
	The goddis wait all your intent full weill."	*understand; very well*

365	Quod scho, "Fair chyld, ga to my father deir	*dear*
	And pray him cum to speik with me anone,"	*speak; at once*
	And sa he did and said, "Douchter, quhat cheir?"	*Daughter; how [is your] mood*
	"Allace," quod scho, "father, my mirth is gone."	*happiness*
	"How sa?" quod he, and scho can all expone	*she explained everything*
370	As I have tauld, the vengeance and the wraik	*retaliation*
	For hir trespas Cupide on hir culd tak.	*offense [that]; had taken*

	He luikit on hir uglye lipper face	*looked upon; leprous*
	The quhylk befor was quhite as lillie flour.	*which; white; lily flower*
	Wringand his handis oftymes he said allace	*Wringing; repeatedly*
375	That he had levit to se that wofull hour	*lived; see*
	For he knew weill that thair was na succour	*well; there; no remedy*
	To hir seiknes, and that dowblit his pane,	*For; sickness; doubled; pain*
	Thus was thair cair aneuch betuix thame twane.	*sorrow enough between; both*

	Quhen thay togidder murnit had full lang,	*had lamented together very*
380	Quod Cresseid, "Father, I wald not be kend,	*do not want to be recognized*
	Thairfoir in secreit wyse ye let me gang	*So help me get away unobserved*
	Unto yone hospitall at the tounis end	*that; edge of town*
	And thidder sum meit for cheritie me send	*there some food; charity send me*
	To leif upon, for all mirth in this eird	*subsist; on this earth*
385	Is fra me gane, sic is my wickit weird."	*departed from me, such; miserable fate*

	Than in ane mantill and ane baver hat	*cloak; hat of beaver fur*
	With cop and clapper, wonder prively	*bowl; rattle, very furtively*
	He opnit ane secreit yet and out thairat	*opened; gate; from there*
	Convoyit hir that na man suld espy	*Guided; should catch sight*
390	Unto ane village half ane myle thairby,	*nearby*
	Delyverit hir in at the spittaill hous	*lepers' lodge*
	And daylie sent hir part of his almous.	*each day; priestly income of donations*

	Sum knew hir weill and sum had na knawledge	*Some; well*
	Of hir becaus scho was sa deformait	*she; so deformed*
395	With bylis blak ovirspred in hir visage	*black boils covering her face*
	And hir fair colour faidit and alterait,	*complexion faded; altered*
	Yit thay presumit for hir hie regrait	*surmised from; loud sobbing*
	And still murning, scho was of nobill kin.	*unceasing; noble family*
	With better will thairfoir they tuik hir in.	*greater eagerness*

400	The day passit and Phebus went to rest.	*passed*
	The cloudis blak overheled all the sky.	*black clouds blanketed*
	God wait gif Cresseid was ane sorrowfull gest,	*knows whether; guest*
	Seing that uncouth fair and harbery.	*unfamiliar food; lodging*
	But meit or drink scho dressit hir to ly	*Without food; prepared herself; lie*
405	In ane dark corner of the hous allone	*alone*
	And on this wyse, weiping, scho maid hir mone:	*in; manner; made her lament*

The Complaint of Cresseid

	O sop of sorrow, sonkin into cair,	*wafer; dipped deep in care*
	O cative Cresseid, now and evermair	*wretched*
	Gane is thy joy and all thy mirth in eird!	*Gone; on earth*
410	Of all blyithnes now art thow blaiknit bair,	*bleached bare*
	Thair is na salve may saif or sound thy sair,	*ointment; cure; heal your disease*
	Fell is thy fortoun, wickit is thy weird,	*Cruel; fate*
	Thy blys is baneist and thy baill on breird.	*bliss; banished; sorrow in first bud*
	Under the eirth God gif I gravin wer	*God grant that I were buried*
415	Quhair nane of Grece nor yit of Troy micht heird!	*Where no one; hear of it*

	Quhair is thy chalmer wantounlie besene	*lavishly furnished chamber*
	With burely bed and bankouris browderit bene,	*fine; well embroidered cushions*
	Spycis and wyne to thy collatioun,	*for your repast*
	The cowpis all of gold and silver schene,	*cups; gleaming gold and silver*
420	The sweitmeitis servit in plaittis clene	*desserts; on clean plates*
	With saipheron sals of ane gude sessoun,	*saffron; seasoning*
	Thy gay garmentis with mony gudely goun,	*many a fine gown*
	Thy plesand lawn pinnit with goldin prene,	*linen [dress]; brooch*
	All is areir, thy greit royall renoun.	*in the past; renown*

425	Quhair is thy garding with thir greissis gay	*garden; such pretty grasses*
	And fresche flowris, quhilk the quene Floray	*which; queen Flora*
	Had paintit plesandly in everie pane,	*painted; separate part*
	Quhair thou was wont full merilye in May	*accustomed; merrily*
	To walk and tak the dew be it was day	*collect; as soon as*
430	And heir the merle and mawis mony ane,	*hear; thrush; blackbird*
	With ladyis fair in carrolling to gane	*singing and dancing to go*
	And se the royall rinkis in thair ray,	*see; princes; splendor (array)*
	In garmentis gay garnischit on everie grane?	*ornamented; stitch*

	Thy greit triumphand fame and hie honour	*triumphant; high*
435	Quhair thou was callit of eirdlye wichtis flour,	*worldly people the flower*
	All is decayit, thy weird is welterit so	*decayed; fate; overwhelmed*
	Thy hie estait is turnit in darknes dour.	*high rank; turned into; grim*
	This lipper ludge tak for thy burelie bour	*leper's lodge in the place of; fine bedroom*
	And for thy bed tak now ane bunche of stro,	*straw*
440	For waillit wyne and meitis thou had tho	*choice wine; foods [which]; then*

Tak mowlit breid, peirrie and ceder sour.   *moldy; pear and apple cider*
Bot cop and clapper, now is all ago.   *Except; over and gone*

My cleir voice and courtlie carrolling,   *clear*
Quhair I was wont with ladyis for to sing,   *In which; accustomed*
445   Is rawk as ruik, full hiddeous, hoir, and hace.   *raucous; crow; most hoarse; harsh*
My plesand port, all utheris precelling,   *bearing; surpassing*
Of lustines I was hald maist conding,   *attractiveness; fitting*
Now is deformit the figour of my face,   *appearance*
To luik on it na leid now lyking hes.   *look; no man; takes pleasure*
450   Sowpit in syte, I say, with sair siching,   *Steeped; grief; bitter sighing*
Ludgeit amang the lipper leid, allace!   *Lodged; leper folk, alas*

O ladyis fair of Troy and Grece, attend   *consider*
My miserie quhilk nane may comprehend,
My frivoll fortoun, my infelicitie,   *unstable; lack of felicity*
455   My greit mischeif quhilk na man can amend.   *great distress which; alleviate*
Be war in tyme, approchis neir the end,   *Be prepared; the end draws nigh*
And in your mynd ane mirrour mak of me.   *use me as a mirror*
As I am now, peradventure that ye   *perhaps you*
For all your micht may cum to that same end   *power*
460   Or ellis war, gif ony war may be.   *else worse, if; could*

Nocht is your fairnes bot ane faiding flour,   *Nothing; flower*
Nocht is your famous laud and hie honour   *praise; high*
Bot wind inflat in uther mennis eiris;   *puffed up; other; ears*
Your roising reid to rotting sall retour.   *rosy red; rottenness; revert*
465   Exempill mak of me in your memour   *make; memory*
Quhilk of sic thingis wofull witnes beiris.   *such; bears*
All welth in eird, away as wind it weiris,[1]
Be war thairfor, approchis neir the hour,   *the hour draws near*
Fortoun is fikkill quhen scho beginnis and steiris."   *fickle; begins to move*

470   **T**hus chydand with hir drerie destenye,   *complaining against; cruel*
Weiping scho woik the nicht fra end to end   *she stayed awake; from*
Bot all in vane, hir dule, hir cairfull cry   *vain; distress; sorrowful*
Micht not remeid nor yit hir murning mend.   *Could; cure; heal*
Ane lipper lady rais and till hir wend   *got up; went over to her*
475   And said, "Quhy spurnis thow aganis the wall   *Why do you dash yourself against*
To sla thyself and mend nathing at all?   *kill*

"Sen thy weiping dowbillis bot thy wo,   *Since; only redoubles; woe*
I counsall thee mak vertew of ane neid,   *advise; to make a virtue of necessity*
To leir to clap thy clapper to and fro,   *learn to shake; rattle*

---

[1] *All prosperity on earth, it blows away like the wind*

480	And leif efter the law of lipper leid."	*live following; leper folk*
	Thair was na buit, bot furth with thame scho yeid	*There; no use; out; went*
	Fra place to place quhill cauld and hounger sair	*until; grinding hunger*
	Compellit hir to be ane rank beggair.	*Forced; full-fledged beggar*

That samin tyme of Troy the garnisoun   *same; defending army*
485   Quhilk had to chiftane worthie Troylus   *Which; as chieftain*
        Throw jeopardie of weir had strikken doun   *Through exploit; war; cut*
        Knichtis of Grece in number mervellous.   *Knights; in prodigious numbers*
        With greit tryumphe and laude victorious   *great; exultant praise*
        Agane to Troy richt royallie thay raid   *Back; very regally; rode*
490   The way quhair Cresseid with the lipper baid.   *By the route; lepers waited*

        Seing that companie, all with ane stevin   *in one voice*
        Thay gaif ane cry and schuik coppis gude speid,   *gave; shook cups promptly*
        Said, "Worthie lordis, for goddis lufe of hevin,   *for the love of the gods in*
        To us lipper part of your almous deid!"   *give some; donations*
495   Than to thair cry nobill Troylus tuik heid   *Then; paid notice*
        Having pietie — neirby the place can pas   *pity — did pass near the place*
        Quhair Cresseid sat, not witting quhat scho was.   *realizing what*

        Than upon him scho kest up baith hir ene   *she raised; both her eyes*
        And with ane blenk it come into his thocht   *in a glance; his mind*
500   That he sumtime hir face befoir had sene   *at some time; before; seen*
        Bot scho was in sic plye he knew hir nocht,   *such straits*
        Yit than hir luik into his mynd it brocht   *But even so; look; brought*
        The sweit visage and amorous blenking   *expression; glances*
        Of fair Cresseid, sumtyme his awin darling.   *once; own*

505   Na wonder was suppois in mynd that he   *if mentally*
        Tuik hir figure sa sone, and lo now quhy: *Perceived; form so readily; why*
        The idole of ane thing in cace may be   *mental image; by chance*
        Sa deip imprentit in the fantasy   *deeply imprinted; imagination*
        That it deludis the wittis outwardly   *frustrates; outer senses*
510   And sa appeiris in forme and lyke estait   *thus appears; equivalent state*
        Within the mynd as it was figurait.   *as it was perceived mentally*

        Ane spark of lufe than till his hart culd spring   *then into; heart did leap*
        And kendlit all his bodie in ane fyre,   *kindled his whole body*
        With hait fevir ane sweit and trimbling   *A sweat and tremor with hot fever*
515   Him tuik quhill he was reddie to expyre,   *Overcame him until; die*
        To beir his scheild his breist began to tyre,   *carry; shield; chest; tire*
        Within ane quhyle he changit mony hew,   *In a short time; hues*
        And nevertheles not ane ane uther knew.   *neither recognized one another*

        For knichtlie pietie and memoriall   *pity; remembrance*
520   Of fair Cresseid, ane gyrdill can he tak,   *belt did; take*

Ane purs of gold and mony gay jowall,   *many a fine jewel*
And in the skirt of Cresseid doun can swak,   *onto; did hurl down*
Than raid away and not ane word he spak,   *rode; he spoke not a word*
Pensive in hart, quhill he come to the toun   *until; town*
525   And for greit cair oft syis almaist fell doun.   *sorrow often nearly*

The lipper folk to Cresseid than can draw   *did approach*
To se the equall distributioun   *make sure about*
Of the almous, bot quhen the gold thay saw,   *when they saw the gold*
Ilkane to uther prevelie can roun,   *Each one; whispered quietly*
530   And said, "Yone lord hes mair affectioun,   *That; more fondness*
However it be, unto yone lazarous   *might be, for yonder leper*
Than to us all, we knaw be his almous."   *for; know; donation*

"Quhat lord is yone," quod scho, "have ye na feill   *What lord is that; any notion*
Hes done to us so greit humanitie?"   *[Who] has; kindness*
535   "Yes," quod a lipper man, "I knaw him weill,   *know; well*
Schir Troylus it is, gentill and fre."   *noble; generous*
Quhen Cresseid understude that it was he,   *When*
Stiffer than steill thair stert ane bitter stound   *Harder; steel; shot; pain*
Throwout hir hart, and fell doun to the ground.   *Straight through; [she] fell*

540   Quhen scho ovircome with siching sair and sad,   *recovered; bitter and sad sighing*
With mony cairfull cry and cald ochane —   *sorrowful; gloomy "alas"*
"Now is my breist with stormie stoundis stad,   *by; beleaguered*
Wrappit in wo, ane wretch full will of wane!" —   *very far from home*
Than swounit scho full oft or ever scho fane   *swooned; before; stopped*
545   And ever in hir swouning cryit scho thus,   *she cried*
"O fals Cresseid and trew knicht Troylus!

"Thy lufe, thy lawtie, and thy gentilnes   *loyalty; nobility*
I countit small in my prosperitie,   *regarded as; during*
Sa elevait I was in wantones   *exalted; lustfulness*
550   And clam upon the fickill quheill sa hie.   *climbed; fickle wheel so high*
All faith and lufe I promissit to thee
Was in the self fickill and frivolous,   *in itself; superficial*
O fals Cresseid, and trew knicht Troilus!"

"For lufe of me thow keipt continence,   *practiced self-restraint*
555   Honest and chaist in conversatioun.   *Honorable; chaste; conduct*
Of all wemen protectour and defence   *defender*
Thou was and helpit thair opinioun.   *sustained their reputation*
My mynd in fleschelie foull affectioun   *sensuality*
Was inclynit to lustis lecherous,   *given over*
560   Fy fals Cresseid, O trew knicht Troylus!"

"Lovers be war and tak gude heid about   *be alert; take careful thought*
Quhome that ye lufe, for quhome ye suffer paine,   *Whom*
I lat yow wit thair is richt few thairout   *I'll have; know there; around*
Quhome ye may traist to have trew lufe agane.   *can trust; in return*
565   Preif quhen ye will, your labour is in vaine,   *Try when; wish*
Thairfoir, I reid ye tak thame as ye find   *advise; judge; find [them]*
For thay ar sad as widdercok in wind.   *they; stable; weather vane*

"Becaus I knaw the greit unstabilnes   *know; great unreliability*
Brukkil as glas into myself I say,   *Brittle; within; declare*
570   Traisting in uther als greit unfaithfulnes,   *Expecting; others as great an*
Als unconstant and als untrew of fay,   *As disloyal; faith*
Thocht sum be trew, I wait richt few ar thay,   *Although; know they are very few*
Quha findis treuth, lat him his lady ruse;   *Whoever; loyalty; let; praise*
Nane but myself as now I will accuse."   *No one; at this time*

575   Quhen this was said, with paper scho sat doun   *When*
And on this maneir maid hir testament.   *in; manner made her last will*
"Heir I beteiche my corps and carioun   *Here; bequeath; dead body*
With wormis and with taidis to be rent.   *toads; lacerated*
My cop and clapper and myne ornament
580   And all my gold the lipper folk sall have   *shall*
Quhen I am deid to burie me in grave.   *dead*

"This royall ring set with this rubie reid   *red ruby*
Quhilk Troylus in drowrie to me send,   *as a love token gave to me*
To him agane I leif it quhen I am deid   *leave*
585   To mak my cairfull deid unto him kend.   *make; sorrowful death known to him*
Thus I conclude schortlie and mak ane end:
My spreit I leif to Diane quhair scho dwellis   *spirit; Diana where; resides*
To walk with hir in waist woddis and wellis.   *among deserted forests; springs*

"O Diomeid, thou hes baith broche and belt   *you have both brooch*
590   Quhilk Troylus gave me in takning   *in token*
Of his trew lufe!" and with that word scho swelt.   *died*
And sone ane lipper man tuik of the ring,   *at once; took off*
Syne buryit hir withouttin tarying.   *Then buried; delay*
To Troylus furthwith the ring he bair   *immediately; brought*
595   And of Cresseid the deith he can declair.   *he reported*

Quhen he had hard hir greit infirmitie,   *heard about; great*
Hir legacie and lamentatioun
And how scho endit in sic povertie,   *ended her life; such*
He swelt for wo and fell doun in ane swoun,   *fainted*
600   For greit sorrow his hart to brist was boun,   *was ready to burst*
Siching full sadlie, said, "I can no moir: *Sighing; am able to do nothing more*
Scho was untrew, and wo is me thairfoir."   *unfaithful*

Sum said he maid ane tomb of merbell gray *Some; made; marble*
And wrait hir name and superscriptioun *inscription*
605 And laid it on hir grave quhair that scho lay *where*
In goldin letteris conteining this ressoun: *statement*
"Lo fair ladyis, Cresseid of Troyis toun
Sumtyme countit the flour of womanheid
Under this stane, lait lipper, lyis deid." *stone; at the end a leper*

610 Now worthie wemen, in this ballet schort, *poem*
Maid for your worschip and instructioun, *Made; honor*
Of cheritie I monische and exhort *For; admonish [that you]*
Ming not your lufe with fals deceptioun; *[That you] mix*
Beir in your mynd this sore conclusioun *Bear; bitter*
615 Of fair Cresseid as I have said befoir. *declared it previously*
Sen scho is deid, I speik of hir no moir. *Since; more*

The nobilnes and grit magnificens	*nobility; great glory*
Of prince or lord quhai list to magnifie,	*whoever should wish to praise*
His ancestre and lineall discens	*ancestry; direct descent*
Suld first extoll and his genolegie	*Should; as well as his genealogy*
5 So that his harte he mycht inclyne thairby	*his will he might direct*
The moir to vertew and to worthines	*more; virtue; worthiness*
Herand rehers his elderis gentilnes.	*Hearing narrated; elders' nobility*
It is contrair the lawis of nature	*contrary to*
A gentill man to be degenerat,	*man of noble birth*
10 Nocht following of his progenitour	*Not following his father's*
The worthe rewll and the lordly estait.	*Worthy leadership; state*
A ryall rynk for to be rusticat	*prince of the royal blood; boorish*
Is bot a monsture in comparesoun,	*only a monstrosity in the comparison*
Had in dispyt and foule derisioun.	*Held; scorn; foul derision*
15 I say this be the grit lordis of Grew	*prove; by; great; Greece*
Quhich set thair hairt and all thair haill curage	*Who; their whole energies*
Thair faderis steppis justly to persew	*fathers'; rightly; follow*
Eiking the wirschep of thair he lenage.	*Augmenting; honor; high lineage*
The ancient and sad wyse men of age	*serious wise; good age*
20 Wer tendouris to the yung and insolent	*guides; undisciplined*
To mak thame in all vertewis excellent.	*make; virtues*
Lyk as a strand of watter of a spring	*stream; from a spring*
Haldis the sapour of the fontell well	*Retains; flavor; original source*
So did in Grece ilk lord and worthy king,	*every*
25 Of forbearis thay tuk tarage and smell	*From; they took quality; character*
Amang the quhilk, of ane I think to tell.	*Among; whom, about one; intend*
Bot first his gentill generatioun	*But; noble lineage*
I sall rehers with your correctioun.	*shall recite subject to*
Upone the mountane of Elicone	*Upon; Helicon*
30 The most famous of all Arrabea,	*Arabia*
A goddes dwelt, excellent in bewté,	*goddess; beauty*
Gentill of blude, callit Memoria	*Of noble descent, called*
Quhilk Jupiter that god to wyfe can ta	*Whom that god Jupiter did take as a wife*

35	And carnaly hir knew, quhilk eftir syne	*coupled with her, who; thereafter*
	Apone a day bare him fair dochteris nyne.	*bore to; daughters [Muses]*

	The first in Grew wes callit Euterpe,	*Greek*
	In our language, "Gud delectacioun."	*Good pleasure*
	The secound maid clippit Melpomyne	*maiden named Melpomene*
	As "Hony sweit" in modelatioun.	*Sweet as honey; song*
40	Thersycore is "Gud instructioun"	*Terpsichore; Good*
	Of everything, the thrid sister iwis	*In; third; indeed*
	Thus out of Grew in Latyne translait is.	*In this way out of Greek into; is translated*

	Caliope that madin mervalous	*maiden with amazing powers*
	The ferd sistir, "Of all musik maistres"	*[Was] the fourth; mistress of all music*
45	And mother to the king ser Orpheous	*mother; sir*
	Quhilk throw his wyfe was efter king of Trais,	*Who through; later; Thrace*
	Clio the fyift that now is a goddes	*fifth*
	In Latyne callit "Meditatioun"	*Contemplation*
	Of everything that has creatioun,	*existence*

50	The sext sister was callit Herato	*sixth; called Erato*
	Quhilk "Drawis lyk to lyk" in every thing,	*Connects*
	The sevint lady was fair Polimio	*seventh; Polyhymnia*
	Quhilk cowth a "Thowsand sangis" sweitly sing,	*Who could*
	Talia syne quhilk can our saulis bring	*Thalia afterwards who*
55	In "Profound wit and grit agilité"	*Into "Deep thought; mental agility*
	Till undirstand and haif capacitie,	*To; mental capacity*

	Urania the nynt and last of all	*ninth*
	In oure langage quha couth it rycht expound	*whoever; properly interpret*
	Is callit "Armony celestiall"	*called "Heavenly harmony"*
60	Rejosing men with melody and sound.	*Gladdening*
	Amang thir nyne Calliope wes cround	*crowned*
	And maid a quene be michty god Phebus	*made; by mighty*
	Of quhome he gat this prince ser Orpheous.	*On whom he fathered*

	No wondir is thocht he wes fair and wyse,	*It is no wonder that he [Orpheus]*
65	Gentill and full of liberalitie,	*Noble; generosity*
	His fader god and his progenetryse	*father a god; mother*
	A goddes, finder of all armony.	*goddess; inventor; harmony*
	Quhen he wes borne scho set him on hir kne	*she; knee*
	And gart him souk of hir twa paupis quhyte	*let; suck from; two white breasts*
70	The sweit lecour of all musik perfyte.	*sweet fluid*

	Incressand sone to manhed up he drew,	*Growing quickly; manhood; rose*
	Of statur large and frely fair of face,	*exceptionally handsome*
	His noble fame so far it sprang and grew	*spread*
	Till at the last the michty quene of Trace	*mighty*

75	Excellent fair, haboundand in riches,	*Surpassingly beautiful, abounding*
	A message send unto this prince so ying	*sent; young*
	Requyrand him to wed hir and be king.	*Requesting*
	Euridices that lady had to name	*for a name*
	And quhene scho saw this prince so glorius	*she*
80	Hir erand to propone scho thocht no schame,	*purpose; declare; considered*
	With wordis sweit and blenkis amorous	*sweet; alluring glances*
	Said, "Welcum, lord and lufe ser Orpheus,	*love*
	In this provynce ye salbe king and lord."	*shall be*
	Thay kissit syne and thus thay can accord.	*kissed then; they did agree*
85	Betwix Orpheus and fair Erudices	*Between*
	Fra thai wer weddit, on fra day to day	*Once; were wedded; from*
	The low of lufe cowth kyndill and incres	*flame; love did kindle and grow*
	With mirth and blythnes, solace and with play.	*and happiness, pleasure and enjoyment*
	Of wardly joy allace, quhat sall I say,	*worldly; alas, what shall*
90	Lyk till a flour that plesandly will spring	*Like to a flower; bud*
	Quhilk fadis sone and endis with murnyng.	*Which fades quickly; sorrow*
	I say this be Erudices the quene	*about*
	Quhilk walkit furth into a May mornyng	*Who; out of doors upon*
	Bot with a madyn in a medow grene	*With only a maid; green*
95	To tak the dewe and se the flouris spring,	*gather; see; bud*
	Quhair in a schaw neirby this lady ying	*Where; wood nearby; young*
	A busteous hird callit Arresteus	*rough herdsman called Aristaeus*
	Kepand his beistis lay undir a bus	*Keeping; beasts; thicket*
	And quhen he saw this lady solitar	*when; on her own*
100	Bairfut with shankis quhyter than the snaw,	*Barefoot; legs whiter; snow*
	Preckit with lust he thocht withoutin mair	*Pricked; decided; more [delay]*
	Hir till oppres and till hir can he draw.	*To rape her; did he approach*
	Dreidand for scaith, sche fled quhen scho him saw	*Fearing; harm; when*
	And as scho ran all bairfute in a bus	*through a thicket*
105	Scho strampit on a serpent vennemus.	*stepped; poisonous snake*
	This cruwall venome was so penetrife	*piercing*
	As natur is of all mortall pusoun,	*As is the nature; deadly poison*
	In peisis small this quenis harte can rife	*pieces; heart did shatter*
	And scho anone fell on a deidly swoun.	*at once; deathlike faint*
110	Seand this cais, Proserpyne maid hir boun,	*Seeing; event; herself ready*
	Quhilk clepit is the goddes infernall,	*Who is called the goddess of hell*
	Ontill hir court this gentill quene can call	*to; did call this gentle queen*
	And quhen scho vaneist was and unvisible,	*when; vanished; invisible*
	Hir madyn wepit with a wofull cheir,	*maiden wept; face*
115	Cryand with mony schowt and voce terrible	*Crying; terrifying voice*

	Quhill at the last king Orpheus can heir	*Until; did hear*
	And of hir cry the caus sone cowth he speir.	*at once did he ask*
	Scho said, "Allace, Erudices your quene	
	Is with the phary tane befoir my ene."	*taken by the fairies; eyes*
120	This noble king inflammit all in yre	*inflamed; ire*
	And rampand as a lyoun revanus	*raging like a ravenous lion*
	With awfull luke and ene glowand as fyre	*fearsome look; eyes glowing*
	Sperid the maner and the maid said thus,	*Asks how it happened*
	"Scho strampit on a serpent venemus	
125	And fell on swoun. With that the quene of fary	*At that moment*
	Clawcht hir up sone and furth with hir cowth cary."	*Seized her at once; did hasten*
	Quhen scho had said, the king sichit full soir,	*When; spoken; sighed very bitterly*
	His hert neir birst for verry dule and wo,	*almost broke; true grief; woe*
	Half out of mynd he maid no tary moir	*made no further delay*
130	Bot tuk his harp and to the wod cowth go	*took; wood did go*
	Wrinkand his handis, walkand to and fro	*Wringing*
	Quhill he mycht stand, syne sat doun on a stone	*As long as he could; then*
	And till his harp thusgait he maid his mone,	*to; in this way; lament*
	"**O** dulfull herp with mony dully string	*doleful harp; dismal*
135	Turne all thy mirth and musik in murning	*into*
	And seis of all thy sutell sangis sweit.	*cease all your subtle, sweet songs*
	Now weip with me thy lord and cairfull king	*weep; sorrowful*
	Quhilk lossit hes in erd all his lyking	*Who has lost; earth; delight*
	And all thy game thow change in gole and greit	*pastime; into wails; sobbing*
140	Thy goldin pynnis with mony teris weit	*golden pegs; tears make wet*
	And all my pane foll to report thow preis,	*pain; strive to express*
	Cryand with me in every steid and streit	*Crying; place; street*
	Quhair art thou gone, my luve Ewridices?"	
	Him to rejos yit playit he a spring	*Himself; cheer; dance tune*
145	Quhill that the fowlis of the wid can sing	*Until; birds of the forest did*
	And treis dansit with thair levis grene	*trees danced; green leaves*
	Him to devoid from his grit womenting	*To draw him away; lamenting*
	Bot all in vane, that vailyeit him nothing,	*vain; availed him not at all*
	His hairt wes so upoun his lusty quene	*so [set] upon; lovely queen*
150	The bludy teiris sprang out of his ene,	*bloody tears; eyes*
	Thair wes na solace mycht his sobbing ses	*that could; cease*
	Bot cryit ay with cairis cauld and kene,	*always; sorrows cold; sharp*
	"Quhair art thow gone, my lufe Euridices?	
	"Fairweill my place, fairweill plesance and play	*home; pleasure; pastime*
155	And wylcum woddis wyld and wilsum way.	*And welcome wild woods; unfamiliar path*
	My wicket werd in wildirnes to ware,	*evil fate; endure*
	My rob ryell and all my riche array	*royal robes; fine clothing*

	Changit salbe in rude russet and gray,	*shall be into rough and undyed homespun*
	My dyademe intill a hate of hair,	*diadem consisting [only] of a hat of [my own] hair*
160	My bed salbe with bever, brok, and bair	*beaver, badger; boar*
	In buskis bene with mony busteous bes,	*sheltering bushes; wild beasts*
	Withowttin sang, sayand with siching sair,	*Without; saying; bitter sighs*
	'Quhair art thow gone, my luve Euridices?'	

	"I thee beseik, my fair fadir Phebus,	*beseech; father*
165	Haif pety of thy awin sone Orpheus,	*pity on your own son*
	Wait thow nocht weill I am thy barne and chyld?	*Do you not know well*
	Now heir my plaint panefull and peteus,	*hear; lament; piteous*
	Direk me fro this deid so dolorus	*Avert from me; death*
	Quhilk gois thus withouttin gilt begyld.	*Who exists thus, beguiled without guilt*
170	Lat nocht thy face with cluddis be oursyld,	*Do not let; covered*
	Len me thy lycht and lat me nocht go leis	*Lend; light; fall short*
	To find that fair in fame that nevir was fyld,	*fair one; who; dishonored*
	My lady quene and lufe Euridices.	

	"O Jupiter, thow god celestiall	
175	And grantser to myself, on thee I call	*grandfather; you*
	To mend my murning and my drery mone,	*alleviate; gloomy lamentation*
	Thow gif me fors that I nocht fant nor fall	*give; strength so that; neither faint*
	Till I hir fynd, for seke hir suth I sall	*Until I find her; seek; indeed*
	And nowther stint nor stand for stok na stone,	*cease or stop; log or stone*
180	Throw thy godheid gyde me quhair scho is gone,	*Through; divine power guide; where*
	Gar hir appeir and put my hairt in pes" —	*Make; at peace*
	King Orpheus thus, with his harp, allone,	
	Soir weipand for his wyfe Euridices.	*Bitterly weeping*

	Quhen endit wer thir songis lamentable	*these mournful songs*
185	He tuk his harp and on his breist can hing,	*took; hung [it] on his chest*
	Syne passit to the hevin as sayis the fable	*Then journeyed; heaven*
	To seik his wyfe bot that velyeid nothing.	*seek; availed*
	By Wedlingis Streit he went but tareing,	*Along the Milky Way; without tarrying*
	Syne come doun throw the speir of Saturne ald	*Then descended; sphere; old*
190	Quhilk fadir is to all the stormis cald.	*Who is called father of all the storms*

	Quhen scho wes socht outhrow that cauld region,	*sought throughout*
	Till Jupiter his grandsyr can he wend	*grandfather did he go*
	Quhilk rewit soir his lamentation	*Who keenly pitied*
	And gart his spheir be socht fro end to end.	*ordered; sphere; searched*
195	Scho was nocht thair, and doun he can descend	*not there; down he did*
	Till Mars the god of battell and of stryfe	*To; battle; strife*
	And socht his spheir yit gat he nocht his wyfe.	*searched; sphere; found; not*

	Than went he doun till his fadir Phebus	*down to his father*
	God of the sone with bemis brycht and cleir,	*sun; rays; clear*

200	Bot quhen he saw his awin son Orpheus	*when; own*
	In sic a plicht, that changit all his cheir	*such a state; face*
	And gart annone ga seik throw all his spheir	*caused at once to go seek through*
	Bot all in vane, his lady come nocht thair.	*vain; did not come there*
	He tuk his leif and to Venus can fair.	*took his leave; did go*
205	Quhen he hir saw, he knelit and said thus,	*When; kneeled*
	"Wait ye nocht weill I am your awin trew knycht,[1]	
	In luve nane leler than ser Orpheus	*no one more loyal*
	And ye of luve goddes and most of micht,	*goddess of love; most mighty*
	Of my lady help me to get a sicht."	*sight*
210	"Forsuth," quod scho, "Ye mone seik nedir mair."	*Indeed; must seek further below*
	Than fra Venus he tuk his leif but mair.	*from; without more*
	Till Mercury but tary is he gone	*without delay*
	Quhilk callit is the god of eloquens,	*Who is called; eloquence*
	Bot of his wyfe thair knawlege gat he none.	*about; there*
215	With wofull hairt he passit doun frome thens,	*down from there*
	Onto the mone he maid no residens.	*At; moon; made no stop*
	Thus frome the hevin he went on to the erd	*from; earth*
	Yit be the way sum melody he lerd.	*along; learned*
	In his passage amang the planeitis all	
220	He hard a hevinly melody and sound	*heard*
	Passing all instrumentis musicall	*Exceeding*
	Causit be rollyn of the speiris round	*rotation; spheres*
	Quhilk armony throu all this mappamound,	*Which harmony; through all this world*
	Quhill moving seis, unyt perpetuall,	*Until motion [should] cease, unites in perpetuity*
225	Quhilk of this warld Plato the saule can call.	*That Plato calls the soul of the world*
	Thair leirit he tonis proportionat	*learned; musical notes*
	As duplare, triplare, and emetricus,	*octave, twelfth; fourth*
	Emolius and eik the quadruplait,	*Fifth; also; double octave*
	Epogdeus rycht hard and curius.	*Second very; abstruse*
230	Of all thir sex sweit and delicious,	*these sweet and delightful six*
	Rycht consonant, fyfe hevinly symphonys	*Very harmonious, five heavenly intervals*
	Componyt ar, as clerkis can devyse.	*Comprised; scholars; devise*
	First diatasserone full sweit iwis	*perfect fourth; sweet indeed*
	And dyapasone semple and dowplait	*octave; doubled*
235	And dyapente componyt with the dys,	*perfect fifth combined; doubled octave*
	Thir makis fyve of thre multiplicat.	*These make five [intervals] derived from three*
	This mirry musik and mellefluat	*melodious*

---

[1] *Do you not know well I am your own true knight*

Compleit and full of nummeris od and evin   *numbers*
Is causit be the moving of the hevin.   *caused; motion; heavens*

240   Of sik musik to wryt I do bot doit,   *About such; only drivel*
      Thairfoir of this mater a stray I lay   *topic I set a limit*
      For in my lyfe I cowth nevir sing a noit,   *could; note*
      Bot I will tell how Orpheus tuk the way   *took the route*
      To seik his wyfe attour the gravis gray,   *seek; across; gray forests*
245   Hungry and cauld our mony wilsum wone   *cold over; desolate country*
      Withouttin gyd, he and his harp allone.   *guide; alone*

      He passit furth the space of twenty dayis   *traveled onward*
      Fer and ful fer and ferrer than I can tell   *very far; further*
      And ay he fand streitis and reddy wayis   *always; found; available paths*
250   Till at the last unto the yet of hell   *gate*
      He come and thair he fand a porter fell   *a fearsome gatekeeper*
      With thre heidis, wes callit Serberus,   *heads; called Cerberus*
      A hound of hell, a monster mervellus.

      Than Orpheus began to be agast   *afraid*
255   Quhen he beheld that ugly hellis hound.   *When*
      He tuk his harp and on it playit fast   *took; played continually*
      Till at the last throw sweitnes of the sound   *through sweetness*
      This dog slepit and fell doun on the ground,   *went to sleep*
      Than Orpheus attour his wame in stall   *tiptoed in across his belly*
260   And neddirmair he went as ye heir sall.   *further down; shall hear*

      He passit furth ontill a ryvir deip,   *to a deep river*
      Our it a brig and on it sisteris thre   *Over; bridge; three*
      Quhilk had the entre of the brig to keip.   *Who; access to; guard*
      Electo, Megera and Thesaphone   *[the Three Fates]*
265   Turnit a quheill wes ugly for to se   *Turning; wheel [that]; horrible; see*
      And on it spred a man hecht Exione   *[was] stretched; named Ixion*
      Rolland about rycht windir wobegone   *Rolling around most utterly beset with woe*

      Than Orpheus playd a joly spring,   *Then; lively dance tune*
      The thre susteris full fast thay fell on sleip,   *asleep*
270   The ugly quheill seisit of hir quhirling,   *wheel stopped; spinning*
      Thus left wes none the entre for to keip,   *no one was left*
      Thane Exione out of the quheill gan creip   *did creep*
      And stall away and Orpheus annone   *stole away; at once*
      Without stopping atour the brig is gone,   *across; has gone*

275   Nocht far frome thyne he come unto a flude   *thence; came; river*
      Drubly and deip that rathly doun can rin   *Turbulent; ran down swiftly*
      Quhair Tantelus, nakit, full thristy stude   *naked, very thirsty*
      And yit the wattir yeid aboif his chin.   *went above; chin*

    Quhen he gaipit, thair wald no drop cum in. — *Though; gaped, there would*

280 Quhen he dowkit, the watter wald discend. — *dipped; run low*

    Thusgat he nocht his thrist to slake no mend.[1]

    Befoir his face ane naple hang also — *In front of; apple hung*

    Fast at his mouth upoun a tolter threde. — *Close to; flimsy thread*

    Quhen he gapit, it rokkit to and fro — *rocked*

285 And fled as it refusit him to feid. — *retreated; refused to feed him*

    Than Orpheus had reuth of his gret neid, — *took pity on; great need*

    He tuk his harp and fast on it can clink. — *and twanged upon it at once*

    The wattir stud and Tantalus gat drink. — *stood still*

    Syne our a mure with thornis thik and scherp — *Then; across a moor; sharp*

290 Wepand allone a wilsum way he went — *a lonely path*

    And had nocht bene throw suffrage of his harp — *not been for the assistance*

    With fell pikis he had bene schorne and schent. — *cruel spikes; pierced and destroyed*

    As he blenkit besyd him on the bent — *looked; field*

    He saw speldit a wonder wofull wycht — *split open; very sorrowful man*

295 Nalit full fast and Ticius he hicht — *Nailed down tight; was called*

    And on his breist thair sat a grisly grip — *breast; horrible vulture*

    Quhilk with his bill his belly throw can boir, — *Which; did dig through*

    Both maw, myddret, hart, lever, and trip — *stomach; diaphragm; liver and bowels*

    He ruggit out, his panis war the moir. — *tugged out; torments were the greater*

300 Quhen Orpheus thus saw him suffir soir, — *When; suffer bitterly*

    He tuke his herp and maid sweit melody, — *took; made*

    The grip is fled and Ticius left his cry. — *ceased his outcry*

    Beyond this mure he fand a feirfull streit — *moor; found a terrifying street*

    Myrk as the nycht, to pas rycht dengerus, — *Dark; to travel upon*

305 For sliddrenes skant mycht he hald his feit, — *slipperiness hardly; footing*

    In quhilk thair wes a stynk rycht odius — *which; stench; offensive*

    That gydit him to hiddous hellis hous — *hideous house of hell*

    Quhair Rodomantus and Proserpina — *Rhadamanthus [Pluto]*

    Wer king and quene, and Orpheus in can ga. — *Were; in did go*

310 O dully place and grundles deip dungeoun, — *gloomy; bottomless*

    Furnes of fyre with stink intollerable, — *Furnace*

    Pit of dispair without remissioun, — *forgiveness*

    Thy meit vennome, thy drink is pusonable, — *food [is] venom; poisonous*

    Thy grit panis to compt unnumerable, — *tortures; count*

315 Quhat creature cumis to dwell in thee — *Whatever being comes*

    Is ay deand and nevirmoir may de. — *forever dying and never again can die*

---

[1] *In this way he [could] not his thirst to slake nor assuage*

Thair fand he mony cairfull king and quene	*There found; miserable*
With croun on heid of brass full hate birnand	*crown; head; hotly burning*
Quhilk in thair lyfe rycht maisterfull had bene,	*Who; lives; tyrannical; been*
320 And conquerouris of gold, riches, and land.	*wealth*
Hectore of Troy and Priame thair he fand	*he found*
And Alexander for his wrang conqueist,	*unjust*
Antiochus als for his foull incest,	
And Julius Cesar for his crewaltie	*cruelty*
325 And Herod with his brudiris wyfe he saw	*He saw Herod with his brother's wife*
And Nero for his grit iniquitie	
And Pilot for his breking of the law,	*Pilate; breaking*
Syne undir that he lukit and cowth knaw	*Then; looked; did recognize*
Cresus that king, none mychtiar on mold,	*Crassus; no one mightier in the world*
330 For cuvatyse yet full of birnand gold.	*greed stuffed; burning*
Thair saw he Pharo for oppressioun	*Pharoah*
Of Godis folk, on quhilk the plaigis fell,	*God's people; whom; plagues*
And Sawll eke for the grit abusioun	*Saul also; abuse*
Of justice to the folk of Israell,	
335 Thair saw he Acob and quene Jesabell	*Ahab; Jezebel*
Quhilk silly Nabot that wes a propheit trew	*Who innocent Naboth; true prophet*
For his wyne yaird withouttin mercy slew.	*vineyard killed without*
Thair saw he mony paip and cardynall	*many a pope*
In haly kirk quhilk dois abusioun	*holy church; commit abuses*
340 And archbischopis in thair pontificall	*their robes of office*
Be symonie and wrang intrusioun,	*By purchase and wrongful claim of a benefice*
Abbottis and men of all religioun	*every religious order*
For evill disponyng of thair placis rent	*spending; the incomes from their benefices*
In flame of fyre wer bittirly torment.	*were*
345 Syne neddirmair he went quhair Pluto was	*Then lower down; where*
And Proserpyne and hiddirwart he drew	*to this place he approached*
Ay playand on his harp quhair he cowth pas	*Always playing; did walk*
Till at the last Erudices he knew	*recognized*
Lene and deidlyk, peteous and paill of hew,	*Lean; corpse-like; hue*
350 Rycht warsche and wane and walluid as the weid,	*Very sickly; pale; withered; weed*
Hir lilly lyre was lyk unto the leid.	*lily complexion; lead*
Quod he, "My lady leill and my delyt,	*loyal; delight*
Full wo is me till se yow changit thus.	*woe; to see; changed*
Quhair is your rude as ros with cheikis quhyte,	*complexion; rose; white*
355 Your cristell ene with blenkis amorus,	*eyes; glances*
Your lippis reid to kis delicius?"	*red lips; delicious*
Quod scho, "As now I der nocht tell perfay	*Just; dare not; indeed*
Bot ye sall wit the caus ane uther day."	*But; learn; another*

360	Quod Pluto, "Ser, thocht scho be lyk ane elf,	*although she looks like an elf*
	Scho hes no caus to plenye and for quhy	*lament, and the reason is*
	Scho fairis alsweill daylie as dois myself	*She does as well*
	Or king Herod for all his chevelry.	
	It is langour that putis hir in sic ply.	*despair; such condition*
	War scho at hame in hir cuntré of Trace,	*If she were; home; country; Thrace*
365	Scho wald refete ful sone in fax and face."	*recover very soon; skin*

	Than Orpheus befoir Pluto sat doun	*in front of*
	And in his handis quhit his herp can ta	*white hands; did take*
	And playit mony sweit proportioun	*sweet melodies*
	With bais tonis in ypodorica,	*bass notes; hypodorian*
370	With gemilling in yporlerica,	*an extra treble line; hyperlydian*
	Quhill at the last for rewth and grit petie	*Until; compassion*
	Thay weipit soir that cowth him heir and se.	*wept; hear*

	Than Proserpene and Pluto bad him as	*commanded; ask*
	His waresoun and he wald haif rycht nocht	*reward; nothing at all*
375	Bot licience with his wyfe away to pas	*permission; to go away*
	To his cuntré, that he so far had soucht.	*whom he had sought so far*
	Quod Proserpyne, "Sen I hir hiddir brocht	*Said; Since; brought her here*
	We sall nocht pairte without conditioun."	*part*
	Quod he, "Thairto I mak promissioun."	*To that I formally agree*

380	"Euridices than be the hand thow tak	*then by; take*
	And pas thi way, bot undirneth this pane,	*subject to this penalty*
	Gife thou turnis or blenkis behind thy bak,	*If; glance*
	We sall hir haif to hell forevir agane."	*shall have her back to hell*
	Thocht this was hard, yit Orpheus was fane	*Although; severe; willing*
385	And on thay went talkand of play and sport	*talking; delight; pastime*
	Till thay almost come to the outwart port.	*Until; outer gate*

	Thus Orpheus, with inwart lufe repleit,	*filled with deep longing*
	So blindit was with grit effectioun,	*blinded; passion*
	Pensyfe in hart apone his lady sweit,	*Concerned about*
390	Remembrit nocht his hard conditioun.	*Did not remember*
	Quhat will ye moir, in schort conclusioun,	*What more do you want?*
	He blent bakwart and Pluto come annone	*glanced backward; came at once*
	And onto hell with hir agane is gone.	

	Allace it was grete hartsare for to heir	*great heartache; hear*
395	Of Orpheus the weping and the wo	
	How his lady that he had bocht so deir	*redeemed at so high a price*
	Bot for a luk so sone wes tane him fro.	*For just a look so soon was taken from him*
	Flatlingis he fell and micht no fordir go	*Down flat; could; further*
	And lay a quhile in swoun and extasy.	*a while; swoon; trance*
400	Quhen he ourcome, thus out on lufe can cry,	*When; awoke; against love*

"Quhat art thou, luve, how sall I thee defyne?   *What; shall*
Bittir and sweit, crewall and merciable,   *cruel and merciful*
Plesand to sum, to uthir plent and pyne,   *grief and torment*
Till sum constant, to uthir variable,   *To; fickle*
405   Hard is thy law, thy bandis unbrekable,   *your bonds unbreakable*
Quho servis thee, thocht thay be nevir sa trew,   *Whoever; though; ever so true*
Perchance sumtyme thay sall haif caus to rew.   *Perhaps; regret*

"Now find I weill this proverb trew," quod he,   *I completely find; true*
Hart on the hurd and handis on the soir,   *Heart; treasure; sore spot*
410   Quhair luve gois, on fors mone turne the e.   *Where; perforce the eye must turn*
I am expart and wo is me tharfoir.   *experienced; woe; therefore*
Bot for a luke my lady is forloir."   *Just; look; lost*
Thus chydand on with luve our burne and bent   *inveighing against; over stream; field*
A wofull wedo hamewart is he went.   *widower homeward; gone*

Moralitas   *Moralization*
415   Now wirthy folk, Boece that senatour   *Boethius; senator*
To wryt this fenyeit fable tuk in cure   *fictional; took care*
In his gay buke of Consolatioun   *fine; [of Philosophy]*
For our doctrene and gud instructioun   *lesson; good*
Quhilk in the self suppois it fenyeid be   *Which; itself, although it is fictional*
420   And hid undir the cloik of poesie,   *cloak*
Yit maister Trivat, doctour Nicholas,   *Trivet*
Quhilk in his tyme a noble theologe was   *distinguished theologian*
Applyis it to gud moralitie,
Rycht full of fruct and seriositie.   *Very; profit; seriousness*
425   Fair Phebus is the god of sapience,   *wisdom*
Caliope his wyfe is eloquence,
Thir twa mareit gat Orpheus belyfe,   *Married, these two begot; without delay*
Quhilk callit is the pairte intellective   *Which is called; intellectual part*
Of manis saule and undirstanding, fre   *man's soul; free*
430   And seperat fra sensualitie.   *separate from*
Euridices is oure effectioun   *our desire*
Be fantesy oft movit up and doun,   *imagination often swayed*
Quhile to ressone it castis the delyte,   *Sometimes; locates; pleasure*
Quhyle to the flesche it settis the appetyte.   *situates*
435   Arestius, this herd that cowth persew   *herdsman who did pursue*
Euridices, is nocht bot gud vertew   *nothing but good virtue*
That bissy is to keip our myndis clene   *is busy*
Bot quhen we fle outthrow the medow grene   *when; flee away across*
Fra vertew till this warldis vane plesans,   *From; world's vain pleasure*
440   Myngit with cair and full of variance,   *Mixed; vicissitude*
The serpent stangis that is the deidly sin   *bites; deadly*
That posownis the saule without and in,   *poisons; outside and inside [completely]*
And than is deid and eik oppressit doun   *is deadened; also forced down*
Till wardly lust all our affectioun.   *To [the level of] worldly; our entire will*

445   Thane perfyte reson weipis wondir sair,   *Then; weeps very bitterly*
        Seand thusgait our appetyte misfair   *Seeing; desire thus go astray*
        And to the hevin he passis up belyfe,   *journeys upward at once to heaven*
        Schawand to us the lyfe contemplatyfe,   *Showing to; life*
        The perfyte will and eik the fervent luve
450   We suld haif allway to the hevin abuve,   *should always have for heaven above*
        Bot seildin thair our appetyte is fundin,   *seldom is what we want found there*
        It is so fast within the body bundin,   *bound so tightly to the body*
        Thairfoir dounwart we cast our myndis e,   *mind's eye*
        Blindit with lust and may nocht upwartis fle.   *cannot fly upward*
455   Sould our desyre be socht up in the spheiris   *Our desire should; spheres*
        Quhen it is tedderit in thir warldly breiris,   *When; tethered; these worldly briers*
        Quhyle on the flesch, quhyle on this warldis wrak,   *Sometimes; trash [goods]*
        And to the hevin small intent we tak.   *we pay little attention*
        Schir Orpheus, thow seikis all in vane   *thou seekest utterly in vain*
460   Thy wyfe so he, tharfoir cum doun agane   *high, so come down*
        And pas unto the monster mervellus
        With thre heidis that we call Cerberus
        Quhilk fenyeid is to haif so mony heidis   *Which is depicted; have so many*
        For to betakin thre maner of deidis.   *represent three sorts; death*
465   The first is in the tendir yong bernage,   *childhood*
        The secound deid is in the middill age,   *death; middle*
        The thrid is in greit eild quhen men ar tane.   *third; great age; taken*
        Thus Cerberus to swelly sparis nane,   *swallow spares no one*
        Bot quhen our mynd is myngit with sapience   *infused; wisdom*
470   And plais upoun the herp of eloquence,
        That is to say, makis persuasioun   *makes an appeal*
        To draw our will and our affectioun
        In every eild fra syn and fowll delyte,   *At every age from sin; delight*
        The dog our sawll na power hes to byte.
475   The secound monstour ar the sistiris thre,   *monsters; three sisters*
        Electo, Migera, and Thesaphany.   *Alecto, Megaera, and Thesiphone*
        Ar nocht ellis, in bukis as we reid,   *[They] are nothing else; books; read*
        Bot wicket thoucht, ill word and thrawart deid: *thought; malicious deed*
        Electo is the bolling of the harte,   *swelling; heart*
480   Mygera is the wikkit word outwert,   *wicked; uttered*
        Thesaphony is operatioun   *the deed*
        That makis fynall executioun
        Of deidly syn, and thir thre turnis ay   *these three perpetually turn*
        The ugly quheill, quhilk is nocht ellis to say   *which is merely to say*
485   Bot warldly men sumtyme ar cassin he   *worldly; are raised aloft*
        Upone the quheill in gret prosperitie   *wheel; great*
        And with a quhirle onwarly or thai wait   *whirl unexpectedly before; realize*
        Ar thrawin doun to pure and law estait.   *cast; poor; humble state*
        Of Exione that on the quheill was spred   *Ixion; spread-eagled*
490   I sall yow tell sum part as I haif red.   *shall tell you; read*
        He was of lyfe brukle and lecherous   *fickle and lecherous in his manner of life*

And in that craft hardy and curagus   *pursuit persistent and bold*
That he wald luve into no lawar place   *did not wish; any lower*
Bot Juno, quene of nature and goddace,   *queen and goddess of nature*
495   And on a day he went upon the sky   *rose up into*
And socht Juno, thinkand with hir to ly.   *sought; intending; have sex with her*
Scho saw him cum and knew his foull entent.   *She; foul intention*
A rany clud doun fra the firmament   *rainy cloud; skies*
Scho gart discend and kest betwix thaim two   *caused to; threw between them both*
500   And in that clud his natur yeid him fro,   *semen went out from him*
Of quhilk was generat the sentowris, *From which were engendered the centaurs*
Half man, half hors, upoun a ferly wis.   *in a remarkable manner*
Thane for the inwart crabing and offens   *deep resentment and offense*
That Juno tuke for his grit violens,   *felt because of his great aggression*
505   Scho send him doun unto the sistiris thre   *sent*
Upone a quheill ay turnyt for to be.   *to be turned forever*
Bot quhen ressoun and perfyte sapience   *when*
Playis upone the herp of eloquens
And persuadis our fleschly appetyte
510   To leif the thocht of this warldly delyte,   *relinquish; thought; delight*
Than seisis of our hert the wicket will,   *ceases; wicked desire*
Fra frawart language than the tong is still,   *From perverse; then; tongue*
Our synfull deidis fallis doun on sleip.   *down asleep*
Thane Exione out of the quheill gan creip,   *wheel did creep*
515   That is to say the grit solicitud,   *great eagerness*
Quhyle up quhyle doun, to win this warldis gud   *Sometimes; world's property*
Seisis furthwith and our affectioun   *Ceases at once when; disposition*
Waxis quiet in contemplatioun.   *Grows*
      This Tantalus of quhome I spak of aire,   *of whom; spoke about earlier*
520   Quhill he levit he was a gay ostlaire,   *While; lived; fine innkeeper*
And on a nycht come travilland thairby   *came traveling that way*
The god of riches and tuk harbery   *wealth; took lodging*
With Tantalus, and he till his supper   *for [the god's] supper Tantalus*
Slew his awin sone that was hym leif and deir, *own son; beloved and dear to him*
525   And gart the god eit up his flesche ilk deill   *caused; to eat; every morsel*
Intill a sew with spycis soddin weill.   *Then; stew well simmered with spices*
For this dispyt quhen he was deid annone   *offense; straightaway*
Was dampnit in the flud of Acherone   *[He] was condemned; river*
Till suffer hungir, thrist, nakit and cawld,   *To; thirst, naked*
530   Rycht wobegone as I befoir haif tould.   *Utterly in despair; told*
      This hungry man and thristy, Tantalus,
Betaknis men gredy and covetous,   *Signifies*
The god of riches that ar ay reddy   *Who are always ready the god of wealth*
For to ressaif and tak in herbery   *To welcome and receive in lodging*
535   And till him seith thair sone in pecis small,   *boil their son; pieces*
That is thair flesch and blud, with grit travell   *great exertion*
To fill the bag and nevir fynd in thair hairt   *fill the wallet; find in their heart*
Upoun thameself to spend nor tak thair pairte. *For themselves; nor take their portion*

	Allace in erd quhair is thare mair foly	*earth where; more folly*
540	Than for to want and haif haboundantly,	*abundantly*
	Till haif distresse on bak, on bed and burd	*To; indigence; [one's] back; table*
	And spair till othir men of gold a hurd	*save up for; hoard*
	And in the nycht sleip soundly thay may nocht,	*sleep; they cannot*
	To gaddir geir so gredy is thair thocht.	*amass property so*
545	Bot quhen that ressoun and intelligence	*But when*
	Smytis upoun the herp of conscience,	
	Schawand to us quhat perrell on ilk syd	*Showing; each*
	That thai incur quhay will trest or confyd	*they; who; trust; put confidence*
	Into this warldis vane prosperitie	*In; world's vain*
550	Quhilk hes thir sory properteis thre,	*these three sorry qualities*
	That is to say, gottin with grit labour,	*gotten; great labor*
	Keipit with dreid and tynt with grit dolour.	*Kept; anxiety; lost; grief*
	This avaris be grace quha undirstud	*Whoever by grace understood this avarice*
	I trow suld leif thair grit solicitude	*believe; renounce their*
555	Of ythand thochtis and he besines	*pressing thoughts; intense endeaveor*
	To gaddir gold, syne leif in distres,	*amass; then live in poverty*
	Bot he suld eit and drink quhenevir he list	*But; should eat; whenever he should choose*
	Of cuvatyse to slaik the birnand thrist.	*relieve; burning*
	This Ticius lay nalit on the bent	*[who] lay nailed; field*
560	And wyth the grip his bowellis revin and rent,	*vulture; pierced and torn*
	Quhill he levit set his intentioun	*While he was alive*
	To find the craft of divinatioun	*discover; art; prophecy*
	And lerit it unto the spamen all	*taught; to all the soothsayers*
	To tell befoir sic thingis as wald befall,	*declare in advance such; were to befall*
565	Quhat lyfe, quhat deth, quhat destany and werd	*What; fate*
	Provydit ware to every man on erd.	*Were in store for; on earth*
	Appollo than for his abusioun,	*then; his [Theseus'] offense*
	Quhilk is the god of divinatioun,	*Who*
	For he usurpit in his facultie,	*branch of knowledge*
570	Put him to hell and thair remanis he.	*into; there he remains*
	Ilk man that heiris this conclusioun	*Each; hears*
	Suld dreid to sers be constillatioun	*seek in the stars*
	Thingis to fall undir the firmament,	*befall beneath; sky*
	Till "Ye" or "Na," quhilk ar indefferent	*For "yes"; which; neutral*
575	Without profixit causis and certane,	*predetermined and certain causes*
	Quhilk nane in erd may knaw bot God allane.	
	Quhen Orpheus upoun his harp can play,	
	That is our undirstanding for to say,	
	Cryis, "O man, recleme thi folich harte!	*call back your foolish heart*
580	Will thow be god and tak on the his pairte,	*take upon yourself his function*
	To tell thingis to cum that nevir wil be	*to come; will never occur*
	Quhilk God hes kepit in his prevetie?	*kept; private knowledge*
	Thow ma no mair offend to God of micht	*can; more; power*
	Na with thi spaying reif fra him his richt."	*Than; prophecy deprive*
585	This perfyte wisdome with his melody	

Fleyis the spreit of fenyeid profecy   *Dispels; spirit; false*
And drawis upwart our affectioun.   *desire*

. . .

Fra wichcraft, spaying, and sorsery,   *witchcraft; sorcery*
And superstitioun of astrolegy,
590   Saif allanerly sic maner of thingis   *Except only such*
Quhilk upoun trew and certane causis hingis,   *Which; depend*
The quhilk mone cum, to thair caus indure,   *must come, while; lasts*
On verry fors and nocht throw avanture,   *By absolute necessity; chance*
As is the clippis and the conjunctioun   *eclipse*
595   Of sone and mone be calculatioun,   *sun and moon by*
The quhilk ar fundin in trew astronomy   *found; true*
Be moving of the speiris in the sky.   *By the motion of the spheres*
All thir to speik it may be tollerable   *To discuss all these*
And none udir quhilk no causis stable.   *no others; no causes make inevitable*
600   This ugly way, this myrk and dully streit   *path; dark; dismal street*
Is nocht ellis bot blinding of the spreit   *else; spirit*
With myrk cluddis and myst of ignorance,
Affetterrit in this warldis vane plesance   *Fettered; world's*
And bissines of temporalite.   *occupation in secular pursuits*
605   To kene the self a styme it may nocht se,   *know oneself even a glimpse it cannot see*
For stammeris on eftir effectioun.   *[it] stumbles; desire*
Fra ill to war ale thus to hell gois doun,   *From bad to worse all; goes*
That is wanhowp throw lang hanting of syn   *hopelessness from a long habit of sin*
And fowll dispair that mony fallis in.   *into which many people fall*
610   Than Orpheus our ressoun is full wo   *very sorrowful*
And twichis on his harp and biddis "Ho,"   *plucks; calls a halt*
Till our desyre and fulich appetyte   *To; foolish*
Bidis leif this warldis full delyte.   *Commands to leave; foul pleasure*
Than Pluto god, and quene of hellis fyre,   *the god; [Proserpina] the queen*
615   Mone grant to ressoun on fors the desyre.   *Must; under compulsion*
Than Orpheus has wone Euridices   *won*
Quhen oure desyre with ressoun makis pes   *makes peace*
And seikis up to contemplatioun,   *goes up*
Of syn detestand the abusioun,   *Detesting the abuses of sin*
620   Bot ilk man suld be wyse and warly se   *each; should; cautiously see*
That he bakwart cast nocht his myndis e   *[should] not turn his mind's eye backward*
Gifand consent and delectatioun   *Giving; pleasure*
Of fleschly lust for the affectioun,   *In; for the desire*
For thane gois bakwart to the syn agane,   *then; again*
625   Our appetyte as it befoir was, slane
In warldly lust and vane prosperite,
And makis ressoun wedow for to be.   *to be a widower*
Now pray we God sen our affectioun   *since; desire*
Is allway promp and reddy to fall doun   *poised*
630   That he wald undirput his haly hand   *place underneath*
Of mantenans and gife us fors to stand   *support; give us the power to remain*

In perfyte lufe as he is glorius
And thus endis the taill of Orpheus.   *tale*

Against Hasty Credence

Fals titlaris now growis up full rank,   *False tattlers; abundantly*
Nocht ympit in the stok of cheretie,   *Not grafted onto; trunk; charity*
Howping at thair lord to gett grit thank,   *Hoping from; earn great*
Thay haif no dreid on thair nybouris to lie.   *have; fear about; neighbors*
5   Than sowld ane lord avyse him weill and se   *should; bethink himself well*
Quhen ony taill is brocht to his presence   *When; tale; brought*
Gif it be groundit into veretie   *If; based in fact*
Or he thairto gif haistely creddence.   *Before; rashly accept as true*

Ane worthy lord sould wey ane taill wyslie,   *A; should weigh; wisely*
10   The taill-tellar and quhome of it is tald,   *tale-teller; of whom; told*
Gif it be said for luve or for invy,   *If; love; envy*
And gif the tailisman weill avow it wald.   *tale-teller will well affirm it*
Than eftirwart the pairteis sould be cald   *persons involved; summoned*
For thair excuse to mak lawfull defence.   *plea; make*
15   Thus sowld ane lord the ballance evinly hald   *maintain the balance evenly*
And gif not at the first haistie creddence.   *not give at the first [hearing]*

It is no wirschep for ane nobill lord   *cause of honor*
For fals tailis to put ane trew man doun,   *Because of; crush a true man*
And gevand creddence to the first recoird,   *giving; statement*
20   He will not heir his excusatioun.   *hear [the true man's] excuse*
The tittillaris so in his heir can roun   *tattlers; ear can whisper*
The innocent may get no awdience.   *can; hearing*
Ryme as it may, thairin is na ressoun   *there is no reason in it*
To gif till taillis hestely creddence.   *give to tales*

25   Thir teltellaris oft tymes dois grit skaith   *These tale-tellers often do great harm*
And raissis mortall feid and discrepance   *stir up deadly feud; dispute*
And makis lordis with thair servandis wreith   *angry with their servants*
And baneist be withowtin cryme perchance.   *be banished without; perhaps*
It is the grund of stryfe and all distance.   *basis for; estrangement*
30   Moir perrellus than ony pestillence,   *More dangerous; plague*
Ane lord in flatterreris to haif plesance   *take pleasure in flatterers*
Or to gif lyaris hestely creddence.   *give liars*

O thow wyse lord, quhen that a flatterrer — *when*
Thee for to pleis and hurt the innocent — *To please you*
35 Will tell ane taill of thy familiar, — *about; close associate*
Thow sowld the pairteis call incontinent — *call the persons at once*
And sitt doun sadly into jugement — *down; solemnly*
And serche the caus weill or thow gif sentence, — *investigate; before you give*
Or ellis heireftir in cais thow may repent — *else later perchance*
40 That thow to tailis gaif so grit creddence. — *paid*

O wicket tung sawand dissentioun, — *wicked; sowing discord*
Of fals taillis to tell that will not tyre, — *About false; speak; tire*
Moir perrellus than ony fell pusoun, — *deadly poison*
The pane of hell thow sall haif to thi hyre. — *torment; have for your reward*
45 Richt swa sall thay that hes joy or desyre — *Just so shall; who have*
To gife thair eirris to heird with patience, — *commit; ears; hear it*
For of discord it kendillis mony fyre — *kindles many a fire*
Throuch geving talis hestely creddence. — *Through*

Bakbyttaris to heir it is no bourd — *To listen to slanderers is no joke*
50 For thay ar planlie curst in everie place. — *publicly cursed*
Thre personis severall he slayis with ane wowrd: — *Three different people; word*
Himself, the heirar, and the man saiklace. — *hearer; innocent man*
Within ane hude he hes ane doubill face, — *one hood; a double*
Ane bludy tung undir a fair pretence, — *bloodthirsty tongue under*
55 I say no moir bot "God grant lordis grace — *more except; grace to lords*
To gife to taillis nocht hestely creddence." — *Not to give to tales*

The Annunciation

Forcy as deith is likand lufe — *Powerful; death; pleasing love*
Throuch quhom al bittir swet is. — *Through whom; sweet*
Nothing is hard, as writ can pruf, — *scripture does prove*
Till him in lufe that letis. — *To; love; lingers*
5 Luf us fra barret betis — *us from trouble relieves*
Quhen fra the hevinly sete abufe — *When from; throne above*
In message Gabriell couth muf — *Bearing a message; did go*
And with myld Mary metis — *meets*
And said, "God wele thee gretis. — *greets*
10 In thee he will tak rest and rufe — *repose*
But hurt of syn or yit reprufe. — *Without; sin; disgrace*
In him sett thi decret is." — *your destiny is firm*

This message mervale gert that myld — *to wonder made; mild one*
And silence held but soundis — *maintained without*
15 As weill aferit a maid infild. — *well suited; undefiled*
The angell it expoundis, — *declares it*

How that hir wame but woundis   *her womb without*
Consave it suld, fra syn exild,   *Conceive; should; exiled*
And quhen this carpin wes compilit,   *when; message; finished*
20   Brichtnes fra bufe aboundis.   *Light from above*
Than fell that gay to groundis,   *lovely one to the ground*
Of Goddis grace na thing begild,   *not at all deprived*
Wox in hir chaumer chaist with child,   *Grew; chaste chamber*
With Crist our kyng that cround is.   *crowned*

25   Thir tithingis tauld, the messinger   *These tidings told*
Till hevin agane he glidis.   *To heaven again; flies*
That princes pure withoutyn peir   *pure princess; equal*
Full plesandly applid is   *is compliant*
And blith with barne abidis.   *with child joyously waits*
30   O wirthy wirschip singuler   *worthy unique honor*
To be moder and madyn meir   *mother and maiden too*
As Cristin faith confidis,   *Christian; trusts*
That borne was of hir sidis   *from her loins*
Our makar, Goddis sone so deir,   *maker; son; dear*
35   Quhilk erd, wattir, and hevinnis cleir   *Who earth, water; bright*
Throw grace and virtu gidis.   *Through; virtue guides*

The miraclis ar mekle and meit   *are great and gentle*
Fra luffis ryver rynnis.   *[That] from love's; flow*
The low of luf haldand the hete   *flame; withholding; heat*
40   Unbrynt full blithlie brinnis.   *Unburnt; burns*
Quhen Gabriell beginnis   *When*
With mouth that gudely may to grete,   *worthy maid; greet*
The wand of Aaron, dry, but wete,   *staff; without moisture*
To burioun nocht blynnis.   *Does not cease to bud*
45   The flesch all donk within is,   *fleece that is all damp inside*
Upon the erd na drop couth fleit.   *[Though] no drop fell on the earth*
Sa was that may maid moder swete   *maiden made a sweet mother*
And sakeles of all synnis.   *innocent; sins*

Hir mervalus haill madinhede   *intact virginity*
50   God in hir bosum bracis   *clasps*
And his divinité fra dreid   *divine power from fear*
Hir kepit in all casis.   *Kept her; circumstances*
The hie God of his gracis   *mighty God in his grace*
Himself dispisit us to speid   *abased to advance us*
55   And dowtit nocht to dee on deid.   *feared not; die indeed*
He panit for our peacis   *suffered; peace*
And with his blude us bacis   *blood washes us*
Bot quhen he ras up, as we rede,   *But when; rose; read*
The cherité of his godhede   *charity; divine power*
60   Was plane in every placis.   *apparent everywhere*

O lady lele and lusumest, *loyal and most lovable*
Thy face moist fair and schene is. *most; bright*
O blosum blith and bowsumest *blossom; most gracious*
Fra carnale cryme that clene is, *From fleshly; who is cleansed*
65 This prayer fra my splene is *comes from my heart*
That all my werkis wikkitest *all the most evil of my deeds*
Thow put away and make me chaist, *purge; chaste*
Fra Termigant that teyn is *[Away] from; is fierce*
And fra his cluke that kene is, *claw; is sharp*
70 And syn till hevin my saule thou haist *afterwards to; hasten*
Quhair thi makar of michtis mast *Where your; greatest in power*
Is kyng and thow thair quene is. *there*

Sum Practysis of Medecyne *Some Procedures*

Guk guk, gud day schir, gaip quhill ye get it, *Cuckoo, good; sir, gape until*
Sic greting may gane weill — gud laik in your hude. *Such; be very suitable; fun; hood*
Ye wald deir me, I trow, becaus I am dottit, *would scorn; guess; crazed*
To ruffill me with a ryme — na schir, be the rude. *upset; no sir, by; cross*
5 Your saying I haif sene and on syd set it *discourse; have seen; aside*
As geir of all gaddering, glaikit, nocht gude, *stuff; borrowing, idiotic, not*
Als your medicyne by mesour I haif meit met it, *And; measure; well measured*
The quhilk I stand ford ye nocht understude *which; aver; misunderstood*
Bot wrett on as ye culd to gar folk wene *wrote; could; make; think*
10 For feir my longis wes flaft *fear; lungs were panting*
Or I wes dottit or daft. *crazed; stupid*
Gife I can ocht of the craft, *If; know anything about*
Heir be it sene. *Let it be revealed here*

Becaus I ken your cunnyng into cure *know; skill at curing*
15 Is clowtit and clampit and nocht weill cleird, *cobbled; patched; polished*
My prectik in pottingary ye trow be als pure *skill; pharmacy; as poor*
And lyk to your lawitnes. I schrew thame that leid. *like; ignorance; curse; lied*
Is nowdir fevir nor fell that our the feild fure, *neither fever; accident(?); across; came*
Seiknes nor sairnes in tyme gif I seid, *Disease; pain; if; see it*
20 Bot I can lib thame and leiche thame fra lame and lesure, *cure them; heal; from; injury*
With sawis thame sound mak. On your saule beid *salves; make; soul be it*
That ye be sicker of this sedull I send yow *sure; prescription; you*
With the suthfast seggis *trustworthy men*
That glean all egeis *smear; eggs*
25 With dia and dreggis *medicine; drugs*
Of malis to mend yow. *malaise; fix you*

Dia Culcakit *Befouled-Rectum Prescription*
Cape cuk maid and crop the colleraige — *Take fresh dung; cut; pepper*
Ane medecyne for the maw, and ye cowth mak it — *stomach, if; could make*

With sweit satlingis and sowrokis, the sop of the sege,	*sweet dregs; sorrel; sap; sage*
30 The crud of my culome (with your teith crak it),	*dirt; anus; teeth crack*
Lawrean and linget seid and the luffage,	*Laurel; flax seed; lovage*
The hair of the hurcheoun nocht half deill hakkit	*hedgehog; not; part chopped*
With the snout of ane selch ane swelling to swage.	*seal; a; soothe*
This cure is callit in our craft Dia Culcakkit.	*called; profession*
35 Put all thir in ane pan with pepper and pik,	*these; tar*
Syne sett in to this,	*Then sit*
The count of ane cow kis.	*Kiss the cunt of a cow*
Is nocht bettir iwis	*nothing; indeed*
For the collik.	*colic*

Dia Longum — *Long Prescription*

40 Recipe thre ruggis of the reid ruke,	*Take three pulls; red rook*
The gant of ane gray meir, the claik of ane gus,	*yawn; mare; cluck; goose*
The dram of ane drekters, the douk of ane duke,	*drake's penis; dive; duck*
The gaw of ane grene dow, the leg of ane lous,	*gall; dove; louse*
Fyve unce of ane fle wing, the fyn of ane fluke,	*ounces; fly's wing; fin; flounder*
45 With ane sleiffull of slak that growis in the slus.	*sleeve-full; algae; on the weir*
Myng all thir in ane mas with the mone cruke.	*Mix; these; mass; crescent moon*
This untment is rycht ganand for your awin us	*ointment; suitable; own use*
With reid nettill seid in strang wesche to steip	*red nettle seed; stale urine; steep*
For to bath your ba cod	*bathe; scrotum*
50 Quhen ye wald nop and nod.	*When; want to nap*
Is nocht bettir, be God,	*nothing; by*
To latt yow to sleip.	*allow; sleep*

Dia Glaconicon — *Pennyroyal (?) Prescription*

This dia is rycht deir and denteit in daill	*very dear; precious; portions*
Caus it is trest and trew. Thairfoir that ye tak	*dependable; true; take*
55 Sevin sobbis of ane selche, the quhidder of ane quhaill,	*sobs; seal; twitter; quail*
The lug of ane lempet is nocht to forsaik,	*ear; limpet; not to leave out*
The harnis of ane haddok hakkit or haill	*brains; chopped; whole*
With ane bustfull of blude of the scho bak	*boxful; blood; female bat*
With ane brewing caldrun full of hait caill	*kettle; hot cabbage*
60 For it wil be the softar and sweittar of the smak.	*gentler; sweeter; flavor*
Thair is nocht sic ane lechecraft fra Laudian to Lundin.	*such; remedy; Lundin (in Fife)*
It is clippit in our cannon	*called; medical canon*
Dia Glecolicon	
For till fle awaye fon	*to chase; folly*
65 Quhair fulis ar fundin.	*Wherever fools are found*

Dia Custrum — *Cough Medicine*

The ferd feisik is fyne and of ane felloun pryce,	*fourth medicine; great cost*
Gud for haising and hosting or heit at the hairt.	*Good; rasping; coughing; heartburn*
Recipe thre sponfull of the blak spyce	*Take three; black pepper*
With ane grit gowpene of the gowk fart,	*big double handful; cuckoo*

70	The lug of ane lyoun, the gufe of ane gryce,	*ear; lion; grunt; pig*
	Ane unce of ane oster poik at the nethir parte	*oyster stomach; lower part*
	Annoynt it with nurice doung, for it is rycht nyce,	*a wet nurse's excrement*
	Myng it with mysdirt and with mustart.	*Mix; mouse droppings*
	Ye may clamp to this cure, and ye will mak cost,	*add; if; pay the extra cost*
75	Bayth the bellox of ane brok	*Both; testicles; badger*
	With thre crawis of the cok,	*crows; rooster*
	The schadow of ane Yule stok:	*shadow; Yule log*
	Is gud for the host.	*good; cough*
	Gud nycht, guk guk, for sa I began.	*Goodnight, cuckoo; thus*
80	I haif no come at this tyme langer to tary,	*have not come; stay longer*
	Bot luk on this lettir and leird gif ye can,	*look at; letter; learn it if*
	The prectik and poyntis of this pottingary.	*method; details; pharmacy*
	Schir, minister this medecyne at evin to sum man	*Sir, administer; evening*
	And or pryme be past, my powder I pary,	*before; I bet my medicine*
85	Thay sall blis yow or ellis bittirly yow ban	*shall bless; else; curse you*
	For it sall fle thame, in faith, out of the fary.	*chase them; a daze*
	Bot luk quhen ye gadder thir gressis and gers,	*watch when; grasses; herbs*
	Outhir savrand or sour,	*Either savory*
	That it be in ane gude oure.	*good hour*
90	It is ane mirk mirrour,	*dark mirror*
	Ane uthir manis ers.	*Another man's rump*

	The Ressoning betwix Aige and Yowth	*Dialogue between Age and Youth*
Yowth	**Q**uhen fair Flora the godes of the flowris	*When; goddess; flowers*
	Baith firth and feildis freschely had ourfret	*Both forest; ornamented*
	And perly droppis of the balmy schowris	*pearly; fragrant showers*
	Thir widdis grene had with thair water wet,	*These woods; their; wetted*
5	Movand allone in mornyng myld I met	*Going by myself; on a; met*
	A mirry man that all of mirth cowth mene,	*merry; was all about mirth did speak*
	Singand this sang that richt sweitly wes sett.	*Singing; very; was set [to music]*
	"O yowth, be glaid into thy flouris grene."	*glad; your flourishing flowers*
Aige	I lukit furth a litill me befoir.	*looked out; little ahead of me*
10	I saw a cative on a club cumand	*wretch; stick approaching*
	With cheikis lene and lyart lokis hoir,	*thin cheeks; frosty gray locks*
	His ene was how, his voce was hes hostand,	*eyes were sunken; hoarsely coughing*
	Wallowit richt wan and waik as ony wand.	*Withered; pale; weak; sapling*
	Ane bill he beure upoun his breist abone	*document; carried; above*
15	In letteris leill but lyis with this legand,	*correct without mistake; inscription*
	"O yowth, thy flowris fedis fellone sone."	*flowers fade shockingly soon*
Yowth	This yungman lap upoun the land full licht	*leapt; very nimbly*
	And marvellit mekle of his misdome maid.	*puzzled greatly over the error made [by Age]*

	"Waldin I am," quod he, "and woundir wicht	*Limber; said; very strong*
20	With bran as bair and breist burly and braid	*brawn like a boar; big; thick*
	Na growme on ground my gairdone may degraid	*man on earth; gifts; belittle*
	Nor of my pith may pair of wirth a prene.	*vigor; diminish in value [by even] a pin*
	My face is fair, my fegour will not faid.	*figure; not worsen*
	O yowith, be glaid into thy flowris grene."	*glad*

Aige	This senyeour sang bot with a sobir stevin.	*senior; stern voice*
26	Schakand his berd he said, "My bairne, lat be.	*Shaking; child, desist*
	I wes within thir sextie yeiris and sevin	*these sixty-seven years*
	Ane freik on fold als frak, forsy, and fre,	*man; earth both keen, strong*
	Als glaid, als gay, als ying, als yaip as ye	*As; young; eager*
30	Bot now tha dayis ourdrevin ar and done.	*passed over*
	Luke thow my laithly luking gif I le.	*Regard; loathsome expression [to see] if I am lying*
	O yowth, thy flowris fadis fellone sone."	

Yowth	Ane uthir vers yit this yungman cowth sing,	*Another verse; still did sing*
	"At luvis law a quhyle I think to leit,	*Under love's rule; while; remain*
35	In court to cramp clenely in my clething	*prance adeptly; clothing*
	And luke amangis thir lusty ladeis sweit	*seek amongst these lovely ladies*
	Of mariage to mell with mowis meit	*talk; suitable jests*
	In secreit place quhair we ma not be sene	*private where; cannot; seen*
	And so with birdis blythly my baillis beit,	*young women; ease my pains*
40	O yowth, be glaid into thi flowris grene."	

Aige	This awstrene man gaif answer angirly.	*stern; gave; angrily*
	"For thy cramping thow salt baith cruke and cowre,	*prancing; shall both bend; shake*
	Thy fleschely lust thow salt also defy	*renounce*
	And pane thee sall put fra paramour.	*pain shall stop you from lovemaking*
45	Than will no bird be blyth of thee in bouir.	*no young woman; glad; you; bedchamber*
	Quhen thy manheid sall mynnis as the mone,	*your manhood; dwindle like; moon*
	Thow sall assay gif that my sang be soure.	*find out if; song is*
	O yowth, thy flowris fadis fellone sone."	

Yowth	This mirry man of mirth yit movit moir.	*still spoke more about mirth*
50	"My corps is clene withowt corruptioun,	*body; clean*
	My self is sound but seiknes or but soir,	*without sickness; sores*
	My wittis fyve in dew proportioun,	*five senses; due*
	My curage is of clene complexioun,	*vigor; healthy constitution*
	My hairt is haill, my levar and my splene,	*healthy; liver; spleen*
55	Thairfoir to reid this roll I haif ressoun,	*read; scroll; have good reason*
	O yowth, be glaid into thy flowris grene."	

Aige	The bevir hair said to this berly berne,	*old gray dodderer; burly lad*
	"This breif thow sall obey sone, be thow bald,	*writ; soon; bold*
	Thy stait, thy strenth thocht it be stark and sterne,	*state; though; strong; keen*
60	The feveris fell and eild sall gar thee fald,	*cruel fevers; age; make you yield*

Thy corps sall clyng, thy curage sall wax cald,   *wither; vigor; grow cold*
Thy helth sall hynk and tak a hurt bot hone,   *stagger; without delay*
Thy wittis fyve sall wane thocht thow not wald.   *do not want [them] to*
O yowth, thy flowris fedis fellone sone."

65   This galyart grutchit and began to greif,   *fine fellow resented; grumble*
     He on his wayis wrethly went but wene   *angrily without delay*
     This lene awld man luche not bot tuk his leif   *did not laugh; took; leave*
     And I abaid undir the levis grene.   *stayed*
     Of the sedullis, the suthe quhen I had sene,   *documents; indeed when*
70   On trewth me thocht thay trevist in thair tone: *In truth; clashed; tunes*
     "O yowth, be glaid into thy flowris grene."
     "O yowth, thy flowris faidis fellone sone."

Robene and Makyne

     Robene sat on gud grene hill   *good*
     Kepand a flok of fe.   *Keeping; flock; sheep*
     Mirry Makyne said him till,   *Merry; to him*
     "Robene, thow rew on me!   *Robin, take pity*
5   I haif thee lovit loud and still   *have loved; quiet*
     Thir yeiris two or thre.   *These years; three*
     My dule in dern bot gif thow dill   *longing in secret unless; soothe*
     Doutles but dreid I de."   *Doubtless without doubt I will die*

     Robene answerit, "Be the rude,   *By the cross*
10   Nathing of lufe I knaw   *about love; know*
     Bot keipis my scheip undir yone wid,   *But keep; sheep under the shelter of that wood*
     Lo quhair thay raik on raw.   *where they wander together*
     Quhat hes marrit thee in thy mude,   *What; upset; mood*
     Makyne, to me thow schaw,   *reveal to me*
15   Or quhat is lufe or to be lude?   *what; love; loved*
     Fane wald I leir that law."   *Eagerly do I wish to learn*

     "At luvis lair gife thow will leir,   *the study of love if; learn*
     Tak thair ane A B C: *Study in it*
     Be heynd, courtas, and fair of feir,   *kind, courteous; manners*
20   Wyse, hardy, and fre,   *determined; generous*
     So that no denger do thee deir.   *rebuff cause you harm*
     Quhat dule in dern thow dre,   *Whatever pain; secret; suffer*
     Preis thee with pane at all poweir,   *Exert yourself; effort; strength*
     Be patient and previe."   *discreet*

25   Robene answerit hir agane,   *her*
     "I wait nocht quhat is luve   *do not understand what*
     Bot I haif mervell in certane   *I cannot understand indeed*

Quhat makis thee this wanrufe. — *What causes you; turmoil*
The weddir is fair and I am fane, — *weather; happy*

30 My scheip gois haill aboif, — *go safely above*
And we wald play us in this plane — *If; were to make love; valley*
Thay wald us bayth reproif." — *rebuke us both*

"Robene, tak tent unto my taill — *pay attention; tale*
And wirk all as I reid — *do exactly; advise*

35 And thow sall haif my hairt all haill, — *shall have; heart entirely*
Eik and my madinheid. — *As well as; virginity*
Sen God sendis bute for baill — *Since; relief; suffering*
And for murning remeid, — *help for sorrow*
I dern with thee bot gif I daill — *In secret; you unless; deal*

40 Doutles I am bot deid." — *Doubtless; just dead*

"Makyne, to-morne this ilk a tyde — *tomorrow; same time*
And ye will meit me heir, — *If; meet; here*
Peraventure my scheip ma gang besyd — *Perhaps; might go astray*
Quhill we haif liggit full neir, — *Until; have lain very close*

45 Bot mawgre haif I and I byd — *I [will] have blame if; stay*
Fra thay begin to steir. — *Once; move away*
Quhat lyis on hairt I will nocht hyd. — *What is sincere I will not hide*
Makyn, than, mak gud cheir." — *then, make the best of it*

"Robene, thow reivis me roif and rest. — *deprive; [of] peace*

50 I luve bot thee allone." — *only you alone*
"Makyne, adew, the sone gois west, — *farewell; sun goes*
The day is neirhand gone." — *nearly over*
"Robene, in dule I am so drest — *sorrow; placed*
That lufe wilbe my bone." — *love will be; cause of death*

55 "Ga lufe, Makyne, quhairevir thow list — *Go and love; wherever; wish*
For lemman I bid none." — *lover; seek*

"Robene, I stand in sic a styll — *exist; such a state*
I sicht and that full sair." — *sigh; very bitterly*
"Makyne, I haif bene heir this quhyle, — *have been here; [long] while*

60 At hame God gif I wair." — *God grant I were at home*
"My huny Robene, talk ane quhyll — *honey; awhile*
Gif thow will do na mair." — *Even if; nothing more*
"Makyne, sum uthir man begyle — *beguile some other man*
For hamewart I will fair." — *homeward; go*

65 Robene on his wayis went — *way*
Als licht as leif of tre. — *As light; leaf; tree*
Mawkin murnit in hir intent — *grieved; mind*
And trowd him nevir to se. — *expected never to see him*
Robene brayd attour the bent, — *hurried over the field*

70	Than Mawkyne cryit on hie,	*Then; cried out loud*
	"Now ma thow sing for I am schent,	*can; because; ruined*
	'Quhat alis lufe at me!'"	*How love troubles me*

	Mawkyne went hame withouttin faill	*without*
	Full wery eftir cowth weip,	*Very tired after after [she] wept*
75	Than Robene in a ful fair daill	*valley*
	Assemblit all his scheip.	*Gathered*
	Be that sum pairte of Mawkynis aill	*By then some; ailment*
	Outthrow his hairt cowd creip.	*Throughout; heart did creep*
	He fallowit hir fast thair till assaill	*followed; to accost [her]*
80	And till hir tuke gude keip.	*paid close attention to her*

	"Abyd, abyd thow fair Makyne!	*Wait*
	A word for ony thing!	*for any price*
	For all my luve it salbe thyne	*shall be*
	Withowttin depairting.	*Without separation*
85	All haill thy harte for till haif myne	*whole; heart; have as mine*
	Is all my cuvating.	*my whole desire*
	My scheip to-morne quhill houris nyne	*until nine o'clock tomorrow*
	Will neid of no keping."	*need*

	"Robene, thow hes hard soung and say	*heard; sung; told*
90	In gestis and storeis auld,	*old tales and stories*
	The man that will nocht quhen he may	*does not want; he has the chance*
	Sall haif nocht quhen he wald.	*Shall not have; may wish*
	I pray to Jesu every day	
	Mot eik thair cairis cauld	*[That] their bitter cares must increase*
95	That first preisis with thee to play	*Who; tries*
	Be firth, forrest, or fauld."	*By wood, forest; field*

	"Makyne, the nicht is soft and dry,	
	The wedder is warme and fair	*weather*
	And the grene woid rycht neir us by	*greenwood [is] very close beside us*
100	To walk attour all quhair.	*in it everywhere*
	Thair ma na janglour us espy	*No tale-teller can see us there*
	That is to lufe contrair,	*Who; hostile to love*
	Thairin Makyne, bath ye and I	*Into there; both*
	Unsene we ma repair."	*Unseen; can go*

105	"Robene, that warld is all away	*world*
	And quyt brocht till ane end,	*completely brought to*
	And nevir agane thairto perfay	*to that point indeed*
	Sall it be as thow wend,	*Shall; supposed*
	For of my pane thow maid it play	*pain; made it a jest*
110	And all in vane I spend.	*I made an effort all in vain*

As thow hes done sa sall I say,   *have; so shall*
'Murne on'; I think to mend."   *Whine away; plan to get better*

"Mawkyne, the houp of all my heill,   *guarantee; well-being*
My hairt on thee is sett   *is fixed on you*
115   And evirmair to thee be leill   *hereafter to be true to you*
Quhill I may leif but lett,   *As long as; without hindrance*
Nevir to faill as uthiris feill,   *others fell*
Quhat grace that evir I gett."   *Whatever favor I receive*
"Robene with thee I will nocht deill.   *not have dealings*
120   Adew, for thus we mett."   *Farewell, since we have met in this way*

Malkyne went hame blyth anneuche   *happy enough*
Attour the holttis hair   *Across; gray woods*
Robene murnit and Malkyne lewche,   *mourned; laughed*
Scho sang, he sichit sair,   *sighed bitterly*
125   And so left him bayth wo and wewche   *both sorrow and injury*
In dolour and in cair   *misery; sorrow*
Kepand his hird under a huche   *flock; cliff*
Amangis the holtis hair.   *Among*

The Bludy Serk   *Bloodstained Shirt*

This hindir yeir, I hard be tald,   *last year; heard it told*
Thair was a worthy king.   *There; honorable*
Dukis, erlis, and barronis bald   *Dukes, earls; bold barons*
He had at his bidding.   *command*
5   The lord was anceane and ald   *ancient; old*
And sexty yeiris cowth ring.   *sixty years did reign*
He had a dochter fair to fald,   *daughter; embrace*
A lusty lady ying.   *lovely young lady*

Of all fairheid scho bur the flour   *beauty she bore; flower*
10   And eik hir faderis air,   *And [was] also; father's heir*
Of lusty laitis and he honour   *charming manners; high*
Meik bot and debonair.   *But meek; gracious*
Scho wynnit in a bigly bour,   *dwelt; imposing dwelling*
On fold wes none so fair.   *In the world was*
15   Princis luvit hir paramour   *loved her in amorous attraction*
In cuntreis our allquhair.   *countries everywhere around*

Thair dwelt a lyt besyde the king   *short distance near*
A fowll gyane of ane.   *one surpassingly horrible giant*
Stollin he hes the lady ying,   *Abducted; has; young*
20   Away with hir is gane   *has gone*
And kest hir in his dungering   *threw; dungeon*

Quhair licht scho micht se nane.   *Where light she could; none*
Hungir and cauld and grit thristing   *cold; great thirst*
Scho fand into hir wane.   *discovered; accommodation*

25   He wes the laithliest on to luk   *most loathsome to look on*
That on the grund mycht gang.   *ground could walk*
His nailis wes lyk ane hellis cruk,   *were like a hook from hell*
Thairwith fyve quarteris lang.   *At that, an ell and a quarter*
Thair wes nane that he ourtuk   *no one; captured*
30   In rycht or yit in wrang   *right; yet; wrong*
Bot all in schondir he thame schuke,   *into pieces he shook them*
The gyane wes so strang.   *giant; strong*

He held the lady day and nycht   *night*
Within his deip dungeoun.   *deep*
35   He wald nocht gif of hir a sicht   *would not allow; a glimpse*
For gold nor yit ransoun   *ransom*
Bot gife the king mycht get a knycht   *Unless; could; knight*
To fecht with his persoun,   *fight; himself*
To fecht with him both day and nycht
40   Quhill ane wer dungin doun.   *Until one [of them] were struck down*

The king gart seik baith fer and neir,   *ordered to seek both far*
Beth be se and land,   *Both by sea*
Of ony knycht gife he micht heir   *Of any; if; could hear*
Wald fecht with that gyand.   *[Who] would fight; giant*
45   A worthy prince that had no peir   *equal*
Hes tane the deid on hand   *Has taken; deed in*
For the luve of the lady cleir,   *love; lovely lady*
And held full trew cunnand.   *kept most loyally [his] vow*

That prince come prowdly to the toun   *came proudly; town*
50   Of that gyane to heir   *To learn about that giant*
And fawcht with him his awin persoun   *fought; [in] his own person*
And tuke him presoneir   *took him prisoner*
And kest him in his awin dungeoun,   *threw*
Allane withouttin feir,   *Alone without companion*
55   With hungir, cauld, and confusioun   *dismay*
As full weill worthy weir.   *deserving were*

Syne brak the bour, had hame the bricht   *Then broke into the chamber; returned; maid*
Unto hir fadir deir.   *father dear*
Sa evill wondit was the knycht   *sorely wounded*
60   That he behuvit to de,   *was bound to die*
Unlusum was his likame dicht,   *Horrible; body made*
His sark was all bludy.   *shirt; bloodstained*

In all the warld was thair a wicht	*there; person*
So peteous for to sy?	*pitiful; see*

65	The lady murnyt and maid grit mone	*mourned; made great lament*
	With all hir mekle micht,	*great strength*
	"I luvit nevir lufe bot one,	*loved; a love except one*
	That dulfully now is dicht.	*sorrowfully; mistreated*
	God sen my lyfe wer fra me tone	*if only; were taken from me*
70	Or I had sene yone sicht	*Before; seen that sight*
	Or ellis in begging evir to gone	*else; forever; go*
	Furth with yone curtas knycht."	*From hence; that courteous*

	He said, "Fair lady, now mone I de,	*must; die*
	Trestly ye me trow.	*Believe you me completely*
75	Tak ye my sark that is bludy	*Take my shirt*
	And hing it forrow yow.	*hang; in front of you*
	First think on it and syne on me	*then*
	Quhen men cumis yow to wow."	*When; come to court you*
	The lady said, "Be Mary fre,	*By gracious Mary*
80	Thairto I mak a vow."	*make*

	Quhen that scho lukit to the serk,	*When; she looked; shirt*
	Scho thocht on the persoun	*thought about; person*
	And prayit for him with all hir harte	*prayed; heart*
	That lowsd hir of bandoun,	*freed her from captivity*
85	Quhair scho was wont to sit full merk	*Where she; used; dark*
	In that deip dungeoun,	
	And evir quhill scho wes in quert	*while she was in health*
	That was hir a lessoun.	*for her; lesson*

	Sa weill the lady luvit the knycht	*So well; loved; knight*
90	That no man wald scho tak.	*would she accept*
	Sa suld we do our God of micht	*So should; our mighty God*
	That did all for us mak,	*Who; everything; create*
	Quhilk fullely to deid wes dicht	*Who foully was put to death*
	For sinfull manis saik,	*sake*
95	Sa suld we do both day and nycht	*So should*
	And prayaris to him mak.	

	Moralitas	*Moralization*
	This king is lyke the Trinitie	*like; Trinity*
	Baith in hevin and heir,	*Both; here*
	The manis saule to the lady,	*soul of man*
100	The gyane to Lucefeir,	*giant; Lucifer*
	The knycht to Chryst that deit on tre	*died; cross*
	And coft our synnis deir,	*paid for; costly sins*

The pit to hell with panis fell,   *dungeon; dreadful torments*
The syn to the woweir.   *sin; wooer*

105   The lady was wowd bot scho said nay   *wooed*
With men that wald hir wed,   *To; wanted to marry her*
Sa suld we wryth all syn away   *As we should deflect*
That in our breist is bred.   *breast*
I pray to Jesu Chryst verrey   *truly Christ*
110   For us his blud that bled   *who gave his blood*
To be our help on Domysday   *the Day of Judgment*
Quhair lawis ar straitly led.   *On which; strictly applied*

The saule is Godis dochtir deir   *dear daughter*
And eik his handewerk   *also; creation*
115   That was betrasit with Lucifeir   *betrayed by*
Quha sittis in hell full merk   *Who sits; dark*
Borrowit with Chrystis angell cleir.   *Rescued by; bright angel*
Hend men will ye nocht herk,   *Kind; not pay heed*
For his lufe that bocht us deir.   *who redeemed us dearly*
120   Think on the bludy serk.

The Garmont of Gud Ladeis   *Clothing; Good Ladies*

Wald my gud lady lufe me best   *If my beloved were to show me the best kind of love*
And wirk eftir my will,   *act according to my wishes*
I suld ane garmond gudliest   *would a most noble garment*
Gar mak hir body till.   *Have made for her body*

5   Of he honour suld be hir hud   *Of high; should; her hood*
Upoun hir heid to weir.   *To wear on her head*
Garneist with govirnance so gud,   *Arrayed; self-command*
Na demyng suld hir deir.   *suspicion; threaten her*

Hir sark suld be hir body nixt   *chemise; nearest to her body*
10   Of chestetie so quhyt   *chastity; white*
With schame and dreid togidder mixt,   *modesty; fear together*
The same suld be perfyt.   *perfect*

Hir kirtill suld be of clene constance   *petticoat; pure faithfulness*
Lasit with lesum lufe,   *Laced; lawful love*
15   The mailyeis of continuance   *eyelets; perseverance*
For nevir to remufe.   *depart*

Hir gown suld be of gudlines   *goodness*
Weill ribband with renowne   *Well ribboned; reputation*

	Purfillit with plesour in ilk place,	Bordered; pleasure; each
20	Furrit with fyne fassoun.	Furred; exquisite style

	Hir belt suld be of benignitie	kindness
	Abowt hir middill meit,	Around; waist well-fitting
	Hir mantill of humilitie	cloak
	To tholl bayth wind and weit.	withstand both; wet

25	Hir hat suld be of fair having	fine behavior
	And hir tepat of trewth,	short cape; constancy
	Hir patelet of gud pansing,	bodice; meditation
	Hir hals ribbane of rewth.	throat-ribbon; pity

	Hir slevis suld be of esperance	sleeves; hope
30	To keip hir fra dispair,	protect her from despair
	Hir gluvis of gud govirnance	gloves; discipline
	To hyd hir fynyearis fair.	conceal her fair fingers

	Hir schone suld be of sickernes	shoes; stability
	In syne that scho nocht slyd	sin so that; not slide
35	Hir hois of honestie, I ges,	stockings; suppose
	I suld for hir provyd.	provide for her

	Wald scho put on this garmond gay,	If she would; fine clothing
	I durst sweir by my seill	dare swear; salvation
	That scho woir nevir grene nor gray	never wore green
40	That set hir half so weill.	suited; well

The Praise of Age

	Wythin a garth under a rede rosere	closed garden; red rosebush
	Ane ald man and decrepit herd I syng.	A feeble old man I heard sing
	Gay was the note, swete was the voce and clere,	Pleasant; tune; voice
	It was grete joy to here of sik a thing,	hear such
5	And to my dome he said in his dytyng	understanding; song
	"For to be yong, I wald not, for my wis,	young; would not want; wish
	Of all this warld to mak me lord and king.	make myself
	The more of age, the nerar hevynnis blis.	nearer heaven's bliss

	False is this warld and full of variance	world; inconstancy
10	Besoucht with syn and othir sytis mo.	Beset; sin; many other ills
	Treuth is all tynt, gyle has the gouvernance,	utterly lost, guile; control
	Wrechitnes has wroht all welthis wele to wo,	Miserliness; turned; benefit
	Fredome is tynt and flemyt the lordis fro,	Generosity; banished
	And covatise is all the cause of this.	covetousness; entirely

15 I am content that youthede is ago.   *youth; past*
    The more of age, the nerar hevynnis blisse.

    The state of youth I repute for na gude   *consider to be no good*
    For in that state sik perilis now I see   *such perils*
    Bot full smal grace. The regeing of his blude   *very little; raging; blood*
20 Can none gaynstand quhill that he agit be,   *withstand until; be aged*
    Syne of the thing that tofore joyit he   *Then; previously he enjoyed*
    Nothing remaynis for to be callit his,   *remains; called his own*
    For quhy it were bot veray vanitee.   *Because; was only utter*
    The more of age, the nerar hevynnis blisse

25 Suld no man traist this wrechit warld, for quhy   *No one should trust; because*
    Of erdly joy ay sorow is the end,   *earthly; always*
    The state of it can no man certify,   *guarantee*
    This day a king, tomorne na gude to spend.   *tomorrow no wealth*
    Quhat have we here bot grace us to defend   *What; without*
30 The quhilk God grant us for to mend oure mys   *which; pay for our crimes*
    That to his glore he may oure saulis send.   *glory; send our souls*
    The more of age, the nerar hevynnis blisse.

The Abbey Walk

Allone as I went up and doun	*Alone; walked*
In ane abbay wes fair to se	*[that] was; see*
Thinkand quhat consolatioun	*Considering what*
Wes best into adversitie,	*Was; in*
5 On cais I kest on syd myne e	*By chance I directed my sight to one side*
And saw this writtin upoun a wall,	*written on*
"Of quhat estait, man, that thow be,	*Of whatever rank; you*
Obey and thank thi God of all."	*your; for everything*
Thy kindome and thy grit empyre,	*kingdom; great*
10 Thy ryeltie nor rich array	*royalty; clothing*
Sall nocht indure at thi desyre	*Shall not endure*
Bot as the wind will wend away.	*But; pass*
Thy gold and all thi gudis gay	*your fine belongings*
Quhen Fortoun list will fra thee fall.	*wishes; fall away from you*
15 Sen thow sic sampillis seis ilk day,	*Since; such examples seest each*
Obey and thank thi God of all.	
Job was moist riche, in writ we find,	*most; scripture*
Thobe moist full of cheretie.	*Tobit; charity*
Job wox peur and Thoby blynd,	*became poor*
20 Baith temptit with adversitie.	*Both provoked by*
Sen blindnes wes infirmitie	*was a disability*
And povertie was naturall,	*inevitable*
Thairfoir in patience baith he and he	*Therefore*
Obeid and thankit God of all.	*Obeyed; thanked*
25 Thocht thow be blind or haif ane halt	*Though you; have a limp*
Or in thy face deformit ill,	*[are] seriously deformed*
Sa it cum nocht throw thy defalt,	*If; through; fault*
Na man sowld thee repreif by skill.	*should condemn you according to reason*
Blame nocht thy Lord sa is his will.	*[that] his will is thus*
30 Spur nocht thy fute aganis the wall	*Kick; against*
Bot with meik hairt and prayar still	*meek heart; continually*
Obey and thank thy God of all.	

God of his justice mon correct   *[because] of; must*
And of his mercy petie haif.   *[must] have pity*
35 He is ane juge to nane suspect   *a judge mistrusted by no one*
To puneis synffull man and saif.   *punish; save*
Thocht thow be lord attouir the laif   *Though; above the rest*
And eftirwart maid bund and thrall,   *made captive and enslaved*
Ane peure begger with skrip and staif,   *poor beggar; pouch; staff*
40 Obey and thank thy God of all.

This changeing and grit variance   *great mutability*
Of erdly staitis up and doun   *worldly ranks*
Cumis nocht throw casualtie and chance   *Happens not by accident*
As sum men sayis without ressoun,
45 Bot be the grit provisioun   *according to the great foresight*
Of God aboif that rewill thee sall.   *above who rule*
Thairfoir evir thow mak thee boun   *make yourself ready*
To obey and thank thy God of all.

In welth be meik, heiche not thyself,   *meek, do not exalt*
50 Be glaid in wilfull povertie.   *glad; willing*
Thy power and thy warldlie pelf   *worldly possessions*
Is nocht bot verry vanitie.   *nothing; utter*
Remembir him that on the tre   *cross*
For thy saik gustit bittir gall   *tasted bitter*
55 Quha hyis law and lawis he.   *Who exalts the low; lowers [the] high*
Obey and thank thy God of all."

Ane Prayer for the Pest   *Plague*

O eterne God of power infinyt   *eternal; infinite power*
To quhois hie knawlege nathink is obscure,   *whose; nothing*
That is or wes or salbe is perfyt   *Whatever; shall be; complete*
Into thi sicht quhill that this warld indure,   *In your sight as long as*
5   Haif mercy of us, indigent and pure.   *Have; on; poor*
Thow dois no wrang to punis our offens.   *wrong in punishing our offense*
O lord that is to mankynd haill succure,   *complete help*
Preserve us fra this perrelus pestilens.   *from; dangerous pestilence*

We thee beseik, O lord of lordis all,   *beseech you*
10 Thy eiris inclyne and heir our grit regrait.   *ears; hear; great distress*
We ask remeid of thee in generall   *aid in general from you*
That is of help and confort dissolait.   *Who are; destitute*
Bot thow with rewth our hairtis recreate,   *Unless; pity; restore*
We ar bot deid but only thy clemens.   *merely dead without; mercy*
15 We thee exort on kneis law prostrait,   *beg; low in humility*
Preserve us from this perrellus pestilens.

We ar rycht glaid thow punis our trespas   *very glad; punish; sins*
Be ony kynd of udir tribulatioun,   *By any; other*
Wer it thy will, O lord of hevin, allais,   *If it were your intention; alas*
20   That we suld thus be haistely put doun   *should; quickly exterminated*
And de as beistis without confessioun,   *die like beasts*
That nane dar mak with udir residens.   *no one dare live with another*
O blissit Jesu that wore the thorny croun   *blessed; crown of thorns*
Preserve us from this perrelus pestilens.

25   Use derth, O lord, or seiknes and hungir soir   *famine; sickness; keen hunger*
And slak thy plaig that is so penetryfe.   *diminish; plague; piercing*
The pepill ar perreist quha may remeid thairfoir.   *killed who could cure it*
Bot thow, O lord, that for thame lost thy lyfe.   *Except you; them; life*
Suppois our syne be to thee pungetyfe,   *Granted; offensive to you*
30   Our deid ma nathing our synnis recompens.   *death cannot; recompense*
Haif mercy, lord, we may nocht with thee stryfe,   *cannot strive against you*
Preserve us fra this perrelus pestilens.

Haif mercy, lord, haif mercy, hevins king,   *Have; heaven's*
Haif mercy of thy pepill penitent,   *on your penitent people*
35   Haif mercy of our petous punissing,   *pitiful punishment*
Retreit the sentence and thy just jugement   *Commute; fitting judgment*
Aganis us synnaris that servis to be schent.   *Against; sinners; deserve; destroyed*
Without mercy, we may mak no defens.   *can; defense*
Thow that but rewth upoun the rud wes rent,   *without pity upon; cross; torn*
40   Preserve us frome this perrellus pestilens.

Remembir, lord, how deir thow hes us bocht   *expensively; paid for us*
That for us synnaris sched thy pretius blude,   *shed; precious blood*
Now to redeme that thow hes maid of nocht,   *what; made out of nothing*
That is of virtew barran and denude.   *barren and naked of virtue*
45   Haif rewth, lord, of thyn awin similitude.   *Have mercy; on; own likeness*
Punis with pety and nocht with violens.   *Punish; pity; not*
We knaw it is for our ingratitude   *know*
That we are punist with this pestillens.

Thow grant us grace for till amend our mis   *respite to; wickedness*
50   And till evaid this crewall suddane deid.   *to evade; cruel; death*
We knaw our sin is all the caus of this.   *the complete cause for*
For opin sin thair is set no remeid.   *manifest; no redress assigned*
The justice of God mon punis than be deid   *must; therefore with death*
For by the law he will with nane dispens.   *make allowance for no one*
55   Quhair justice laikis, thair is eternall feid   *is lacking, there; feud*
Of God that suld preserf fra pestilens.   *who should preserve*

Bot wald the heidismen that suld keip the law   *chief men; should maintain*
Punis the peple for thair transgressioun,   *Punish; their*

	Thair wald na deid the peple than ourthraw,	*There; no death; then destroy*
60	Bot thay ar gevin sa plenly to oppressioun	*addicted so manifestly*
	That God will nocht heir thair intercessioun,	*not hear their entreaty*
	Bot all ar punist for inobediens	*are punished; disobedience*
	Be swerd or deid withouttin remissioun,	*By sword; forgiveness*
	And hes just caus to send us pestilens.	*has*

65	**S**uperne lucerne, guberne this pestilens	*Highest lamp, control*
	Preserve and serve that we nocht sterf thairin,	*Protect; aid; not die*
	Declyne that pyne be thy devyne prudens,	*Reduce; torment by*
	For treuth, haif reuth, lat nocht our slewth us twyn.	*loyalty; pity; sloth part us*
	Our syte full tyte, wer we contryt, wald blin.	*ills very soon; would cease*
70	Dissivir did nevir quha euir thee besocht	*Perish; whoever begged you*
	But grace with space for to arrace fra sin.	*Without [there being] grace with [sufficient] time*
	Lat nocht be tint that thow sa deir hes bocht.	*Let nothing; lost; dearly*

	O prince preclair, this cair quotidiane,	*illustrious; daily trouble*
	We thee exort, distort it in exyle.	*beg you; avert; exile*
75	Bot thow remeid, this deid is bot ane trane	*Unless; help; merely a trap*
	For to dissaif the laif and thame begyle,	*deceive the others; trick them*
	Bot thow sa wyse, devyse to mend this byle,	*contrive; boil*
	Of this mischeif quha may releif us ocht	*From; who can relieve; at all*
	For wrangus win, bot thow our sin oursyle?	*ill-gotten gains unless; cover*
80	Lat nocht be tint that thow sa deir hes bocht.	

	Sen for our vice that justice mon correct,	*As for; must*
	O king most he, now pacife thy feid.	*high; soothe your anger*
	Our sin is huge, refuge we nocht suspect.	*we do not expect protection*
	And thow be juge, dislug us of this steid.	*If; remove; from this plight*
85	In tyme assent or we be schent with deid,	*Relent in time before; ruined by death*
	For we repent, all tyme mispent forthocht.	*misused time regretted*
	Thairfoir evirmor be gloir to thy godheid.	*glory be to your divine power*
	Lat nocht be tint that thow sa deir hes bocht.	

	The Ressoning betwix Deth and Man	*Dialogue between Death*

Mors	**O** mortall man behald, tak tent to me	*Death; behold, pay attention*
	Quhilk sall thi myrrour be baith day and nycht.	*Who shall; both; night*
	All erdly thing that evir tuke lyfe mon de.	*earthly; came to life must die*
	Paip, empriour, king, barroun, and knycht,	*Pope; knight*
5	Thocht thai be in thair ryell estait and hicht,	*Though; royal state; greatness*
	May nocht ganestand quhen I pleis schote this derte.[1]	

---

[1] *May not withstand when I choose to shoot this dart*

| | Waltownis, castellis, towiris nevir so wicht | *Walled towns; ever; strong* |
| | May nocht resist quhill it be at his hart. | *Cannot; until* |

Homo   Now quhat art thow that biddis me thus tak tent   *Man; what; you; commands; pay heed*
10   And mak ane myrrour day and nycht of thee
         Or with thi dert I suld rycht sair repent?   *very bitterly regret*
         I trest trewly of that that thow sall le.   *trust indeed; do lie*
         Quhat freik on fold sa bald dar manniss me   *What man on earth so bold; threaten*
         Or with me fecht outhir on fute or hors?   *fight with me either; foot*
15   Is none so wicht, so stark, in this cuntré   *strong; powerful*
         Nor I sall gar him bow to me on fors.   *That; not make; perforce*

Mors   My name at me forsuth sen that thow speirs,   *from; indeed since you ask*
         Tha call me Deid, suthly I thee declair,   *They; Death, truly*
         Calland all man and woman to thair beirs   *Calling; their biers*
20   Quhenevir I pleis, quhat tyme, quhat plais, or quhair.   *Whenever; please, place; where*
         Is nane sa stowt, sa fresch, nor yit sa fair,   *none so strong; brisk; yet*
         So yung, so auld, so riche, nor yit so pure,   *young; old; poor*
         Quhairevir I pas, outhir be it lait or air,   *Wherever; go; whether; early*
         Man put thaim heill on fors under my cure.   *Must; themselves wholly; rule*

Homo   Sen it is swa that natur can so wirk   *Since; thus; work*
26   That yung and auld, riche and pur man de,   *must die*
         Inn my youtheid allace I wes full irk,   *In; youth alas; stubborn*
         Culd nocht tak tent to gyd and govern me,   *Could not; heed; myself*
         Ay gud to do, fra evill deidis to fle,   *Always good; from; deeds; flee*
30   Trestand ay youtheid wald with me abyd,   *Trusting always; would; stay*
         Fulfilland evir my sensualitie,   *Indulging always*
         In deidly syn and speacialy in pryd.   *mortal; especially*

Mors   Thairfoir repent and remord thi conscience,   *examine your*
         Think on thir wirdis I now upoun thee cry: *about these words*
35   O wrechit man, O full of ignorance,   *wretched*
         All thi plesance thow sall deir aby.   *your pleasure; shall pay dearly for*
         Dispone for thee and cum with me in hy,   *Arrange; yourself; come; haste*
         Edderis, askis, wirmes meit to be.   *Snakes', newts', worms' food*
         Cum quhen I call, thow may me nocht deny   *when; cannot refuse me*
40   Thocht thow wer paip, empriour, and king al thre.   *Though; pope; all three*

Homo   Sen it is swa fra thee I may nocht chaip,   *Since; so [that] from; escape*
         This wrechit warld for me heir I defy   *wretched; here; renounce*
         And to the deid to lurk undir thi caip   *death; your cloak*
         I offir me with hairt rycht hummilly,   *myself; heart; very humbly*
45   Beseikand God the devill my enemy   *Beseeching; [that] the devil*
         Na power haif my saule till assay.   *Have no power; soul; attack*
         Jesus, on thee with peteous voce I cry   *to you; pitiful voice*
         Mercy one me to haif on Domisday.   *on me to have; Doomsday*

The Thre Deid Pollis   *Three Dead Skulls*

    O sinfull man into this mortall se   *in this earthly realm*
    Quhilk is the vaill of murnyng and of cair,   *Which; vale; sorrow; woe*
    With gaistly sicht behold oure heidis thre,   *fearful eyes; three heads*
    Oure holkit ene, oure peilit pollis bair.   *hollowed eyes; skinned; bare*
5   As ye ar now, into this warld we wair,   *you are, in; world were we*
    Als fresche, als fair, als lusty to behald.   *As lively; attractive; see*
    Quhan thow lukis on this suth examplair,   *When; looks; true example*
    Of thyself, man, thow may be richt unbald.   *For; very apprehensive*

    For suth it is that every man mortall   *true; mortal man*
10   Mon thole the deid and de that lyfe hes tane.[1]
    Na erdly stait aganis deid ma prevaill.   *No earthly; against; can win*
    The hour of deth and place is uncertane   *uncertain*
    Quhilk is referrit to the hie God allane.   *Which; entrusted; high; alone*
    Heirfoir haif mynd of deth, that thow mon dy.   *Thus have; must die*
15   This sair exampill to se quotidiane   *painful; see each day*
    Sould caus all men fra wicket vycis fle.   *Should; from wicked; to flee*

    O wantone youth, als fresche as lusty May,   *lascivious; lively; pleasant*
    Farest of flowris renewit, quhyt and reid,   *flowers fresh grown, white*
    Behald our heidis, O lusty gallandis gay.   *Behold; heads; lusty, merry young men*
20   Full laithly thus sall ly thy lusty heid,   *Just as hideously shall lie*
    Holkit and how and wallowit as the weid.   *Eyeless; hollow; faded; weed*
    Thy crampand hair and eik thy cristall ene   *curly; also; crystal eyes*
    Full cairfully conclud sall dulefull deid.   *Very sadly woeful death shall bring to an end*
    Example heir be us it may be sene.   *here in us; seen*

25   O ladeis quhyt in claithis corruscant,   *ladies white; glittering clothes*
    Poleist with perle and mony pretius stane,   *Shining; pearls; precious stone*
    With palpis quhyt and hals so elegant,   *breasts; throat*
    Sirculit with gold and sapheris mony ane,   *Encircled; sapphires many*
    Your finyearis small, quhyt as quhailis bane,   *slender fingers; whalebone*
30   Arrayit with ringis and mony rubeis reid,   *Arrayed; red rubies*
    As we ly thus so sall ye ly ilk ane   *lie; shall; each one*
    With peilit pollis and holkit thus your heid.   *flayed skulls; hollowed*

    O wilfull pryd, the rute of all distres,   *source; distress*
    With humill hairt upoun our pollis pens.   *humble heart about; meditate*
35   Man, for thy mis ask mercy with meiknes.   *wrongs; meekness*
    Aganis deid na man may mak defens.   *Against death; withstand*
    The empriour for all his excellens,
    King and quene and eik all erdly stait,   *also every earthly rank*

---

[1] *Must suffer the death and die who has taken on life*

Peure and riche salbe but differens,   *Poor; shall be without distinction*
40   Turnit in as and thus in erd translait.   *Turned into ash; transformed into earth*

This questioun quha can obsolve, lat see,   *who; answer; may he adjudge*
Quhat phisnamour or perfyt palmester: *What face-reader; palmist*
Quha was farest or fowlest of us thre   *Who; prettiest; ugliest*
Or quhilk of us of kin was gentillar   *which; of more noble a family*
45   Or maist expert in science or in lare,   *most; knowledge; learning*
In art musik or in astronomye?   *musical art*
Heir still sould ly your study and repair   *Here always; lie; destination*
And think as thus all your heidis mon be.   *like this; heads must be*

O febill aige, ay drawand neir the dait   *age, always approaching; date*
50   Of dully deid and hes thy dayis compleit,   *dismal death; has; finished*
Behald our heidis with murning and regrait,   *distress*
Fall on thy kneis, ask grace at God, and greit   *mercy; from; weep*
With orisionis and haly salmes sweit,   *prayers; holy, sweet psalms*
Beseikand him on thee to haif mercy,   *Begging*
55   And of our saulis bydand the decreit   *souls awaiting judgment*
Of his godheid, to rew and glorife.   *divine power; pity; exalt*

Als we exhort that every man mortall,   *Furthermore*
For his saik that maid of nocht all thing,   *sake who made everything from nothing*
For mercy cry and pray in generall   *Cry for mercy*
60   To Jesus Chryst of hevin and erd the king,   *the king of heaven and earth*
Throuch your prayar that we and ye may ring   *Through; reign*
With the hie Fader be eternitie,   *high; for eternity*
The Sone alswa, the Haly Gaist conding,   *son also; Holy Spirit of equal rank*
Thre knit in ane be perfyt unitie.   *Three; one by*

🌿 EXPLANATORY NOTES

ABBREVIATIONS: Bartholomaeus: Bartholomaeus Anglicus, *On the Properties of Things*; **Bs**: the Bassandyne Print; *CA*: Gower, *Confessio Amantis*; **Consolation**: Boethius, *The Consolation of Philosophy*; *CT*: Chaucer, *Canterbury Tales*; *DOST*: *Dictionary of the Older Scottish Tongue*; *DSL*: *Dictionary of the Scots Language*; *Eneados*: Douglas, *Eneados*; **Fox, ed.**: *The Poems of Robert Henryson*, ed. Fox; **Gray**: Gray, *Robert Henryson*; *MED*: *Middle English Dictionary*; **MSc**: Middle Scots; *NIMEV*: Boffey and Edwards, eds., *New Index of Middle English Verse*; **NPT**: Chaucer, *Nun's Priest's Tale*; *OED*: *Oxford English Dictionary*; **OFr**: Old French; *Orpheus*: Henryson, *Orpheus and Eurydice*; **Perry**: Perry, ed., *Babrius and Phaedrus*; *PF*: Chaucer, *Parliament of Fowls*; **Romaunt**: Chaucer, *Romaunt of the Rose*; *RR*: Guillaume de Lorris and Jean de Meun, *Romance of the Rose*; **Testament**: Henryson, *The Testament of Cresseid*; *TC*: Chaucer, *Troilus and Criseyde*; **Whiting**: Whiting, *Proverbs, Sentences, and Proverbial Phrases*.

FABLES (*NIMEV* 3703)

As attested in the print tradition, Henryson's *Fables* is a set of thirteen moralized tales headed by a Prologue. In large part, these tales are drawn from a curricular text of the Middle Ages, a collection of fables in Latin distichs (couplets), which has been identified in various ways: by its supposed author, Gualterus Anglicus (Walter of England); by its first modern editor, *Anonymus Neveleti* ("[Isaac] Nevelet's 'Anonymous'"); or by its medieval name, *Romulus*. The tenth-century *Romulus* is based on the first-century collection of Latin fables by Phaedrus, a Thracian freedman of the emperor Augustus; and Phaedrus begins his collection with the declaration "Aesopus auctor quam materiam repperit" ("Aesop is my source. He invented the substance of these fables"; Perry, pp. lxxiii–lxxxii, 190–91). *Romulus* contributed in the late twelfth century to the *Fables* of Marie de France, and to the French collections known as *Isopets* (Marie, *Fables*, p. 7). The fables in most of these derivations uphold the extreme brevity of the genre — *De gallo et jaspide* (*The Cock and the Jasp*) is a mere four distichs of tale and one of moral in *Romulus*; Marie completes this fable and its moral in eleven octosyllabic couplets. Early in the fifteenth century, John Lydgate turned to *Romulus* for his little sequence of *Isopes Fabules*. As presented in the print tradition, Henryson's *Fables* contains three sequences of fables from *Romulus*: at the beginning, the Prologue, *The Cock and the Jasp*, and *The Two Mice*; in the middle, *The Sheep and the Dog*, *The Lion and the Mouse* with its own prologue, and *The Preaching of the Swallow*; at the end, *The Wolf and the Lamb* and *The Paddock and the Mouse*. As is common to the tradition, each of Henryson's *Fables* ends with a *Moralitas*, a section in which the characters and events in the narrative are subjected to literal and allegorical moralization that sometimes challenges the present-day reader. Henryson draws inventively and learnedly on a rich tradition of scholastic commentary on "Aesop," that is, *Romulus*, especially as that tradition was disseminated in the *Auctores octo morales* ("Eight Moral Authors"): the *Distichs of Cato*, the *Eclogue* of Theodulus, the *Facetus* and *De contemptu*

159

mundi by Bernard of Cluny, the *Liber Floretus*, the *Tobias* of Matthew of Vendôme, Alan of Lille's *Doctrinale altum parabolarum*, and finally the *Romulus* "Aesop." This collection of textbooks underpinned the elementary curriculum in medieval Europe.

In two sections inset into the overarching Aesopian sequence, Henryson's *Fables* in the print tradition include two groups of tales about foxes and wolves, drawn largely from the tradition of Reynard the Fox circulating from the twelfth century in Latin (the mock-epic *Ysengrimus* by Nivardus) and French (the many-branched compilation known as *Le Roman de Renart*, ca. 1175–1250, with later sequels); Chaucer's Nun's Priest's Tale comes from this tradition and provided Henryson a source for the first of his fables about foxes, *The Cock and the Fox*. Incorporation of Reynardian stories into collections of "Aesop" was well established by the time Henryson undertook to do so: Marie de France included such material (Marie, *Fables*, p. 7), as did Odo of Cheriton, whose *Fables* (dated 1225–40) appear to have been available to Henryson. A stimulus to such incorporation came in 1476–77, with Heinrich Steinhöwel's printing of his bilingual (Latin and German) schooltext *Esopus*, translated into French by Julien Macho (1480) and into English by William Caxton (1483–84; Davies, "Tale of Two Aesops"). Steinhöwel included seventeen so-called *fabulae extravagantes* in his collection, among them versions of "The Fox, the Wolf, and the Husbandman" and "The Wolf and the Wether." The term *extravagantes* (literally, "wandering outside") is usually associated with extra-canonical papal decrees, outside the Decree of Gratian and the *Corpus Juris*; in other words, the *fabulae extravagantes* ("non-canonical fables") have the same relation to Aesop as do the *Extravagantes* to the *Decretales* that formed the basis of the canon law for which Henryson, if the records pertain, received a degree at the University of Glasgow and which he appears to have practiced as a notary public in Dunfermline (see Introduction, page 2, above).

Henryson's handling of his sources for the *Fables* thus reveals a deep familiarity with the Aesopic tradition as embodied in the *Romulus* of the medieval curriculum, as well as a keen awareness of recent developments in the incorporation of extra-canonical material into the printed "Aesop" (Wheatley, *Mastering Aesop*, pp. 150–56, 162; Lyall, "Henryson's *Moral Fabillis*," pp. 89–90). The ways in which Henryson's *Fables* were received by generations of Scottish readers can be glimpsed in the short poem with which the young Edinburgh merchant George Bannatyne begins the fifth part of his manuscript anthology, devoted to "the Fabillis of Esop, with divers uthir fabillis and poeticall workis . . . 156[6]8" (fol. 298r):

To the Redar.	
My freindis, thir storeis subsequent,	*these stories*
Albeid bot fabillis thay present,	*Although only*
Yit devyne doctouris of jugement	*Yet learned doctors of theology*
Sayis thair ar hid, but dowt,	*there; without doubt*
Grave materis wyis and sapient	*Serious; thoughtful*
Under the workis of poyetis gent.	*noble poets*
Thairfoir be war that thow consent	*be careful that you [don't] fall into the habit(?)*
To blame thir heir set owt.	*criticize these [that are] set forth here*

The allusions to "devyne doctouris" and concealed "Grave materis" indicate that, with a century and the Reformation separating him from Henryson's original composition of the *Fables*, Bannatyne still relishes the propriety of scholastic commentary's revealing the sudden conceptual leaps from within the vivid, even racy narrative.

Though still a matter for debate, the structural integrity of the *Fables* is being rediscovered in, for instance, the thematic significance of numbers: the thematic focus of the midmost lines in *The Preaching of the Swallow* and *The Lion and the Mouse*; the symbolic value of the numbers of stanzas, as in *The Fox, the Wolf, and the Cadger* (see the Explanatory Notes to lines 1461, 1754, and 2021–22). Indeed, the thematic consistency that emerges as the *Fables* unfold provides a powerful argument for their structural integrity (Greentree, *Reader*, pp. 81–89). Also subject to continued debate is the topicality of the *Fables*, the argument having been proffered that some passages allude to specific events. Summarizing Denton Fox's "brilliant account of the overall meaning of Henryson's selection and arrangement," Annabel Patterson notes that the structure of the *Fables* "illustrates the tragic ambivalence of Aesopian tradition with respect to its own powers of persuasion" (*Fables of Power*, p. 162n25).

A consideration of the text of the *Fables* should take as its primary tenet that "quite different textual traditions" are represented by the Bannatyne Manuscript and the Bassandyne print respectively (Fox, ed., p. lxxv). The text provided here follows modern practice (e.g., Wood, Fox, Kindrick, Gopen) in using the Bassandyne print as its base. However, credence has been given to the arguments advanced by Jamieson, MacQueen, and Burrow for the importance of the Bannatyne Manuscript as a witness to readings explainable as having been deemed linguistically obscure or doctrinally offensive by the late sixteenth-century Scottish printers. The present editor has noted the simplifications, modernizations, and expurgations that characterize Charteris, Bassandyne, and their descendants, and at such junctures has paid particular attention to the variant readings Bannatyne offers. As well, the present text follows Fox in occasionally preferring a reading from the Charteris and Lekprevik print of the *Fables*, on the grounds that variants between the text of this print and that of Bassandyne "should be judged solely on their merits" (Fox, ed., p. lxxiv); such variants sometimes occur because one or the other printer, faced with an unfamiliar word, has substituted a familiar one with a very different meaning (e.g., *manfully* in Bs for *mane full*, line 285), or because a common sort of mistake in transcription or typesetting has occurred (e.g., *thus* in Bs for *this*, line 1873).

Prologue
Several distinguished analyses have been made of this Prologue in relation to its brief source (twelve distichs long), the Prologue to the verse *Romulus* (e.g., Fox, "Henryson's *Fables*," pp. 338–41; Fox, ed., pp. 187–94; Kratzmann, "Henryson's Fables," pp. 50–57; Spearing, *Medieval to Renaissance*, pp. 187–92). See Aaron E. Wright's edition, *The Fables of "Walter of England"* for the text of the distichs with a medieval commentary (pp. 19–23).

title. The title provided in the early printed editions shows the influence of the printed Aesops derived from Steinhöwel (including Caxton's), headed by the story of Aesop the Phrygian: for Henryson, however, Aesop is a Roman, Christian lawyer, and poet, not an illiterate, pagan Phrygian slave (lines 1371–74n; compare Gopen, *Moral Fables of Aesop*, p. 17).

1   Here and elsewhere in the edition, an initial capital letter in boldface corresponds to the marking of sections in the principal witnesses with ornamented or otherwise amplified initials.

1–7   *feinyeit fabils.* The collocation of "feign" and "fable" recurs in Scots, often with the connotation of lying (*DOST fenȝeit* 2; compare *Fables*, line 1389); that "fable" and "falsehood" might be taken as synonymous can become realized as if in passing, as the work unfolds (e.g., the apparently straight-faced aside "but fabill," "without a lie" [line 2308]); as a whole, this stanza bears comparison with the discussion of fiction in lines 1379–97 and in *Testament* (64–70n).

3   *polite termes of sweit rhetore*. For later Middle Scots poets such as Gavin Douglas and Sir David Lyndsay, this line defines the high literary style: polished words and delectable eloquence (*DOST polist* 2; *polit* 2); compare Henryson's criticism of the lawyers who "under poleit termis falset mingis" (*Fables*, line 2716).

7   *Figure* is used, as elsewhere in the *Fables* (lines 59, 1258, 1400, 1451, 1614, 1971, and *figuris* 2593; compare *figurall*, 587, 1099; *figurate*, 600, 2935), to refer to the allegorical status of a fiction in relation to the truth it in some way represents; compare *Testament* lines 506, 511.

8–14   In comparison to Chaucer with his "olde feldes" out of which "newe corn" simply "cometh" (*PF*, lines 22–23), Henryson emphasizes the sheer labor of cultivating the rich but intractable ground of fiction and language in order to produce a wholesome lesson; this work must be done repeatedly, with the reader coming after the writer like a pupil following the teacher (compare line 1734n).

10–12   In this organic image of the production and reception of a meaningful text, both the flowers and the grain are "springing"; hence, the adjectives "Hailsum and gude" refer to both as well (compare line 1904n).

15–16   Fables are traditionally justified in terms of the allegory — here, highly compressed — of the fable and moral as akin to the nutshell and its contents (compare lines 586–89). James Simpson suggests that the reading "The nuttis schell . . . is delectabill" should not be discarded hastily: "For the moralist who seeks abstract meanings in fiction, the shell is tough and the kernel sweet. For the lover of narrative, however, it's the other way around" ("Faith and Hermeneutics," pp. 225–26); the classic discussion of this figure remains Bernard Huppé and D. W. Robertson, *Fruyt and Chaf*.

17–19   Denton Fox (ed., p. 190) suggests that Stephen Hawes, an English poet at the court of Henry VII, may have imitated these lines in *The Pastime of Pleasure* (1509; lines 713–14).

20–25   In contrast to the allegory of the nutshell, the second, recreational, justification for fables may seem commonsensical but has its own curricular place (Boas and Botschuyver, *Disticha Catonis* 3.6). The allegory of the unbent bow is the latest in Henryson's sequence of brief figures; on this figure, see Glending Olson, *Literature as Recreation*, pp. 90–93.

26   *sad materis*. The mixture of merriness and seriousness seems at this juncture simply to be a matter of comic relief; subsequent events will deepen the ethical significance of the blend as a mirror of the pattern of existence (e.g., lines 193n, 331–33n, 345n, 368n, 642–43n).

28   Henryson is quoting the second line from the Prologue to *Romulus* (A. Wright, *Fables*, p. 19). H. Harvey Wood notes that "this quotation has been used as a clue in the attempt to discover Henryson's original for the fables" (*Poems and Fables*,

p. 225). It also appears on the title page of the Charteris text of the *Fables*. As becomes clear in the course of the *Fables*, mixing (which denotes augmenting but also corrupting and throwing into confusion) is a thematic as well as a stylistic principle underpinning the whole work (compare *Testament* 610–16n).

29–30   *my maisteris . . . your correctioun.* The mode of address changes (compare *thee, thi* in line 6 and *we* in line 22); modesty becomes the topic in a passage that exemplifies Machan's perception: "A diminished sense of self for both narrators and authors informs and, more importantly, *enables* Middle English writing" (*Textual Criticism*, pp. 97–98). Wheatley notes that *maisteris* is a term of address "appropriate to the classroom" (*Mastering Aesop*, p. 152); the poet is writing as if he is at school.

31–32   *In mother toung . . . translatioun.* The reference to "ane maner of translatioun" alludes tersely to the vernacular poet's power of invention: "What Henryson dramatizes, in effect, is the birth of the vernacular author whose father is literary authority and whose mother is vernacular language" (Machan, *Textual Criticism*, p. 130). Given the recent advance of Scots into the forum of official discourse (Introduction, p. 14, above), Henryson's reference to the "mother toung" is less self-deprecating than it is a tactical claim that, as a translator from Latin, the vernacular poet is advancing the right of his language to function at the center of public discourse — and the right of poetry to be situated at that center.

33–35   Lyall considers this "a typically Henrysonian touch, displacing responsibility for the idea but then declining to identify its true begetter" ("Structure," pp. 93–94); for Wheatley, the avoidance of *vane presumpcioun* entails suppression of a patron's name in the interest of a higher aim, "to glorify the spiritual [lord]" (*Mastering Aesop*, p. 153).

36–42   Such language recalls the *bustious eird* that demands cultivation if the flowers and grain are to grow (line 8, above; compare "rude and hamelie dite," line 119). The witty denial of eloquence is traditional: compare the Franklin's polished apology, *CT* V[F]718–20. Chaucer provides a precedent for the request, replete with ornate terms, for correction: *TC* 3.1331–36. Gray observes that "in asking for correction [Henryson] uses a cluster of words which are far from homely" (*Robert Henryson*, p. 83, note 13).

45–47   Priscilla Bawcutt and Felicity Riddy observe that the scholastic terms in these two lines (*dispute, argow, sillogisme, propone, conclude, exempill, similitude*) "suggest that Aesop's animals behave remarkably like academics of Henryson's day" (*Selected Poems of Henryson and Dunbar*, p. 212).

47–49   Henryson thus demonstrates the capacity of an allegory to work through inversion: people behaving like animals might be predicted to be the opposite of animals behaving like people, and yet the latter become an allegory of the former; and both phenomena involve an inversion of the proper working of creatures in their proper spheres of being.

50 ff.   "Men like beasts" is scriptural (Psalm 49 [48]:12; 2 Peter 2:12) and Boethian (*Consolation* 3.pr5; 4.pr3, me3). This statement of the unreinable tendency to sensuality anticipates but does not articulate the proverb "Like a dog to its

vomit," from 2 Peter 2:22 (compare Proverbs 26:11), the memorably graphic
conclusion of a scriptural passage that underpins this stanza; see also line 2972n.

56   The topic of humanity rendered bestial appears in the Prologues to the *Auctores
      octo*, the curricular compilation that featured "Aesop"; by this means, Henryson
      follows his source in emphasizing "the figurative nature of the poet's project"
      (Wheatley, *Mastering Aesop*, pp. 153–54).

58   Aesop's *gay metir and facound purpurat*, the distichs of *Romulus*, implicitly find
      their counterpart in Scots rhyme royal; Henryson is alluding to the legitimate
      descent from his source to his *translatioun* even as he alludes to the gulf between
      them.

59–60 Henryson indicates that fables decorously conceal topics that might otherwise
      offend classes of people, high or low; raising the topic by appearing to dismiss
      it, he refers to the satirical and polemical capacity of this sort of narrative.

61   The Prologue ends by announcing the topic of the ensuing fable; thereby the
      textual link between the two sections is strengthened, and the location of *The
      Cock and the Jasp* at the start of Henryson's *Fables* explicitly parallels its location
      in *Romulus*.

The Cock and the Jasp
Henryson's source is the first fable in the verse *Romulus* (A. Wright, *Fables*, pp. 23–26), which
is a mere four distichs long plus a single one for the *Moralitas*.

69   The term *jasp* (Latin, *jaspis*) tends to refer to various kinds of semiprecious chal-
      cedony, a stone consisting of silica and quartz: the green (prase, chrysoprase,
      plasma), green with red (heliotrope), white, banded, and multicolored (onyx),
      banded brown (agate), or gray-blue varieties have been referred to as jasp, but
      not the red varieties sardonyx and carnelian. These stones were used for seal
      impressions because wax does not stick to their lustrous, smooth surface.
      Especially in Egypt, the Middle East, and Central Asia, these stones have been
      carved into intaglios and cameos since ancient times. If, as is typical, the jasp in
      this fable is thought of as a seal, it is to be regarded as not just a valuable item
      but an authentication of the identity of its owner — like modern guarantees of
      identification, crucial but difficult to replace.

81   Specifying an "ideal possessor" for a jewel is a topic in medieval texts about
      jewels, the lapidaries (Bishop, "Lapidary Formulas," p. 476).

82   The contrast between *pietie* and *mydding* deserves comparison with Hary's diction
      when his hero Wallace is thrown onto the midden at Ayr: "Thai kest him our out
      of that bailfull steid . . . In a draff myddyn quhar he remaynt thar" (McKim,
      Wallace, 2.255–57). Also in the background is the tercel's rebuke of the duck in
      PF: "Out of the donghil cam that word ful right" (line 597).

83   *muke and mold*. With the primary sense of "dung and dirt" goes a second
      meaning by which *muke* is wealth and *mold* is the humus from which the human
      body was created (*OED muck* n.1.II.4; *mould/mold* n.1.I.2.a). In regard to the

wrongful setting of the jewel, Bishop notes the parallel with the Middle English poem *Pearl* (lines 22–24; see "Lapidary Formulas," p. 476).

86   Here and in line 100, the cock insistently rejects the allure of *cullour*; compare the "gay metir and facound purpurat" of Aesop's style (line 58).

102   An instance in which the "mother toung" (line 31) turns out to be more subtle than its user realizes, the proverb might be translated, "Looking is easy work," though the rooster, thinking only of filling his stomach, assumes that "light" means "unsubstantial"; for other instances in which the wisdom of proverbs ironically reflects on its user, see lines 1763n and 1997n.

106–12 Here is the "anaphoric climax" of the rooster's specious speech, in which he has used lapidary topics such as the ideal setting as "a substitute for thought . . . to justify his leaving well alone." In the last line of the stanza, Bishop notes especially the rooster's "self-centred" completion of his earlier remark that "thow ganis not for me" (line 80) with "nor I for thee" (line 112; see "Lapidary Formulas," p. 477).

120–26 However many properties are actually listed here (and the stanza may have been incompletely revised; Fox, ed., pp. 197–98), Henryson's account of the jasp is comparable with the discussion of this precious stone in the great medieval encyclopedia *De proprietatibus rerum* ("On the Properties of Things") by Bartholomaeus Anglicus: though "the chief colour therof be grene it hath many othere colours ymedlid among. . . . [It] dryveth away fantasies, and maketh a man siker in periles. . . . And me troweth that it hath as many vertues as dyvers colours and veynes" (XVI.52, Seymour-Smith, *On the Properties of Things*, 2:853).

129–30 The "deidis of vertew" are being described as surpassingly "excellent" in that they, like the jasp, derive from heaven.

139   In "Schir, ye have mony servitouris," Dunbar alludes to this scripturally redolent line (Matthew 6:19–20) in his insistence that his well-made verse is proof against "wering or consumptioun, / Roust, canker, or corruptioun" (lines 31–32); compare Aesop's frustration with a *roustit*, cankered world (lines 1396–97).

142–45 The passage is rich in scriptural reminiscences, beginning with the commonly cited epitome of the ignorantly mocking fool: "The fool has said in his heart, 'There is no God'" (Psalm 13 [14]:1).

146–47 Unlike the scriptural pigs goaded to violent retaliation by a diet of pearls (Matthew 7:6), this sow merely gets sick; the moralist does not engage in a preacher's full-scale denunciation of obdurate ignorance.

151   The scriptural allusion to the surpassingly valuable pearl for which the merchant sold all he owned (Matthew 13:45) makes the connection explicit between the jasp and the kingdom of heaven.

159   *Of this mater to speik, it wair bot wind.* One of many junctures at which the moralist pulls back from explicitly applying the fable to present circumstances; implicit, however, is a warning to the reader not to assume that the moral lessons to be uncovered in this work are inapplicable.

161   *thair* refers to the midden in the fable, in which the jasp was unexpectedly and
             unprofitably uncovered, but also to the actual lines of the fable in which the jasp
             is mentioned, as well as the lines in the moral in which it is interpreted.

The Two Mice

Henryson's source is the twelfth fable in the verse *Romulus* (A. Wright, *Fables*, pp. 45–49),
which at fifteen distichs for the story and one for the *Moralitas* is a trifle more expansive
than were either the Prologue or *De gallo et iaspide*. Fox surveys the key differences between
the version in *Romulus* and Henryson's: in the latter, the mice are sisters and they
experience two interruptions to their feast, one by a steward and one by a cat; both these
changes from *Romulus* occur in other versions of the fable (Fox, ed., p. 201).

166–68   No mere rehash of *Romulus*, this opening provides a telling anticipation, the
             quhyle / Quhilis construction (compare lines 331–33), as well as an emphasis on
             crime that is only partly developed in the ensuing narrative; for the latter,
             compare the eighteenth-century poet Allan Ramsay's version of this passage
             (Introduction, p. 11); the opposition of briers to corn suggests an alternation of
             good times and bad that will assume depth as the *Fables* proceed (lines 184,
             2541, 2545; compare line 2941).

172   In fifteenth-century Dunfermline the burgh *gild* was open to both artisans and
             merchants: "to judge by the expenditure on food and drink, conviviality was a
             principal function of its meetings" (Whyte, *Scotland before the Industrial Revolution*,
             p. 70); compare line 1558n.

173   "The mouse was exempt from the usual tolls, which were levied both on exports,
             such as wool and hides (the *magna custuma*), and on goods entering the burghs
             for sale in the markets (the *parva custuma*)" (Bawcutt and Riddy, *Longer Scottish
             Poems*, p. 355).

180–85   Resemblances are to be traced between the burgh mouse and Henryson's
             Orpheus, who traverses woods and *wilsum wayis* in search of Eurydice (lines 130,
             155, 290, 414); compare the more explicitly penitential motive that almost
             convinces the shepherd mourning his dead dog to wander into the countryside
             (lines 2472–73n; compare *Testament*, lines 94–95n).

193   The mingling that will feature thematically at the end of the fable and again at
             the outset of the *Moralitas* (345n, 368n) emerges briefly at this apposite moment;
             indeed, the stanza includes some structural markers — the phrase *fute for fute*,
             for instance — that will recur more ominously in the final fable (line 2875).

204   The saying that thieves — evildoers generally — hate the light, ultimately
             scriptural (John 3:20; Whiting E184), assumes thematic importance as the *Fables*
             proceed (lines 618–20, 2294) and may be connected to the comparison between
             the soul and the eye of the bat, both of which can function only when the light
             is failing (lines 1636–40n); Gavin Douglas performs a self-reflexive variation on
             this theme in concluding *The Palis of Honoure* with the declaration that the poem
             is plagiarized, and "Thyft lovys lycht but lyte" (line 2167; also Dunbar, *The
             Goldyn Targe*, line 279).

206   The contrast between the two diets, one crude, the other dainty, becomes a theme of Cresseid's Complaint (*Testament*, lines 418, 440–41).

217   The burgh mouse has not come by her high standards by right of birth but is that frequent target of satire, the overweening commoner (compare Chaucer's guildsmen, *CT* I[A]361–78).

223   It is to strengthen the reader's exegetical teeth to work through textual tough nuts that the *Fables* have been written (lines 15–18, 1559n; compare Augustine, *On Christian Doctrine* 2.6.7).

229–31   The remonstration of the "rurall mous" assumes a sententious strain (line 225; Proverbs 15:17, 17:1; Whiting C176–78, M700).

248   To get her way, the burgh mouse inverts lavish Lenten fasting in the burgh and paltry rural Easter feasting; Dunbar reworks the theme in "Dumbaris Dirige to the King"; for further elaboration of the Lent-versus-Easter theme, see lines 2000–06n. Towards the end of the present fable, the rural mouse will return to this theme and set it right-ways-up (line 320n).

251   Though the burgh mouse has no fear of spring traps or box traps, she seems to know enough about them to distinguish between them; not so much can be said for Henryson's copyists (Textual Notes, line 251n).

257, 262   Henryson's reference to the nocturnal activity of the mice is a realistic detail but also suggests that this mode of travel involves a inversion of the usual scheme; likewise, the omission of the usual decorous greeting intensifies the sense of an increasingly offensive neglect of proprieties; see also line 268.

264   In the version of this fable by Marie de France, the foodstuffs are limited to "Plenté de farine e de miel" ("Plenty of flour and honey"; Marie, *Fables*, 9.27).

279   John A. Burrow notes the omission of an unstressed syllable in the first foot of the line; for Henryson, this is an unusual departure from the metrical norm, but may be an instance of poetic foregrounding: "The headless line may be original, reflecting the town mouse's emphasis" (*English Verse*, p. 343, note 118).

281   The unusual word *subcharge*, "additional course in the meal," recurs with irony in line 346.

285   This line caused the copyists difficulty; Bannatyne calls the *pièce de résistance* of the feast *furmag*, cheese (a word nowhere else attested in Middle Scots); that the difficult reading *mane*, fine white bread (compare *MED* pain-demeine; *OED* pandemain), is authoritative is suggested by its prominence in Odo's version of the fable (Jacobs, *Fables*, p. 87).

286   The whiteness of the candle is an indication of the good quality, and hence higher price, of the tallow used to make it.

287   Spices would be the expected serving at the end of a feast, but the mice have their own preferences. Lured to the sensation of eating spices, the print witnesses provide "gust thair mouth" for the mousier delight in B's reading "creisch thair teithis."

289   In interposing these common moralizing proverbs at this juncture (Whiting Y39, J58), Henryson makes a mock-heroic narrative transition (compare NPT, *CT* VII[B²]3205: "For evere the latter ende of joye is wo").

295   *They taryit not to wesche.* The alacrity of the mice is contrasted, appropriately, to the lavishing of time on preparations as in the ceremonious washing before the meal (line 268; compare *CT* I[A]3821–22: "And doun gooth al; he foond neither to selle, / Ne breed ne ale, til he cam to the celle / Upon the floor"). The present omission reflects ironically on the greedy omissions of proper etiquette mentioned earlier ("Withowt godspeid," "Withowtin grace," lines 262, 268); the inevitable lapse of etiquette shows the terror-stricken mice suddenly stripped of their pretensions. Compare the burlesque romance *Rauf Coilyear* (line 268), in which failure to wash indicates more straightforwardly a lack of refinement.

296–97   The form *to ga* instead of the expected past tense (*yeid* or *hyit* or *haistit*) indicates a lowering of the style and a related acceleration of the narrative: "But get out, whoever could get to the front of the crowd!" In their crowded haste, the mice are frustrating each other's efforts to escape (compare *CT* III[D]572–74: "I holde a mouses herte nat worth a leek / That hath but oon hole for to sterte to, / And if that faille, thanne is al ydo"). As often in Henryson's narration of action, the sudden shift from past to present tense indicates a further stylistic lowering to enhance the immediacy of the event.

320   *thir fourty dayis* suggests that these events are taking place during the long fast of Lent, or perhaps that the upland mouse feels the need to undertake penance — a whole Lent's worth — for her excesses and narrowly averted disaster.

326   In *Romulus* and its French derivations, it takes only one threat of capture to convince the country mouse to go home; Henryson's "rurall mous" attempts to regain her nerve and stay the course, only to suffer a more drastic encounter.

326, 329   *Gib* (an abbreviation of *Gilbert*) and *Bawdronis* are conventional Scots names for cats, the latter described as "affectionate" (*DOST Gib* n.; *DSL Baudrons*).

328   The simile alludes comically combat (*Amis and Amiloun*, line 1321; *Golagros and Gawain*, line 758; Whiting F190); the burlesque is augmented by the alliteration with *fled* (compare line 552).

331–33   The kittenish but deadly behavior is made emblematic of fortune (Greentree, *Reader*, p. 78; Lyall, "Structure," p. 95); the "Quhylis" (sometimes) topic associated with fortune recurs in similar circumstances (lines 166–68n, 1525n, 2892, 2939; *Orpheus*, line 516). The mingling of play and predation is like *buk-heid* (line 333), a rough version of "blindman's buff" (*DOST buk-hid*; compare lines 970, 2383).

336   The copyists differ as to where the rural mouse has gone: Bannatyne has her behind a *dressour* and the printers place her behind the *burde*. Asloan's reading, which has been adopted, implies that the chase is taking place in a hall, hung with curtains (Bawcutt and Riddy, *Longer Scottish Poems*, p. 358).

345   *guse is gude.* The contrast between the wished-for tasty goose and the unexpectedly sour garlic sauce becomes proverbial in later Scots (*DOST gansel*); if Henryson

is not the author of the saying, he certainly infuses it with unprecedented thematic significance, exemplifying the principle of mingling that runs through this fable and out into the *Fables* as a whole.

365   At this point the stanza form changes from rhyme royal to the ballade (*ababbcbC*).

368   The intermingling of joy and adversity plays against the intermingling of fable and "gude moralitie." Implicitly, learning to read morally is an ethical practice in deciphering potentially deceptive appearances (line 2716n).

372   *small possessioun*. In the refrain, this repeated phrase reflects wittily upon a fable about the belongings proper to a mouse.

381–82   *O wantoun man . . . Thy wambe . . . a god to be*. The direct scriptural allusion (Philippians 3:19) opens a sequence of relevant concepts that emerge in the next two verses of the epistle: one's proper living place (compare the rural mouse's *kith*, line 351 and *this cuntrie*, line 379; Philippians 3:20); and the potential parallel between small, humble bodies and higher ones (Philippians 3:21). Compare the Pardoner's Tale, *CT* VI(C)520–33.

391–93   *As Solomon sayis*. Citing Solomon as an authority need not indicate a precise source in one of the books ascribed to him, though the lines here do paraphrase Ecclesiastes 3:12; as in the *Moralitas* to *The Trial of the Fox* (lines 1130–31), the prestige of his name adds luster to the reworking of a conventional theme.

395   *maist degree*. The distinction between worldly excess and true nobility, alluded to at various points in the fable, is emphasized at its endpoint.

The Cock and the Fox
Henryson's main source is Chaucer's Nun's Priest's Tale, though for the hens' speeches *The Parliament of Fowls* is an important contributor, as is the Wife of Bath's Prologue.

397–400   The concession to fiction that was indicated in the Prologue (lines 44–46), that animals may with propriety be represented as reasonable and articulate, appears now to be abandoned in favor of a more factually based principle: even though animals are without reasoning power, they still exemplify a diversity of natural inclinations.

407–10   The prospect of an unknowable infinity of animal natures, and thereby an infinity of fables, elicits a seemly gesture of incapacity from the poet. His avowed intention to write about the fox and the rooster thus seems a defeat on two levels: it has proven impossible to write inventively about nature; and the alternative is simply to retell an anecdote about a *cais*, an anecdote recalling an event "this ather yeir" (line 409). Assuming the guise of a dutiful old dog without the *cunning* to perform new tricks, Henryson may in fact be writing more like a "fenyeit, craftie, and cautelows" fox (line 402).

410   Chauntecleer is the name of the rooster in the Nun's Priest's Tale and also in *Le Roman de Renart*; this is only the second instance in the *Fables* of an animal

having a name (after Gilbert, "Gib Hunter our jolie cat," line 326), and it signals a change in the generic affiliations of the ensuing tale.

411–13   In contrast to this curt dismissal, the widow in NPT is the subject of a little encomium of the simple life (*CT* VII[B²]2821–46); having been elaborated in the previous fable (e.g., lines 358–63, 373–80) this rustic theme would be redundant here.

415–17   Like the widow, the rooster is disposed of in a few lines; compare Chaucer's circumstantial portrait (*CT* VII[B²]2849–64); Henryson's Chantecleir will be described later, but through the varying perspectives of three of his wives (lines 495–543).

419–20   While Chaucer mentions the "yeerd . . . enclosed al aboute / With stikkes" before describing the rooster, Henryson places the description of the thicket after, in order for it to serve as the setting for the fox. In NPT, by contrast, many lines of discussion about dreams must pass before the description of the fox waiting "in a bed of wortes" (*CT* VII[B²]3221). Henryson gives the fox prominence: his character is no more or less than was predicted at the outset (line 402).

428   Chaucer's Chauntecleer cannot "ryde" Pertelote on their perch at night; "ful of joye and of solas," he does so in the daylight (*CT* VII[B²]3167–78). In contrast, Henryson's Chantecleir has been at work all night, and no mention is made of the narrowness of the perch — which is likely located under the roof of the widow's cottage (lines 584–85n). Klaus Bitterling reads *for nicht* as a compound adverb ("Robert Henryson, *The Fables*"): "Exhausted, having stayed up all night, Chantecleir flew from his nest" — one might suppose he is escaping.

429   As the name for the fox (compare *Russell* in NPT and *Renard* in the French sources), *Lowrence* occurs earliest in Henryson's *Fables*. The fox is unique in the *Fables* for the recurrence of his name, which has been explained as a pun on another word appearing earliest in this work, *lour*, "skulk" (line 952; *DOST lour*, v.; *Lowrence*). Breeze suggests, however, that the word *lowry* for "fox" derives from Brythonic Celtic, a language spoken in lowland Scotland and the north of England into the medieval period, with derivations surviving in place-names; compare early Welsh *llewyrn*, "foxes" ("Henryson's Lowrence the Fox," p. 300).

438–40   The fox broaches his offer of service, which will become the keynote of his appeal to Chantecleir; Chaucer's fox, in contrast, claims to have visited the yard "oonly for to herkne how that ye synge" (*CT* VII[B²]3290). Lowrence, meanwhile, claims that he owes duty to Chantecleir because of the bond of loyalty he shared with Chantecleir's father. Such bonds between lords and men were becoming increasingly formalized in fifteenth-century Scotland (Wormald, *Lords and Men in Scotland*, pp. 17–18).

449   The fox claims to have recited the *dirge*, the Matins of the Office of the Dead, "the liturgical text intoned daily for the souls of the dead" (Fein, *Moral Love Songs*, p. 289); knowledge of the dirge was spreading due to its inclusion in the medieval primer, the prayer book for lay people; the fox is flaunting his

devotion but also his value as a literate and even clerkly servitor. The topic of the fox mourning is ubiquitous in the *Roman de Renard*.

462–63   Having neglected to crow according to his natural *inclinatioun*, the *werie* Chantecleir has declined from the proper *conditioun* of being a rooster; so claims the fox (lines 400, 428).

483   The hens' names each contain a diminutive suffix, *-ok*: "Bold little hen" (Pertok), "Speckled little hen" (Sprutok), and "Crested little hen" (Toppok). These names provided the occasion for inventiveness, if not occasional confusion, among later poets, copyists, and editors (*Eneados* 12 prol.159; *Colkelbie Sow* 3.105, 117; Fox, ed., p. 215).

491   Chaucer's widow remains conscious; Henryson prefers to let the focus shift to the hens' debate, a strikingly inventive amplification in a telling characterized by its compression.

498   Pertok's comparison between Chantecleir's voice and the clock tower bell corresponds to the detail in Chaucer's initial portrait of Chauntecleer (*CT* VII[B²]2854).

513–15   A forthrightly merry widow, Sprutok anticipates Dunbar's inventive elaboration in *The Tretis of the Tua Mariit Wemen and the Wedo*: "I wald me prunya plesandly in precius wedis, / That luffaris mycht apon me luke and ying lusty gallandis" (Bawcutt, *Poems of William Dunbar*, poem 3, lines 374–75).

533   From the wives' accumulated perspectives, Chantecleir combines apparently contradictory vices: having been called impotent and jealous (lines 517, 519), he is now an insatiable frequenter of prostitutes; he is a compendium of the more bestial *inclinatiouns* of husbands.

546–47   In later Scots, *birkie* denotes extreme bareness and paleness, like the white birch in winter (*DSL birkie* n3), so that *Birkye* may be a dog with short white fur. *Berrie* is assumably deep brown (like the Monk's horse, *CT* I[A]207); *Bell* has a fine ringing voice; and then there is poor *Bawsie Broun* — in Dunbar's *Fasternis Evin in Hell*, one of the devils is named "Bawsy Broun" (Bawcutt, *Poems of William Dunbar*, poem 47, line 30).

551–53   Alliteration functions here to enhance the impression of increasing force and speed. The first line starts slowly with double alliteration in the second foot; the pace increases in the third foot, with the recurrence pitched forward on the stressed syllable; then the *b*-less fourth foot produces a spurt towards *bent*, at the end of the line. In line 552, the conventional simile (line 328n) produces top speed. The lines move like the hounds, *full wichtlie* (line 553).

558   Chaucer's Chauntecleer speaks "In al his drede" (*CT* VII[B²]3406) and urges the fox to exult in his superior skill; Henryson's Chantecleir advises Lourence to defend his action as arising from a bond of friendship. In each case, the rooster is practising the very trick that had previously fooled him, but here the theme on which it is based has become the false assurance of loyalty.

582   The lesson the fox derives from his loss is that a thief ought not to engage in formal dispute mechanisms like honest people, but just be a thief and make off

with the goods. He has been fooled into acting on the values he had previously manipulated in order to catch Chantecleir.

584–85 Chantecleir is finally depicted as an ordinary farmyard bird, flying back to the place from which he emerged at the outset of the story (line 428), in at the *lever* (the outlet through which the smoke escaped from the fireplace) to his home under the thatched roof of the widow's cottage.

586–89 Henryson picks up the discussion, itself typically allegorical, about the relation between the narrative of a fable and its moralization (compare lines 15–18).

595–99 Pride in kin leaves one "without a leg to stand on"; the ensuing comparison to the Fall of the Angels (Revelations 12:7–9) reduces faith in one's lineage to a type of devilish self-love; the hounding of the *feyndis infernall* recalls the memorable episode, just read, of the hounding of the fox (lines 546–54).

600–13 In contrast to Chaucer, whose denunciation of flattery occurs digressively (*CT* VII[B²]3325–30), Henryson allows the theme sequential development in the *Moralitas*, where it can be treated allusively without loss of clarity: note the motif of sugar and gall, implicitly connecting flattery to Venus and Fortune (compare *Testament* lines 225–29) but also to Boethius' false Muses (*Consolation* 1.pr1).

The Fox and the Wolf

Sources: for the confession of the fox, *Roman de Renart* passim; for the baptism of the kid, Perry no. 655 (in a *Romulus* recension). "Many analogues to the two main actions can be found in earlier fable literature, but they are not known to have been combined before Henryson" (Fox, ed., p. 222).

614–17 The allusions to the widow, Chantecleir, "this foxe," and his abortive daylight raids all indicate that the ensuing fable is to be taken as the integral second part of an inset sequence within the *Fables*; more than *The Cock and the Fox, The Fox and the Wolf* is to feature Lowrence as its antihero.

621–24 The level of style rises suddenly with this chronographia, a stylized indication of time that sets the ensuing narrative off from the preceding material; at the outset, the mythology (Thetis the sea, Phoebus the sun, Hesperus the evening star) seems burlesque — a fox is waiting for nightfall.

628 The fox proceeds into a rougher landscape than those encountered so far in the *Fables* (though one should make allowances for the difference of scale affecting the mice); this hill, on which he perceives his likely fate, anticipates the *craig* (line 664) from which the wolf emerges and the *heuch* in which the fox lies in wait for suitable prey (lines 745, 747).

629–34 The preceding chronographia has in fact served to prepare for Lowrence's learned interest in astronomy, comparable to that shown by the poet at the outset of the *Testament* (lines 8–14); and in this regard, the poet claims Lowrence as his teacher.

635–36   MacQueen notes the propriety to the ensuing events of maleficient Saturn associated with the sign of the goat and justice-dealing Jupiter with the sign of the archer (*Robert Henryson*, p. 146).

639   Noting the atronomical impossibility of this alignment, Alison Hanham and J. C. Eade suggest that the opposition of Venus to Mars and Saturn is a purely thematic device connecting the fable to the denunciation of sensuality in the *Moralitas*, thereby preparing for the reference to to fox's fornication in the next fable (lines 799–800; "Foxy Astrology in Henryson," pp. 25–29).

642–43   Scanning the heavens, this fox appears to balance between reason and instinct; the first is his as an outcome of the fictional form (lines 47–48); the second is an outcome of his special place in the plenitude of nature (lines 407–10); in this mingled state, Lowrence is deeply versed in celestial signs even though he lacks an astronomer's instruments and charts.

649–55   "The reader is asked here to contemplate not the usual fox of fable to whom we may conveniently assign the human characteristics of guile and deceit and whom we may then satisfyingly frustrate or punish. This fox is stretched on the dilemma of the opposition between his natural and spiritual instincts" (Roerecke, "Integrity and Symmetry," pp. 78–79).

666–69   Drawing on Renardian sources, Odo also depicts the wolf as an imperfect cleric (Perry 539.595, 52.628); with propriety, Henryson's wolf has the guise of a Franciscan, a gray friar (line 679), precedent for which is interpolated into the *Romance of the Rose* (11222.lvi1–lviii9); as a doctor of theology, he should be on a par with those best qualified to apply moral precept to lived experience (1100–03); such moralizing and its learned practitioners do not always warrant respect (lines 1052–53, 2971–72). Still, the poet's attitude to such doctors is complicated: after all, they are "the teachers who interpret fables" (Wheatley, *Mastering Aesop*, p. 179).

676   The contraction *dude* ("do it"; *DOST dude*) provides the stanza with a pertly colloquial ending, one that belies the obsequious reverence the fox is showing his "gostlie father" (line 672) the wolf.

677   As a *lanterne*, he is taken to be a "guiding light" of moral instruction (*MED lantern(e* 4).

693   *Benedicitie*, the customary friar's greeting and, more generally, a common exclamation (e.g., *CT* III[D]241, 280, 1087), but also a metonymy for the rite of confession (e.g., CA I[A]205).

697   Gopen argues that "the narrator's sensitive withdrawal does not hinder him from giving a word-for-word account" (*Moral Fables of Aesop*, p. 12); by omitting to report the fox's actual confession, however, the poet has upheld the letter of his principle.

710   "Like Langland [*Piers Plowman* C.5.24: 'I am to wayke to wirche . . .'] and Hoccleve (*Regement*, 976–85) in similar situations, the fox alludes to Luke 16:3" (Pearsall, *Chaucer*, p. 492).

712–13   The elements necessary for *perfyte confessioun* that the fox lacks are "verray sorwe that a man receyveth in his herte for his synnes" and "sad purpos . . . neveremoore to do synne" (*CT* X[I]127–29).

719–21   Amenability to such negotiation is a theme of medieval satire against the friars (the so-called antimendicant satire; compare *CT* I[A]221–24).

731   *neid may haif na law.* Proverbial. See Whiting N51. Compare *Piers Plowman* B.20.10; Gower, *CA* 4.1167, 8.75; or variations like Chaucer, CTI[A]4026: "nede has na peer"; or Gower's frequent "nede he mot that nede schal" (*CA* 1.1714, 3.352, 8.1020).

734   The wording of this line recalls the title Asloan gives to the now-lost poem he ascribes to Henryson, "Master Robert Hendersonnis Dreme On Fut by Forth" (Introduction, p. 5); the Firth of Forth is the estuary on the north shore of which Dunfermline lies.

736   The fox's frustration on the shore offers a concise reenactment of the deflection of moral awareness that has been traced through the events of the fable so far.

751   Gray wittily and learnedly surveys the "splendid folk-motif" of the renaming of forbidden food, which is attested in *Romulus* (Gray, p. 116; Perry 569.655).

757–60   Always with ironic effect, the sensual impulse to warm one's belly recurs in Henryson's poems (line 1407; *Testament*, line 36), though this is the one time when the consequences are fatal. For the fox to make the wry assertion that it would be fitting to have an arrow in his belly seems an extreme provocation to an avenging thunderbolt of justice. On the other hand, this line may be a predecessor of the idiomatic expression "to make a bolt" of — that is, to take a risk on — something (Shakespeare, *Merry Wives* 3.4.24 qtd. *OED bolt* n.I.1.b); if so, the fox means to say, "My stomach is worth the risk"; but, as elsewhere in the *Fables* (e.g., line 2244), the literal meaning of his words comes unexpectedly uppermost.

775   The sudden, unprepared-for death is just the sort of *schamefull end* the fox had read for himself in the stars (line 653).

786–88   Having declared that fables provide symbolic instances of the ways in which certain kinds of people become like certain species of animals (lines 48–49, 399–40), the poet now indicates the circumstances in which both sorts of beings are *neidlingis* (necessarily) destroyed, namely through *consuetude and ryte* (line 782).

The Trial of the Fox
The motifs of the animals' parliament, the absent animal (a donkey rather than Henryson's mare), and the kicked wolf are assembled in Odo of Cheriton's fable *De asino nolente venire ad parliamentum leonis* (Perry no. 638). The trial of the fox occurs in the *Roman de Renart*, though there he is not executed (Branch 1.62–63, 279–82, 458).

827–28   A characteristic Scots proverb about the fox (Whiting F 592; see also Dunbar's satire on the Gaelic chieftain *Donald Owyr*, ending "Ay rynnis the fox / Quhill he fute hais") leads into a typical detail of Scottish landscape, beyond the margins of arable soil: a *peitpoit* is a deep, waterlogged hole in a peat bog from which peat has been cut, mainly for fuel.

834–37 The poet exclaims on the familiar theme of the the executor's disloyalty (*Piers Plowman* B.15.128; *OED secutor*), leading toward emphasis on their neglect of the duty to pray for the testator's soul; the Protestant printers rewrote this passage, which had become offensive for its devotional practice; in the process they emphasized the need to protect wealth, a theme at odds with the tenor of the passage (Textual Notes 836n, 837n).

839–40 The fanfare seems to shake the world, as it does in the *Testament* when Mars blows his horn (lines 195–96): "It is as though the tallies have been taken; the 'busteous Bugill' of the summoning Unicorn is highly suggestive of the trump of doomsday, as is the generally ominous tone the poet achieves in his description of the assemblage of beasts" (Roerecke, "Integrity and Symmetry," p. 85). The fox later takes up this apocalyptic theme (line 952).

842, 848 Decisively but not unchangeably, the arrival of the unicorn associates the animal kingdom with heraldry. In Scotland, heraldry was the concern of the court of the Lyon King of Arms, in which one of the junior heralds was the Unicorn Pursuivant. *Oyas* (Old French *oiez*, "Hear ye!") is the Scottish heraldic officer's proper cry before making an announcement to a gathering including knights and squires (*DOST Oyes*).

855–65 The lion's proclamation epitomizes and may parody the stiffly ceremonious style, ornamented with the stylized phrases and terms (*celsitude, Lattis yow to wit, evin incontinent, Thinkis . . . to hald*) typical of royal public discourse: a failure of proportion may occur in sending greeting to God and *brutall beistis* as if both were *my subjectis grit and small*.

866–72 The chronographia of a spring morning is decorously kingly, not least in its alliteration marking the stresses in the third line and following; to heighten the courtliness of this "pleasant place," indications of privilege (the sheer wealth, "as the gold" of vegetation, the buds of "spyce," the conspicuous consumption involved in cultivating grasses; compare Dunbar, *The Goldyn Targe*, lines 1–45) are interspersed with no less decorous scenic elements (the moisture-distilling clouds, the lark, merle, and mavis; compare lines 1321–27n).

873–79 Commencing with the nice detail of the three attendant leopards (the lions in the arms of England being known as leopards; Fox, ed., p. 237), the stanza depicts a series of royal appurtenances, in phrases marked by ornamental alliteration and a characteristic [modifier +] noun + modifier syntax.

887–920 By comparison with the catalogue of "mony diverse kynd" of beasts in *The Kingis Quair* (stanzas 155–57), Henryson's depiction is much longer, more syntactically variegated, semantically more negative, and more fanciful — arcane, even — in its names and details; it is a passage bound to give its copyists and editors headaches (e.g., lines 895n, 906n, 914n). As placing mythological beasts at the head of the list makes obvious, the passage is rhetorically encyclopedic; the reader need not be alarmed to encounter species repeated under various names.

893   Henryson depicts the camel in a way that recalls an Aristotelian association between gluttony and the neck of a crane, famously employed by Spenser (*Nichomachean Ethics* 3.10; *Faerie Queene* 1.4.21).

895   *anteloip*. The copyists may have made two animals out of one: the heraldic antelope has ax-like horns (*OED antelope*), and a *sparth* is literally a broad ax — "*his* sparth"? That something has gone amiss in the line is suggested by the lack of an unstressed syllable in the third foot.

903   In the *Flyting*, Dunbar combines Henryson's terms for the hedgehog and hare into a single insult: in his appearance and gait, Dunbar's opponent Walter Kennedie resembles a "Hard hurcheoun hirpland" (Bawcutt, *Poems of William Dunbar*, poem 65, line 179; compare Alexander Montgomerie, *Cherrie and the Slae*, second version, line 286).

906   The printed texts diverge markedly from the manuscript witness at this point (Textual Notes to line 906); Fox speculates that the manuscript reflects misunderstanding of a rare name like *bonnacon* (bison): this animal, with its reputedly "noxious excrement, could appropriately be linked to the notoriously stinking badger" (ed., p. 242).

914   The obscure names in this line have occasioned much speculation: *ane* refers elsewhere in MSc to the donkey, so that the second element of *lurdane lane*, Bannatyne's reading, becomes notionally plausible and thus is marginally preferred over the printers' apparently garbled *bowranbane*.

928   The widely distributed distich "Parcere prostatis scit nobilis ira leonis; / Tu quoque fac simile, quisquis dominaris orbe" (Bawcutt, *Poems of William Dunbar*, 2:398: "The noble lion's wrath knows how to show mercy to the abject; do thus, each of you who reign in the world"); the theme is literally central to the midmost of the *Fables*, in which the mouse restates the proverb and the lion learns it (lines 1486–88, 1503–05).

943–46   In Dunbar's *The Thistle and the Rose* (lines 106–12), the lion is advised to prevent the stronger animals from oppressing the weaker; the messianic prophecy (Isaiah 11:6–7) provides the context for this emblem of ideal peace, which turns out inevitably to be unsustainable.

951–58   *Fensit the court*. The necessary preliminaries to be undertaken by an officer of the court, "fencing included a demarcation of the bounds of the assembly, a proclamation of its authority and an announcement of the peace of the court"; usually the senior herald, Lyon King of Arms, fenced a new session of Parliament, the highest court in Scotland (Walker, *Legal History*, pp. 466, 233).

991   *gray stude meir*. In Odo's version of this tale (Perry 557.638), the absent animal is a donkey, an animal with a reputation for solitariness, stubbornness, and irritability; making the change to the mare, Henryson draws attention to the animal's belonging to a "stud" (enclosure) of horses, a valuable, productive community, the values of which she embodies (lines 1111–17; Fox, ed., p. 231); as a result of the change, her kick will be an altogether weightier, more considered, less merely temperamental, act.

1004   *contumax.* Despite having insisted on his ignorance in his plea to be excused from the errand of carrying the message to the mare, the fox (like Chaucer's Summoner; *CT* I[A]639–46) is now keen to show off what command he possesses of legal terminology; still, it is a scrap the lion cannot resist citing later (line 1050).

1013–14   Like the Robert Henryson who graduated from Glasgow University, the wolf is recommended as a *venerabilis vir*, a "man of age." The fox's gibe about the wolf's expertise has particular relevance to the task at hand: in fifteenth-century Scotland, the chancellor, usually a cleric, kept the great seal, the insignia by which various royal documents were authenticated (Walker, *Legal History*, p. 138; compare lines 1890n, 2970n).

1031–33   Though these lines may be read as the poet's interjection, they are taken here as part of the fox's rejoinder to the mare; flaunting his scraps of learning and his experience with "scrolls," he is insouciantly in character in saying what suits the moment — only a few moments after he found it prudent to claim to be illiterate. The proverb the fox cites ("Happy are those who take warning from the perils of others") works like a cliché, springing to mind automatically when the circumstances fit: thus the lion will intone it in Scots when he hears about the wolf's discomfiture (line 1065). As for the parenthetical assurance that the message on the scroll is not worth forfeiting (*MED forfeten*), the price of obedience, five shillings, would be a standard large amount for a poor person (line 1183).

1052   The wolf in the previous fable was also a "doctour of divinitie" (line 666). The joke about the doctoral red cap (the wolf's bloodied head), which is evidently so rich that the fox repeats and the lion echoes it (lines 1061–62), may pertain to the academic costume of non-theology doctors at Glasgow (Fox, ed., p. 247).

1064   *greitest clerkis ar not the wysest men.* Proverbial. See Whiting C291.

1079   The apparent intersection between aggression and fun with regard to the wolf has just brought the lion and his court to gales of laughter; caught out in his offense against the peace of the court, the fox is left feebly asserting the entertainment value of his attack on the lamb as his justification (compare lines 2558–77).

1089   Treason, an offense to be tried in parliament, was broadly defined in fifteenth-century Scotland; the fox is liable to the charge because he disobeyed the royal command to keep the peace and specifically that "tod Lowrie luke not upoun the lam" (line 945; Walker, *Legal History*, pp. 305, 527).

1091   In a Scottish court, the sentence would be pronounced, not by the judge, but by the *dempster* (Walker, *Legal History*, p. 340).

1101   "[T]he reference to the 'doctouris of devyne' . . . in support of his method rather encourages our scepticism because it reminds us of the vain outwitted Wolf whom the Fox mockingly addresses as 'new-maid doctour off divinitie'" (line 1052; Mehl, "Robert Henryson's *Moral Fables*," p. 97). On the other hand, given the bruising the profession of "doctouris of devyne" has received in the tale, it may be poetic justice to cede interpretive authority to them.

1102   For *apply* meaning "apply an allegory or moralization," see *MED, ap(p)lien* 3.c.

1104–10   Gavin Douglas amplifies this quick survey of a world going mad for profit, *Sum wanting one thing, and sum another* (*Eneados* 8.prol.44–52, 92–105). Henryson and Douglas give a satirical edge to an influential scriptural review of trades and crafts, Ecclesiasticus 38:24–31.

1111–17   This stanza and the two ending this *Moralitas* were subjected to a thoroughgoing Protestant revision in the printed texts; as well, the order of the stanzas may have been changed at an early stage of the textual tradition (Textual Notes, lines 1111–41 *passim*).

1118–24   Thus moralized, the mare sustains a commitment to a value higher than that of royal command; while taking the higher stakes and her greater integrity into account, she is still to be compared to that altogether smaller being the rural mouse, who surrendered to the blandishments of the burgh, was nearly destroyed, and regained her integrity in returning to her own country (lines 343–56). Though the switch from female to male may distract present-day readers in the equation of contemplative men to the nurturing, independent mare, that animal's strengths typify these men's commitment to interpret the world allegorically, as a penitential wilderness.

1145   The expression "The Talking of the Tod" could be taken to refer to the three tales concerning foxes (*The Cock and the Fox*, *The Fox and the Wolf*, and *The Trial of the Fox*); these three tales stand as a unit even in the Bannatyne Manuscript, where the sequence is otherwise strikingly at odds with that in the prints (Introduction, p. 7, above).

The Sheep and the Dog
Source: *Romulus* 4 (A. Wright, *Fables*, pp. 31–33).

1147   One element that distinguishes the present fable from the one to which it appears analogous, the penultimate *The Wolf and the Lamb*, is that the antagonist is a dog and not a wild predator, is poor and not powerful, and thus should be above dishonesty and oppression; compare the standard character of the loyal dog that Henryson alludes to earlier (line 403).

1148   In fifteenth-century Scotland, the consistory was an ecclesiastical court, usually presided over by the bishop's Official, a canon lawyer; this court had jurisdiction over moral offenses, especially those committed by clerics, but also over a variety of secular offenses. Since the procedure depended heavily on sworn statements, perjury was regarded as an especially damaging offense: "False accusations, if malicious, could give rise to the accusers being charged with defamation" (Walker, *Legal History*, pp. 405, 542–43).

1160   Making the raven the messenger of the court alludes to his wide reputation for untrustworthiness in such endeavors; sent out for news, the raven failed to return to Noah's Ark (Genesis 8:7; Holland, *Buke of the Howlat*, line 812).

1166   *Perrie* (in the Bannatyne Manuscript, *Burry*) may recall *Berrie*, one of the widow's dogs in *The Cock and the Fox* (lines 546–47n).

1174   The fox assumes the function that would have been the responsibility of the historical Robert Henryson, notary public of Dunfermline.

1175–79 The *gled*, or kite, had a reputation for cowardice and cruelty (Bartholomaeus XII.27, Seymour-Smith, *On the Properties of Things*, 1:634–35); like the *graip*, the vulture, it is a scavenger, though it also eats small animals, as in *The Paddock and the Mouse* (lines 2896–2902); the collusion between these two advocates is only natural.

1189–94 The charge of bias is serious and, if proven, would incur heavy punishment. In Scotland, "[t]he amount of legislation against judicial corruption in the fifteenth century shows how widespread the problem was" (Walker, *Legal History*, p. 543; also pp. 483–85); compare lines 2657–61, *Abbey Walk* line 35.

1199   In Scottish legal procedure, if a trial took place on a holiday, in feriate time, the judgment was liable to a parliamentary decree that it was "of no avail, strength, force or effect" (Walker, *Legal History*, p. 467).

1203–07 According to procedure, if the authority of the court is deemed to be compromised, arbiters were to be appointed by those in authority — the bishop in a case between clerics, the provost and burgh council if between townspeople — and not the parties themselves (Walker, *Legal History*, p. 181); in any case, one wonders what input the sheep had been able to exert if the two arbiters selected turned out to be the bear and the badger.

1216–17 The legal procedure appears to have shifted from canon to civil law. In Scotland, "civil law" meant Roman law, based on the Code of Justinian (the imperial statutes) and the Digests, principally the three compilations of legal opinions given the force of the law.

1221   The Decrees were the body of Roman law as commented upon by two principal groups of Italian jurists, the glossators and the later commentators, resulting in a weighty array of apparatus, collections of cases, opinions, and interpretations, and summaries, all composing an expanding body of law, the Corpus Juris Civilis. The arbiters are involved in a laborious, potentially endless, scholarly enterprise.

1246   Earlier (line 1157), *interdictioun* occurred in the context of a church court and refers to being banned from access to certain church sacraments; in the context of civil law, it refers to a prohibition from various kinds of public places and transactions. "By making his readers think of both types of courts," Gray comments, "Henryson is broadening his attack into one on legal injustice in general" (p. 147).

1265–71 Likening the wolf to a powerful sheriff (the king's chief administrator of justice in a county, with large and often sweeping powers of security, war, and taxation) completes the transition from church law to civil, noted above; this transition makes notional sense in a legal system in which the sheriff is bound "to support the church courts." In various counties, the office of the sheriff was inheritable, a tradition not conducive to competence; opportunities were plentiful to exploit the position, and corruption seems, as Henryson indicates, to have been widespread (Walker, *Legal History*, pp. 333–34).

1269–75   Rather than being associated with inquests as became the practice in England, the medieval Scottish coroner is to be considered a royal officer who summoned those charged with offenses to appear at trial; Henryson depicts the coroner touching the accused person with his *wand*, his staff of office (*DOST wand* n. 6). Earlier (line 1160) named as an *apparitour*, a summoner for a church court, the raven is now (line 1272) identified as the *crownair*, the coroner of a sheriff court, no less corrupt than the presiding judge.

1279–81   "Henryson informs us that we must wait until later — the second half of the work, as it turns out — to learn the allegorical significance of the Fox and Glede. He does this in a passage which looks both backward and forward in the work" (Roerecke, "Integrity and Symmetry," p. 120, citing lines 2205 and 2431–33 for the fox, and line 2962 for the *gleid*, the kite).

1286–1320 The stylistic, situational, and thematic strengths of this displaced complaint have been perceptively discussed (e.g., Jamieson, "Poetry," p. 104; Mehl, "Robert Henryson's *Moral Fables*," pp. 95–96; Wheatley, *Mastering Aesop*, p. 161). The sheep's mythological reference (*Boreas*) and his prominently alliterative allusion to the flowers faded by frost refer eloquently to the disorder of the *cursit consistorie*. His having been "counted as [a] sheep for the slaughter" justifies his quotation of the desperate question that immediately follows that verse, "quhy sleipis thow" (Psalm 43 [44]:22–23); his demand that God "discerne" his "cause" draws polemically on the opening of the previous psalm ("Iudica me Deus et descerne causam meam a gente non sancta"; "Judge me O God and distinguish my cause from the nation that is not holy").

1309–12   Allegory achieves compression (compare lines 237–38): poor people are naked sheep; gentleness, the value of true nobility, is murdered; mercy is exiled.

1314–20   The conclusion to the sheep's complaint involves an austere acceptance of responsibility for suffering (compare *Testament* line 574, and *Prayer for the Pest* lines 17–22).

The Lion and the Mouse
The principal source is *Romulus* 18 (A. Wright, *Fables*, pp. 58–61). "The opening section of the fable is apparently original, though of course the [devices and gambits] are all traditional" (Fox, ed., p. 263).

1321–27   The kingly associations of this Chaucerian stanza, brilliant in themselves, have been prepared for by the linking of the lion to the season and the scene, in *The Trial of the Fox* (lines 866–72n); they further prepare for the arrival of the "imperious" Aesop (Machan, *Textual Criticism*, p. 129) and his evocation and subsequent moralization of the kingly pleasant place in the tale proper (lines 1346–47, 1408, 1580n; compare *Eneados* 13.prol.1–88).

1349–60   David Laing speculated that Henryson's description of Aesop "might in some measure be applicable to himself" (*Poems and Fables*, p. xi; compare line 1373, "In civile law studyit"; also line 1384, "my maister venerabill"; Introduction, above), a speculation analogous to that of Aesop as "an image not of the Other but of the writerly Self in an ideally productive, famous form" (Patterson, *Fables of Power*, p. 32); in this regard, Aesop is to be compared with Henryson's witty portrait of the planetary god Mercury in the *Testament* (see especially lines 239, 242). A prominent article of Aesop's clothing is the camel's hair "chimar," (a loose, short robe) which is dyed a deep purple; the unusual color recalls the violets mentioned only a few lines earlier, but also Aesop's own *purpurat* verse style as evoked in the opening Prologue (lines 58, 1335).

1363–69   In spite of the stanza's abundant indications of paternal benevolence (sitting down beside the dreamer) and filial regard (the reverent mode of address), Henryson diplomatically asks his "gude maister" to identify himself, as if aware of the needs of his own audience even in the midst of his dream.

1370–74   Aesop's noble descent, Roman birth "withoutin nay," university education in civil law, and eternal salvation in heaven all contrast with the depiction in the printed Aesop of the author as a "dyfformed and evylle shapen" churl, unschooled but with a surprisingly "grete wytte" (Caxton fol. ii), a depiction reflected, for example, in the image of Aesop "the Phrygian" that is used in the frontispiece to the Bassandyne print of Henryson's *Fables*. Aesop is also a Roman "poyet laureate" for John Lydgate (*Isopes Fabules*, lines 8–14). The "cunning" clerk who appears earlier in the *Fables* is the wolf in *The Trial of the Fox* (lines 998, 1026).

1398–1403 "[T]aillis may lytill succour mak" in a corrupted world (line 1397), but with the most delicate courtesy, the dreamer can still persuade the laureate author to provide one more fable, in the hope that this one listener may yet carry away something that will help "heirefter"; as in his request for a *curriculum vitae* from Aesop, he is playing at being his own ideal reader — and, by implication, is assuring that reader that receiving and keeping the kernel of the fable may help mightily hereafter.

1431–46   "[T]he pleas of the mouse . . . deploy in small compass and with great felicity every possible argument to excuse the impertinence of the mice. In this stanza the disciplines of rhetoric and the bar combine to yield a delectably lively economy of utterance, clinched by the typically decisive final rhyme" (Burrow, "Dunbar," p. 115).

1449–53   The image of authority deserves the same respect as the person; on the one hand, the lion upholds the principle of the awe that should be shown to images of royalty; on the other, he cannot help implying that all authority is like a stuffed lion-skin.

1460   On the punishment decreed for treason, see line 2634n.

1461–66   The central stanza of the forty-three comprising *The Lion and the Mouse* has at its center the appeal to the king to "mak thy mynd to mercy inclinate" (Spearing, *Medieval to Renaissance*, p. 198); the same emphasis occurs in the central line of the entire *Fables*, line 1488, the completion of a sentence recapitulating the proverb "Parcere prostratis scit nobilis ira leonis" (line 928n).

1475–78   Following *Romulus*, Henryson alludes to a classical triumph, "in which the honour gained by the victorious triumphator depends on the prestige of the captives who are displayed in his procession" (Spearing, *Medieval to Renaissance*, p. 198; compare Shakespeare, *Julius Caesar* 1.1.37–39). The mouse's point is that honor arises from the indomitability of one's adversary and does not redound to the victor who kills those who have surrendered to him.

1493   The mouse is reckoned scripturally among the unclean beasts (Leviticus 11:29).

1525   The "Quhyle . . . quhyle" pattern reduces the lion to a plight like those experienced by two mice in the *Fables*: the rural mouse in the paws of the cat, and the mouse struggling to keep afloat while tied to a frog (331–33n, 2929ff.n; compare 166ff.n).

1531–41   The lion gives vent to a formal complaint rhetorically and even verbally akin to those uttered by Cresseid (*Testament*, lines 407–10) and Orpheus (*Orpheus*, lines 134–83).

1558   The mice calling their female leader "brother" has perplexed Henryson's editors, who have adduced the demands of rhyme for explanation; still, the word may pertain to any fellow Christian, fellow member of a religious order or guild, or close friend (*MED brother* 3, 4); given the emphasis elsewhere in the *Fables* on members of religious communities protecting and correcting wayward secular authority (lines 991, 1118–24, 1616–19), the arresting detail of the possible sex-change demands the reader's attention.

1559–63   These mere rural mice are equipped and willing to get a king out of an insoluble bind; they are to be contrasted to the burgh mouse with her sensitive teeth (line 223n) and perhaps compared to the moralization on the mare whose duties are not to be disturbed by royal command (lines 1118–24n).

1566–69   Aesop's immediate conclusion is that the king's safety depends on the principle that the bestowal of mercy instills loyalty; the dreamer's request for "ane moralitie / In this fabill" does not indicate his obtuseness but rather his desire for a fuller explication of the signification of each of the narrative elements.

1573–79   Though this stanza has been taken to refer to James III (e.g., Nicholson, *Scotland*, pp. 500–20), it is couched in general terms. Henryson's accusation of *sleuth* does stick, however: rarely calling parliaments outside Edinburgh, James was unprecedentedly sedentary; he earned opposition by his sale of remissions to people convicted of robbery and murder (Walker, *Legal History*, p. 190; Macdougall, *James III*, pp. 160–80; Wormald, *Court, Kirk, and Community*, pp. 10–12).

1580   Aesop is teaching the dreamer, and thus the reader, to interpret such seasonally "lowne and le" landscapes as allegories of mutability (compare lines 1321–27n).

1598–1600 The point of this textually complex passage (Textual Notes, line 1599n) is that by showing mercy, lords set an example for those "of small degree," so that the social damage and disruption involved in the retaliatory violence of the bloodfeud can be avoided through the kin offering and accepting *kinbute* (financial compensation for manslaughter or injury; *DOST kinbut*); as the master shows mercy and reason, so does the man. In fifteenth-century Scotland, *kinbute* is a traditional way of averting full-scale bloodfeud: it involves "the acceptance by the kin [of the person killed] of pecuniary compensation," analogous to *wergild* in Anglo-Saxon England. Still, *kinbuit* was a term "used more generally, for compensation for other kinds of losses" (Walker, *Legal History*, p. 616; *Acts of the Parliament of Scotland* 2.3.7 [1424]).

1608–11   Though generally skeptical about specific political allegory in this fable, Gray comments that this stanza "strongly suggests a veiled reference to some well-known contemporary event . . . the generalizing 'oftymes hes bene sene' may suggest to some that it is a deliberate piece of mystification" (p. 143).

1615–19   Aesop assigns the dreamer a task to persuade, not the lords to be loyal to the king, but the *kirkmen* to pray that the lords remain loyal; it is a line of approach that suits a poet based in an ecclesiastical center like Dunfermline; such a poem properly addresses and instructs politically responsible churchmen.

1618   In 1482, a band of lords captured James III at Lauder. McKenna reviews the debate over whether this reference to unfaithful lords may allude to that event ("Legends of James III").

The Preaching of the Swallow
The principal source is *Romulus* 20 (A. Wright, *Fables*, pp. 63–65). Henryson adapts "his source markedly — adding new forms (the *chanson d'aventure*, the debate, the preaching), expanding the tale ('realistic' detail), omitting an incident that does not suit his purpose (the Swallow does not live with the Fowler)" (Jamieson, "Poetry," pp. 162–63).

1623–42   Studying the language and style of this passage, Jeremy J. Smith notes that it can exemplify the value of French terms to denote ethical and religious concepts (*prudence, mervelous, profound, omnipotent, perfyte, ingenious*), and "a marked tendency to adopt the characteristically French post-modifying adjective construction, even when a Germanic word is used as the headword: *wirking mervelous*." These stanzas exemplify Henryson's philosophical style, to be contrasted to the courtly manner in which the preceding fable began (lines 1321–27n) by its more "complex syntax, flagged by subordinating conjunctions and non-finite verb phrases acting as the predicators of subordinate clauses" ("Language of Older Scots Poetry," pp. 205–06).

1626–28   "[P]rudence, according to an ancient and widely received tradition, consists precisely in the ability to hold in mind not merely the present time, but also the past and the future" (Burrow, *"Preaching,"* p. 154). The emphasis on the instantaneous divine perception of time is Boethian (*Consolation* 5.pr6).

1629   "The logic of Henryson's 'thairfoir' is that the 'presoun corporall' is a limitation placing man far beneath a God 'sa perfyte and sa ingenious'" (Schrader, "Henryson and Nominalism," p. 7; compare *Eneados* 10.prol.86–95); the furthest the shackled mind can go towards understanding divine wisdom, perhaps, is to employ fictional analogies drawn from creation, what Douglas calls "rude exemplys and figuris" (*Eneados* 10.prol.83), thereby making a virtue of necessity.

1636–40   The Aristotelean comparison between human reason and the weak eyesight of a
          noctural animal in the daylight (*Metaphysics* 2.1.3; compare 204n) here becomes
          elaborated into a miniature figure replete with naturalistic and regional detail;
          Henryson complicates the figure by having the bat venture forth in the *gloming*,
          in the vestiges of daylight, not quite in the nocturnal realm of *fantasie*. From
          another perspective, "The illusory 'reality' of the natural world prevents our
          seeing the true realities of God manifest in it" (Burrow, *English Verse*, p. 325).

1650–51   To illustrate the tradition from which Henryson derives his compensatory assur-
          ance that creation offers ways to perceive God's qualities, "the eclectic *Sentences*
          of Peter Lombard" have been cited ("For from the continuity of creatures the
          Maker is known to be eternal, from the greatness of creatures omnipotent, from
          order and arrangement wise, from governance good," 4.1.3.101.36, qtd. and
          trans. Schrader, "Henryson and Nominalism," p. 11).

1657–60   The *firmament* "represents the furthest limit of human perception" and the
          nearest approach to divine perfection. Concentric below it, the "spheres" —
          Saturn, Jupiter, Mars, the sun, Venus, Mercury, the moon, all in their fixed
          paths — revolve around the earth. "All eight spheres are carried each day
          through one complete revolution from East to West by the Primum mobile,
          which contains them all, although their own proper motions are from West to
          East" (Burrow, *English Verse*, p. 326). From the "chirkinge of the mevinge of the
          cerclis and of roundnesse of hevene . . . cometh most swete melodye and acorde"
          (Bartholomaeus VIII.17, Seymour-Smith, *On the Properties of Things*, 1:493);
          Henryson returns to the theme of this music in *Orpheus* (lines 218–39n), though
          he avoids mentioning it in the darker cosmology of the *Testament*.

1661   The descent and consequent degradation of order is inscribed in the descending
          sequence of the four elements, "since the movement of the passage is from God
          to man" (Fox, ed., p. 278); compare *Testament*, line 147n.

1663   Glimpsed thus, God perfects the author function, a connection that the theologian
          Hugh of St. Victor characterized thus: "the whole world which is knowne by
          sence is as it were a booke written with the fynger of God . . . and every the
          creatures be as it were certaine letters . . . ordeyned by the judgement of God,
          to make knowne, and as it were after a certaine maner to signify the invysible
          wisdome of God" (*Patrologia Latina* 176.814; sixteenth-century English trans.
          qtd. Gray, p. 125).

1671–74   In a passage abounding with commonplace scriptural echoes, these lines make
          especially prominent and explicit allusions to Wisdom 9:2 (God "fitted human
          beings to rule the creatures") and 11:20 (God "ordered all things by measure,
          number, and weight"), the latter "a key text in medieval cosmology" (Burrow,
          English Verse, p. 327n53); at the virtual nadir of the descent of meaning and
          order, humanity is also depicted as its focus.

1675   Attention shifts toward order in seasonal time; Boethius is an important source
          for the concept that the cycle of the seasons exemplifies divine benevolence
          (*Consolation* 4.m4).

1692–1705 In the Prologue to Book 7 of his *Eneados,* Douglas responds enthusiastically to Henryson's set-piece descriptions of the onset of winter, here and in lines 1832–38: see, for example, Douglas' variation on the topic of the stripping of the leaves:

The grond stud barrant, widderit, dosk or gray,	*barren, withered, dark*
Herbis, flowris and gersis wallowyt away.	*grasses faded*
Woddis, forestis, with nakyt bewis blowt,	*bare, barren branches*
Stude stripyt of thar weid in every howt.	*Stood stripped; garments; forest*
(*Eneados* 7.prol.63–66)	

Of Aeolus, god of the winds, Priscilla Bawcutt comments that "[i]n Scottish tradition he absorbs the character of Boreas, the north wind" (*Poems of William Dunbar,* 2:397).

1697–98 The detail of the birds' mourning in winter foreshadows the events of the fable (lines 1836–38); compare the winter scene in *Sir Gawain and the Green Knight,* in which the knight is "Ner slayn wyth the slete" and "mony bryddez unblythe upon bare twyges . . . pitosly ther piped for pyne of the colde" (lines 729; 746–47). Gower, by comparison, couches the effects of seasonal change on avian behavior in terms of the myth of Philomela, the bare trees of winter intensifying the shamed nightingale's wish to hide (*CA* 5.5946–53; compare lines 1832–38). Douglas amplifies this detail in his description of winter:

Smale byrdis, flokkand throu thik ronys thrang
In chyrmyng and with cheping changit thar sang
Sekand hidlis and hyrnys thame to hyde
Fra feirfull thuddis of the tempestuus tyde
(*Eneados* 7.prol.69–72)

[Small birds, flocking through thickly overgrown bushes
Into chirping and cheeping change their song
Seeking hiding-places and nooks to hide themselves
From terrifying gusts of the stormy season]

1707–08 The depiction of spring as the servant of summer is an original twist on the personification of the seasons: as the chief servitor and representative, spring bears the official insignia and thus ensures everything is ready for the arrival of his lord the summer (line 1681); still, Henryson draws back from too close an association between the increasingly pleasant scene and the theme usually associated with it, of kingship (compare 1321–27n): to see the clay underneath the wild columbine is to recognize that this is not the courtly pleasant place (lines 1713–19n).

1710–11 "The small birds of the vivid *descriptio* of spring take their place in the spring opening of the story, to become later [line 1730 and following] its chief actors. The same spring which is the last of one series of seasons becomes the first of another" (Burrow, "*Preaching,*" p. 153). The passage bears comparison with the depiction of the birds in the Prologue to Chaucer's *Legend of Good Women,* except that Chaucer's birds anticipate the fate still in store for Henryson's:

The smale foules, of the sesoun fayn,
That from the panter and the net ben scaped,   *snare*
Upon the fouler, that hem made awhaped   *terrified*
In wynter, and distroyed hadde hire brood,
In his dispit, hem thoghte yt did hem good
To synge of hym, and in hir song despise
The foule cherl that, for his coveytise,
Had hem betrayed with his sophistrye.   *deception*
(F Prol.130–37)

1713   Echoes of the Prologue to Langland's *Piers Plowman* cluster in this fable, here to
            the opening line, "In a somer seson, whan softe was the sonne"; see also line
            1775 (compare *Piers Plowman* Prol.6, "Me bifel a ferly, of Fairye me thoghte";
            Burrow, *English Verse*, p. 332n153–4).

1713–19   The poet's motives contrast with those that impel Amans into the wood at the
            outset of *CA*, "Noght for to singe with the briddes" (1.111) but to lament his
            misfortune in love. Like the figure of the poet in Chaucer's Prologue to the
            Legend of Good Women (G 40–50), Henryson's visitor to the springtime scene
            wants to hear the birds and see the flowers and "the soill that wes richt
            sessonabill," a collocation that, like the "clay" previously (lines 1707–08n), recalls
            the trope in the Prologue of the soil as the ground for the text (lines 8–14n).

1725   Those "that luifit corne" include both birds and farmers; in the hard world of
            this fable, that shared love does not draw them into harmony but pits them in
            competition.

1729   Typically shrubby, its blossoms an early sign of spring, the hawthorn tree
            provides cover in several Middle English and Middle Scots poems to observe
            unusual goings-on undetected (e.g., *Winner and Wastoure*, line 36; Dunbar, *Tretis
            of the Tua Mariit Wemen and the Wedo*, line 14). Gray comments on the "magical
            reputation of the tree" (p. 89n19).

1734   Associations between swallows and prophecy were available to Henryson
            (Isidore, *Etymologiae*, XII.vii.70, p. 268; Vincent of Beauvais, *Speculum naturale*
            16.97.1213, qtd. Hill, "*Hirundines Habent Prescium*," p. 30). In scholastic com-
            mentaries on *Romulus*, the swallow is commonly interpreted to be a preacher
            (Wheatley, *Mastering Aesop*, p. 169). In her exhortation to her flock to work the
            soil for their own future well-being (line 1750), the swallow, like the poet (lines
            8–14n), is also a teacher.

1741   Henryson infuses significance into varieties of laughter: often, as here, a laugh
            or derisive chuckle bespeaks an assumption of superiority and a lowering of
            one's guard — a spontaneously revealed failure to recognize what is at stake
            (e.g., lines 446, 684, 1054; compare line 2329); compare line 1558n.

1754   *Disticha Catonis* 2.24: "Prospice qui veniant, hos casus esse ferendos; / Nam levius
            laedit, quidquid praevidimus ante." The swallow has already provided a trans-
            lation (lines 1738–40). Burrow comments that this maxim "stands at the mathe-
            matical centre of the poem . . . excluding the Moralitas. . . . Perhaps it was
            Henryson's custom, when expounding this passage of [*Romulus*] in the school at

Dunfermline, to use the parallel with Cato as a way of introducing discussion of the fable's moral significance" (*"Preaching,"* pp. 157–58).

1755–58   The passage, as Schrader points out, is strongly Boethian (*Consolation* 2.pr1, qtd. Fox, ed., p. 282). Burrow translates lines 1757–58 thus: "But prudence is an interior process of reasoning (?) which makes a man foresee in advance and observe" (*English Verse*, p. 331n136–7).

1763   As Burrow notes, most of these proverbs will come to pass in ways that lead to the destruction of the lark and her fellows (*English Verse*, p. 332).

1825–31   The fowler and his wife follow an ancient procedure in the making of flax (Fox, ed., pp. 283–84). The pods are raked off at the outset in order to harvest the seeds for oil and planting. While many medieval flax-makers retted the stalks in troughs, the *burn* is convenient for the purpose here. The stalks are then beaten, scraped and raked to extract the fibers, which are spun into thread. The documentary realism of this passage, conveyed by a poet who seems entirely conversant with the activity he is summarizing, forms a precedent for the authenticity in the depiction of rural life in the next two fables, as for instance the description of ploughing in *The Fox, the Wolf, and the Husbandman* (lines 2233–43n).

1846–50   Roerecke contrasts the birds' scraping to the ignorant rooster's search for food in the first fable ("Integrity and Symmetry," pp. 92–96); unlike the rooster, the flock has been taught to read the signs; these birds' "persistence in error, then, is obviously perverse and thus the more blameable" (p. 110).

1887   The abruptness may pertain to the violent catastrophe, after which a return to the consolatory mode of the prologue to the fable would been ill-advised (McKenna, *Henryson's Tragic Vision*, p. 189).

1890   Work that is *autentik* is of enduring importance (*DOST*); it involves truth unadorned by a surface of fiction; compare lines 1013 and 2971–72 for the further possibility that the purveyors of such authenticity are not always to be trusted.

1897   The devil is often depicted as a fowler, and not least when a bird is speaking: Dunbar's blackbird advises "every man that he / With lufe nocht in the feindis net be tone" (Bawcutt, *Poems of William Dunbar*, poem 24, lines 101–02; compare Chaucer, *Legend of Good Women* F Prol.130–37, qtd. lines 1710–11n). Of particular relevance in the comparison is the depiction of the devil as sower of tares (compare lines 366–70; Matthew 12:25), but the reference to the devil as a fallen angel (compare lines 596–99) conveys a motive of particular envy for the birds, which are still blessed with the capacity to fly upwards.

1902–08   By the fifteenth century, the analysis of the process of sin into three parts was conventional; compare Chaucer's Parson's Tale: "deedly synne hath, first, suggestion of the feend . . . and afterward, the delit of the flessh . . . and after that the consentynge of resoun" (*CT* X[I]330–35).

1904   Note the antitype here to the sprouts of knowledge and eloquence in the Prologue to the *Fables* (lines 10–12n).

1908   As elsewhere in the *Fables*, the moral implications of human behavior cause fact
        and fiction to converge: habit likens humanity to the *brutall beistis* (line 397;
        compare lines 54–56, 215–17; see also 786–88n).

1921   The ungodly are conventionally compared to chaff or dust in the wind (e.g.,
        Psalms 1:4, 35:5); adjacent to one such comparison is a no less relevant analogy
        between ephemerality and the flight of a bird (Wisdom 5:14; compare 5:10).

1932   The memorably grisly image of the grave as the worms' kitchen neatly achieves
        an inversion of worldly values: it is a mark of social distinction to be served from
        a kitchen.

1949   Fellowship with the angels in heaven articulates a factor to the delight of this
        fable: the energetic flight of the birds draws out the more fiendish aspects of the
        fowler's hatred for them (line 1897n).

The Fox, the Wolf, and the Cadger
Arthur Richard Diebler identified a source for this fable to be *Roman de Renart, branche* 14,
episode 10 (*Henrisone's Fabeldichtungen*, pp. 65–68). Henryson appears to have been especially
inventive here; his "account merely follows the outlines of the story" (Jamieson, "Poetry,"
242–43). Agreeing that the two versions resemble each other only slightly, Fox speculates
that "Henryson may well have known an oral version" (ed., p. 289).

1955   Anger is the element in which the characters of this fable operate: the wolf, who
        is its principal exponent at the outset, seems to pass it to the fox, who takes
        offense at having to swear an oath of loyalty (line 2023); and by stealing the fish
        and then cursing his victim, the fox passes it along to the cadger (line 2098); it
        is not until the penultimate fable, *The Wolf and the Lamb*, that the wolf again
        becomes chiefly identified by wrath. The association between rage and wind
        present in *breith* returns in the simile for the cadger's anger, "wraith as ony
        wind" (line 2168; compare Dunbar, "I maister Andro Kennedy," line 26).

1956   The alliterative collocation "feud or favor" recurs in Scots, most early in official
        documents (*DOST fede*, n.1c; compare 2165).

1962   Elsewhere in the *Fables*, foxes are called *Lowrence* or *Lowrie* (429n); here, the
        name *Russell* appears for the only time in the work (compare *CT* VII[B²]3334).
        The wolf may be making a clumsy pun on the expression *russat gray*, meaning
        "undyed homespun cloth" (line 679, *Orpheus* line 158), in which case he is
        alluding to the fox's comparative poverty; or he may be using *russel*, meaning
        "red thing" (*MED russel*, n.a; *DOST russell*, 2n), as in "you gray red thing"; if so,
        this is the first of several references to actual or supposed characteristics of the
        animal (compare lines 1982n, 1991, 2001) — the fox tends to have a silver-gray
        cast to the fur on its haunches and under its tail.

1966–68 As steward, the fox is to be the wolf's chief executive officer, though the term can
        be used, as in England, to refer to a household administrator responsible for
        provisions. The term also has high political associations, the Stewart of Scotland
        being the "officer of state next after the king," and, since Robert II, a title of the

king's eldest son (*DOST stewart*). The parodic usage of the term is compounded by the fox's reluctance; he is compelled to take his place as a tricky servitor, not, as in *The Cock and the Fox*, as an outcome of his flattery, but at the insistence of the wolf; strategically or not, Lowrence plays hard to get.

1967   The expression "knap doun caponis" recalls a line from the Scots burlesque romance *Rauf Coilyear*, "Knap doun capounis of the best, but in the byre" ("Knock down some of the best capons out in the barn," line 111); perhaps the wolf is being associated in passing with the boorish, overbearing hero of that romance, who is calling for the capons; the echoic *knap* begins a sequence of vividly rendered sounds in this fable: *swak* (lines 2076, 2146), *swakkit* (line 2081), *trimmillit* (line 2098), *hakkit* (line 2103), *battis* (line 2182), *dungin* (line 2196).

1982   Foxes are notorious for their odor, emitted from glands under the tale and on the feet; again, as with the verbal echoing of sounds noted above (line 1967n), the representation of the keen sensory apprehension of the world, this time through smell, conveys both danger and desire; compare line 2030.

1997   This is one of several instances in the *Fables* in which a proverb rebounds upon its user (e.g., lines 102n, 1031–33n, 1763n, 2063–69n). See Whiting F49.

2000–06   The fox's disinclination to fish makes an allusion to *The Fox and the Wolf*, in another situation in which penance is required and dodged (lines 719–21); the fox in that fable was killed, which may suggest that chronology has not been maintained — or, more significantly, that all foxes are the same in regard to penance and fishing. MacQueen notes the relation between the numerical structure of the fable and the season of Lent: forty stanzas for forty days ("Lent" p. 117; compare line 248n and lines 2034, 2120, 2153).

2002   The size of a minnow, the stickleback has spines on its back and armor plates on its sides; it would not make an appetizing morsel for a fox, let alone a wolf.

2010   Bawcutt translates the line thus: "You expect to manipulate me, playing with me as if I were a cat that would chase a straw" (*Poems of William Dunbar*, 2:364).

2021–22   "The additional oath of loyalty demanded by the Wolf is particularly relevant to fifteenth-century Scottish circumstances; in effect it is a bond of manrent" (MacQueen, "Lent," p. 115); on such bonds between lords and servitors, see lines 438–40n.

2025–27   "Errour of naciouns and feynynges of poetis menen that Jubiter was highest fadir of goddis" (Bartholomaeus VIII.12, Seymour-Smith, *On the Properties of Things*, 1:480); to swear by Jupiter is to swear falsely; compare lines 2869–71.

2028   The spelling *cadgear* is typical of late sixteenth-century MSc orthography; the spellings current in the 1490s are *cagger, kegger*. Henryson's is the earliest use of the word in Scots (*DOST, cadge(a)r, cage(a)r*).

2042   In English, the pejorative significance of *pelf* is taken to emerge in the sixteenth century (*OED pelf*, n); In "Abbey Walk" the expression "warldlie pelf" (line 51) is used with such a connotation, which may be an indication of the poem's having been written by someone other than Henryson. Here, the fox means it to refer admiringly and avidly to prospectively stolen goods.

2045   *not worth ane fle*. Proverbial. See Whiting F263. Compare *Fables*, line 2286.

2046   Bawcutt and Riddy note "a subdued irony, since the bee is usually a type of honest industry" (*Longer Scottish Poems*, p. 364).

2052–55   The "unliklie" posture of the fox playing dead inspires the cadger to dance his grotesque little jig of triumph (lines 2060–62); the exchange of emotions and sensory experiences, noted above as a narrative technique in this fable (lines 1967n, 1982n) appears to be realized in an exchange of distorted gestures, which in turn will ensnare the wolf (lines 2161–67); the sequence represents a development of the technique employed in the depiction of the exaggerated pose the fox urges on Chantecleir (lines 462–80) and of the languorous loll affected by the fox himself just before he is shot (757–60n).

2063–69   The mishandling of proverbs indicates the supreme readiness of the speaker for a comeuppance (e.g., 1997n): the cadger mangles two sayings in rapid succession: the devil seldom lies dead in a ditch and the fox prospers when the farmer's wife curses him (Fox, ed., p. 293; Bawcutt and Riddy, *Longer Scottish Poems*, p. 364).

2074   Though not as economically important as wool, hides were a staple of Scottish trade with Flanders (Whyte, *Scotland before the Industrial Revolution*, pp. 59, 73–74).

2083   The rousing morning song "Hunt's up" was being sung in England in the early sixteenth century (*OED hunt's-up*); Henryson's is the earliest reference, though, as in English, there are several occurrences in sixteenth-century Scots (*DOST hunt* n.1.b). The word *hunt* to refer to the pursuit rather than the pursuer is earliest attested in Scots, although a strikingly early English example appears in Chaucer (*CT* I[A]2628).

2089   The word *nekhering* has two meanings in Scots: a heavy hit to the nape of the neck (a translation of the Latin *colaphus*) and a kind of herring, the shad (Latin *collacus*; *DOST nekhering*).

2127   The appeal to the senses produces a redolent line: *callour* is an adjective applied to fine salmon in which the flesh is richly flecked with jellied fat (*MED calver*; compare *OED calver* a. and v.); the simile of the partridge's eye "might be used appropriately to describe the glistening skin of a fresh-caught salmon" (Fox, ed., p. 296). The key to all this distracting vividness of sensory appeal is that it is entirely a ruse — the fox is conjuring up a fantasy fish for the greedily willful wolf.

2154   *In principio*, "In the beginning," the opening words of both Genesis and the Gospel of John, used as a greeting by begging friars and as a charm (*CT* I(A)254; Bloomfield, "Magic of *In Principio*," pp. 559–65). This detail of satire against the friars reverses the roles played in *The Fox and the Wolf*.

2189–90   The proverb is borne out by the wolf's comeuppance but not by the fox's success; the discrepancy is resolved in the *Moralitas*, in which the fox is the supreme trickster, the world (line 2205; compare lines 2063–69n).

2228   The proverb (Whiting P421, 423) clinches the sensory appeal and its disastrous frustration traced in the language and narrative structure of the fable: lured by the worldly fox, the wolf and the cadger have proceeded without perception and have come to confusion.

The Fox, the Wolf, and the Husbandman
A source for this fable has been identified in Steinhöwel's *Esopus* (8.10; Lyall, "Henryson's *Moral Fabillis*," p. 375) or one of its translations; in Steinhöwel, this is the tenth in a series of in twelve fables derived from a widely-distributed compilation, the *Disciplina Clericalis* of Petrus Alfonsi. Fox adds that "the greater part of Henryson's version is original: it is only the bare bones of the plot and a few details which can be parallelled in the earlier works" (ed., p. 300).

2233–43   The documentary precision of this description of ploughing with oxen creates the impression of a strong contrast with the preceding fable with its dizzying sensory appeal; looking back across that tale of illusion, this opening recalls the description of flax-making in *The Preaching of the Swallow* (lines 1825–31n).

2234   "Streiking tyme" ("ploughing time") is ambiguous: this could be autumn (as soon as late August), early winter, or early spring; the simile of the angry hare (line 2242n) may imply the latter. However, if the fox's vision of a "somer cheis" (line 2355) indicates the freshness of the item, the autumn would make better sense.

2235, 2241 The ploughman's view of the furrow contrasts with that of the burgh mouse, toiling "Fra fur to fur" in search of her sister (line 185).

2237   The ploughman's religious interjection *Benedicité* deserves comparison with the earlier misuse of this holy greeting (line 693n). Perhaps the world of this fable is not so far after all from one in which a wolf in friar's clothing blesses a possibly penitent fox, or in which a supposedly solicitous fox utters *In principio* as a charm to avert bad luck (line 2154n). The opening realism may be nothing but a ruse; after all, the complete hoax of the big cheese lies ahead.

2242   The Scots proverbial depiction of the hare as an epitome of anger corresponds to the expression more usual in English, "mad as a March hare" (Fox, ed., p. 301).

2246   Compared to Steinhöwel and Petrus Alfonsi, in both of which versions the fox is a latecomer to the dispute, here the fox is at the center of the scene from the outset; "it is Lowrence who instigates the action, encouraging the Wolf to take the Husbandman's cursing of his oxen seriously" (Lyall, "Henryson's *Moral Fabillis*," p. 366); the same decisive shift of focus toward the fox occurs when he volunteers to judge the dispute (line 2310).

2251   The wolf will treat the plowman's words as if they were as binding as a king's *verbum* or judgment (Hill, "*Stet Verbum Regis*," p. 129), a position made valid by the medieval perception that "the mental faculty most readily associated with promises was not intention but will"; in other words, "one was felt to be

answerable for the performative power of one's own words even when one had
no intention of making them perform anything" (Green, *Crisis of Truth*, pp. 310,
312). An outcome of the wolf's position is that the plowman is placed on equal
footing with the sovereign in terms of the weight of his utterances; a moral lesson
about controlling one's speech is implicit, but so is a political one about the
responsibilities shared by individuals at all ranks in society. In effect, integrity
is true nobility; compare *Testament*, lines 551–53n.

2253–54   At this point, Henryson's phrasing resembles that found in several versions of
Steinhöwel's *Esopus*, Caxton's among them: "And whanne the nyght was come
/ the labourer vnbonde his oxen / and lete them goo to his hows / And thenne
whanne the wulf sawe them comynge homeward . . ." (Lenaghan, *Caxton's Aesop*,
p. 206; qtd. Lyall, "Henryson's *Moral Fabillis*," p. 367).

2255   The wolf is depicted with a limp; with Henryson's depiction of the "hirpilland
hair" in mind (line 903n), one might suppose that the wolf is ready to be "angrie
as ane hair," as the plowman was previously (line 2242n); but more likely this
awkward pace indicates his hesitancy to approach the man, even now that the
hour is "weill lait" (line 2253); the same can be said for the *lourand* approach of
the fox when he emerges from cover (line 2294).

2259   Gray comments that "We feel no more surprised when the wolf accosts the
husbandman . . . than we do in the ballad when Thomas the Rhymer meets the
Queen of fair Elfland. This is the result of a confident and consummate skill in
narrative art" (p. 82).

2270   The *plank*, a coin of small value, was first minted in Scotland about 1470 (*DOST
plak*, n.). The occurrence of the word offers evidence of a date after which the fable
was written or at least revised; compare the date of publication of the Aesopic
tradition likeliest to have provided its source — Steinhöwel (1476–77), translated
into French by Macho (1480), translated in turn into English by Caxton (1483–84).

2280–83   Again (compare line 2251n) the wolf insists on the fundamental parity between
the word of a lord and that of a farmer.

2285–86   *But lawte . . . nocht worth ane fle*. Proverbial. See Whiting F263. Compare *Fables*,
line 2045.

2329   In the role of a judge, Lowrence exemplifies the corruption of the office
depicted in *The Sheep and the Dog* (line 1265n); see also line 1741n on the
possible significance of the fox's laugh.

2332   Lowrence's allusion to the scriptural theme of the sleep of God underscores the
relation between the present parody of judicial procedure and that which is
featured in *The Sheep and the Dog*, in the *Moralitas* to which it was the suffering
victim who cried out "O lord, quhy sleipis thow sa lang?" (lines 1286–1320n).
Now the sleep of God is complacently assumed by the wicked.

2335   The Wife of Bath also uses this proverb (*CT* III[D]415).

2346   To rave "unrocked" is to act wildly without provocation (*DOST rok* v.). In *The
Testament of the Papyngo*, Lyndsay uses the phrase in a Henrysonian dialogue

between scavenging birds (line 969). The repeated association between the expression and low-life characters suggests that it is markedly coarse, a quality Henryson sharpens by Lowrence's uttering it in the same breath as a blasphemous oath (*OED rock* v1.6a; *DOST rok* v. 2; compare *Orpheus* line 284).

2362   The comparison between the worthless outcome of further dispute and a withered turnip has its counterpoise in a cheese promised to be "Quhyte as ane neip" ("white as a turnip," line 2395), especially when that cheese is later moralized as the vice of covetousness (line 2448).

2392   Though the expression "shadow of the moon" has been taken as evidence that Henryson had read Caxton's version of the fable (Jamieson, "Poetry," p. 257; MacQueen, *Robert Henryson*, p. 219), the word *schadow* is "Henryson's normal term for 'reflection', or 'reflected image' (compare *Testament*, line 348)" (Fox, ed., p. 306).

2408   As in the preceding fable, the fox lures the wolf into the final stage of the trick by appealing to his superior strength (compare lines 2124–25).

2418–19   The question whether Henryson copied "if one goes up, the other must come down" from Caxton can be answered by noting that this proverb is widely distributed by the late fifteenth century and would have occurred to more than one reteller of this fable (Whiting B575).

2427–30   As noted above (line 1955n), Henryson gives much more prominence to the wicked oppression of the wolf in his version of *The Wolf and the Lamb* (Wheatley, *Mastering Aesop*, p. 183).

2437–39   Scholars have often expressed perplexity with the apparent arbitrariness of the interpretations offered in this *Moralitas*. Foremost among the problematic details is the identification of the hens with the good works by which a medieval Christian avoids falling into the devil's clutches. Kratzmann regards the topic of the hens as "ridiculously far-fetched," speculates about its "playful mockery," and, relenting, concludes that "Henryson manages to have it both ways, and to give the game a serious edge" ("Henryson's *Fables*," p. 67; for further comment, see Lyall, "Henryson's *Moral Fabillis*," p. 371). Jamieson speculates that Protestant revision has been so extensive that it is not even "certain that we have Henryson's own *moralitas* to this fable," at least in regard to specific details ("Poetry," p. 272). Wheatley is less disturbed by the hens: "Much ink has been spent deriding the allegory of the hens as good deeds; scholastic commentators recurrently gloss various characters in fables thus" (*Mastering Aesop*, p. 184).

The Wolf and the Wether
Steinhöwel's *Esopus* and its translations contain the source for this fable (5.15; Perry no. 703).

2465   The simile is a conventional indication of the pallor and gauntness of grief (*Orpheus*, line 350; *DOST wed(e* n.2).

2471   The shepherd's lament may have burlesque associations: *darling* is a word typical of love and marriage, as when Troilus mourns Cresseid, "sumtyme his awin darling" (*Testament*, line 504) or Pertok bewails the loss of Chantecleir, "our drowrie and our dayis darling" (line 497).

2472–73   The decision to leave home and wander into the countryside has penitential undertones; compare the burgh mouse going to visit her sister (lines 180–87).

2475   The verb *schute* establishes the threat of deadly violence (*DOST* s(c)hute v.1.b) but later (line 2567) signals the success of coarse humor in reversing that threat.

2480–89   "[T]he sheep disguised in a dog's skin is a living and comic image of the meaning hidden within the deceptive outer form of fiction" (Spearing, *Medieval to Renaissance*, p. 194; compare lines 15–16n); it is also a reminder of the assertion made by the lion in *The Lion and the Mouse*, that the image of power — a skin stuffed with straw — should be honored as much as the powerful person whose image it represents (lines 1449–53n); in the recurrence of the theme, Henryson is not far from King Lear's dog in office.

2495   The collocation "wanton of his weed" may appear to suggest that the ram becomes self-indulgent or extravagant because of his new clothes; more likely, this is an early example of the word to refer to insolence or even mercilessness (*OED wanton* a.4b. compare 5a.; *MED wantoun* a, b); his declared lack of fear for the wolf reveals that his appearance has made a fool of him already.

2518–25   Alliteration and "carefully chosen visual details" heighten the rendering of violent action (Gray, p. 106); the passage deserves comparison with the description of an earlier dog-chase (lines 551–53n).

2537   In the landscape of the chase, the *rekill* appears to mark a boundary between farmland and wilderness; the peats would be stacked after being dug out from the bog (lines 827–28n). Now the chase is in the wolf's territory.

2555–56   The topic of mingled play and earnest, which now gains prominence in the final stages of the narration (lines 2558, 2560, 2564, 2577, 2583) is initiated by the wolf; he sees the game as an instrument of *scorne* that will lower his standing.

2575   The ram's excuse that he intended no harm to the person of the wolf makes clear that he understands the damage done thereby to the respect owed the wolf; his only excuse, a feeble one, is that he did not intend to cause this damage.

2584   "The wolf is more upset about his little accident than anything, and returns to it again and again; it seems he cannot get over the needless indignity of it. (He is a gentleman, after all)" (Pearsall, ed., *Chaucer*, p. 497; compare lines 2562–63, 2567).

2588   Wondering how to distinguish between surface ornament and meaningful core in this stanza, MacQueen calls it "one of the most Lydgatean stanzas [Henryson] ever wrote" (*Robert Henryson*, p. 186); Mehl compares it to the stanza at the start of the *Moralitas* to *The Cock and the Fox* and adds that "in both cases there is a certain self-consciousness and a contrast of tone that is quite unlike Lydgate" ("Robert Henryson's *Moral Fables*," p. 98); after the sudden violence of the previous stanza, this ceremonious retreat into latinate abstraction is diplomatic and prepares for the safely orthodox meaning about to be derived from the fable; high rhetorical style is being donned like a robe of office.

2598–2601   That an overweening "pure man" can "counterfute ane lord in all degree" indicates a flaw in the system of badges of rank, one that can be repaired only by its expansion to an unsustainable prominence ("clym sa hie") and a subsequent correction through inversion ("tit thair heillis over thair heid"). Events in fifteenth-century Scotland bore out this principle: for example, under James I, the Parliament of 1430 passed an act that "grouped persons into classes of society and prescribed the permitted standards of dress for each" (Walker, *Legal History*, p. 183).

2599   Compare lines 371–72.

2610–11   For Pearsall, "there seems a particular uneasiness in the relation of fable and *Moralitas* when the reference is to social rather than religious obligations" (*Chaucer*, p. 498). However, the moral might also be seen as a counter to the situation of the previous fable, with which it is closely linked in terms of their common source in Steinhöwel; the potentially inexpedient emphasis there on a nobility based on integrity rather than blood is here covered by an insistence on the necessity for rigidly maintained ranks. But in his bodily reaction to fear, the lordly wolf has already submitted perforce to the common circumstances of animal nature, in a memorable reduction of natural equality into parity with beasts (lines 48–50).

The Wolf and the Lamb

The *Fables* return to their principal source, *Romulus*: *De lupo et agno* ("The Wolf and the Lamb") is the second in the Latin sequence (A. Wright, *Fables*, pp. 26–28). The simple, long-established narrative elicits special inventiveness in the *Moralitas*, "although of course the fable was commonly used to show how the powerful unjustly oppress the poor" (Fox, ed., p. 315). Henryson's foregrounding of dialogue has been likened to Lydgate's in his version of the fable (Davenport, *Medieval Narrative*, p. 90); however, Lydgate begins with the wolf's accusatory comparison between the "false and double" lamb and his "contrary" father (lines 260–66); Lydgate's lamb, much less eloquent than Henryson's, simply repeats helplessly that he stood downstream (lines 272–84; Lydgate, *Minor Poems*, 2:574–76). Dialogue is central to all versions deriving from *Romulus*, including those of Marie de France (*Fables*, pp. 32–35) and Odo of Cheriton (Jacobs, *Fables*, p. 95).

2634   Drawing (being dragged to the gallows) and hanging constituted a punishment notoriously enacted by Edward I in Scotland for treason; as perpetuated under Robert I, it has been deemed "less brutal than the contemporary English practice in that it omitted disembowelling and quartering of the victims' bodies, but was grim enough" (Walker, *Legal History*, p. 528; see also Bellamy, *Law of Treason*, p. 23; Walker, *Legal History*, pp. 85, 88; *Fables*, line 1460).

2650   The *Ergo* reveals the logician in sheep's clothing: evidently the lamb has been well-schooled; all the more does he irritate the wolf.

2657–61   Compare lines 1191–94; in the order in which they appear in the sixteenth-century prints, the order followed in this edition, the generational progression of relationships and hostilities — the rising feuds of the fable world — take form.

2663–68   The lamb proceeds to a higher level of authority, citing Ezekiel 18 on the limits of retribution.

2672   The question whether the father's guilt is visited upon the son opens up a scriptural discrepancy that the wolf is quick to exploit in his allusion to Exodus 20:5; St. Thomas Aquinas comments on the conflicting interpretations of guilt (*Summa theologiae* I–II, q.81, a.2; qtd. Fox, ed., p. 317); in insisting on the unforgiving pursuit of vengeance from generation unto generation, the wolf is upholding the principle of the feud.

2676–78   The wolf's accusation that the lamb's father planned to poison the water advances his attack on three fronts: it makes a distractingly scandalous diversion from the minutiae of textual debate (in which the lamb has already demonstrated his skill), a tactical response to the lamb's assertion that his lips are not *contagious* but *sweit* (lines 2652, 2654), and a sharpening of the actual charge according to Scots criminal law, the Poison Acts of 1450 having made the importation of such substances a capital crime (Walker, *Legal History*, pp. 527; 550, note 58).

2693–94   In a striking personification, the wolf is accusing the lamb of "intruding reason" as if the action were like asserting the right of a false claimant for a property; this "propertie" should be shared by those already in possession, the wolf's preferred "wrang and reif." Laying aside all his previous fantastic theories about spewing poison and the crimes of the father (lines 2672 and following), the wolf now declares that the real treason is that the lamb's insistence on mercy, *reuth*, is overturning the custom of *crueltie* in these parts.

2702   The grim parody of the Mass renders the wolf's inversion of values blatant.

2716   The wielders of "polished terms" are here the corrupt lawyers; the only other occurrence of the phrase in the *Fables* is in the Prologue (line 3), in which it refers to "feinyeit fabils of ald poetre"; blending terms is what poets do, like lawyers; it is an activity that mirrors the nature of existence in the world, with adversity *intermellit* with joy (line 368n); and, like fine clothes on the backs of churls, it often produces confusion and corruption (lines 2598–2601n); the theme reemerges in the first part of the *Moralitas* to *The Paddock and the Mouse* (lines 2910–25, 2912n.; compare *Testament* line 241).

2728–34   Landlords' oppression of tenants is a topic of complaint in Middle Scots poetry, occurring, for example in Dunbar, "Efter geving I speik of taking" (Bawcutt, *Poems of William Dunbar*, poem 46, lines 11–20; 2:382).

2745–48   Though the Leases Act (1449) and Diligence Act (1469) had done much to alleviate the problems of tenants, legal disputes over landlords' wrongful claims were rife in later fifteenth-century Scotland (Walker, *Legal History*, pp. 676–80); one such case, in Traquair (south of Edinburgh, some distance from Dunfermline) involved a group of tenants that included a Robert Henryson (Mathews, "Land," p. 46).

The Paddock and the Mouse

For his source, Henryson turns to the fable immediately following *De lupo et agno* in *Romulus*, *De mure et rana* ("The Mouse and the Frog"; A. Wright, *Fables*, pp. 29–31). The *Moralitas* follows the tradition of the commentaries in focusing on key elements of the narrative: "Henryson has taken the image of the paddock and mouse struggling in the water and then caught up unawares by the kite, and has made it into a powerful and gloomy symbol for man's earthly life" (Fox, ed., p. 325).

2785   Given its aquatic setting, the *paddok* (*OED paddock* n.1: *pad* n.1 + the diminutive suffix *-ock; MED paddok(e* n.) is not a toad but a frog, "watery and morische, crying and slymy, with a grete wombe and ysplekked therunder and is venemous and abhominable therfore to men and most yhated. And bothe in water and in londe he lyveth" (Bartholomaeus XVIII.91, Seymour-Smith, *On the Properties of Things*, 2:1243).

2795–97   Compare the burgh mouse's refusal of her sister's rustic meal (lines 222–23); a reluctance to work one's way through nutshells suggests a parallel reluctance to see beyond the surface of things (lines 15–16n).

2830   In the *Flyting* with Walter Kennedie, Dunbar recalls this sentiment, "Thocht I wald lie, thy frawart phisnomy / Dois manifest thy malice to all men" (lines 81–82); perhaps the mouse is so easily deflected from her justifiable suspicion because she bases it solely upon the frog's physiognomy.

2832   A translation (line 2830) anticipates the Latin proverb (Walther, *Proverbia Sententiaeque Latinitatis Medii Aevi*, no. 6026).

2842   The frog is alluding not to Absalon in the Miller's Tale but to the biblical Absalom, the handsome, rebellious son of King David (2 Samuel 13–19).

2865   The "murthour aith" is recorded only here and in line 2884; the phrase seems to refer to a pledge to protect the life of one for whom one is undertaking a service of carriage: Walker notes that such oaths were considered binding by both divine and natural law (*Legal History*, p. 600).

2869–71   MacQueen reads this oath "subjecting the pair to the god of nature" as an emblem of "the binding together of body and soul" (*Complete and Full with Numbers*, p. 97); compare lines 2025–27n.

2892   Compare lines 331–33n, 1525n.

2896   "The kite is evoked with the same kind of savagery as the fiendish churl in *The Preaching of the Swallow*" (Kratzmann, "Henryson's *Fables*," p. 64). Throughout the fables, Henryson's birds of prey (compare *gled* and *graip*, lines 1175–79n) have been scavengers; the Scottish poet refuses to emulate Chaucer's interest in noble eagles and hawks.

2901   The kite "hath a voys of pleynynge and of mone as it were messenger of hungir, for when he hungrith he sechith his mete pewlynge with voys of pleynynge and of mone" (Bartolomaeus XII.27; Seymour-Smith, *On the Properties of Things*, 1:635).

2903–05   In his translation of this fable, Seamus Heaney mutes the alliteration but does
           not soften the grisliness of this climactic passage:

> That butcher disembowelled them with his bill,
> Flayed them, stripped the skin off inside out
> Like taking off a sock, but guts and all,
> Their flesh only half-filled that greedy kite.

2904   From this starkly memorable line, it is possible to look back at what Rosemary
           Greentree describes as a "recurring motif . . . that of stripping away the outer
           covering, in a metaphorical or a literal sense. . . . Thus the literal references to
           skinning and stripping carry at least the threat of death, and we see a change in
           the creatures affected as the *Fables* proceed" (*Reader*, pp. 79–80; compare
           15–16n, lines 774, 812, 1309, 1450).

2910–33   The first three stanzas of the *Moralitas* are in the ballade with refrain (*ababbcbC*),
           the stanza used for the *Moralitas* to *The Two Mice* (lines 365–96); as there,
           Henryson varies the phrasing in the refrain. The ballade befits a passage in which
           the moralization is straightforward and static: avoid committing yourself to a
           dishonest partner; many have been ruined by such relationships; it is better to
           be alone than to be bound in such a partnership — Henryson properly refers to
           the passage as "This simpill counsall" (line 2930). Nevertheless, he is about to
           enter a zone of discourse in which it is revealed that all is not as it seems in this
           fable.

2912   As in "Against Hasty Credence," flattery and lying are judged to be "Moir
           perrellus than ony pestilence" (line 30).

2923   Geoffrey of Vinsauf, *Poetria nova* line 201 (Wheatley, *Mastering Aesop*, pp.
           174–75); Henryson's fox might not agree with this line (line 760).

2934   Kratzmann observes the double marking of a change of direction at this point
           in the *Moralitas*: not only does the stanza revert to rhyme royal after three
           stanzas of ballade, but the new stanza begins with "explicit authorial comment"
           ("Henryson's *Fables*," p. 63).

2939–47   Although Henryson delays making explicit the commonplace "waves of
           tribulation" (line 2956), he is imitating that ebb and flow in his anaphora on
           "Now." Early in this "Now" sequence (line 2939) appears a brief reversion to the
           "quhylis" formula that has previously signified mutability in both narrative and
           exclamatory modes (line 1525n); Kratzmann notes the gravity of Henryson's
           style, "masterly alliterative colloquialism within the control of an insistently
           rhetorical form" ("Henryson's *Fables*," p. 63).

2948   The binding of the soul to the body is a theme also present in the *Moralitas* to
           Orpheus (lines 451–54). Spearing adds perceptively that "it is tempting also to
           see [the frog and mouse] as the literal and the allegorical, 'Standand distynit in
           thair opinioun' (line 2958), yet unbreakably linked" (*Medieval to Renaissance*, p.
           194).

2966   The reduction of the audience to a single person, "my freind" (also line 2969), may reflect a pessimism akin to that expressed by Aesop in the prologue to *The Lion and the Mouse* (lines 1391–97), concerning the capacity of fables to hold and teach an audience (Wheatley, *Mastering Aesop*, p. 187); noting a parallel occurrence in Dunbar ("He hes anewch that is content," line 11), Bawcutt points out, however, that "Such addresses were common in didactic verse" (*Poems of William Dunbar*, 2:401).

2970   Wheatley (*Mastering Aesop*, p. 188) hears the voice of a "sadder and a wiser man" who is preparing to undertake what Aesop earlier referred to as "mair autentik werk" (line 1890). In the assertion that this fable is ending "schortlie," Kratzmann and Mehl perceive an irony that may involve a dig at the friars ("Henryson's *Fables*," p. 65; "Robert Henryson's *Moral Fables*," p. 93); compare lines 1890n, 2154n.

2972   A gesture of closure can be traced in this echo of a passage in the Prologue (lines 47–49n) in which the superficial function of fables — to show animals behaving like people — is inverted; the repetition recalls the "initial announcement" (Roerecke, "Integrity and Symmetry," pp. 96–97).

THE TESTAMENT OF CRESSEID (*NIMEV* 285)

The Testament of Cresseid, an inventively tragic completion in 79 rhyme royal stanzas with an inset complaint in seven nine-line (*Anelida*) stanzas of Chaucer's *Troilus and Criseyde*, can fairly be called Henryson's most controversial poem. A brief review of the narrative may be helpful. In the prologue, an aging man, forced by bitter wind to abandon his place at his window where he has been bestowing delighted attention on the ascent of the planet Venus, retreats to his chamber with its warming fire and begins to read in order to pass the time on a wintry Lenten night. First he reads the fifth book of Chaucer's *Troilus and Criseyde*; then he takes up another little book (a *quair*, "quire") about the fate of Cresseid, the story he proceeds to narrate. Diomeid's repudiation of Cresseid and the reader-poet's conflicted response to Cresseid's consequent degradation lead rapidly to Cresseid's withdrawal to the residence of her father Calchas, here depicted as a priest of Venus (lines 103–05n). In a private chapel, Cresseid rebukes her patron gods Venus and Cupid for not honoring what she considers their commitment to keep her in a perpetual springtime of desirability. On uttering these words, Cresseid falls into a trance, during which the planetary gods (Saturn, Jupiter, Mars, Phoebus the sun, Venus, Mercury, and Cynthia the moon, each described in memorable detail) descend at Cupid's eerie bell-ringing summons. Cupid utters his complaint about Cresseid's disloyalty, and Mercury appoints Saturn and Cynthia to determine the punishment, which is to be leprosy. Cresseid awakens and departs for a lepers' hospital in a village nearby, where she spends much of the night lamenting her changed circumstances, in a formal complaint; a "lipper lady" advises her to accept her new life. The scene shifts out-of-doors, to the return of Troilus from battle along the road where the lepers are begging. Though neither Cresseid nor Troilus recognizes the other, Troilus, stirred by the recollection of the deeply-imprinted image of his beloved, hurls a quantity of money and jewels down upon Cresseid's "skirt" and rides on. Learning that the benefactor was Troilus, Cresseid is transfixed with pain, repeats her newfound realization of her falseness in contrast to Troilus' loyalty, composes her last testament, and dies. The poem ends with the reader-poet pointing the moral to "worthie wemen," not to mix love with deception.

Recent work on the poem has addressed some perennial topics of contention: Henryson's relation to Chaucer, the function of the narrator, the propriety of the planetary gods, and the attitude towards Cresseid. To begin with, the relation between the *Testament* and *TC* is the debatable land of Henryson scholarship. Condemnations of Henryson for being a flawed, "univocal" reader of Chaucer (Bennett, "Henryson's *Testament*"; Strohm, "Writers as Readers," pp. 100–01) have stimulated attention to the boldness of Henryson's "antithetical misreading" (Spearing, *Medieval to Renaissance*, p. 168) — fitting qualities given the prominence of debate in the *Parliament of Fowls* and the *Canterbury Tales* — in contrast to the voluminous responses to Chaucer by his English follower John Lydgate (Watson, "Outdoing Chaucer"). Explicitly connecting his poem to Chaucer's, Henryson initiated what became the dominant English response to the *Testament*, namely as a tailpiece to *TC*. Its inclusion in Thynne's edition of Chaucer's works, pendant to *Troilus and Criseyde* and preceding the *Legend of Good Women*, ensured that for English readers it would remain closely associated with Chaucer during the sixteenth century and after, notably in Gascoigne's "Dan Bartholomew his second Triumphe," Turbervile's *Epitaphes, Epigrams, etc.*, and Whetstone's *The Rocke of Regard* (Forni, *Chaucerian Apocrypha*, p. 114), as well as Heywood's *A Woman Killed with Kindness* and Shakespeare's *Troilus and Cressida* (Fradenburg, "Henryson Scholarship," p. 68). Indeed, the late sixteenth-century "Laste Epistle of Creseyde to Troyalus," despite its Scottish provenance, may best be seen as an element of this English reception of the *Testament* as virtually indistinguishable from *TC* (McKim, *Laste Epistle*, introduction; Kelly, *Chaucerian Tragedy*, pp. 232–33).

Well-worked as the question of literary relations may be, it offers scope for development. Anna Torti notes promisingly that the complementary relation between *Testament* and *TC*, Henryson's poem standing as "a parenthesis within Chaucer's narrative," is "severed by the end of Henryson's poem. The *Testament* is no longer an ideal parenthesis of *TC*, but a variation on it — a 'continuation' which radically changes its source's narrative sequence and meaning" ("From 'History' to 'Tragedy,'" pp. 186, 187). Finally, Cresseid's fate is not the least significant contrast Henryson makes to *Troilus and Criseyde*, which ends with Troilus' ascent "Up to the holughnesse of the eighthe spere" from whence he "fully gan despise / This wrecched world" (5.1809, 1816–17).

Considerations are ongoing over the implications for Scottish poetry, and for Henryson's authorship in particular, of his notorious question "Quha wait gif all that Chauceir wrait was trew?" with its emphasis on the moral ambiguity inherent in the poet's making of fiction. Between Denton Fox's edition of Henryson in 1981 and the present edition, essays and studies on *The Testament of Cresseid* have redefined the role of the poet in the work. The poem with its occasional "disjunctions" and "awkwardness" has been taken to project the "attitudes of sorrow, sympathy, understanding, and forgiveness" of an "imperfect, and vulnerable, author" (Kelly, *Chaucerian Tragedy*, p. 259). Of help in reading the passages of direct discourse in the first person is the perception that the "I" assumes a choric role, "not only the tale teller, but also a witness of the action" (McKenna, *Henryson's Tragic Vision*, p. 118). The *Testament* presents a first-person perspective at rhetorically apt junctures: the opening depiction of an old man's "retrospection on youth" shows "an 'I' that is explicitly brought into being by the act of writing" that establishes a "'comic' aspect of the poem" (Riddy, "'Abject Odious,'" p. 245; Torti, "From 'History' to 'Tragedy,'" p. 190). A more austere estimate of the narrative perspective emerges in considerations of the stanzas in which the poet apostrophizes his protagonist (lines 77–91): "a Chaucerian note of febrile sympathy for Cresseid which deliberately leaves us unsure of how to judge her" befits an ongoing effort to correlate the merged vices of pride and lechery with the "abhominabill" person of Cresseid (Godman, "Henryson's Masterpiece," p. 296; Riddy, "'Abject Odious,'" pp. 232, 234, qtd. line 308).

Early readers had no qualms about condemning Cresseid. The first allusion to her appears in *The Spektakle of Luf* (1492; Asloan MS fol. 141r), in a list of disloyal women: she "went common amang the Grekis and syn deid in gret mysere and pane" (qtd. Fox, ed., p. xix). Likewise, the early seventeenth-century Latin translator of *TC* and the *Testament*, Sir Francis Kinaston, observed that Henryson "learnedly takes uppon him in a fine poeticall way to expres the punishment and end due to a false unconstant whore, which commonly terminates in extreme misery" (qtd. Fox, ed., p. xiv; Rollins, "Troilus-Cressida Story," pp. 397, 400; compare Mieszkowski, "Reputation of Criseyde"). Taking Kinaston as authoritative, Susan Aronstein argues that Henryson vindicates traditional misogyny against Chaucer's many-sided, open-ended depiction of Criseyde ("Cresseid Reading Cresseid," p. 5; Strohm, "Writers as Readers," pp. 100–01). The continuing debate indicates that for some readers, Henryson's Cresseid has a complexity like that of Chaucer's Criseyde: for Sally Mapstone, it is possible to discuss Chaucer, Henryson, and Shakespeare (and behind them all, the *Roman de Troie* of Benoit de Saint Maure) as "a group of writers who utilize to great effect [the] contrast between what Criseyde may say and what may be said of her" ("Origins," p. 143). For such readers, "*The Testament of Cresseid* is not a text which is circumscribed, closed off, or finite in its interpretive scope but rather one which constantly undermines its apparently authoritative stance" (Dunnigan, "Feminizing the Text," p. 120).

No reader of the *Testament* can fail to be arrested by the punishment of leprosy the gods visit upon on Cresseid. Given the medieval belief that the disease could be contracted through sexual contact (Bartholomaeus VII.65, Seymour-Smith, *On the Properties of Things*, 1:426), the punishment seems to fit the crime, but the venereal associations are of secondary importance: the gods punish Cresseid for her verbal abuse of Venus and Cupid (Spearing, *Medieval to Renaissance*, p. 173; Torti, "From 'History' to 'Tragedy,'" p. 189; Grigsby, *Pestilence*, p. 99). From this perspective, she exemplifies the bringing low of pride. However, the gods themselves are imperfect: "[t]heir procedure is in accordance with legal forms, but (as is often the case too in Henryson's *Moral Fables*) the legal process merely serves the interest of the powerful" (Spearing, *Medieval to Renaissance*, p. 174). Not all readers have been impressed by the long passage in which the gods assemble in judgment over Cresseid. Seamus Heaney comments that "the roll-call of the immortals can feel a bit too operatic" (*Testament*, p. 9; Burrow, "Dunbar," p. 114). It would be a mistake to discount the gods: Bawcutt and Riddy cogently argue that "The large amount of space devoted to the planetary gods is far from being superfluous ornament. They have 'power of all thing generabill' (line 148) and symbolize certain natural forces or physical laws of the universe" (*Longer Scottish Poems*, pp. 135–36). Jill Mann writes attentively about "a sinister effect of claustrophobia" in the descent of the gods, whereby "the cosmos seems to be bearing down on Cresseid" ("Planetary Gods," p. 96).

The assembly of the gods articulates the extent and the limits of divine power in the poem; Cresseid is "not punished by God but only overwhelmed by the natural forces of mutability embodied in the planets" (Kelly, *Chaucerian Tragedy*, p. 257; MacQueen, *Robert Henryson*, p. 70). The machinery of power is of more than historical interest for a late medieval Christian reader: "As Chaucer does in the Knight's Tale or in *Troilus and Criseyde*, Henryson suggests that his pagan characters have a faith that they take seriously, in part by having them couch some of the utterances in which they refer to it in recognizably formal modes such as prayers" (Boffey, "Lydgate," p. 56; further, Watson, "Outdoing Chaucer," p. 105). Given this assumed parity of belief and practice between the character and the reader of *Testament*, it is not surprising that the poem can be read as an exemplary tale (Kindrick, *Rhetoric*, pp. 229–33). As in the *Fables*, the fiction enables a searching review of the ways law is practiced in order to protect the privileges of the powerful; it is all a fiction, after all. The odd chronology, the inconsistent narrative perspectives, the incomplete characterization may indeed make it a "flawed masterpiece," as J. A. W. Bennett called it thirty years ago; but a masterpiece it remains ("Henryson's *Testament*").

1–2	Henryson makes vast and literal Chaucer's decorously "sory chere" for a "sorwful tale" (*TC* 1.14): not just a *chere* but a properly pathetic *sessoun*.
4	Terming his work a *tragedie*, Henryson again indicates a contrastive relation between it and Chaucer's *Troilus and Criseyde*, in which the term appears only near the end (5.1786); see also Dunbar, *Timor mortis conturbat me*, line 59, where the word is linked to "balat making" (compare *Testament*, line 610–16n; Kelly, *Chaucerian Tragedy*, pp. 217, 218n4).
5	In mid-March the sun enters the zodiacal sign of Aries, "the colerike hoote signe" (*CT* V[F]51); according to the medieval encyclopedist Bartholomaeus Anglicus, "in Marche tyme is ful chaungeable and unstedefast" (IX.11, Seymour-Smith, *On the Properties of Things*, 1:530); calling the season *Lent*, Henryson stresses its penitential character (compare lines 248n, 320n, 2000–06n).
6	Bartholomaeus Anglicus provides a standard explanation for hail as the result of a clash between cold and warmth, "colde vapour and moist, ichasid and idryve by coolde to the innere partie of the cloude, and that by maystrie of hete that is aboute" (XI.10, Seymour-Smith, *On the Properties of Things*, 1:587); likewise in *The Flower and the Leafe*, "the sonne so fervently / Waxe whote [hot]" that "there came a storme of haile" (lines 355–56, 368).
8	That the poet has an *oratur* indicates privilege and education, as well as clerical status; the word can refer to a private chapel (as it does in line 120; *DOST oratour*; *MED oratori(e)*.
11–14	The opposition of Venus to the sun at this initiatory moment may recall the poet-dreamer's prayer to Venus in *PF*, "As wisly as I sey the north-north-west, / Whan I began my sweven for to write, / So yif me myght to ryme, and endyte!" (lines 117–19).
17	The north wind, according to Bartholomaeus, "for they ben colde and drye, maketh bodies harde and spereth poores and purifieth humours, and clerith spiritis and wittis . . . [This] wynd is colde and drye and cometh out of streight contrey into large contreye and maketh the eyre sotile and thinne, cliere and drye, and fresith the moist partyes bothe of erthe and of watir" (XI.3, Seymour-Smith, *On the Properties of Things*, 1:577).

19   According to Martin J. Duffell and Dominique Billy, this line provides evidence of Henryson's awareness of the lyric caesura (inversion of the second foot) in French verse ("From Decasyllable to Pentameter," p. 389).

29–35   The expression "man of age" (*venerabilis vir*) also features in the fox's recommendation of the wolf (*Fables*, line 1013; compare Introduction, p. 2, above); with his amatory interests, the narrator has been compared to Pandarus in *Troilus and Criseyde*, to the "nasty narrator" of the Merchant's Tale, and to Amans in *CA* (Benson, "Critic and Poet," p. 39; Watson, "Outdoing Chaucer," p. 102).

34   Skill with *phisike* anticipates the leading role to be assigned in the tale proper to Mercury, "Doctour in physick" (line 250; J. Strauss, "To Speak," p. 11); for the use of *phisike* to stimulate *nature*, compare *CT* 4.1807–11.

39   Compare *The Book of the Duchess* line 49; as does Chaucer in the beginnings of his dream poems, Henryson here depicts the figure of the poet seeking a respite from the night in reading.

40   That this reading material is a *quair* (*OED*, quire, n.) may indicate that it is indeed a "litel boke" (*TC* 5.1786), a single gathering of four sheets into eight leaves; the reading material may thus consist of the concluding Book 5 of *Troilus and Criseyde* (compare *DOST quair* 4).

43–56   For Spearing, these two stanzas, summarizing a whole book of Chaucer, exemplify Henryson's compendious conciseness (*Medieval to Renaissance*, p. 170).

57–63   William Stephenson notes that the initial letters of the lines in this stanza spell out "O FICTIO," a phenomenon he argues to be a signal that the "uther quair" is a fabrication ("Acrostic 'Fictio'"). These letters are accordingly provided here in boldface.

61–63   Occasionally identifications are made of the "uther quair," though the reference is usually taken to be fictitious (Kindrick, "Henryson's 'Uther Quair' Again"; compare, e.g., Kelly, *Chaucerian Tragedy*, p. 216, Spearing, *Medieval to Renaissance*, pp. 166–67, Bawcutt and Riddy, *Longer Scottish Poems*, p. 367).

64–70   The opening question raises afresh a central concern of the *Fables*. A. C. Spearing notes that Henryson's "is apparently the first use in English of the term *inventioun* . . . to apply not to the 'finding' of material in existing sources but to a poet's 'making-up' of an untrue story" (*Textual Subjectivity*, p. 23; see also MacQueen, *Robert Henryson*, p. 55); Torti regards this stanza as "a milestone in the passage from the Middle Ages to the Renaissance in terms of their conceptions of poetry" ("From 'History' to 'Tragedy,'" p. 191; also Benson, "Critic and Poet," p. 34).

74   According to scripture, a "lybell of repudie" is a document of divorce, issuable by a man after having "taken a wife and consummated the marriage; but she has not pleased him and he has found some impropriety of which to accuse her"; the document is also issuable by that woman's second husband if he "takes a dislike to her"; in both cases, the woman is dismissed from the house of her former husband (Deuteronomy 24:1–4).

75   The recurrence of *exclude* in Saturn's sentence (*Testament*, line 315) may indicate
        an implied analogy between "the legal consequences of divorce" and "the
        destructive effects of leprosy" (Mathews, "Land," p. 59).

77   This line, pivotal to any interpretation of the poem, is ambiguous: crucially,
        commoun may modify "scho" (Cresseid; line 76) or "court," an uncertainty height-
        ened by the placement of the adjective after the noun: vice versa, "common
        court" would refer to a courtyard or residence of general access to everyone in
        a noble or royal household (*DOST court* n.1, 2; *commoun*; *MED court* n.1.); given
        this ambiguity, a pejorative reading develops from *commoun*, "unsavory, notorious;
        promiscuous" (*MED commun(e* adj.9).

78–84   Elizabeth Allen notes that the interchange of active and passive verbs in this
        stanza bespeaks an unresolved conflict between sympathy and condemnation
        (*False Fables*, p. 143).

83   With the adverb *giglotlike*, "lasciviously" (*MED gigelot, gigelotrie*; *DOST giglot,
        giglotry*), the pejorative implications lurking in the previous stanza become
        explicit.

87   The impulse to excuse Cresseid recalls but does not parallel the wish to excuse
        Criseyde "For she so sory was for hire untrouthe / Iwis, I wolde excuse hire yet
        for routhe" (*TC* 5.1098–99).

92–98   The stanza epitomizes that variety of conciseness in which "specific emotional
        effects" are achieved by means of verbal compression: the effect Spearing
        identifies is "the cold relentlessness of suffering" (*Medieval to Renaissance*, p. 170).

94–95   Bennett notes the parallel with the departure of the burgh mouse in search of her
        sister, in "The Two Mice" (*Fables*, lines 180–85n; "Henryson's *Testament*," p. 8).

101   Cresseid's report contrasts with the scriptural conditions for the "lybell of
        repudie" (line 74n); it was Diomeid's mere sensuality that doomed her and no
        fault in herself.

103–05 In his effusive good will, worldly-wise sententiousness, and ineffectuality,
        Henryson's Calchas has justly been compared with Chaucer's Pandarus (Benson,
        "Critic and Poet," p. 36), a comparison that also draws him into a parallel with
        the figure of the poet here (lines 29–35n). Of significance is Henryson's innova-
        tion in making Calchas a priest of Venus (lines 107–09); elsewhere, as in Chaucer,
        he serves Apollo.

110–21 Kelly notes an apparent disjunction in the temporal sequence, Cresseid having
        just arrived at the mansion of Calchas and now being depicted habitually and
        sorrowfully visiting the temple until "at the last" she chooses to go to the private
        orature instead (*Chaucerian Tragedy*, pp. 229–30).

132   Cresseid's "failure to discriminate between her loss of Diomeid and Troilus is
        clear in the co-ordinating syntax, despite the perfunctory extra-metrical
        attribution of nobility to Troilus" (J. Strauss, "To Speak," p. 8).

135   When Gower's Thisbe rhetorically expands Cupid's blindness to include Venus by implication (*CA* 3.1465), her outcry can be read as an exculpation of the gods, "blinde / Of thilke unhapp" of her lover's death — that is, unknowing and therefore not responsible; in contrast, Cresseid deliberately calls Venus blind and blames her and her son for making false promises.

136–39   The reversion of spring into winter in Venus and Cupid's abandonment of Cresseid parallels the climatic inversion and hopes for Venus' reviving influence with which the poem began (*Testament* lines 4–7, 19, 24), and predicts the punishment, "Thy moisture and thy heit in cald and dry" (*Testament* line 318) Cresseid will undergo for her rebellious outcry. Bawcutt and Riddy note the antecedent in the *Romance of the Rose* (line 1588; *Romaunt* line 1616; *Longer Scottish Poems*, p. 368).

141–43   Citing Steven F. Kruger (*Dreaming in the Middle Ages*, pp. 136–37), Kelly describes Cresseid's *extasie* as "a miraculous 'action dream,' in which a usually supernatural figure does something physical to the dreamer" (*Chaucerian Tragedy*, p. 235); the passage is comparable to the dream concluding Gower's *CA*, in which Cupid summons a "Parlement" (8.2454ff.) and pulls "a fyri lancegay" from Amans' heart (8.2798); Venus anoints Amans and shows him a "wonder mirour" (8.2821), in which he sees his face "riveld and so wo besein" with age (8.2829); and when he awakens, "loves rage was aweie" (8.2863). In *The Palis of Honoure*, Douglas parodies Henryson when a prayer to Venus for guidance results in a sudden "extasy," at the onset of which "As femynine so feblyt fell I doun" (Prol.106, 108).

147   The order of appearance of the planets is from highest to lowest, as in *Orpheus* (lines 189–216).

148   The planetary gods rule all things "capable of being generated or developed" (*MED gendrable*), or, to complete the philosophical phrase, "all things generable and corruptible" (*OED generable*); in Henryson's indication of this power, the present tense of the verb *hes* deserves attention: ascending, descending, opposing, and aligning in turn, these gods also rule over the poet's world, as demonstrated in the opening scene of the poem.

153   Fox cites Raymond Klibansky et al. (*Saturn and Melancholy*, p. 203) for the late medieval iconographic emphasis on Saturn the "ragged peasant"; Henryson's passing emphasis on Saturn's lack of "reverence" and "busteous" manner connect this depiction to the theme of the rebelliousness of peasants (compare *CT* I[A]2459), a theme which anticipates the display of the churlish, thieving man in the moon on the dress of Cynthia, Saturn's co-adjutor (lines 260–63n).

154   To describe Saturn's manner of arrival, "crabitlie" (angrily) expresses his boorish rebelliousness, senile peevishness, and planetary imperiousness; Cresseid applies the adjective "craibit" to all the gods (*Testament*, line 353; compare Dunbar, *The Goldyn Targe*, line 114).

155ff.   Though the "wysdom and usage" of "elde" are not evident in Henryson's description as they are in Chaucer's (*CT* I[A]2448; compare 2467–69), Saturn exhibits the characteristics of old age, in which "kynde hete quenchith, the vertu of governaunce and of reuleynge failith, humour is dissolved and wastid, myght and strengthe passith and faileth, fleisch and fairnes is consumpt and spendith, the skyn rivelith, the sinewis schrinken, the body bendith and croketh, fourme and schap is ilost, fairnes of the body brought to nought"; "by fablis," Saturn "is ipeyntid as an olde man . . . and is pale in colour othir wan as leed, and hath tweye dedliche qualitees, cooldnes and drynes" (Bartholomaeus VI.1, Seymour-Smith, *On the Properties of Things*, 1:293; VIII.12 [1.479]; compare *Fables*, line 2819; *Orpheus*, line 351).

160–64   Though Henryson's description of Saturn includes the icicles found in the description of this god in *The Assembly of Gods* (Chance, *Assembly of Gods*, lines 279–87), the fifteenth-century English poem does not emphasize the aspects of suffering, illness, and decrepitude featured here; Gray observes that Henryson's portrait "makes other fifteenth-century English descriptions of Saturn seem very feeble" (Gray, p. 183; e.g., *Reason and Sensuality*, line 1438; compare Mann, "Planetary Gods," p. 97).

165   By tugging the clothing "fra him," the wind is wearing it out (*DOST wer* v.3.3; *MED weren*, v.2.5a); the worn-out, weatherbeaten clothing compactly realizes the Saturnian associations with storms and decrepitude; compare the contrasting use of *weir* in line 182, where it means "repel" or "avert" (*DOST wer* v.1.2; *MED weren* v.1.1–2; compare line 467n, but also *Fables*, lines 2465n).

171   As Riddy observes, "nureis" is markedly feminine in its associations ("'Abject Odious,'" p. 247; *DOST nuris* n.); the term is also applied to Phebus (*Testament*, line 199).

174   The garland of flowers associates Jupiter with Cupid (*Legend of Good Women* G.Prol.160).

176–79   The simile "hair like gold wire" pertains to Venus in both *The Assembly of Gods* (line 373) and *The Kingis Quair* (line 4); in John Lydgate's *Troy Book*, Criseyde's own hair is "Like to gold wyr" (3.4125). Jupiter's conventionally attractive voice, eyes, and hair, and his predictably sumptuous clothing, all find their correlatives in Cresseid's losses, as she and her judges measure them (lines 337–38, 422–23, 443–45).

183–88   Mars "is an hoot planete and drye . . . and so hath maistrie over colera and fire and colerik complexioun. . . . Undir him is conteyned werre and bataille, prisoun, and enemie, and he tokeneth wraththe and swiftnesse and woodnesse, and is reede, and untrewe, and gilefulle" (Bartholomaeus VIII.13, Seymour-Smith, *On the Properties of Things*, 1:481; compare Chaucer, *Complaint of Mars*, lines 97–103; *CT* I[A]1995–2040); his falchion is appropriately rusty, "for iren taketh rust of nothing so soone as of mannes blood" (Bartholomaeus XVI.44, Seymour-Smith, *On the Properties of Things*, 2:849).

195–96   The terms in which the blast of the horn is depicted echo those used for the horn-call that announces the arrival of the unicorn in *The Trial of the Fox* (*Fables*, lines 839–40n), although the use of the perfect tense deprives Mars' fanfare of the figural significance noted in the fable.

197–203   "The lines describing [Phebus] are placed exactly in the middle of the overall *descriptio* . . . [but] his sovereignty is affirmed only to be undermined" (Spearing, *Medieval to Renaissance*, p. 176).

205   Phaethon disastrously mishandled the chariot of the sun; see Ovid, *Metamorphoses* 2.31–328.

209–17   In a "touching example of how the schoolmaster-poet's imagination struck roots in the textbooks of his trade" (Burrow, "Dunbar," p. 120), Henryson draws on Eberhard of Béthune's versified Latin grammar *Graecismus* (9.226–27): "*Erubet Eous aurora, pallet Ethous, / Fervet Pyrous, se mergit aquis Philogeus*" (qtd. Fox, ed., p. 357); "Eous reddens in the dawn, Ethous is pale, / Pyrous glows, Philogeus immerses himself in the sea." Spearing notes the repetition in this stanza of a trajectory already marked at the beginning of the poem (lines 8–14), "Titan" the sun disappearing, "leaving only Venus visible in the wintry sky" (*Medieval to Renaissance*, p. 176).

221   Green is inherently ambiguous: alone and in the right circumstances, it proclaims youth, nature, and festive celebration (Bawcutt, *Poems of William Dunbar*, 2:418); set beside fatal black, its threatening, even demonic associations rise to the fore. Noting the arrangement of the planetary gods in contrasting pairs of malice and benevolence, Mann resolves the apparent anomaly of the partnerless Venus, who "fits into the pattern by virtue of containing a whole set of oppositions within herself" ("Planetary Gods," p. 97). Torti observes that "In the three stanzas describing *Venus* we find all the reasons for the fault for which *Cresseid* should be condemned" ("From 'History' to 'Tragedy,'" p. 189).

223–31   Venus "hath colour whight and schinynge . . . For among alle sterres Venus schinith most comfortabilly and whitly" (Bartholomaeus VIII.14, Seymour-Smith, *On the Properties of Things*, 1:482); into this portrait of Venus, however, Henryson infuses Cresseid's features along with those of Fortune. A precedent for such merging occurs in John Lydgate's *Troy Book*, in which the tale of Cryseide's disloyalty is initiated by a portrait of "chaungable" Fortune with her "stormy face" (3.4078–79), and Cryseide, "ful of doubilnes," utters "wordis white, softe, and blaundyshynge . . . For under hid was al the variaunce," "The sugre aforn, the galle hid behynde": in sum, "Thei can outward wepyn pitously, / The tother eye can laughe covertly" (3.4269, 4272, 4275, 4283, 4291–92; compare MacQueen, *Robert Henryson*, pp. 51–54; Mann, "Planetary Gods," p. 105n25). At one moment provocative, at the next envenomed, Venus encapsulates the fates of both Cresseid and Henryson's Eurydice (*Orpheus*, lines 75–84n, 105, 349–51n).

239–50   The portrait of Mercury as a rhetorical poet and "Doctour in phisick" recalls the presentation of the poet at the outset of the *Testament* and is strikingly similar to the depiction of Aesop in the prologue to *The Lion and the Mouse* (line 34n; *Fables*, lines 1349–60n; compare *Eneados* 13.prol.87; MacQueen, *Robert Henryson*, p. 80; Gray, p. 187).

252   Henryson's recurrent concern with the relation between fiction and lying in poetry arises to clinch the portrait of Mercury as god of poetry (*Fables*, lines 1–7n, 397–400n, 1629n, 2480–89n; Mann, "Planetary Gods," p. 101).

253–59   "Amonge planetis the mone fulendith hire cours in most schort tyme . . . [and]
          passith in most uncerteyn and unstedfast mevinge . . . The mone in rewlinge
          hath most power over disposicioun of mannes body, for . . . under the mone is
          conteyned sikenesse, losse, fere and drede, harm and damage" (Bartholomaeus
          VIII.17, Seymour-Smith, *On the Properties of Things*, 1:491–93).

260–63   The churlish, rightly punished rebel (Numbers 15:32–36) features significantly
          in the depiction of Cynthia's spotted, leaden paleness (compare lines 339–40);
          like the churl, the rebellious Cresseid will be displayed perpetually as an example
          and warning.

266   Mercury is chosen to be an advocate for the plaintiff, not a judge (*DOST
          forspekar*). The court is a "parliament": an assembly "of the higher nobility and
          clergy, and of townsmen," the late medieval Scottish parliament "was the highest
          court in the land" (Wormald, *Court, Kirk, and Community*, p. 21; Walker, *Legal
          History*, pp. 223–24).

270   This statement embodies the ideal it depicts, and has been taken as Henryson's
          goal of eloquence, "fullness of matter with strong formal control" (Burrow,
          "Dunbar," p. 114; see also Spearing, *Medieval to Renaissance*, p. 169).

271–73   Like a pursuer (i.e., plaintiff) in a Scottish bishop's court, Cupid offers an oral
          petition "giving his grounds for raising the action" (Walker, *Legal History*, p. 408).

274–87   Cresseid's offense is comparable to false accusation, an offense that in late
          medieval Scotland fell under the jurisdiction of the bishop's court; investigation
          involved the bishop's Official summoning the supposed offender; as did the
          pursuer, the accused had a right to legal counsel; and a plea of not guilty was to
          be supported by the sworn testimony of "at least six compurgators"; if deemed
          to have been a malicious act, this offense could lead to a charge of defamation,
          punishable by penances — from this perspective, the arbitrary procedure and
          hasty sentence of the gods' parliament would have occasioned readerly head-
          shaking. However, Cresseid's blasphemy may be considered as apostasy or
          heresy, which were "more harshly dealt with": during 1407–33, Lollards were
          burnt at Perth, Glasgow, and St. Andrews (Walker, *Legal History*, pp. 405–07).

295–300   Mercury's counsel is that Saturn and Cynthia serve as if they were commissaries
          in a bishop's court, and act together "to impose fines and penance"; in cases of
          heresy, the officer with this authority was the inquisitor (Walker, *Legal History*,
          p. 407). As Mann observes, it was under Saturn and Cynthia — and Jupiter —
          that Troilus and Criseyde consummated their love ("Planetary Gods," p. 95; *TC*
          3.624–25).

311   According to Scottish procedure, the coroner lays a wand upon an accused
          person to signify an arrest (compare *Fables*, lines 1269–75n); Saturn performs
          this gesture in pronouncing sentence.

322   The punctuation of this line as a separate sentence follows Bawcutt and Riddy's
          advice that prominence and emphasis are improved thereby: "As a beggar thou
          shalt suffer *and* die" (*Longer Scottish Poems*, p. 372).

323–29   "At this point the narrator breaks in like a chorus, with an urgent exclamation expressing the audience's horror and *pite*" (Gray, p. 189).

344   Repetition of the adjective "doolie," previously found in the first line of the poem, indicates that the dream that has just ended is in some sense analogous to the circumstances in which the poem is depicted as having originated; this repetition substantiates Fradenburg's claim that, like *The Kingis Quair*, the *Testament* involves breaking "apart the structure of the dream-vision without discarding the fragments" ("Henryson Scholarship," p. 88n47), the possibility arising that Cresseid's plight "Suld correspond and be equivalent" (line 2) to that of the poet.

349   For readers who perceive a growth of moral insight in the later stages of the poem, this moment is significant: "the limits of her understanding are apparent in the fact that she sees only a physical deformity, without connecting it to the wrong she committed against Troilus" (Allen, *False Fables*, p. 145). For readers who find themselves less comfortable with the validity of such a pattern, "From this moment on Cresseid is a *speculum* and an *exemplum*: Henryson the moralizer takes over" (Torti, "From 'History' to 'Tragedy,'" p. 193). Kelly, however, refuses to grant the planetary gods the sort of reverence by analogy that these perspectives imply: for him, they are not so much "representatives of divinity as representatives of the natural world," they are "deificait" (line 288), "deified in the eyes of men" (*Chaucerian Tragedy*, p. 240).

350   Chaucer employs a similar circumlocution in the Merchant's Tale, when May watched her slack-necked bridegroom singing in bed; both poets indicate that the sensation is unknowable, at least by them — and then they proceed to describe it in terms of what the female character said or did not say (*CT* IV[E]1851–54). From this point on, increasingly emphatic references to an unnamed God begin to crop up in the poem (lines 402, 414, 493; Kelly, *Chaucerian Tragedy*, p. 241).

353   Spearing translates *craibit* as "touchy and callous" (*Medieval to Renaissance*, p. 174); Heaney, "ill-set" (*Testament* 28); either way, it is as if, from the perspective of Cresseid's initial horror and outrage at her punishment, *all* the gods are like querulous, doddering Saturn (line 154).

358   Considering "the child's arrival to announce supper," Mann admires Kurt Wittig's sense of Henryson's "tightlipped reticence": "When pathos seems to rise to the highest pitch, the poet looks away and sees the common reality of every day" (Wittig, *Scottish Tradition*, p. 46, qtd. Mann, "Planetary Gods," p. 99).

382–83   Scottish burgh law provided for the disposal of lepers: "if anyone were put out of the burgh for leprosy but have goods and gear sufficient for his clothing and sustenance, he should be put in the burgh hospital"; except at specified times, lepers should gather at the burgh ports and beg for alms; by 1466, no fewer than three parliamentary acts had provided for reform of the Crown's hospitals for lepers and other unfortunates (Walker, *Legal History*, pp. 587–88).

386   Another character is noted for wearing a voluminously concealing hat made of beaver pelts: Chaucer's unnamed, secretive Merchant (*CT* I[A]272).

392   At this point, despite his "daylie" provision of goods from those bestowed on him
           in his priestly capacity — his "almous" — Calchas ceases to provide any effective
           support to Cresseid. Kelly (*Chaucerian Tragedy*, p. 230) relates the resulting
           discrepancy between Calchas' promise and Cresseid's subsequent indigence
           (lines 441, 481–83) to an apparent flaw in chronology: Calchas' "daylie" support
           implies that Cresseid has spent "a good deal of time" with the lepers, but this
           implication is countered by Troilus' appearance the "samin tyme" (line 484) as
           Cresseid's first night in the hospital (line 230).

397–99   The lepers' opportunistic response to Cresseid's excessive grief arises from an
           attitude similar to that which produces the sardonic comment in the Franklin's
           Tale on Dorigen's weeping, "As doon thise noble wyves whan hem liketh" (*CT*
           V[F]818, 1348, 1462).

407–69   "The Complaint of Cresseid" is marked off from the narrative in various ways: the
           lead-in formula "scho maid hir mone" (also *Orpheus*, line 133); its exclamatory
           direct discourse in Cresseid's person; the title (compare the headings *Litera* and
           Canticus in *Troilus and Criseyde*); and also the change from rhyme royal to the
           Anelida stanza (so named from its use in Chaucer's experimental *Anelida and
           Arcite*) of nine lines, *aabaabbab*. The Complaint has been read as an indication of
           Cresseid's current lack of insight into the reasons for and conditions of her present
           situation; her complaint has been compared to Dorigen's (*CT* V[F]1355–1456;
           Spearing, *Medieval to Renaissance*, pp. 184–85) and also to the rhetorically
           elevated speeches of warning made by figures exemplifying pride brought low,
           such as the revenant corpse of Guinevere's mother in *The Awntyrs off Arthure* (lines
           95–195) and the chastened owl in Sir Richard Holland's *Buke of the Howlat* (lines
           958–84; Riddy, "Alliterative Revival," p. 45; Spearing, *Medieval to Renaissance*, p.
           183); Gray regards this "elaborate *planctus*" as "perhaps Henryson's finest piece
           of rhetorical writing, a great tragic *aria* for his heroine at the lowest ebb of her
           fortune" (p. 197).

413   Depicting the onset of a new stage of life as if it is a crop sprouting out of the
           ground recalls Cresseid's rebuke of Cupid and Venus (lines 136–39); it also
           recalls comparable transformations in the *Fables* (lines 8–14, 1793–96).

416–33   The ensuing two stanzas exemplify the topic *Ubi sunt* ("Where are they now?"),
           a deeply-seated theme, often with explicitly Christian penitential associations, as
           illustrated by various lyrics in the Vernon Manuscript; Chaucer allusively reworks
           the theme in passages of complaint in *The Book of the Duchess* (lines 599–616) and
           Troilus and Criseyde (e.g., 5.218–21). Boffey notes the distortion of the theme in
           Cresseid's complaint, which she describes as "a kind of perverted final testament"
           in which "she specifies some of her losses in terms that persuasively recall the
           items listed in many actual wills" ("Lydgate," p. 54).

425–33   Comparing this passage to its counterpart in Lydgate's *Testament* (lines 325–27,
           367), Boffey perceives that "the alluring and carefree delights of spring are
           shown in retrospect to be empty of moral direction, and the juxtapositions of
           youth and age, or of beauty and decay, are used to point to the unalterably
           mutable condition of earthly life" ("Lydgate," p. 54).

429 A traditional Maytime pastime for young women in Scotland was to gather the morning dew with which to wash one's face for beauty (Fox, ed., pp. 372–73); compare *Orpheus* line 95.

434–42 "The middle stanza of Cresseid's complaint, the fourth, is the only one that contains any reference to triumph . . . but what it goes on to say is that all this is reduced to the leper's 'cop and clapper'" (Spearing, *Medieval to Renaissance*, p. 183).

452–60 Kelly contrasts this *memento mori* to other Henrysonian admonitions about the imminence of death (*Thre Deid Pollis* lines 5–6, 16–23, and especially 25–32; *Ressoning betwix Deth and Man* lines 1–3, 35–39); where the lesson elsewhere is to repent, Cresseid "is not warning the ladies to take preventive action against change, but only to be aware that change will come" (*Chaucerian Tragedy*, pp. 241, 246; compare *TC* 4.837–40). "The projection of her disfigured self as a 'mirror' to warn others of the physical decay that awaits them is . . . perhaps not entirely altruistic; Cresseid seems partly to seek consolation in anticipating the fragility of others' beauty" (Boffey, "Lydgate," p. 55).

467 This detail takes on added meaning given the mention earlier of Saturn's frayed, faded clothing twisting in the wind (line 165n).

471 As at the outset of the complaint, Cresseid's emotions take an ironic hue with an allusion to Dorigen's excess of lamentation, lasting "a day or tweye" (*CT* V[F]1457; compare 397–99n).

475 Kicking against a wall typifies the futile, destructive outlay of energy characteristic of anger; compare Chaucer, *Truth* lines 11–12, "Be war therefore to sporne ayeyns an al; / Stryve not, as doth the crokke with the wal"; *Abbey Walk* line 30.

478 Again the leper woman's remonstrance assumes a Chaucerian quality: "To maken vertu of necessitee" is Theseus' advice in the Knight's Tale (*CT* I[A]3042; compare *CT* V[F]593).

484–90 Benson upholds E. M. W. Tillyard's contention that the significance of the ensuing scene, culminating in the mutual "nonrecognition" of Cresseid and Troilus, depends on the reader's recollection of Criseyde's sighting of Troilus riding back from battle ("Critic and Poet," p. 35; *TC* 2.1247–1274; compare Bennett, "Henryson's *Testament*," pp. 5, 11).

498 Cresseid's effort to see has occasioned much comment: Burrow remarks that "The reference to '*both* her eyes,' conventional in verse, acquires extra implications here: Cresseid shifts and focuses her bloodshot eyes (cf. . . . 337) with difficulty" (*English Verse*, p. 317n; Bawcutt and Riddy, *Longer Scottish Poems*, p. 374); John MacQueen interprets the failure of perception allegorically — "appetite, deformed by sin, cannot recognize Virtue" (*Robert Henryson*, p. 91).

505–11 Bennett ("Henryson's *Testament*," pp. 13–14) compares this stanza to the scientific explanations the Eagle foists upon the dreamer in Chaucer's *House of Fame*; more sympathetically, Burrow considers it "part of the scene's horror and pathos that a learned explanation is required for the fact that Troilus recognizes Cresseid at all, and that his recognition can only be explained as a form of delusion" (*English Verse*, p. 317n). The classic commentary on the passage is Marshall Stearns' (*Robert Henryson*, pp. 98–105); compare *TC* 5.1158–62.

507   Burrow comments on the scholastic context for the term *idole* and notes that in the *Romance of the Rose*, "Jean de Meun couples *ydoles* with *fantasie* in the same technical sense" (*RR* 18229–37; *English Verse*, p. 318n507–8); Chaucer offers a convenient, significant precedent in Troilus' initial meditation on Criseyde, "a mirour of his mynde, / In which he saugh al holly hire figure" (*TC* 1.365–66).

512–15   Compare Dido's admission that she is falling in love with Aeneas ("agnosco veteris vestigia flammae"; Virgil, *Aeneid* 4.23; Bennett, "Henryson's *Testament*," p. 13). The verb *kendlit* contrasts Troilus with the "man of age" at the outset of the poem, for whom love "kendillis nocht sa sone as in youtheid" (line 30); thus, the flame inside Troilus epitomizes his "youthful, sexual, and male" state, realized at the moment in which "loathing of and desire for the feminine can be seen to collapse into one another" (Riddy, "'Abject Odious,'" p. 245).

515   Here and again in line 525, Henryson is alluding to Troilus' extreme suscepti-bility to violent emotion (e.g., *TC* 3.1092, 5.197–203): after his first prayer to Cupid, "the fyre of love . . . brende hym so in soundry wise ay newe, / That sexti tyme a day he loste his hewe" (1.436, 440–41).

522   The colloquialism and the rough action it denotes make a shocking contrast to the refined styles in which the scene has been depicted so far: *swak* is typically associated with a powerful blow in combat or a heavy impact in the course of manual labor (e.g., Barbour, *Bruce* 5.643; *Fables* 2076; compare *MED swap* n); the violence of *swak* briefly articulates various levels of disgust, some less conscious than others, towards Cresseid.

537   It is unstated how much Cresseid "understude": she cannot know that Troilus did not recognize her and therefore cannot know that his gift lacked elements of volition and awareness; the compounding of misunderstanding is productive of ironies. Still, the problem is academic: this is what Troilus did, and this is how Cresseid understood it. Henryson has devised an instructive, emblematic situation in which motives matter less than the actual consequences.

538   *Stound* usually denotes a period of time with the potential for specialization into "a pang, shock" (*MED stound(e* 3: *DOST stound* n.2); as Burrow notes, "The *stound*, or pang, is imagined as a steel blade piercing Cresseid's heart — and, in effect, killing her" (*English Verse*, p. 319n538–9); Heaney translates this line, "A stun of pain, a stroke sharper than steel" (*Testament*, line 39); compare *Fables*, line 311.

547–74   "Although many critics have argued that this 'redemption' signals the author's humane and gentle treatment of his heroine," Aronstein will have none of it: "Henryson's Cresseid pays the price of complete self-denigration to perform his poem's double redemption" ("Cresseid Reading Cresseid," p. 9); Kelly finds room for enlightenment in Cresseid's reinterpretation of that "prosperitie" in which she set little worth on Troilus' gifts of love, loyalty, and gentleness (*Chaucerian Tragedy*, p. 247); L. M. Findlay interprets Cresseid's "coming to rest in personal accountability" as exemplary ("Reading and Teaching," p. 71).

550   Fortune's "fickle wheel" — a phrase that apparently originates here — becomes an Elizabethan cliché: Thomas Whythorne, "Who so that list" (*Triplex of Songs*, 1571) Shakespeare, *Henry V* 3.6.26 (it is Pistol's phrase); *Locrine* 2.6.44.

551–53   For Kelly, Cresseid admits to having made a promise to Troilus, equivalent to a vow of marriage, frivolously (*Chaucerian Tragedy*, p. 249); by extension, her defamation of the gods stands at the climax of a sequence of momentous utterances made without thought. There is a sense in which her never having meant it really does not matter; and in that sense, Cresseid is comparable to the Husbandman of Henryson's *Fables*, caught out by the efficacy of a promise meant as little more than an expletive (line 2251n; Green, *Crisis of Truth*, p. 312).

573   In reading this line as Cresseid's declaration "that there are fewer women than men who are worthy of trust," Kelly approaches Aronstein's perception that Henryson's depiction of his protagonist is inherently misogynistic; but Kelly proceeds to argue that the poet is about to expound "a more benign view of women than Cresseid does" (*Chaucerian Tragedy*, pp. 250–51).

577–88   Bawcutt and Riddy tersely observe that "Cresseid's testament observes three points of the common medieval formula: *Terra terram tegat; demon peccata resumat; / Mundus res habiat; spiritus alta petat*" (*Longer Scottish Poems*, p. 374; "May the earth cover [my] earth; may the devil take back [my] sins; may the world receive [my] goods; may [my] soul seek heaven"); on the possibility that the second and fourth points are left indistinguishable, see lines 587–88n. Christian Sheridan makes a case for treating the testament proper as an "embedded text," analogous to the earlier Complaint (lines 407–69), signaled in both the Charteris and the Anderson prints with a subhead; ornamental capitals mark the beginning of the embedded text and the return to the narrative proper ("Early Prints," p. 26). Here these capital letters are thus indicated in boldface.

583   On the night of consummation, Troilus and Criseyde exchange rings; she gives him a brooch "in which a rubye set was lik an herte" (*TC* 3.1368, 1371); elsewhere, Chaucer gives the jewel sentimental and sexual qualities, especially when Troilus bathes the ruby in his signet with his tears (*TC* 2.1086–90; discussed by McKim, "Tracing the Ring," p. 449); it "originally represented Troilus' gift of his heart to her" (Hodges, "Sartorial Signs," p. 242; *TC* 2.585, 5.549). Henryson changes the circumstances of the ring-giving; having Troilus give Cresseid the ring as a pledge of their union, he provides a counterbalance to the "libell of repudie" that is "send" to Cresseid by Diomeid (line 74n).

587–88   Cresseid's bequest of her spirit to Diana (whom Chaucer's Emelye called "chaste goddesse of the wodes grene" and "Queene of the regne of Pluto"; *CT* I[A]2297, 2299) poses challenges to the reader: according to canon law, for a woman to believe in Diana was tantamount participation in the nocturnal rites of witchcraft (Gratian, *Decretum* 2.26.5.12 [cols. 1030–31] qtd. Kelly, *Chaucerian Tragedy*, p. 255); irony may be detected in Henryson's revision of Criseyde's testament (4.785–91;

Spearing, *Medieval to Renaissance*, p. 167); so, recalling Emelye's prayer to Diana, might pathos (*CT* I.2297–2310; Bawcutt and Riddy, *Longer Scottish Poems*, pp. 374–75). Not every reader has been impressed by these lines: Bennett deprecates Henryson's "fondness for the set alliterative phrase" ("Henryson's *Testament*," p. 15); nevertheless, Heaney elicits a ballad-like quality from these lines: "I leave my spirit to stray by paths and springs / With Diana in her wildwood wanderings" (*Testament*, 40). *Orpheus* and *Robene and Makyne* both end with title characters in deserted woods.

589–90   Compare *TC* 5.1037–43, 1660–66, 1688–94.

601–02   Troilus abruptly confirms Cresseid's estimate of her disloyalty; he suppresses full vituperation with the same turn of phrase as in the parallel moment in *Troilus and Criseyde*, "I kan namore seye" (5.1743); Henryson echoes these words in the last line of the poem.

603–09   Boffey notes that Troilus' epitaph "stresses at once Cresseid's physical degeneration and the possibility that her story, given visible form in the written letters, may have some kind of salutary afterlife in the minds of its readers" ("Lydgate," p. 53).

606   *Goldin letteris* commonly illuminate the names of triumphant heroes like Marcus Manlius (Lydgate, *Fall of Princes* IV.371) or Dunbar's Bernard Stewart (Bawcutt, *Poems of William Dunbar*, poem 56, lines 94–95).

610–16   Like a *moralitas* of the more literal sort — the one to *The Two Mice* or the first part of the one to *The Paddock and the Mouse*, for example — the closing stanza makes explicit the lesson with which the narrative concluded: the lesson the "worthie wemen" of Henryson's audience are to draw appears simple: do not mix love with deception; in other words, do not mix truth with fiction (compare 252n).

ORPHEUS AND EURYDICE (*NIMEV* 3442)

Some confusion lingers over the title of this poem. In the last line of the *moralitas* to Henryson's retelling of the myth of Orpheus and Eurydice, the poet identifies the poem: "And thus endis the taill of Orpheus." In 1508, the poem was printed by the first Scottish printers, Walter Chepman and Andro Myllar, who provided the heading "Heire begynnis the traitie of Orpheus kyng." In his commentary to the opening sections of his translation of Virgil's *Aeneid* (1513), the Scottish poet Gavin Douglas cites the poem as the "New Orpheus" by "Maister Robert Hendirson" (*Eneados* 1.19n13). A few years later, the poem was inscribed into the Asloan Manuscript, where its heading reads "Heir followis the tale of Orpheus and Erudices his quene." Only late in the textual tradition did the poem acquire the title *Orpheus and Eurydice*, under which it has consistently appeared in its modern editions. As well as the virtue of consistency, the modern title offers a certain justice in giving billing to Eurydice: for one thing, the much-discussed double structure of the poem is thereby suggested.

Orpheus and Eurydice consists of two parts, the narrative proper and the *Moralitas*. Since this is the least familiar of Henryson's longer poems, a survey of its structure may be helpful.

In the first part, seven stanzas of rhyme royal (the lineage of Orpheus; Eurydice's invitation to him to marry her; the death of Eurydice while fleeing her boorish attacker Aristaeus; Orpheus' departure into the forest) are followed by the lament of Orpheus (five ten-line stanzas) and then the story is completed in 33 stanzas of rhyme royal (in search of news about Eurydice, Orpheus rises to the sphere of the fixed stars and then descends through the spheres of the planetary gods; he hears the music of the spheres; he journeys into hell, where his music charms the torments of hell so that three victims — Ixion, Tantalus, and Tityus — are released; he enters the palace of hell, where he sees hosts of kings and prelates; finally he approaches Pluto and Proserpina, sees Eurydice, plays his harp beautifully, earns permission to leave with his wife under the condition that he not look back at her while she is following him, does so, loses Eurydice permanently, and utters a final complaint before he returns home). The remaining 219 lines, in pentameter couplets (at least one line is missing at 585), comprise the *Moralitas*, in which many of the characters and some of the events are given allegorical signification: first (lines 425–58) Phoebus, Calliope, Orpheus, Eurydice, and notoriously Aristaeus ("gud vertew," line 436); Eurydice's death, Orpheus' celestial journey; then some of the denizens of hell are given increasingly expansive, circumstantial allegorical treatment: Cerberus, the Furies, Ixion, Tantalus, Tityus; each of these vignettes except the last is concluded by noting that when reason (and/or sapience or intelligence) plays on the harp of eloquence, the torment ends; the final section of the *Moralitas* concerns Orpheus and his loss of Eurydice. Reason plays effectually on the harp of eloquence but cannot resist the call of "affection."

The principal source is the very widely distributed commentary on Boethius' *Consolation of Philosophy* by the thirteenth-century Dominican friar Nicholas Trivet (for the relevant portion, see Fox, ed., pp. 384–91; Johnson, "Hellish Complexity," p. 414), with its source in the *Consolation* itself (3m.12); less acknowledged but demonstrably pervasive is the influence of Chaucer, especially the dream poems. An inventive adapter, Henryson has produced "a poetic compendium of sorts, a tissue of familiar materials which stands in a densely mediated relationship to the text of the classical *auctor*, Boethius" (Copeland, *Rhetoric*, p. 228); Alessandra Petrina notes that "the convergence of literary modes, the conflation of genres, seems the key-note" for reading the poem ("Aristeus Pastor Adamans," p. 391). In recent considerations, two topics have been recurrent: the fraught relation between the tale and the *Moralitas*; and the celebration of learning, as revealed through the liberal arts of rhetoric, music, and astronomy, a celebration tinged with irony only inasmuch as the poet — and, by implication the reader — can get little more than a drily theoretical, jargon-ridden glimpse of the ideal perfections envisioned through these disciplines.

The most problematic aspect of the poem has to be the *Moralitas*, which several modern readers have viewed to be in conflict with the narrative. So uncomfortable has it made some readers that an attempt has been made to demonstrate on stylistic grounds that, in whole or part, Henryson did not write it (D. Strauss, "Some Comments," pp. 7, 10). The most influential principle of criticism has been that the first part has vernacular roots (romance, proverbs, courtly complaint), the second is steeped in the practices of scholastic commentary (see Petrina, "Aristeus Pastor Adamans," p. 390, and Johnson, "Hellish Complexity," pp. 412–13 for critical reviews of this approach); the narrative skill of the first part of the poem makes the second seem "dull and ineffectual" (Gros Louis, "Robert Henryson's *Orpheus*," p. 646; compare Friedman, *Orpheus*, pp. 199–200); it is worth noting in passing that the lack of alliteration that has been cited at the start of the *Moralitas* is also a factor at the outset of the narrative (Fox, ed., p. 392). Various attempts have been made to justify this conflict as significant tension: as in Ovid or Chaucer, "generic instability" — taken as an intrinsic virtue — results from the establishment of "one set of generic expectations, only to undermine them by shifting genre," and hence arises the "strain" between romance and allegory (Marlin, "'Arestyus,'" p. 143). A distorting consequence of seeking a simplistic dualism has been to read the poem in the light of subsequent cultural and literary developments, as if it were more like Gavin Douglas' *Palis of Honoure* or the Child ballads than it is.

More subtly, *Orpheus and Eurydice* has been read as very much a fifteenth-century poem, an implicit debate of genres marked by convergences of style and matter so extreme that they entail "outright contradiction" (Petrina, "Aristeus Pastor Adamans," p. 391). To restrict this principle to the relation between the narrative and the *Moralitas* is to miss some of its most striking effects. For example, two technical stanzas reviewing the elements of music Orpheus learned on his celestial journey lead into a first-person, colloquial admission of ignorance about the subject; as Fox notes (ed., p. 403), the moment is an amplification of a very Chaucerian gesture.

Arguably, the *Moralitas* pursues the narrative as Aristaeus pursued Eurydice: it does not quite catch its prey. On the one hand, the *Moralitas* comments outright on the meaning of the narrative, but on the other, the narrative "raises points which reflect critically on the *moralitas'* hermeneutic mode and which reconfigure and question the validity of the poem's patriarchal structuring of literary activity" (McGinley, "'Fenȝeit' and the Feminine," pp. 79–80). It is important to remember, as Ian Johnson has shown ("Hellish Complexity," pp. 414–15), that the source for the *Moralitas*, Nicholas Trivet's commentary on Boethius' *Consolation of Philosophy*, is also the source for the narrative: the commentary contributes episodes only briefly alluded to in Boethius' brief lyric on Orpheus; the stanzas on Tantalus are an obvious example. Evidently, the debate between the modes is ongoing; narrative and moral, for the time being, still mean too much to one another for one to overthrow the other.

1–7   The prologue opens abruptly with advice about addressing a noble audience; praise of high ancestry is to encourage emulation; underlying this beginning is a Boethian principle of nobility realized in the effort to live up to ancestral traditions of virtue (*Consolation* 3.6, qtd. Fox, ed., p. 391); but the emphasis on the poet's role in stimulating such ambition is a topic characteristic of late medieval literary prologues; Gray notes the same topic at the outset of the Scottish chronicle *The Book of Pluscarden* (tr. Felix J. H. Skene, 2 vols. [Edinburgh: T. and A. Constable, 1877–80]; qtd. p. 228).

8–14   After the conventional motives perfunctorily laid out in the first stanza, the particular concerns of the poem with debasement and "foule derisioun" begin to come into view; some complex, potentially troubling implications are presented, having to do with varieties of offense that will be given full exposition in the upcoming depiction of the denizens of hell.

12   This line is made arresting by its drastic juxtaposition between the archaic alliterative word for "man," *renk* (*DOST renk* n.2), and Henryson's latinate neologism *rusticat*; this is the first line in the poem in which alliteration is prominent.

13   The word *monsture* is used with reference to its Latin origin, *monstrum*, a portent or warning; the word will reappear in reference to Cerberus (lines 253, 461) and the Furies (line 475).

19–21   As in the first stanza, the emphasis shifts toward the role of the poet as an advisor to princes, comparable to Sir Gilbert Hay's depiction (1456; translated from Ramon Llull) of the "worthy wyse anciene knycht yat [that] lang tyme had bene in the excercisioun of honourable weris" who instructs a noble squire in the "hye and noble order of knychthede" (*Boke of the Order of Knychthede*, p. 3).

22–23   Fox suggests that the image of the wellspring may "be a reminiscence of the beginning of the Boethian metre which Henryson is following" (*Consolation* 3.12, qtd. ed., p. 392).

28   The poet's submission of the work to the correction of the reader is a conventional gesture, and Henryson offers it as if in passing; compare *Fables*, line 30.

29–30   Mount Helicon is in Boeotia, a region of Greece: from it sprang the Hippocrene spring, source of poetic eloquence; despite having been located in Arabia, the mountain thus provides an ideal location epitomizing the values of the noble audience envisioned in the opening lines, the protagonist (who is about to be introduced), and the poet.

36–63   Fox cites Dorena Allen Wright's discovery of the source for Henryson's list of the Muses in the widely distributed Latin grammar *Graecismus* by Eberhard of Béthune ("Henryson's *Orpheus and Eurydice*," p. 44; qtd. Fox, ed., p. 393; compare *Testament*, lines 209–17n). McGinley notes the gendered attributes in the etymologies (which Eberhard derived from the mythographer Fulgentius) provided for the Muses' names: for example, Euterpe ("delectatioun") and Melpomene ("hony swete") are rendered feminine, in contrast to Terpsichore ("'Fenȝeit' and the Feminine," p. 78).

69–70   Calliope's enspiriting *lecour* recalls Chaucer's use of the word (*CT* I[A]3; a further Chaucerian connection may be made to the eloquent praise performed by children "on the brest soukynge" (*CT* VII[B²]458); the image has associations with medieval depictions of the Madonna and Child, founded on Luke 11:27, "a verse not uncommon in religious lyrics on the Nativity theme" (MacDonald, "Robert Henryson, Orpheus, and the *Puer Senex* Topos," p. 119); compare *Eneados* 1.prol.463–70.

71   Considering the beginning of this line in the Asloan Manuscript ("Quhen he was auld"), MacDonald cites *MED old* 1a to adduce "a special sense of 'old,' as applied to children" and suggests that the word may further "express an intellectual sense of *senex*, implying that Orpheus was 'fully nourished in wisdom, to a level normally associated with an old man'" ("Robert Henryson, Orpheus, and the *Puer Senex* Topos," pp. 118, 119).

75–84   According to Charles Elliott, Eurydice "is given certain secular and sensual touches; she is *haboundand in riches* (line 75), and feels no shame (which suggests emotion raised above reason) in offering to Orpheus *wordis sweit and blenkis amorus* (line 81)" (*Robert Henryson: Poems*, p. xviii). Fox suspects that the "account of the courtship is perhaps Henryson's invention" (ed., p. 396); the alluring glances Eurydice casts toward Orpheus are what he misses when he sees her in hell (line 355); compare *Testament* lines 226, 503.

92–98   Petrina notes the modulation into a lower style in the previous stanza, so that the scene already shows "affiliations with Middle English romance" ("Aristeus Pastor Adamans," p. 392); in this scene, the shepherd "is further from the princely Orpheus and nearer to the Robene of *Robene and Makyne*" (p. 391); "rustic" qualities have already been deprecated as degenerate (line 12n).

95   Compare *Testament*, line 429n.

98   The setting recalls the hiding place of the fox in the *Fables* (lines 756, 2246).

100   Petrina observes that this line suddenly abandons "any pretence of Arcadian prettiness and establish[es] a rough and urgent tone of primal desire and flight for survival" ("Aristeus Pastor Adamans," p. 389). Ogling at "schankis quhyte, withouttin hois" rouses a lusty squire to assail a lady in Lyndsay's *Squyer Meldrum* (line 949).

110   Through Chaucer's Knight's Tale, Henryson alludes to a conjunction between Diana and Proserpina (compare *Testament*, lines 587–88n); Eurydice and Cresseid are richly comparable characters.

113   The detail of Eurydice's vanishing recalls the parallel moment in *Sir Orfeo* (lines 192–93); note, however, the deferral of the relation between Proserpina and *the fary* (with a precedent in *CT* IV[E]2236) until the maid's speech (lines 124ff.), where it takes on the quality of an unsophisticated, "'folk' interpretation" of the event (Gray, p. 222); compare line 359n.

127–33   Fox notes the translation "by Henryson or by a scribe" (ed., p. 397) of these rhyming words into English (compare *sair, wa, mair, ga, fra, stane, mane*).

131–32   In his *Dirige to the King*, Dunbar similarly depicts James IV doing penance in Stirling: "Solitar walking your alone, / Seing no thing bot stok and stone" (lines 17–18).

134–43   This stanza refines the ten-line ballade (*aabaabcddc*) in "The Compleint to his Lady" attributed to Chaucer; a ten-line stanza with the same rhyme scheme as Henryson's appears in *The Quare of Jelusy* (Symons, *Chaucerian Dream Visions and Complaints*, lines 572–81).

135   Job 30:31.

143   The lamenting refrain stands "in stark contrast to the *contemptus mundi* approach of the *moralitas*" (McGinley, "'Fenʒeit' and the Feminine," p. 80). "The modulation in the central complaint of Orpheus, with its refrain not slavishly kept . . . is quite an extraordinary thing for a poet in the very dawn of his special dialect-division of literature" (Saintsbury, *History of English Prosody*, 1:272)

144–53   Henryson refines on his sources at this point: while the Boethian Orpheus plays sorrowful music, Henryson's plays a lively tune to relieve himself of his misery;

though it delights the birds and trees, the "spring" fails to comfort its performer (compare line 268).

158   In the guise of a friar, the wolf wears the same humble cloth (*Fables*, line 679).

161   In effect, Orpheus anticipates living like the "bustuous hird" Aristeus (line 97; compare lines 92–98n).

186   Henryson, with daring originality, has Orpheus ascend into the heavens (for a discussion of the possible sources, see Gray, p. 231, note 51). Fox reports the suggestion of Russell Poole that "*as sayis the fable* may, like the reference to *ane uther quair* (*Testament*, line 61), be a reference to a pretended authority at precisely the point where the author is relying on his own invention" (ed., p. 399); compare *Fables*, lines 33–35n.

190   The key characteristic of Saturn is his bringing of stormy weather (e.g., Dunbar, *The Goldyn Targe*, lines 114–15); compare the more detailed portrait in the *Testament*, lines 155ff.n, 160–64n, 165n.

210   Of all the planetary deities, Venus is the only one who has any sense of where to seek Eurydice.

218–39   The "melody" learnt by Orpheus pertains to the Pythagorean concept of *musica universalis*, the "music of the spheres," by which the distances of the planets from the earth and their "proportionate speeds of revolution" were considered to be related according to musical intervals; Plato bases the concept of the world-soul on the Pythagorean proportions of the spheres (Haar, "Music of the Spheres"); the theory of this music is expounded in Macrobius, *Commentary on the Dream of Scipio* (pp. 73–74, 193). Given the prominence of Pluto elsewhere in the poem, the substitution of that name for the philosopher's in each of the witnesses is perhaps appropriate.

226–32   This stanza displays musical jargon but does so in order to give some substance to the musical intervals according to which the planetary spheres are related; six tones are named, corresponding perhaps to the six spheres in which Orpheus has spent time (lines 185–216), those of all the planets except the moon. As in Henryson's learned depiction of the mental process by which Troilus reacts unconsciously to the presence of Cresseid (*Testament*, lines 505–11n, 507n), a matter of fundamental significance can be approached by imperfect human understanding only through the abstruse complexities of jargon and theory.

233–39   This stanza has given editors much difficulty, especially if line 235 is taken to refer to a single, dissonant interval, *disdiapente*. A simpler reading finds the five intervals Henryson indicates: *diatesseron*, *diapason*, *duplate*, *diapente*, and *dis*. These are "of thre multiplicat" because they are all derived from three perfect intervals, the fourth, the fifth, and the octave — the foundations of consonance as expounded by Boethius in *De institutione musica* (2.18; Bower, "Boethius").

240–42   The admission of ignorance in the midst of a display of learning recalls the Franklin's self-deprecating gesture about rhetoric (*CT* V[F]717–27; compare *Book of the Duchess* line 1170); in this witty stanza, the alliterative tags *gravis gray* and *wilsum wone* appear as self-consciously naive (*DOST grave* 2n2; *MED wilsom* 1; see also lines 155, 290, and *Fables* 180–85n); following Henryson, the expression to "lay a straw" indicating a limit to a topic becomes idiomatic in Scots poetry (*DOST stra* n.1.4). Douglas ends a passage of musical theory with a comparatively exaggerated admission of ignorance (*Palis of Honoure*, lines 517–18).

248   Gray compares the style of this line to a recurrent motif in the ballads (p. 221; e.g., Child 2.2, 33.1); the female protagonist of "The Cruel Brother" (Child 49B) "harped both far and near / Till she harped the small birds off the briers / And her true love out of the grave" (lines 38–40).

256–58   The harp now comes into its own as a bringer of harmony; in *De regimine principum bonum consilium*, a Middle Scots poem of advice to princes (texts of which are preserved in the Chepman and Myllar prints and the Maitland Folio Manuscript), the analogy is made explicit between the sweet sound of a well-tuned harp (line 4) and a king's proper rule over a realm (line 9); compare lines 469–70.

259   The proportion of Orpheus to Cerberus the three-headed guard-dog of the underworld recalls that in *The Lion and the Mouse*, when the mice traverse the belly of the sleeping animal (*Fables*, line 1411); the protagonist is rendered insignificant in size.

272   Marlin notes an apparent anomaly here and again in lines 286 and 300: with his music, Orpheus is freeing those who are being justly punished; "If the tormented represent wrong desires, Orpheus' music actually quiets the guards that hold these desires in check — exactly opposite to the *moralitas'* interpretation" ("'Arestyus,'" p. 144). As in the *Fables*, mercy, *reuth* (*Orpheus*, line 286), outshines justice (lines 1461–66n; further, Johnson, "Hellish Complexity," p. 415).

275–88   Henryson is using details in Trivet to expand a mere two lines of comment about Tantalus in Boethius (lines 36–37) into two stanzas; as Johnson indicates, "Henryson adds to Trivet a more elaborated dramatic narrative, with appropriately uncomfortable details of the process of the torment" ("Hellish Complexity," p. 415); similarly, Thomas Rutledge comments that "The appetite is safely sated rather than repudiated. Orphic music seems to offer appetitive happiness rather than moral admonition. The balance of 'instruction' and 'consolacion' [lines 416–17], momentarily, has shifted" ("Henryson's *Orpheus*," p. 408).

284   Compare *Fables*, line 2346n.

286   Petrina notes that "The medieval treatments of the story frequently show a tendency to transpose it into courtly terms — a process certainly reflected in the protagonist, whose attempt to rescue Eurydice from Hades is easily ranged, along with Alcestis' sacrifice, among the supreme examples of devotion" ("Aristeus Pastor Adamans," p. 385).

288   This line, Johnson notes, "departs significantly from what both Boethius and Trivet say at this point in the metrum. They make no mention of the water standing, nor of Tantalus getting drink"; Henryson appears to have reapplied

the detail in Boethius (*Consolation*, 3.m.12.7–9) that Orpheus stilled rivers ("Hellish Complexity," p. 415).

303–05   The slipperiness of the road to hell is conventional (Horstmann and Furnivall, *Minor Poems*, p. 616, line 149; qtd. Fox, ed., p. 406; compare Psalm 35 [34]:6).

310–16   In his depiction of the "painefull, poysonit pytt of hell," Sir David Lyndsay draws heavily on this passage (*The Dreme*, lines 189, 190–280).

321   As Fox points out (ed., p. 406), Hector and Priam of Troy are punished for upholding adultery (e.g., Lydgate, *Fall of Princes*, 1.6308–21).

322   For Gower, the conquests of Alexander the Great mark the passage from the age of silver to the age of brass (*CA* Prol.699–700).

323   Henryson could have read the story of Antiochus and his incestuous relations in Gower (*CA* 8.271–347); Chaucer also contributes to the notoriety of this story (*CT* II[B^1]82–83); see Archibald, "Incestuous Kings in Henryson's Hades."

324   Chaucer depicts Caesar as a bloodthirsty conqueror despite all the Roman hero's love of "honestee" (*CT* VII[B^2]2671–726).

325   Herod married Herodias, his brother's wife, and was reproved by John the Baptist (Mark 6:17–18).

326   For Nero, the exemplar of imperial depravity, material was to hand in Chaucer (*CT* VII[B^2]2463–2550) and, with emphasis on "glotonie / Of bodili Delicacie," Gower (*CA* 6.1151–1234; qtd. lines 1161–62).

327   Pontius Pilate broke the law by handing Jesus over for crucifixion even though he found no case against him (Matthew 27:24, Mark 15:12–15, Luke 23:20–24, John 19:4–6).

329–30   Gower depicts Crassus as a covetous emperor whom the Romans punished by making him drink molten gold (*CA* 5.2068–2224).

331–32   Pharoah's oppression of the Israelites results in the ten plagues (Exodus 7:14–12:34).

333–34   Saul, first king of Israel, disobeys God's command regarding the Amalekites and thereby breaks his allegiance; he massacres the priests (1 Samuel 15:7–23; 22:17–19).

335–37   Ahab and Jezebel, king and queen of Israel, coveted the vineyard of Naboth (who is not usually referred to as a prophet); Jezebel had Naboth stoned to death on trumped-up charges (1 Kings 21:1–16).

338–44   This stanza provided Lyndsay, circa 1526, with the source for a greatly expanded, forthrightly anticlerical depiction of the damnation of the religious in *The Dreme* (lines 162–238); Lyndsay's "In haly kirk quhillk did abusioun" (line 182) is identical to line 339 as it appears in the Bannatyne Manuscript. Fox points out that all the witnesses read *bischoppis* in line 343; he admits *archbishoppis* on Lyndsay's evidence for topical reasons: "There were no archbishops in Scotland until 1472, when Patrick Graham succeeded by simony in having papal bulls issued which raised St. Andrews, his see, to an archbishopric. Graham was widely attacked, and was deposed in 1478" (ed., p. 408). In line 342, "men of all religioun" is attested by Lyndsay, *Dreme*, line 181, "Thare was sum part of ilk religioun."

349–51   With her ghastly, withered, leaden appearance, in obvious contrast to her alluring appearance when she was on earth (line 75), Eurydice can be compared with Cresseid (*Testament*, line 461); compare Criseyde in the Greek camp (*TC* 5.708–14).

359   The connection between the *fary* and hell, previously articulated by a mere serving woman, is now confirmed by no less a personage than Pluto.

369–70   MacQueen notes that "Hypodoria and Hyperlydia were the lowest and highest of the fifteen classical Tonoi or Keys. . . . The choice of these *tonoi* implies that Orpheus in his playing utilised the full range from lowest to highest, and so by producing a 'proporcioun' which corresponds to the music of the spheres" ("Neo-platonism," p. 83); see also Caldwell, "Robert Henryson's Harp of Eloquence," p. 149.

377–83   Boethius gives this speech to Pluto (Fox, ed., p. 406); "Proserpine seems to get the last word in Henryson's hell, just as she does in January's garden" (Marlin, "'Arestyus,'" 146; *CT* IV[E]2236).

401–12   Johnson ("Hellish Complexity," p. 417) compares this "tragically tainted declaration" with Troilus' equally Boethian "despairingly determinist monologue of love-loss" (*TC* 4.974–1078) and notes the excessive pessimism of Orpheus' assertion that love's "bandis" are "unbrekable" (compare *Consolation* 3.m12.3–4).

405   Compare *Consolation* 3.12.47–48.

415–633   Copeland has argued for the dependency of the ensuing *Moralitas* on the "fable" of Orpheus, a dependency that she considers to operate in the *Fables* (*Rhetoric*, p. 228). The stylistic changes, Marlin notes, are "accompanied by a shift in address: the third-person narration that dominates the tale gives way to a direct address to the reader . . . suggesting a fictive rhetorical situation wherein a lecturer addresses several auditors" ("'Arestyus,'" p. 147); in this regard, Henryson's style diverges from the impersonal exposition adopted by Nicholas Trivet (for instances of the plural first person, lines 431, 437, 444, 451, 453, 455).

426   The association between Calliope and eloquence secures the allegorical connection between music and eloquence; in the narrative, Calliope is associated with "all musik" and "musik perfyte" (lines 44, 70); given the relation expounded between music, celestial harmony, and perfect proportion (218–39n, 226–32n, 233–39n), these are the values of Calliope's eloquence, uncompromised by Mercury's associations with lying (compare *Testament* line 252; compare Marlin, "'Arestyus,'" p. 142).

431–34   For Mann, interpreting Eurydice as the appetitive part of the soul clarifies the "downwards and inwards movement" of the the quest of Orpheus, "forced to descend from heaven to the depths of the earth to which its appetitive part, represented by Eurydice, is by nature confined" ("Planetary Gods," p. 96); Mann likens this movement to the way the "cosmos seems to be bearing down on Cresseid" in the parliament of the planetary gods (*Testament*, lines 143–264).

435–36   "Aristeus' 'lust' (line 101) is very far from the virtue he is supposed to represent" (Petrina, "Aristeus Pastor Adamans," p. 390); the distance is acknowledged in Henryson's protesting "noucht bot." As Petrina notes, this ethical clash has been prepared for by Henryson's apparently non sequitur insistence, at the poem's outset, on maintaining nobility against rustic degeneracy (lines 8–14; "Aristeus," p. 390).

445–46   Marlin notes a discrepancy at this point between the *Moralitas* and Nicholas Trivet's commentary: "while Nicholas' commentary mentions the intellect weeping for the affect, he figures it not as a sign of contrition; rather, he holds the intellect culpable" ("'Arestyus,'" p. 143).

456–57   "These 'breris' characterise the fallen condition of the *affectus* in this world, its fleshly attachments and its 'wrak'. Intriguingly, 'wrak' is glossed by Fox as 'worldly possessions' and also as 'rubbish' — a soundly Boethian pairing of senses showing Henryson's brilliant lexical tact" (Johnson, "Hellish Complexity," p. 416).

469–70   The harp is a ubiquitous figure of harmonious proportion, one that features in the Scots *De regimine principum*, texts of which appear among the Chepman and Myllar prints and in the Maitland Folio (Gray, pp. 229–33).

490   Marlin sees this as an indication of Henryson's emulation of Chaucer's bookishness ("'Arestyus,'" p. 146)

531–44   As he did in the narrative, Henryson treats Tantalus expansively: he "translates two clauses of Nicholas . . . into a fourteen line invective on miserliness" (Marlin, "'Arestyus,'" p. 147).

546   Rutledge observes that "Orpheus only loses Eurydice because he forgets, for a moment, to rely on his 'harp of eloquence' . . . It is male virtue rather than poetic power which fails" ("Henryson's *Orpheus*," p. 403).

559–76   Marlin finds Henryson's allegory of the myth of Tityus especially telling; in place of Nicholas Trivet's "dry, scholastic etymologies," here is an "outburst against divination, witchcraft, and sorcery," at the end of which the formula appears to be omitted that has ended each of the previous passages about monsters and their victims, namely that the harp of reason and eloquence allays the torment that has been described ("'Arestyus,'" pp. 147–48). Though the texts of this *Moralitas* are rife with lacunae, Marlin's conclusion deserves consideration: Henryson is inveighing against divination, at the very moment "he is striving to divine intellective meaning from a poetic text" ("'Arestyus,'" p. 148).

582   This recollection of Chaucer's "Goddes pryvetee" also recalls a warning against searching into secrets in the prologue to *The Preaching of the Swallow* (lines 1647–49).

616–27   The conclusion has elicited divergent responses. On the one hand, Marlin
          maintains a reading of the *Moralitas* that entails an ironically depicted narrator
          who "fulfils his own picture of Orpheus: a widowed reason (line 627), an intellect
          out of touch with its affections" ("'Arestyus,'" p. 148). On the other, Rutledge
          asserts that the poet succeeds, finally, in turning his attention to God and away
          from earthly things: "poetic eloquence (Henryson's, if not Orpheus'), bolstered
          by divine grace, is able to turn our 'affection' to heaven" ("Henryson's *Orpheus*,"
          p. 404).

SHORTER POEMS: STRONGER ATTRIBUTIONS

The twelve remaining poems ascribed to Henryson in one or more of the early manuscripts
and prints are presented here in two groups, Stronger and Weaker Attributions; in each of
these groups, the poems are arranged alphabetically by their first lines. Among the whole
group of twelve, moral ballades predominate, with seven poems in this stanza and with a
clear lesson to expound: *The Abbey Walk*, *Against Hasty Credence*, *Ane Prayer for the Pest*, *The
Praise of Age*, *The Ressoning betwix Aige and Yowth*, *The Ressoning betwix Deth and Man*, and *The
Thre Deid Pollis*. Of these seven ballades, the last five concern the imminence of death and
the timeliness of repentance, while *The Abbey Walk* upholds the need for humility and
gratitude in the face of the changing circumstances of life. *Against Hasty Credence* stands
apart from the other moral ballades in that its theme, the imperative that lords behave
judiciously with regard to accusations, is expounded without reference to God until the
penultimate line. Refrains feature in five of the moral ballades (and in the *Moralitas* to "The
Two Mice," also in this form): *The Abbey Walk*, *Against Hasty Credence*, *Ane Prayer for the Pest*,
The Praise of Age, and *The Ressoning betwix Aige and Yowth*, the last of which has two refrains,
one for each of the competing speakers.

      The competitive element in *The Ressoning betwix Aige and Yowth* also associates it with the
group of dialogues and debates, which, though formally diverse, constitute a subgroup.
Together with *The Ressoning betwix Aige and Yowth* deserve to be grouped *Robene and Makyne*
and probably *Sum Practysis of Medecyne*: *Robene and Makyne* because it is made up mostly of
dialogue between two fictional characters; and *Sum Practysis* because of its use of a dramatic
persona, an apothecary, who addresses an opponent (who remains silent). Unlike the first
group of moral ballades, the thematic associations of these dialogue/debates are diverse, as
are the verse forms, with *Robene and Makyne* in eight-line stanzas in alternating four- and
three-stress lines and alternating *a* and *b* rhymes, and *Sum Practysis* in the alliterative
thirteen-line stanza, a form that remained in specialized use in Scotland well into the
sixteenth century.

      Remaining are three quite diverse poems: *The Annunciation*, *The Bludy Serk*, and *The
Garmont of Gud Ladeis*, the first of these a devotional poem in an innovative refinement of
the Middle English twelve-line stanza form, the second an exemplary tale with *Moralitas* in
the same stanza form as *Robene and Makyne*, and the third — the nearest approach to a love-
lyric among the poems ascribed to Henryson — a sumptuary allegory in a quatrain that is
essentially the *Robene* stanza divided in half.

      As is often the case with shorter poems that are associated with a named poet of repute
in a particular literary culture, the authorship of each of the above poems is open to debate.
Perhaps the doubt is greatest with regard to *The Thre Deid Pollis*, ascribed to Henryson in

the Maitland Folio but to Patrick Johnston in the Bannatyne Manuscript. Bannatyne is the sole witness for *The Bludy Serk*, *The Garmont of Gud Ladeis*, *Ane Prayer for the Pest*, and *The Ressoning betwix Deth and Man* (both in the Draft Manuscript as well as the main manuscript), *Robene and Makyne*, and *Sum Practysis of Medecyne*; and though *The Abbey Walk*, *The Praise of Age*, and *The Ressoning betwix Aige and Yowth* appear elsewhere, Bannatyne is alone in ascribing these poems to Henryson. In fact, for only *Against Hasty Credence* of all the shorter poems is Henryson's authorship attested by more than one witness. The one Henrysonian poem not found in the Bannatyne Manuscript, *The Annunciation* (the unique copy of which is in the Gray Manuscript) does not shed much light on the problem, since it is generically and formally anomalous. The fact that moral ballades predominate among the shorter poems ascribed to Henryson does not strengthen the evidence for authorship of any one of them; indeed, his reputation for writing just such poems, often with refrains, might well have drawn extra items into the orbit of his name: suspicion lingers over the particularly weak attributions for *The Abbey Walk*, *Ane Prayer for the Pest*, *The Ressoning betwix Deth and Man*, and *The Thre Deid Pollis*.

In the shorter poems, Henryson draws on a fair range of sources. *The Annunciation*, as MacDonald has shown, is a translation of a Latin hymn, *Fortis ut mors dilectio*. *The Abbey Walk* has strong affinities to a poem in the Vernon Manuscript (Ramson, "'Lettres,'" p. 44). *Against Hasty Credence* has affinities to passages in Lydgate's *Fall of Princes* and "The Churl and the Bird." Some of these poems allude to, but are not confined by, specific generic conventions: thus *Robene and Makyne* reveals "a distinct air of familiarity with the genre" of the *pastourelle*, the medieval dialogue of pastoral courtship (Petrina, "Deviations," p. 113; Jamieson, "Poetry," p. 297); likewise, the *chanson d'aventure*, a medieval genre in which (as in "The Preaching of the Swallow") the poet goes out one spring morning and hears a wondrous speech or dialogue, provides only the opening gambit for *The Praise of Age* and *The Ressoning betwix Aige and Yowth*. In fact, the same inventiveness with respect to sources that has been noted in the longer poems can also be traced here. Alessandra Petrina comments perceptively that these shorter poems exemplify Henryson's "constant reflection on the tools of his trade" and show that fine rhetoric can be "Rycht plesand" (*Fables*, line 4), "provided the reader was aware of the presence of fiction, and of the interpreting problems this would create" ("Deviations," p. 107). For the reader who is becoming acquainted with Henryson's poems, insight into his stylistic and thematic concerns can be found in the brief compass of *The Bludy Serk*, *Against Hasty Credence*, and, of course, *Robene and Makyne*: the play with levels of style, the elegant turn of phrase, the memorable cadences, and the sure moral sense that calls for no heavy emphasis.

AGAINST HASTY CREDENCE (*NIMEV* 758)

ababbcbC5; seven ballade stanzas

A moral ballade with refrain: rumormongers are springing up like weeds around lords, so that lords are advised to evaluate information in terms of the motives of its provider and subject, and then call the parties to speak on their own behalf; for a lord to do otherwise is to lose honor; heeding slander produces disorder and violence (stanza 5 essentially repeats stanza 2, about the lord's responsibility to summon and judge the parties); an exclamation on "wicked tongue" follows; the backbiter damages himself, his victim, and the lord who hears his slander; the poem ends with the arresting images of the double face and the bloody tongue. The theme of corruptive slander is well attested in Middle English verse (e.g., Sandison, "*Chanson*," pp. 121–23; Lydgate, *Fall of Princes*, 1.4243–4844, and "The Churl and the Bird," lines 197–203 [*Minor Poems*, 2:468–85]); Henryson shapes this theme towards an emphasis on the need for lords to proceed according to legal principles in their search for the truth.

30   Compare Lydgate: "For there is noon mor dreedful pestilence / Than a tunge that can flatre and fage" (*Fall of Princes* I.4621–22)

36–40   While defamation was an ongoing irritant in fifteenth-century Scotland (Ewan, "'Many Injurious Words'"), perjury was punishable by the church; given the crucial importance of oaths in testimony, it was "a question whether perjury was a mortal sin" (Walker, *Legal History*, p. 543); to bring an accusation to court, therefore, was to make it a matter of gravity with heavy consequences to the false accuser. Compare Lydgate: "Leve no talis nor yive no credence, / Till that the parti may come to audience" (*Fall of Princes* I.4584–85).

THE ANNUNCIATION (*NIMEV* 856)

The twelve-line stanza in which this poem is cast has an ambitious rhyme scheme: *a4b3a4bb3aa4bb3aa4b3*. "[I]n recognizing that both William Dunbar [in "Ane Ballat of Our Lady"] and Robert Henryson created idiosyncratic twelve-line stanzas for hymns of praise to the Virgin, one must consider the possibility that there was a tradition of or devotional reason for Marian adulation in twelve-line songs" (Fein, "Twelve-Line Stanza Forms," p. 385). *The Annunciation* is a devotional lyric: the power of love is epitomized by Gabriel's message from God to Mary; without sin, Mary will bear a child, who will be Christ; glad of the news, Mary is exalted by the honor of giving birth to the son of God; love, like a river or an unquenchable flame, brings continued miracles to pass, with Gabriel's annunciation fulfilling the coming into leaf of Aaron's staff and the dew of Gideon's fleece; as God protected Mary, so he submitted to degradation and even death for us, moistening us with the blood of his passion and manifesting his love in the resurrection; Mary, avert my sins and hasten my soul to heaven. As MacDonald reveals, *The Annunciation* is a close translation of a Latin lyric that "enjoyed a certain popularity in the late fifteenth century"("Latin Original," p. 54), *Fortis ut mors dilectio*; MacDonald provides an edition and translation of this poem (pp. 55–60). Four manuscript copies of *Fortis ut mors dilectio* are extant, one in a book (National Library of Scotland, MS 10270, at fols. 61–62) owned by James Brown, "student at St Andrews in the 1470s, and dean of Aberdeen from 1484 until his death in 1505" (MacDonald, "Latin Original," p. 51).

5–6   Punctuating these lines as part of one sentence bestows a clear grammatical function to the conjunction "Quhen" and draws attention to the typology of present existence given precedent and meaning by the Annunciation; alternations between tenses continue to feature in the telling of the scriptural event.

15–18   Henryson translates *pudicam* as "maid infild"; the original emphasis on modesty has been intensified into one of lack of pollutive sin; a more striking adjustment occurs in "fra sin exild," for which no precedent exists in the Latin poem.

37–40   Adding the image of the running river, Henryson renders concrete the Latin verb *manant*. In comparing the translation to the original at this juncture, MacDonald comments that "Though the number of syllables remains the same, the number of words, and thus the possibility of alliteration, is considerably increased; this contributes to the lapidary style of the Scottish version" ("Latin Original," p. 62).

43–46   As Fox notes, three typological figures for Mary follow: the burning bush, the flourishing rod, and "the most famous of all the symbols of the virginity of Mary," Gideon's fleece (Exodus 3:2, Numbers 17:8, Judges 6:37; Raby, *History of Christian-Latin Poetry*, p. 371, qtd. Fox, ed., p. 431).

68   As MacDonald notes, "A change typical of the vernacular is that of 'demon' . . . to 'Termigant'" ("Latin Original," p. 61); this common name for a false god was firmly established in Middle Scots as a devil's name (*DOST termigant*).

71–72   Henryson's allusion to the coronation of the Virgin is not present in the Latin original.

SUM PRACTYSIS OF MEDECYNE (*NIMEV* 1021)

In seven thirteen-line alliterative stanzas (rhyme scheme *ababababc4ddd3c2*), this is an invective in the person of an apothecary; Fox compares it to the French *herberies*, "parodies of a quack's promotional speech" (ed., p. 475); mock prescriptions also feature in Middle English verse (Jamieson, "Minor Poems," pp. 140–41; Gray, pp. 244–45). The first stanza announces the speaker's readiness to counter the boasts and insults of a competitor; in the second, the speaker contrasts his rival's incompetence to his own incomparable skill in preparing medicines, some examples of which he will provide in order to heal his rival of "malis"; four grotesque prescriptions follow, one per stanza — for digestive upset ("Dia Culcakit"), for impotence (or insomnia, "Dia Longum"), for folly ("Dia Glaconicon"), and for a cough ("Dia Custrum"); the final stanza offers an assurance of the efficacy of the preceding medicines and ends with a coarse gibe.

Reviewing the whole performance, Jamieson observes that "the irregularity of the metre serves to illustrate the confusion of the speaker's mind, confusion shown also by the studied difficulty of the diction" ("Minor Poems," p. 141). The alliterative thirteen-line stanza already had an association with flyting and grotesquery in Sir Richard Holland's *Buke of the Howlat*. It may be that Scots poets continued to have recourse to alliterative forms (e.g., Dunbar's *Tretis of the Tua Mariit Wemen and the Wedo*) as a way of distinguishing their handling of comic and satiric material from that of a recurrent exemplar in these genres, the notably non-alliterative Chaucer.

1   So cry the worm-fowls in frustration — "'Kek, kek!' 'Kukkow!' 'Quek quek!'" — after which the goose declares "I can shape hereof a remedye" (*PF* lines 499, 502).

44   Gray enjoys the "mad precision" of *fyve unce* (p. 248).

85   "To *blis* or *ban*," to bless or curse: a conventional pairing, as in *Wallace* 2.292 or Dunbar, *Tretis of the Tua Mariit Wemen and the Wedo*, line 154.

THE RESSONING BETWIX AIGE AND YOWTH (*NIMEV* 3942)

The rhyme scheme is *ababbcbC5*. A debate in nine alternating stanzas witnessed by the poet between two speakers, Age and Youth, each of whom has his own refrain, Youth's addressed delightedly to himself ("O youth, be glaid into thi flouris grene") and Age's addressed warningly to Youth ("O youth, thi flouris fedis ferly sone"); the last stanza brings the encounter to a close and restates the two refrains.

A synopsis follows: walking outdoors after rain one spring morning, I met a merry man who sang "O youth . . ."; towards us, an ugly old wretch was approaching with a sign on his chest that read, "O youth . . ."; stirred up by this admonition, which he considers erroneous, the young man declared that he was strong and handsome; the old man retorts that he was too, sixty years ago; the young man announces that he intends to enjoy love as long as possible; irritated, the old man points out that age will cost him his virility and attractiveness; the young man declares that he is healthy; the old man tells him that he will lose his health and vitality; upset, the young man departs, as does the old, leaving me with their conflicting messages.

Citing John W. Conlee (*Middle English Debate Poetry*), Priscilla Bawcutt notes that "This particular structure, with an alternating refrain, and a stanza rhyming *ababbcbC*, occurs in several late medieval debate poems" (*Poems of William Dunbar*, 2:340); in Middle Scots verse, see, for example, Dunbar's debate between the Merle and the Nichtingall, "In May as that Aurora did upspring." MacDonald places this poem alongside other debates in Scots, among them *The Ressoning betwix Deth and Man* (see Weaker Attributions, below) and Walter Kennedy's "At matyne houre, in midis of the nicht" ("Lyrics" 255–56).

8, 16, etc.   Scripture subordinates flowering youth to the superior wisdom of age: likened to a flower, youth is emphatically brief and insubstantial (Job 14:2; compare *Pricke of Conscience*, lines 704–17).

10–12   Henryson's description of *Aige* differs from that in a Middle English debate between the ages of man, the alliterative *Parlement of the Thre Ages*, in which the figure of old age is described in markedly pejorative terms — his grotesque ugliness ("ballede and blynde and alle babirlippede," line 158) seems of a piece with his low rank — which rather compromises his religious fervor ("And ever he momelide and ment and mercy he askede," line 160).

38   This line might be taken as the seed for the grotesque clandestine wooing depicted in Dunbar's "In Secreit Place."

ROBENE AND MAKYNE (*NIMEV* 2831)

Robene and Makyne is a dialogue of love in sixteen eight-line ballad-meter stanzas (*a4b3a4b3a4b3a4b3*) in which the two speakers, "Robene" the shepherd and "Mirry Makyne," speak by alternating stanzas until the seventh stanza, in the last two lines of which Robene retorts curtly to Makyne's appeal; the eighth stanza involves a rapid exchange of two-line speeches; the ninth stanza shifts into third-person narration until the last two lines, in which Makyne utters a brief lament; the tenth stanza likewise proceeds in the third person, but with the attention turning to Robene, who now begins to feel love stir; the eleventh, twelfth, thirteenth, and fourteenth stanzas revert to the alternation of voices that predominated in the earlier part of the poem, though now Robene is trying to persuade Makyne; the fifteenth stanza mirrors the seventh, with Robene making his last appeal for six lines and Makyne replying curtly in the last two; the final stanza, like the tenth, contrasts the positions of the two, only this time the contrasts proceed rapidly, with two lines to Makyne's departure, the third and fourth contrasting his mood to hers, the fifth and sixth to the plight Makyne has left Robene in, and the seventh and eighth to a final picture of Robene alone, keeping his sheep "under a huche."

   Robene and Makyne alludes to various generic associations without quite being drawn into their orbit. Associations with the ballad have been adduced (e.g., Gray, p. 265; Fox, ed., p. 470), but, as Alessandra Petrina has noted, the poem lacks the "incremental repetition of motifs" characteristic of ballads, so that "the popular patina we seem to detect is the result of Henryson's craftsmanship rather than a clue to the spontaneous folk origin of the poem" ("Deviations," p. 110). Connections have also been sought between this poem and the medieval *pastourelle*, typically a wooing of a shepherdess by a courtly lover, but, again, Henryson conveys "a distinct air of familiarity with the genre" without having a specific source therein (Petrina, "Deviations," p. 113). Though *Robene and Makyne* has been described as a burlesque (e.g., Cornelius, "Robert Henryson's Pastoral Burlesque"), its blend of elegance and rusticity contrasts sharply with Dunbar's far more outrageous "In Secreit Place." The Bannatyne Manuscript, sole witness for Henryson's poem, contains a group of so-called "erotic dialogues," of widely varying tone: for example, "Jok and Jinny" (fol. 137), "In somer quhen flowris will smell" (fol. 141), and "The Commonyng betwix the mester [scholar] and the heure [prostitute]" (fol. 264).

1–3	The names are typical of medieval depictions of rustic wooing, *Makyne* (the diminutive of *Matilda*) in particular often given a coarsely pejorative cast (*TC* 5.1174; *CT* II[B[1]]30; *MED malkin*, "a. Woman's name, often used as jocular or contemptuous term for a servant woman . . . [b] a mop or bundle of rags used for cleaning; esp. for cleaning ovens; [c] an impotent man"). Henryson has Robin live down to his boorish associations, while Makyne rises decisively above hers.
17–24	The enduring theme of advice to lovers takes definitive form in the *Romance of the Rose* (*Romaunt*, lines 2175–20; Neilson, *Origins and Sources*, pp. 168–212); instances in Middle Scots verse include Dunbar's "Be ye ane luvar."
37–40	Fox (ed., p. 473) notes a parallel between this desperate appeal and one uttered by a similar female protagonist in the Middle Scots poem *The Murning Maiden*: "I may not mend bot murning mo / Quhill God send sum remeid / Throw destany or deid" (Craigie, *Maitland Folio*, 1:360–61, lines 31–33).
89–96	This "unsentimental evaluative view of love," Mapstone observes, "invites . . . consideration — not often attempted — alongside Henryson's *Testament of Cresseid*, another of his poems in which a female figure comes to dispense a new appraisal of things amatory" ("Older Scots," p. 10). From a contrasting perspective, Greentree points out that Makyne's "sharpest lesson" has homiletic associations: "The warning to mend one's ways while time remained was a familiar one . . . enforced through the genre of *memento mori*" ("Literate," pp. 68–69).

THE BLUDY SERK (*NIMEV* 3599)

The rhyme scheme is *a4b3a4b3a4b3a4b3*; twelve eight-line ballad-meter stanzas in the narrative, three in the *Moralitas*. An exemplary tale with *Moralitas*: an old king had a lovely young daughter; heir to the kingdom, she had many noble suitors; nearby dwelt a hideous giant, who abducted the princess and cast her into a dungeon; he was formidably powerful and violent; the only possible relief would be for the king to find a knight willing to fight to the death with the giant; a wide search produced a peerless prince who loved the princess and was willing to fight the giant; the prince defeated the giant and threw him in his own dungeon; the prince rescued the princess but was fatally wounded, his shirt soaked with blood; grief-stricken, the princess would rather have died than see the prince thus, or she would rather have lived the life of a beggar if she could have lived it with him; ready to die, the prince gave the princess his shirt and bade her to keep it in her view and her thoughts when other men came to court her; she did so, recollecting her rescue from the dungeon; henceforth she remained true to the prince, and so should we remain to God who died for our sins. In the *Moralitas*, the king is likened to the Trinity, the princess to the soul, the giant to the devil, the prince to Christ, the dungeon to hell, and the other wooers to the temptations of sin; as the princess refused her suitors, so should we avert sin — may Christ protect us on the Day of Judgment; because the soul, God's daughter, betrayed by the devil, was rescued from hell by Christ, who paid dearly to redeem us, think about the bloody shirt.

The Bludy Serk is a version of the "extremely widespread" story of Christ as a knight who fights for his lady the soul, but dies of his wounds (Woolf, "Theme of Christ the Lover-Knight," p. 14; qtd. Fox, ed., p. 437); a version is found in the *Gesta Romanorum*, a collection of "entertaining moralized stories," drawn on by Chaucer, Gower, and Lydgate as well as Henryson (Salisbury, *Trials and Joys of Marriage*, p. 16). This poem may be related to a traditional song with the same title among "the chief amusements of the old people" in late eighteenth-century Dumfries and Galloway (Heron, *Observations Made in a Journey*, 2:226).

28   The giant's nails are an ell and a quarter long; an ell is about forty-five inches, so these talons measure almost five feet!

62   The arresting, memorable image of the bloody shirt functions traditionally as a reminder to uphold loyalty; it is produced to incite kin and followers to support a family cause in a feud (Brown, *Bloodfeud*, p. 29; compare Malory, *Le Morte Darthur* [Caxton's version], Book 10, chapter 34; *Njal's Saga*, chapter 116). As befits an advocate of mercy and civility (e.g., *Fables*, line 1598n) Henryson wrests the image away from these retaliatory associations and reorients it towards the devotional tradition of the Image of Pity, the depiction of the tortured Christ (Gray, *Themes and Images*, pp. 124–34).

103   As Fox notes, this line does not rhyme: "It is possible that the line is corrupt: B wrote *gyane*, then cancelled it and wrote *pit*" (ed., p. 441).

119   The phrase *bocht us* [or *so*] *deir* regularly features in allusions the Passion of Christ: *Fables*, line 1901; *Ane Prayer for the Pest*, line 41; also Dunbar's lament for Bernard Stewart, "Illuster Ludovick," line 27.

THE GARMONT OF GUD LADEIS (*NIMEV* 4237)

The rhyme scheme is *4b3a4b3*; ten four-line ballad-meter stanzas. A synopsis follows: The poet declares, "If my beloved would love me the best and obey me, I would make her the finest clothing: a hood of honor, a chemise of chastity, a petticoat of faithfulness, a gown of virtue, a belt of kindness, and a cloak of humility; (in the next three stanzas, hat, cape, bodice, ribbon, sleeves, gloves, shoes, stockings all are moralized thus); were she to put on this outfit, it would suit her better than anything she ever wore." Gray succinctly comments that "in this case in a very real sense, 'clothes make the woman'" (p. 262).

In fifteenth-century Scotland as elsewhere in late medieval Europe, sumptuary laws were passed, restricting the kinds of clothing people below the nobility were allowed to wear. In 1458, for example, the Scottish Parliament issued sumptuary legislation "which defined the permissible kinds of dress for daughters as well as wives"; a standard justification for such laws was that the waste of money on fine clothes was impoverishing the realm (Walker, *Legal History*, p. 187; compare *Fables*, lines 2598–2601n).

The allegory of a good person's clothing derives from scripture, Paul's epistles containing an itemized list of the accoutrements in the armor a Christian is to wear in the battle with the devil (Ephesians 6:11–17), as well as a decree about the modest dress proper to devout women (2 Timothy 2:9–10). Henryson adapts these concepts: the garments he lists are to be bestowed on his "gud lady" as a reward for the best sort of love, namely, obedience (lines 1–2).

1   While *gud lady* can mean "virtuous woman" (as in the scriptural source) or "beautiful" or "noble" woman, it is also a standard idiom for "wife" (*MED ladi(e* 1, 9; *DOST lady*); as well, this is the strong woman beyond price of scripture (Proverbs 31:10). In the Bannatyne Manuscript a poem appears on the same theme that echoes Henryson's: "Wald my gud ladye that I luif / Luiff me best for ay / I suld gar mak for hir behuif / Ane garmond gude and gay" (lines 1–4; Ritchie, *Bannatyne Manuscript*, 3:295).

29   Sleeves were commonly separate garments, laced onto a dress when it was to be worn; compare *TC* 5.1043 for an instance of the bestowal of a sleeve as a sign of inconstancy.

39   The line might be translated, "That she never dressed in either gaudy or muted colors" (compare Fox, ed., p. 445).

THE PRAISE OF AGE (*NIMEV* 1598)

The rhyme scheme is *ababbcbC5*; four ballade stanzas. In a summer garden, the poet listens to an old man singing: growing old, one approaches heaven; in this wicked world, the rulers in their greed have exiled generosity; the delights of youth pass away without leaving a trace; in this unstable world, God's grace is all we can have, by which we draw near to heaven. Thematically related to this poem is "Honour with Age" (*NIMEV* 429) by Henryson's younger compatriot Walter Kennedy.

11–14   The allegory of the vices ousting the virtues from a kingdom; compare Chaucer, *Lak of Stedfastnesse*, lines 15–21; also *Fables*, lines 1300–03.

SHORTER POEMS: WEAKER ATTRIBUTIONS

THE ABBEY WALK (*NIMEV* 265)
ababbcbC4; seven eight-line stanzas
A moral ballade with refrain: consolation in adversity is to be gained by giving thanks to
God; scriptural examples are adduced (Job, Tobit); adversity is the working of God's justice,
and pity is his mercy; all comes from God. The penultimate line, "Quha hyis law and lawis
he" is key: inversion is the proper working of divine will.

1–5	The setting gives moral point to the opening gambit of reading an inscription (Sandison, *Chanson*, 121); Kelly comments on the value of this "an open-ended or unfinished framework" as a precedent for *The Testament of Cresseid*: here, "the inscription forms not only the body but also the end of the poem" (*Chaucerian Tragedy*, p. 226).
8, etc.	"Bi a Way Wandryng as I Went," a moral ballade in the Vernon Manuscript, has a comparable refrain, "Evir to thonke God of al."
17–24	The paired examples of Job and Tobit present two "tightly interlaced" sorts of adversity: this stanza is "stylistically the poem's high point" in Ramson's opinion, and "the best pointer to the poem's art: its balance which spreads into the two sets of three stanzas, is carried through to the level of single lines, the prominent caesura, in the first four stanzas particularly, giving the lines a formal poise which is part of the poem's meaning but is also part of its decorative patterning" ("'Lettres,'" pp. 44, 45).
25–32	Compare "Bi a Way Wandryng as I Went" (lines 9–11): "Thaugh thou waxe blynd or lome / Or eny seknesse on the be set, / With such grace God hath the gret."
30	The "lipper lady" used this saying to give point to her remonstrance to Cresseid (line 475n); in the present poem, fuller use is made of a Chaucerian precedent, *Truth*, which contains not only this saying (lines 11–12) but also the proverb that lies behind Henryson's refrain, in Chaucer's words, "Know thy contree, look up, thank God of all" (*Truth*, line 19).
33–40	Kelly notes the centrality to *Testament* of the theme that "natural afflictions are temptations, which must be endured in patience. At other times, to be sure, adversity is recognized as deserved, but it is also corrective, and serves to save as well as to punish" (*Chaucerian Tragedy*, p. 238).
35	Compare *Fables*, lines 1190, 1194, 2689.
41	The moralizing phrase "change and vary" crops up in Dunbar's *Timor mortis conturbat me* (line 9).
51	For the emergence in the sixteenth century of a pejorative connotation to *pelf*, see *Fables*, line 2042n.

ANE PRAYER FOR THE PEST (*NIMEV* 2420)

The rhyme scheme is *ababbcbC5*; eleven ballade stanzas, the three last with internal rhyme (lines 65–72 completing each of the first, second, and third feet; lines 73–80 and 81–88 completing the second and third feet). *Ane Prayer for the Pest* is a penitential ballade with the refrain "Preserve us fra this perrelus pestilens": God most powerful and perfect, have mercy on us in punishing us for our offenses, save us from the plague; hear our lament, because unless you mercifully restore us, we will die; we would gladly submit to any other punishment, but is it your will that we die like beasts, so that we dare not live together? Choose famine, but remove your plague because our deaths will not make up for our sins; have mercy, without which we are defenseless; you redeemed us dearly on the cross, so now take pity on your likeness; give us grace to atone for our sins, for without atonement the only justice is death; rulers, who should punish wrongdoers, are wholly corrupt, so that God will not heed their appeals; diminish this plague — if we were contrite, our sorrows would cease — none who seeks grace is destroyed; without your aid, we are in a deathtrap — no one can overlook our greed but you; calm your hostility — we can expect no relief — soon we will all be dead — do not let what you so dearly bought be lost. Bengt Ellenberger notes the exceptionally "high style, the intricate rhyme scheme, and the non-technical character of the words" that differentiate *Ane Prayer for the Pest* from Henryson's attested styles (*Latin Element*, p. 63). Drexler notes that the Draft portion of the Bannatyne Manuscript presents *Ane Prayer* as two poems: after line 64 appears the colophon *Finis*; and the ensuing stanzas have a new refrain ("Henryson's 'Prayer for the Pest'"; compare Textual Notes 64an).

17–22	The theme of plague as punishment is scriptural (Numbers 14:11–12; 2 Samuel 24:13–17); compare Conscience's sermon, in which he "preved that thise pestilences were for pure synne" (Langland, *Piers Plowman*, B.5.13).
29	The term *pungetyfe* appears to be Henryson's own Latinism (*DOST pungitive* 1a); compare *Testament*, line 229, where the adjective refers to the hostility shown by Venus.
65–72	Dunbar's "Ane Ballat of Our Lady" (lines 1–3) also features the aureate terms *superne* and *lucerne*.
81–82	In their edition of the poem, Robert L. Kindrick and Kristie A. Bixby suggest that *Sen* should be interpreted to mean "As for": "As for our sins, which justice must correct, O King most high, now pacify your anger" (*Poems of Robert Henryson*, p. 265).

THE RESSONING BETWIX DETH AND MAN (*NIMEV* 2520)

A dialogue in six alternating ballade stanzas (*ababbcbc5*): Death demands man's attention and asserts that no creature, regardless of earthly station, can resist death; Man, incredulous and uncomprehending, wants to know his challenger's identity and asserts that he will defeat anyone who challenges him; Death identifies himself and repeats that he cannot be resisted by anyone; realizing the imminence of death, Man admits to a sinful youth; Death calls for repentance in readiness for the inevitable; Man repents submissively and appeals to God for mercy. While skeptical about any connection between this poem and the Dance of Death, Gray detects "echoes of an earlier type of poem, the *Vado mori* ('I go to die') in which a number of 'estates' are confronted by Death and overcome by him. . . . Here he is an awesome and mysterious figure" (*Selected Poems of Henryson and Dunbar*, p. 380).

4   The formula "reges pontifices imperatores" ("kings, popes, emperors") commonly refers to the highmost ranks of power in the world, especially in relation to their vulnerability to death.

33–40   Compare the *Moralitas* to "The Fox and the Wolf" (lines 789–95), in which "gude folke" are warned to "feir this suddane schoit" and "remord your conscience."

THE THRE DEID POLLIS (*NIMEV* 2551)

In eight ballade stanzas (*ababbcbc5*), this is a moral ballade in which the reader, "sinfull man," is addressed by three skulls (reminiscent of the theme of the Three Living and the Three Dead; Fox, ed., p. 487): they invite him to look at them and realize that as he is now, so they were once; everyone must suffer death and therefore should keep it in mind in order to avoid sin; the young man is to think of his head in the same state; finely dressed ladies will turn out thus; the proud must seek mercy because all ranks of society will turn to dust; no scholar can distinguished between the skulls in terms of beauty, nobility, or learning; the aged should learn from the skulls to request mercy for himself and also for their souls; everyone should seek mercy in order to reign forever with the Trinity.

The copy of this poem in the Bannatyne Manuscript has an ascription to Patrick Johnston (d. 1495), "a notary, land-owner, and official receiver of revenues from Crown lands in West Lothian [who] produced court entertainments" (Bawcutt, *Poems of William Dunbar*, 2:336).

4   The hollowed-out eye sockets of the skulls find their way into Dunbar's insulting depiction of Walter Kennedie, his opponent in *The Flyting* (line 164).

14–16   The *memento mori*; compare *The Flyting of Dunbar and Kennedie* (lines 162–67).

17–24   Compare *The Ressoning betwix Aige and Yowth*, lines 41–48 and 59–64.

 **TEXTUAL NOTES**

ABBREVIATIONS: A: the Asloan Manuscript; **An**: *The Testament of Cresseid* (Anderson); **B**: the Bannatyne Manuscript; **Bd**: the Bannatyne Manuscript Draft; **Br**: Bawcutt and Riddy, *Longer Scottish Poems*; **Bs**: *The Morall Fabillis of Esope the Phrygian* (Bassandyne); **Bu**: Burrow, *English Verse 1300–1500*. **C**: *The Morall Fabillis of Esope the Phrygian* (Lekprevik and Charteris); **Ch**: *The Testament of Cresseid* (Charteris); **Cm**: the Chepman and Myllar Prints; ***DOST***: *Dictionary of the Older Scottish Tongue*; **Fox**: Denton Fox, ed., *The Poems of Robert Henryson*; **G**: The Gray Manuscript; **H**: Harley 3865; **Ht**: *The Morall Fabillis of Esope* (Hart); ***MED***: *Middle English Dictionary;* **Mf**: the Maitland Folio; **Mk**: the Makculloch Manuscript; ***OED***: *Oxford English Dictionary*; **R**: the Ruthven Manuscript; **T**: *The Testament of Creseyde*, ed. Thynne.

FABLES

title	Bs (base text throughout), C: *The Morall Fabillis of Esope the Phrygian*.

THE PROLOGUE: Mk, B, Bs [C, H, Ht], Fox

title	Mk omits. B: *The Cock and the Jewell*. [new line] *Prolog*. Bs: *The Prolog*.
4	*plesand ar*. Mk, B: *Ar rycht plesand*.
5	*quhy that*. Mk, B, Fox: *quhy*. Bs: *that*. Fox notes the support of Mk and B in 2344 but suggests that *quhy that* "may have been the original reading" (ed., p. 189); on the grounds that metrical regularity is a hallmark of Henryson's style, especially at the outset of each of the *Fables*, Fox's suggestion has been adopted here.
6	*of thi*. B: *vyce of*. Bs: *haill*.
7	*O*. Mk, B, Bs: *Off*. Taking a cue from G. Gregory Smith's emendation of Mk from *Off* to *O* (*Specimens*, p. 267) and noting the reading *of thi* in line 6 of the same witness, Fox regards Mk's apparent redundancy as the best pointer to the meaning and rhetorical stance of this passage (ed., p. 189).
8	*a*. Bs: *the*. The reading shared by Mk and B refers to a particular kind of heavy soil, hard to cultivate but fertile; the implications are richer than in the reading in Bs, which refers to soil generically.
12	*springis thar a*. Bs: *dois spring ane*.
16	*Haldis*. Bs: *aldis*.
	sweit and. Bs: *and is*. For Kratzmann, the reading in Mk and B is "clearly preferable, because it gives a sense which provides a logical relation to the second part of the simile" ("Henryson's *Fables*," p. 53).

21   *blyth*. Bs: *light*.

22   *For as we se*. Mk: *For as*. Bs: *Forthermair*.

24   *ay is*. Bs: *is ay*.

29   *authour*. Mk, Fox: *poete*. Aesop is one of the Eight Authors (*Auctores octo*) of the medieval curriculum; to call him an *authour* is more meaningful, therefore, than to refer to him as a *poete*; it is understandable that in Mk, which provides the text of only one fable, this point is less significant than it is in the more ambitious compilations in B and especially Bs.

40   *Gif ye find ocht that*. Bs: *Gif that ye find it*.

43   *his fabillis*. Mk: *this fabill*. B: *his fable*. The variation is of considerable import for readings of the *Fables*: either this is a general prologue to the whole sequence of tales or it introduces specifically and only the ensuing tale, *The Cock and the Jasp*; here a crucial difference arises between Bs, in which the ensuing fable is indeed the first, and B, in which it appears in the middle of what seems to be a much looser sequence.

45   *And to*. Bs: *In to*.

47   *Puttyng*. Bs: *Put in*.
                 and. Bs: *and in*.

52   *him renye nor*. B: *nocht derenye nor*. Mk: *nocht derenye and*. Both *derenye* (*OED deraign* v.1; *DOST derenȝe* v.) and *renye* ("call to account"; *OED arraign* v.1) are precisely apposite here; since the next verb, *arreist*, has precisely legal associations, the reading in Bs is preferred here.

54   *Quhilk*. Bs: *And that*.
                 the. Bs omits.

55   *the mynd*. Bs: *thair myndis*.

56   *he*. Bs: *thay*.
                 beist is. Bs: *beistis ar*.

58   *and facound purpurat*. Mk, Fox: *and in facund purpurat*. B: *facound and purpurat*. Bs: *as poete lawriate*. Fox notes that *facund* was a noun in fifteenth-century Scots and points out that the preposition *in* introducing this phrase may be a scribal error (*DOST facund* n.; ed., p. 193).

60   *Tak*. Bs: *Lak*.

63a   Bs: *Finis*.

THE COCK AND THE JASP: MK, B, Bs C [H, HT], FOX

title   Mk, B, C omit. Bs: *The Taill of the Cok and the Jasp*.

74   *Quhat be thairin*. Mk: *Tak no tent so at*. Bs, C: *Thay cair na thing*.

81   *lord or*. B: *only warldly*.

82   Bs, C: *Pietie it wer thow suld ly in this mydding*.

83   *muke and*. Bs, C: *muke on*.

87   *I may*. Mk: *It may*. Bs, C: *It may me*.

89   *leif and*. Mk: *haldyne*.

92	*ga skraip.* Bs: *ga scrapit.* C: *haif scraipit.*
98	Bs: *For les availl may me as now dispyis.* C: *For thyne availl may as now dispyis.*
99	*I had.* Bs, C: *haif I.*
102	*wyfis.* B: *wyse men.*
	that. Bs omits.
	werk is. B: *wark was.* Bs, C: *werkis ar.*
103	B omits.
	sum meit have. Bs, C: *have sum meit.*
104	*not weil leif.* Bs, C: *not leue.*
111	*fen.* B: *as.* Bs, C: *midding.*
118	*fabill.* Bs, C omit.
title	*Moralitas.* Mk, Bs, C: precedes line 127. B [marginal, in a different hand]: *Moralite.*
120–26	In Bs, some confusion seems to have arisen about the proper location of this stanza, which is in the same *civilité* font as the fable proper, not the Roman font of the following stanzas of the *Moralitas.*
120	*hes.* Bs, C: *had.*
122	*is lyke.* Bs, C, Fox: *lyke to.*
125	*hap.* Mk: *hoip.*
126	*Of fyre nor fallis.* Mk: *and noi sal.* Bs, C: *Or fyre nor water.* Lists of terms typically pose difficulties for copyists; the difficulty of *fallis* has arguably produced simpler readings in Mk, Bs, and C.
131	*ay.* Bs, C: *for.*
132	*haif.* Bs, C: *wyn.*
139	*can freit.* Mk: *fre.* B: *nor ket.* Bs: *can screit.*
143	Mk, Bs, C, Fox: *Quhilk at science makis bot ane moik and scorne.*
145	*argumentis.* Bs: *argumenti.*
147	*the.* Bs, C omit.
150	Mk, Bs, C: *Quhilk is sa nobill, sa precious and sa ding.*
151	*it.* B omits.
	with na. B: *nocht with no.* Bs, C: *not with.*
	thing. Mk: *gud.*
154	*neidit.* Bs, C: *neidis.*
156	*it nocht.* Mk: *it.*
	for. Mk: *nocht.* B omits.
159	*it wair bot.* Mk, Fox: *I wair bot.* B: *I do bot waistis.* Bs, C: *it wer bot.*
161a	B: *Explicit quod mr R. H.* Bs, C: *Finis.*

THE TWO MICE: A, B, Bs, C [H, Ht]; FOX, Bu, Br

title	A: *Heir begynnes the tale of the uplandis mous and the borowstoun mous.* B (in a later hand): *The Twa Myss.* Bs, C: *The Taill of the Uponlandis Mous and the Burges Mous.*
164	*eldest.* B, Bs, C: *eldest duelt.*
165	*yungir.* Bs, C: *uther.*

166   Bs, C, Br: *Soliter, quhyle under busk, quhyle under breir.*

167   *in.* Bs, C: *and.*

168   *levit on hir.* B, Bs, C: *levis on thair.*

171   *tother.* Bs, C, Fox, Br: *uther.*

            that in. A: *into.*

            couth. Bs, C, Fox, Br: *can.*

175   Bs, C, Br: *Amang the cheis in ark and meill in kist.* The arrangement of nouns in compound phrases, as elsewhere in the *Fables*, produces variant readings.

179   *led.* Bs, C, Br: *had.*

183   *Throw.* Bs, C, Br: *Furth.*

184   *mure and mosse.* A: *mure mos.* Bs, C, Fox: *mosse and mure.*

185   A: *Cryand on hir fra balk to balk.* Bs: *Scho ran cryand quhill scho come to a balk.* C: *Scho ranne with mony ane hiddeous quaik.* Bawcutt and Riddy consider both A and B to be "weakened by the absence of a reference to the *fur* or 'furrow', which vividly conveys the different scale of the mouse's world" (Br, p. 356). Burrow observes that "The sudden switch to the Lilliputian world of the mouse, labouring up and down the ridge and furrow of a ploughed field, puzzled scribes" (*English Verse*, p. 339).

186   *sweit.* B, Br omit.

187   *couth.* B: *quod.* Bs, Fox, Br: *culd.* C: *cryit.*

188   *kinnismen.* Bs, C, Fox: *kinnisman.*

190   *cheir, lord.* Bs, C, Br: *joy.*

191   A, B, Bu: *Was kithit* [B: *kyid*] *quhen thir sisteris twa war met.* Bs, Br: *Beis kith quhen that thir sisteris met. ythit.* Fox: *Beis kithit quhen thir sisteris twa war met.*

192   *Quhilk that oft syis.* A, Bu: *The welcummyng.* Bs, C, Br: *And grit kyndnes.*

197   *semple.* Bs, C, Br: *sober.*

198   *misterlyk.* B: *maisterlig.* Bs, C: *febillie.*

199   *erdfast.* Bs, C: *steidfast.* Bawcutt and Riddy note that *erdfast* is "distinctive but perhaps slightly archaic" (*Br*, p. 356).

202   *Withoutin.* Bs: *Without.*

205   *hyid.* Bs: *glyde.* C: *yeid.*

206   *peis.* Bs, C: *candill.*

207   *thair wes weilfair.* Bs, C, Br: *this wes gude fair.*

208   *prompit.* B: *prunnigit.* Fox: *prunyit.* Though the logical reading in Bs is arguably a simplifying substitution of a more for a less familiar term, Fox's emendation has not been followed; the meaningful, idiomatic, unusual *prompit* has good textual support.

210   *Think ye this meis* [A, Bu, Fox: *meit*] *nocht.* Bs, C, Br: *Is nocht this meit rycht.*

213   *efter that.* Bs, C: *sister quhen.*

215   *ryte.* Bs, C: *rate.*

216   *syre.* B: *schyr.* Bs, C omit.

	levand in. Bs, C: *leving into.*
221	*quhy.* Bs, C: *quhylis.*
224	*usit wes before.* A, Bu: *usit is befor.* B: *usit wer befoir.* Bs, C: *wes before usit.*
226	*yow pleis.* Bs, C: *pleis yow.*
229	*hartlie.* Bs, C: *mery.*
231	*tender, sweit, and.* Bs, C: *tender and wonder.*
232	*plesans.* Bs, C: *plesure.*
	in. Bs, C: *in the.*
235	*visage.* Bs, C: *curage.*
239	*this.* Bs, C: *his.*
247	*trewe.* B: *gude.* Bs, C omit.
251	*na fall, na trap.* A: *na trape na fall.* Bs, C: *nor fall trap.* According to Bawcutt and Riddy, "A and B seem to make a distinction between two kinds of mouse-trap (*MED falle*; *DOST fall*, n. 2) which is lost in Bs" (*Br*, p. 357).
252	*on togidder yeid.* B, C, Fox, Br: *on togidder thay yeid.* The loss of metrical regularity in the alternate reading does not seem justified.
253	*skugry ay.* A: *stowthry ay.* Bs, C: *stubill array.* Bawcutt and Riddy comment that "Scribal misunderstanding of a rare word, together with the common c/t confusion, could have led to A's *stowthry*" (*Br*, p. 357).
	rankest. Bs, C omit.
254	*Under covert full.* B: *And wondir sly full.* Bs, C: *And under buskis.*
262	*Withowt godspeid.* A: *Intill ane innes.* The lack of proper etiquette has greater thematic import than the identification in A of a specific destination.
264	*upon.* Bs, C: *upon thair.*
265	*Flesche.* B: *With fische.* Bs, C: *And flesche.*
266	*grotis, meile, and.* Bs: *meill and eik off.*
278	*bot how lang.* A, Bu: *how lang now.* Bs, C, Br: *how lang.*
281–87	A omits this stanza.
285	*mane full.* B, Bu: *furmag.* Bs: *manfully.* This crux appears to Fox to depend on the failure of B and Bs to identify *mane* as fine white bread. Burrow, however, bases a case for *furmag* on the common association between mice and cheese (*English Verse*, p. 344).
287	*gust thair mouth.* B, Bu: *creisch thair teithis.* As Burrow notes, the reading in B is delightfully specific (*English Verse*, p. 344); however, it may provide an instance of Bannatyne's enthusiastically imaginative involvement in the poem he is copying, with something of a mixed metaphor resulting in the unwanted implication that the spices would have been greasy as well as the substitute the mice prefer.
289	*thay.* Bs, C, Fox, Br omit.
300	*all.* A, Bs, C, Fox, Br: *ane.*
304	*nor serche.* A: *to char.*
	to char nor. A: *nor yit to.* B: *nor char no.* Bs, C, Br: *to sker nor.*

306	*This.* Bs, C, Fox: *The.*
	passage. Bs, C, Br: *passing.*
309	*flatlingis.* Bs, C, Fox, Br: *flatling.*
311	*wofull.* A, Bu: *wilsome.*
312	*fever.* Bs, C: *fever scho.*
318	*answerit.* Bs, C: *answerit hir.*
324	A, Bu: *And unto burde togidder baith thay sat.* Bs, C, Fox: *And to the burde thay went and togidder sat.*
328	*fled.* Bs, C: *went.*
	of. Bs, C: *on.*
331	*tait.* Bs, C: *cant.*
335	*fair.* Bs, C. omit.
336	*the dosor.* B: *the dressour.* Bs, C: *ane burde.* Bawcutt and Riddy comment that the reading in the printed texts may "derive from a memory of line 324" (*Br*, p. 358).
337	*Syne.* Bs, C: *And.*
338	*So hie scho clam.* Bs, C. *Scho clam so hie.*
339	*And.* Bs, C: *Syne.*
	clukis. A, Bu: *clukis richt.* Bs, C, Br: *cluke thair.*
342	*Apon.* Bs, C: *And to.*
346	*sair.* Bs, C: *fair.*
347	*ma.* A, B, Fox: *may.* Bs, C: *na.*
352	*I suld.* Bs: *suld I.* C: *suld.*
356	*scho.* B, Bs, C, Fox, Br omit.
357	*eftirwart.* Bs, C: *weill thairefter.*
361	A, Bu: *Of nutis, pes.* B, Fox: *Off peis and nuttis.* The variants for this line exemplify the copyists' difficulty with lists of topically related terms.
365	*heir.* Bs, C omit.
	will ye. A: *quhill ye.* Bs, C, Br: *and ye will.*
366	*In.* Bs, C: *In to.*
368	*intermellit.* Bs, C: *interminglit.* The prints appear to substitute a more modern for an older form of the word.
372	*And.* Bs, C: *That ar.*
381–88	C omits this stanza.
383	*Luke.* Bs: *Lieke.*
	ondeid. Bs: *but dreid.*
387	Bs: *Best thing in eird, thairfoir I say for me.* The syntax of the manuscript readings is more idiomatic.
388	*merry hart.* A: *sekerness.* Bs, Br: *blyithness in hart.* The metrical irregularity of the reading in Bs encourages a preference for the reading in B.
389	*freind, thocht.* Bs, C, Br: *my freind sa.*
392	*I.* Bs: *thair.* C: *it.*
	se. Bs, C: *be.*
396a	A: *Heir endis of the twa mys.* B: *Explicit quod mr. R. H.* Bs, C: *Finis.*

THE COCK AND THE FOX: B, BS [C, H, HT]; FOX

title	B (in a later hand): *The Fox and the Cock.* Bs: *The Taill of Schir Chantecleir and the Foxe.*
405	*and.* Bs: *and sa.*
407	*it excedis.* Bs: *is excludit.*
423	*hir pultrie.* Bs, Fox: *pultrie baith.* The line in B is more metrically regular than that in Bs, and as idiomatic.
430	*juparteis.* Bs: *jeperdie.*
438	*yow service for.* Bs, Fox: *service to you.*
441	*oft fulfillit.* Bs: *full oft fillit.*
447	*forsuth I held.* Bs: *I held up.*
456	*warmys.* Bs: *is warme.*
457	*Yow for to serve.* Bs: *To mak yow blyith.*
462	*Me think yow.* Bs, Fox: *Ye are me think.*
463	*and.* Bs: *off.*
472	*Quhat.* Bs: *For.*
	cok. Bs: *fox.* Capturing the speed and zest of the interchange at this key moment, Fox's two emendations here are irresistible.
477	*walkit.* Bs: *wawland.* The image, conveyed by Bs's *wawland*, of Chantecleir rolling his eyes seems weakly associative: his eyes are shut.
482	*countermaund.* Bs: *that cryme.* The reading in B is more specifically, wittily apposite.
486	*reylok.* Bs: *hay.* The printed text makes a characteristic substitution here of a familiar for an unfamiliar word.
494	*of.* Bs: *in.*
527	*yow.* Bs omits.
	ye. Bs: *he is.*
533	Bs: *"He had," quod scho, "Kittokis ma than sevin."*
536	*Adulteraris that list.* Bs: *For adulterie that will.*
546	*Birkye.* Bs: *Berk.*
	Bell. Bs omits.
555	*raches.* Bs: *kennettis.* The variant terms are roughly synonymous; the reading in B produces a formulaic alliteration that befits the scene of vigorous motion that is beginning.
558	*spak.* Bs: *said.*
570	*unto a.* Bs: *out off the.*
576	Bs: *Na fals theif and revar, stand not me neir.* The variant presents an instance of the copyists' recurrent difficulty with lists, a difficulty that in Bs produces metrical irregularity.
578	*love.* Bs: *freindschip.*
581	*mair.* Bs: *mais.*
	coud nocht be. Bs: *to be sa.*
582	*But spake.* Bs: *Quhairthrow.*
585	*In.* Bs: *And in.*

592   *ar.* B, Fox: *is.*
602   *mynd maist toxicate.* B: *mouth mellifluate.*
606a   B: *Flattery.*
607   *The wickit mynd and.* B: *This wikkit wind of.* The imaginative reading in B
              produces a mixed metaphor arguably characteristic of the scribe —
              a wicked wind is not like sweet sugar; see the Textual Note to *Fables,*
              line 287.
609   *fell.* Bs omits.

THE FOX AND THE WOLF: B, BS [C, H, HT]; FOX

title   B (in a later hand): *The Fox and the Wolf.* Bs: *The Taill how this foirsaid Tod
              maid his confessioun to Freir Wolf Waitskaith.*
614   B (LH margin): *Incipit aliam fabulam.* Thus begins an explicit connection
              between the fox fables in B that is arguably stronger than the linkage
              between the group of ten of the *Fables* intermingled in this manu-
              script compilation with other poems.
616   *fatal.* Bs: *subtell.*
618   *miching.* Bs: *waitting.*
621   *Thetes.* Bs omits.
623   *off.* Bs: *up.*
648   *the.* Bs: *my.*
649   *wait.* B, Fox: *watt.* Bs: *ken.*
651   *fait.* Bs: *men.*
652   *bot.* Bs: *bot gif.*
653   *Deid.* Bs: *It.*
              and. Bs: *ane.*
655   *all.* Bs: *my.*
657   *lyif is.* Bs: *lyifis.*
659   *alyk ar.* Bs: *ar lyke.*
665   *thence.* Bs: *hence.*
666   *of.* Bs: *in.*
668   *cum.* Bs: *cummit.*
677   Bs: *Ye ar mirrour, lanterne, and sicker way.*
684   *Na.* Bs: *A.*
697   *But to.* Bs: *Unto.*
              mele. Bs: *kneill.*
714   *pennance.* Bs: *penitence.*
716   *A.* Bs: *Na.*
717   *Seikly.* Bs: *Selie.* B: *And seikly.*
723   *hyne to.* Bs: *untill.*
729   *faut of.* Bs: *fall no.*
736   *walterand.* Bs: *watter and.*
737   *All stonist.* Bs: *Astonist all.*

| 741 | *boittis, net, nor bait*. B: *net, bottis, nor bate*. Bs: *boittis nor net bait*. This line exemplifies the difficulties posed to copyists by lists of terms. |

741   *boittis, net, nor bait*. B: *net, bottis, nor bate*. Bs: *boittis nor net bait*. This line exemplifies the difficulties posed to copyists by lists of terms.

769   *gane*. Bs: *gang*.

772   *The hird him hynt*. Bs: *He harlit him*.

776   *contritioun*. Bs: *provisioun*. Here and again in 778, 779, and 794, the prints show signs of Protestant expurgation of explicit references to the moral conditions leading to penitence in the sacrament of confession; it is one thing to satirize confession in the fable itself, and another to indicate the ongoing importance of the ritual for the reader.

777   *mend*. Bs: *amend*.

778   *conclusioun*. Bs: *confusioun*.

779   *gois now to confessioun*. Bs: *now hes gude professioun*.

780   *Cannot repent*. Bs: *Yit not repentis*.

794   *Do wilfull pennance here*. Bs: *Obey unto your God*.

795a   B: *Explicit exemplum veritatis et falsitatis*. In B, the reader is invited to read the trio of fox thus, as contrasts of truth and falsehood.

THE TRIAL OF THE FOX: B, Bs [C, H, Ht]; FOX

title   B [in a later hand]: *The Fox Tryed Before the Lyon*. Bs: *The Taill of the Sone and Air of the foirsaid Foxe, callit Father wer: Alswa the Parliament of the fourfuttit Beistis, haldin be the Lyoun*.

798   Bs: *Till airschip be law that micht succeid*.

799   *the*. Bs omits.

      lemanrie. B: *lenanrye*. Bs: *adulterie*.

802   *pultrie tig*. Bs, Fox: *pultrie to tig*. The infinitive is implicit without *to*; the more concise version in B preserves metrical regularity.

806   *get*. Bs: *geir*.

      wrang. Bs: *fals*.

812   *is*. Bs: *hes*. The use of *is* as the auxiliary here for the present perfect of the verb of motion accords with grammatical practice in fifteenth-century Scots.

822   *stouth*. Bs, Fox: *thift*. *Stouth* is a specific kind of theft; B's reading is thus marginally preferable.

      he had done. Bs, Fox: *did his father*. B's reading preserves metrical regularity.

824   *throw naturall*. B: *for faderlye*. Here is an instance of B's imaginative involvement in the text producing a shift in perspective (from the son's motivation to the father's) that does not fit logically.

832   *wrangwis guidis, gold*. Bs: *warldlie gude and gold*.

836   Bs: *To execute, to do, to satisfie*. In Bs, the traditional secular theme of the greedy, disloyal executors of a will has taken the place of the reference, preserved in B, to the medieval ritual, discredited under Protestantism, of prayers for the dead; see also line 837.

837   Bs: *Thy letter will, thy det, and legacie*.

                is thy devotioun. B: *is thy devotioun*; *thy* produces a metrical confusion and may be "a spurious addition" (Fox, ed., p. 235).

838   *he carit*. Bs: *him, he passit*. B, Fox: *him carit*. Fox's emendation is unnecessary: B's reading preserves a use of *carry* in Scots as a transitive verb meaning *go* (*Fables* line 1767; *DOST cary* v); compare *Fables* 2029 and its Textual Note.

840   *him*. Bs: *he*.

841–42   Bs: these two lines are transposed; the sequence in B preserves a logical and chronological sequence.

848   *Oyas, oyas*. Bs: *on this wyis*. The herald's conventional cry *Oyez* ("Listen!") has been misunderstood by the printer.

851   *Govand*. Bs: *Gritlie*. Again, the printer substitutes a current, familiar word for an archaic one.

852   *his buste*. Bs: *ane bus*.
                bill. Bs: *bull*.

855   *We*. Bs: *The*.

856   *ay lestand but ending*. Bs: *helth everlestyng*.

868   *as the*. Bs: *als as*.

869   *gresis*. Bs: *gers*.

872   *trippand*. Bs: *creippand*. B's birds are more sprightly than those in Bs.

873   *a*. Bs: *with*.

881   *fut all*. Bs: *all four futtit*.

898   *jonet*. Bs: *gillet*. The *jonet* is a fine light saddle horse, while *gillet* is synonymous with "mare"; a case could be made for either reading; the decision here is to side, as Fox does, with B because the scribe tends to preserve more unusual terms — if also to fabricate them on occasion (as found in *Fables* 824, Textual Note).

902   *wodwys*. Bs: *tame cat*.
                wild wolfyne. Bs: *wildwod swyne*. "Some of the strange names may have defeated early copyists as well as modern editors" (Gray, *Selected Poems of Henryson and Dunbar*, p. 374); here and elsewhere, too insistent an avoidance of redundancy and apparently arbitrary association (why mention a she-wolf here when the wolf was named elsewhere?) may impose a principle of organization foreign to the work.

906   *baver, bakon, and the*. Bs: *wyld once, the buk, the*.
                balterand. B: *batterand*. Bs: *welterand*. Burrow considers this emendation one of Fox's most perceptive and skilled ("Dunbar," p. 121).

908   *gray*. B, Fox: *gay*. B's reading may arise from the wish to avoid an apparent redundancy; B's seems grounded on the etymological difference involved — in *greyhound*, the first element has nothing to do with color but derives from Old Norse *grøy*, "bitch" (*OED greyhound*).
                with. B, Fox: *the*.

910   *globard*. B: *globert*. Bs: *glebard*.

914	*bowranbane.* B: *lurdane lane.* The reading in Bs has not been defined convincingly; but in spite of its alliterative tidiness and relative obviousness (*lane* from *l'âne,* Fr. "donkey"), B's reading looks like a desperate stopgap.
919	Bs: *With haist scho haikit unto that hill off hicht.* In the version of the line in B, the a lyric inversion of the second foot conforms to Henryson's common practice (Introduction, p. 22).
923	*blenkit.* Bs: *luikit.* B's reading is more specific; Bs's anticipates *lukit* in line 926.
926	*The lyoun lukit quhen.* Bs: *He lukit quhen that.*
945	Bs, Fox: *The tod Lowrie luke not to the lam.* Within the zone of normal variation (see the Textual Note to 919, above), B offers a metrically more regular line than does Bs.
949	*call.* Bs: *callit.*
952	*Tod Lowrie lukit up.* Bs, Fox: *Than Tod Lowrie luikit.* Jamieson argues for the superiority of B because of the richer implications there in the placement, physically and psychologically, of the fox ("Poetry," p. 232n1).
954	*rarit.* Bs, Fox: *cryit.*
966	*far doun.* Bs: *laich.*
967	*the.* Bs omits.
969	*thoill.* Bs: *bene.*
971–84	B omits these stanzas. "The other [sources] provide two additional stanzas . . . of direct condemnation by the author . . . The alliterative pattern seems Henrysonian though the metre is very rough indeed" (Jamieson, "Poetry," p. 234).
986	*stait.* Bs: *estait.*
989	*beist into this.* Bs: *kynd of beistis in.*
991	*gray stude.* Bs: *stude gray.*
993	*My lord.* Bs: *Now see.*
999	*ye.* Bs. omits.
1035	*wretchit.* B and Fox omit.
	on his wayis. Bs: *thus on he.*
1042	*a bank.* Bs: *abak.*
1052	*This new-maid.* Bs: *Speir at your.*
1067	*garray.* Bs: *merines.* B's reading is more archaic; Bs prefers the word common to Scots and English.
1072	*He werryit.* Bs: *Devorit.*
1087	*sis.* Bs: *assyis.* The aphetic variant (missing the first syllable *a-*) in B is attested elsewhere (in French, Dutch, and Latin as well as Scots and English; *OED size* n1); it maintains metrical regularity better than does the explicitness of *assyis* in Bs.
1089	*and party.* Bs: *pyking and.*

1095	*basare.* Bs: *bowcher.* Bs provides a simple, common substitute for the specialized term in B.
1102	*Apertly be oure leving.* Bs: *That to our leving full weill.*
1103	Bs, Fox: *And paynt thair mater furth be poetry.* The printed text arguably provides a Protestant revision of a potentially unacceptable subordination of preaching to the authority of *poesye.*
1104	*liklynace.* Bs: *liknes.*
1106	*mare grace.* Bs: *incres.* The printed text substitutes an inoffensive secular term to avoid even the possibility that the line might be read to refer to the earning of grace in spiritual terms.
1107	*And gapis.* Bs: *Thinkand.*
1111–24	B, Bs, Fox all present these two stanzas in the opposite order, which inverts the topical and grammatical coherence of the passage (e.g., the antecedent of "Hir," line 1125); if this analysis is correct, the inversion would have taken place at a stage in the textual transmission prior to the divergence of the manuscript tradition represented by B from the print tradition represented by Bs.
1118	*contemplatioun.* Bs: *gude conditioun.* A Protestant revision has occurred here in Bs; the rest of the stanza is marked by similar substitutions.
1119	*Of pennance.* Bs: *As pilgrymes.*
1120	Bs: *Approvand that for richt religioun.*
1121	*That presis God.* Bs: *Thair God onlie.* Concern that the idiom *presis God to pleis* will be misread (not "endeavors to please God" but "forces God to be pleasant") may have resulted in the attempt at a correct explicitness in Bs.
1123	Bs: *Fechtand with lust, presumptioun, and pryde.*
1129	Bs, Fox: *Fra thow begin thy mynd to mortifie.* In the last word of the line in Bs, note the false rhyme with *fle* in 1128.
1130	Bs, Fox: *Salomonis saying thow may persaif heirin.* The delay in Bs of the reference to Solomon enables the Protestant copyist to avoid the reference, preserved in B, to the penitent believer's capacity to *wyn* "thy sely saull."
1134	Bs: *Assaultand men with sweit perswasionis.* Thus Bs avoids mentioning the religious orders disestablished in reformed Scotland.
1135	Bs: *Ay reddie for to trap thame in ane trayne.*
1137	*with ithand.* Bs: *draw neir with.* B presents a more archaic, precise phrase than does Bs.
1139	B [line cancelled, with the following correction interlined]: *Lord eternall medeator for us mast meke.* Bs: *O mediatour mercifull and meik.* If B's correction is to be taken as editorial, then the apostrophe to Mary sounds a doctrinal alarm for even the maker of a manuscript anthology in Edinburgh in the late 1560s.
1140	B [line cancelled, with the following correction interlined]: *Sitt doun before thy fader celestiall.* Bs: *Thow soveraigne lord and king celestiall.*

1141   Bs: *Thy celsitude maist humillie we beseik.*

1143   *that.* Bs: *thy.*

The Sheep and the Dog: B, Bs [C, H, Ht]; Fox

title   B [in a later hand]: *The Dog, the Scheip, and the Wolff.* Bs: *The Taill of the Scheip and the Doig.*

1148   *unto.* Bs: *to.*

1158   *straitly.* Bs: *for.*

1164   *the dayis.* Bs: *twa dayis or.*

1172   Bs, Fox: *The oure off cause quhilk that the juge usit than.* The reading in B is metrically more regular than the version in Bs.

1175   *up.* Bs omits.

1186   *Avysitlie.* Bs: *The scheip avysitlie.* Greater explicitness is achieved by the indication of the subject phrase in Bs, but a hypermetric line is thus produced; omission of the subject phrase in B seems based on a looser, less formal sense of syntactic relations than holds in Bs.

1190   *enter pley.* B: *interply.* Bs: *enter in pley.*

1194   *as juge.* Bs: *juge as.*

1200   *In quhilk no jugeis.* Bs, Fox: *Quhairfoir na juge.*

1208   *eftir.* Bs: *efterwart.*

1211   *or.* Bs: *nor.*

1214   *decreitis.* B, Fox: *decretalis.*

1216   *civile mony volum.* Bs: *civile law volumis full mony.* The adjective *civile* can be used alone to denote civil law (*MED civile* adj. as n.).

1218   *Pro and contra, strait argumentis resolve.* B: *Prowe and contra strait argument thay resoll.* Bs: *Contrait prostrait argumentis thay resolve.* Fox: *Contra et pro, strait argumentis thay resolve.* Fox proposes that *thay* may be a "spurious addition, made by analogy with 1216" (ed., p. 258).

1219   Bs: *Sum objecting and sum can hald.*

1220   *ye, thay.* Bs: *ye that thay.*

1221   *held.* Bs: *hald.*

1222   *schrew.* Bs: *beschrew.*

1224   *summar and.* Bs: *sweirand.*

1242   *and.* Bs: *and eke.*

1251   *persecutioun.* Bs: *the executioun.*

1252   *and.* Bs: *he.*

1256   *he forjugeit.* Bs: *it commandit.*

1270   Bs: *Thocht he wer trew as ever wes Sanct Johne.*

1273   *porteous.* Bs: *portioun.*

1276   *be.* Bs: *wes.*

1278   *swa.* Bs: *tak.*

    skat. Bs: *tat.*

1289   *frawart.* Bs: *hard.*

1292   *hair.* Bs: *sair.*

1295   *O lord*. Bs: *Lord God*. The divine reference is made explicit in Bs at the cost of rhetorical emphasis.

1300   *syn*. Bs: *sone*.

1301   Bs: *Loist hes baith lawtie and eik law*. As elsewhere, lists of terms result in textual variation (e.g., textual notes to lines 126, 576, 741).

1304   *jugis*. B: *juge*. Bs: *juge it*.

1305   *Thay ar*. Bs: *He is*.

1306   *meid thay thoill*. Bs: *micht he lettis*.

THE LION AND THE MOUSE: B, Bs [C, H, HT]; FOX, BR

title   B [in a later hand]: *The Lyon and the Mous*. Bs: *The Taill of the Lyoun and the Mous*.

            Prologue. B, Bs omit.

1321   *joly*. Bs omits.

1324   *lemis*. Bs: *bemis*.

1331   *gresis*. Bs, Br: *gers*. The explicitly disyllabic variant in B underlines the metrical regularity of the line.

1335   *arrayit rone*. Bs, Br: *arrayit on rone*.

1336   *viola*. Bs: *violat bla*. In Bs, the preference for common, straightforward terms (*violat* for *viola*) has produced a distracting inappositeness of color — a livid violet — and a hypermetrical line.

1340   *and the*. Bs, Br: *and of*.

1345   *maid a cors*. Bs: *cled my heid*. As elsewhere (e.g., *Fables*, lines 776, 836, 1103, 1118, 1130, and Textual Notes), the Protestant printer expurgates explicit references to Catholic religious practices.

1350   *chymmeris*. Bs: *chemeis*. The printer substitutes the name of a more familiar article of clothing for a garment specific to a scholar or cleric (Fox, ed., p. 266).

1359   *he weir*. Bs, Br: *can beir*. The reading in Bs may arise from a confusion, not infrequent in Scots secretary script, between *b* and *w* (or *v*); B's reading presents *weir* as a form of the past tense of *weir*, "wear."

1386   *dedene*. Bs: *not disdayne*. Fox notes that *dedene* "was falling out of use in the 16th c." (ed., p. 267); further, the reading in Bs is hypermetrical.

1395   *e*. Bs, Br: *hart*.

1398   *Yit*. Bs: *Yis*.

1404a   B omits. Bs: *The end of the Prolog, and beginnis the Taill*.

1405   *wery*. Bs: *war*. In support of B's reading, Bawcutt and Riddy adduce Langland's *wery forwandrit* (*Piers Plowman* A.prol.7); however, they ingeniously suggest that C's reading *verray* is superior: "*verray* is not an adverb but an adjective describing the lion's true and rightful prey, the venison which is later contrasted with the 'unhailsum' flesh of mice" (*Br*, p. 360; compare lines 1490–95). The location of the adjective *verray* after the noun it modifies is rare but occasionally appears as an indicator of a heightened, religious style, as in

Henryson's *Bludy Serk*, line 109 (*DOST verray* adj.); in the present context, such worshipful eloquence seems inapposite, while the Langlandian implication of culpably wearying wandering may be closer to the mark.

1438   *prodissioun*. B: *promissioun*. Bs, Br: *presumptioun*. Fox bases this emendation on the clue provided by the otherwise semantically weak reading in B.

1439   *Erer*. Bs, Br: *The rather*. B provides a rarer, less modern reading.

1460   *Onto*. Bs, Br: *Upon*. The action of dragging calls for the preposition in B.

1461   *A*. Bs, Br: *Na*.

1463   *thi yre*. Bs, Br: *it*.

1471   *spirituall*. Bs: *speciall*. Fox suggests that Bs makes "a Protestantizing emendation" here (ed., p. 269).

1477   *conqueist*. B, Fox: *compair*. Spearing argues incisively for *conqueist*, the reading in Bs in a "precise classical sense" comparable to *tribunall* (line 1472) and *honour triumphall*" (line 1475; *Medieval to Renaissance*, p. 352n52).

1527   *he knet*. Bs, Br: *the net*.

1530   *thus*. Bs, Br: *and*.

1548   *thy*. Bs, Br: *off thy*.

        gentilnes. Bs, Br: *gentrace*.

1549   *with that*. Bs, Br: *this way*.

1552   *same*. Bs, Fox, Br: *samin*.

1562   *abone*. Bs: *about*.

1563   *mastis*. Bs, Br: *net*.

1577   *and*. Bs, Br: *that*.

1599   *kinbute baith for*. B, Fox: *commoun baith for*. Bs, Br: *kinbute baith of*. Especially when used figuratively, B's term is the difficult reading (note the uncertainty with the idiom in Bs) and has been retained.

1612   *expone*. Bs, Fox, Br: *expound*.

1616   Bs: *I the beseik and all men for to pray*. Here is another instance of the printers' removal of references to medieval religious practices.

1619   *lord*. Bs, Br: *king*.

THE PREACHING OF THE SWALLOW: B, Bs [C, H, HT]; FOX, BU

1625   B: *Excelland*. Bs, Fox: *Excellent*. Though *excellent* can function in Scots northern English as an adjectival present participle (Fox, ed., p. 277; *OED excellent* a.), the *-and* suffix is correct.

        argument. Bs, Fox: *jugement*.

1632   *a thing*. Bs, Fox: *nor thingis*. Burrow speculates that the reading in Bs may arises from a determination "to avoid calling God 'a thing'" (*English Verse*, p. 325).

1633   *materiale*. Bs: *naturall*. The reading in B is more emphatic and specific.

1649   *dirk ressounis*. Bs: *all ressoun*. Fox posits that B's reading "attempts to soften Henryson's statement" (ed., p. 278); Schrader argues that

Henryson "was not trying to do away with all reasoning" and hence B should be preferred ("Henryson and Nominalism," p. 9n32).

1653	*takis*. Bs: *tak*.
1664	*we*. Bs, Fox: *weill*.
1665	*we*. Bs, Fox: *weill*.
1678	*grene*. Bs: *off grene*.
1688	*Hir tume*. B: *Hir louid*. Bs, Br: *The tume*. Fox emends this phrase to conform with the pronoun *hir* in line 1690 and to take account of the more specific adjective in Bs.
1701	*ar bethit*. Bs: *bene laifit*.
1711	*smale*. Bs: *haill*.
1744	*lo se, and*. Bs: *and gude*.
1754	*praevidimus*. B: *providimus*. Burrow notes that B's reading follows that provided in some manuscripts of *Disticha Catonis* (*English Verse*, p. 331).
1758	*befoir and see*. Bs: *and foirse*.
1760	*thingis at*. Bs: *thing behald*.
1761	*ethar*. Bs: *the better*.
1770	*ferslye*. Bs, Fox: *ferlie*. The violence of the flight is rhetorically significant; the reading in Bs appears to echo the occurrence of this word and its related forms elsewhere in this fable (lines 1730, 1775).
1797	*young*. Bs omits.
1829	*swingillit*. B: *scutchit*. The variants are synonymous.
1841	*hes*. Bs, Fox omit.
1851	*into a branche litill*. Bs, Fox: *on ane lytill branche neir*. Burrow observes that "*litill by* may represent a rare expression meaning 'not too close', otherwise unrecorded; *branch* here means 'seedling tree'" (*English Verse*, p. 336; *MED braunch* 4c).
1856	*lyit heir*. Bs, Fox: *heir layit*.
1860–66	In addition to appearing in the complete text of this fable in B, this stanza also occurs as a separate item in B (f. 76b), in the section of "ballatis Full of wisdome and moralitie" (f. 43b).
1874	*rycht grit hertis*. Bs, Fox: *grit hart sair for*.
1879	Bs: *Off sum the heid he straik, off sum he brak the crag*. Fox: *Off sum the heid, off sum he brak the crag*. Fox corrects the hypermetrical line in Bs; in the present edition, the line in B is preferred — anacoluthic purpose is detected in the semantically clashing *off*'s.
1903	*in*. Bs: *unto*.
1911	*stark*. Bs, Fox: *scharp*.
1920	*vaill*. Bs: *availl*. The aphetic form in B is metrically superior to its more explicit counterpart in Bs.
1923	*thus*. Bs, Fox: *is*.
1928	*warld calf dois*. Fox: *warldis calf dois*.
1931	*partit*. Bs: *departit*.

1934	*helpis*. Fox: *help is*.
1946	*to seis*. Bs: *fra*.

THE FOX, THE WOLF, AND THE CADGER: BS, C, H, HT; FOX, BR

title	Bs: *The Taill of the Wolf that Gat the Nekhering throw the Wrinkis of the Foxe that Begylit the Cadgear*.
1957	*breith*. Bs, H, Ht: *wraith*.
1958	*waithing*. Bs, C: *watching*. H: *wetching*.
1983	*thay suld*. Bs, C: *I*.
1995	*sonyeis*. Bs, H: *senyes*.
2001	C, Ht: *And I can nouther fische with huke nor net*.
2013	*rude*. Bs, C, H, Br: *reid*.
2029	*caryand*. Bs, C, H, Fox, Br: *carpand*. The emendation *caryand* was proposed by A. J. Aitken (Br, p. 364).
	Lowrence culd him spy. C: *drew this boucheour by*.
2087–88	C transposes these two lines.
2103	*hakkit*. C: *snakkit*. Like Fox, Bawcutt and Riddy prefer *snakkit*, "broke with a snapping sound" (Br, p. 364) but it is not recorded until the late sixteenth century (*DOST snak* v.).
2148	*dow not*. Bs, H: *he will*. The reading in B denotes lack of capacity; that in Bs involves a redundant subject.
2168	*als wraith as ony*. Bs, H, Ht: *wavering as the*.
2171	*revenge him best*. Bs, H: *revengit on him*.
2177	*bat*. Bs, C: *bot*.
2192	*myne*. Bs, C: *syne*.
2193	*a stewart fyne*. Bs, C: *efterwart syne*. H, Ht, Fox: *efterwart fyne*. For the emendation to *a stewart*, see Poole, "Henryson, *Fables* 2193."

THE FOX, THE WOLF, AND THE HUSBANDMAN: BS, C [H, HT]; FOX

title	Bs, C: *The Taill of the Foxe that begylit the wolf in the schadow of the Mone*.
2284	*contrufit*. So Fox. Bs, C: *contrusit*.
2310	*juge*. Bs, C: *ane juge*.
2372	*hous*. Bs, C: *hors*.
2432	*Arctand*. Bs: *Actand*.
2434–38	Because no text survives except those in the Protestant printed editions, it is impossible to judge the extent to which these four lines have been adjusted to tone down unwanted references to medieval religious practices.

THE WOLF AND THE WETHER: BS, C [H], HT; FOX

title	Bs, C: *The Taill of the wolf and the wedder*.
2474	*that*. Bs, C omit.
2476	*wichtlie*. Bs, C: *wretchitlie*. Ht: *wightlie*. Fox cites the emendation to *wichtlie* proposed by Craik ("Emendation"), but notes these witnesses' lack of

trouble with this word in its earlier occurrence (line 553) and offers another, "less apt" alternative, *wrethlie*, "angrily" (ed., p. 311); while the reservation about Craik's emendation is persuasive, the alternative is not.

2537   *till ane rekill*. Bs, Ht: *still quhill ane strand*.
2548   *Syne*. Bs: *Tyne*.

THE WOLF AND THE LAMB: B, Bs, C [H, Ht]; FOX
title   B: *The Wolff and the Lamb*. Bs: *The Taill of the Wolf and the Lamb*.
2628   *him*. Bs, C: *he*.
        presomyng. Bs, C: *belevand*. Fox notes that *belevand*, while current in sixteenth-century Scots, is nowhere else attested in Henryson (ed., p. 316).
2629   *this*. Bs, C: *him*.
2630   *angrie, austre*. Bs, C: *awfull angrie*.
2632   *this*. Bs: *and*.
2668   *pyne*. Bs, C: *pane*.
2673   *cheris*. Bs: *refuse*.
2677   *into*. Bs: *in*.
        spew. Bs: *did spew*.
2682   *audiens*. Bs, C: *evidence*. Fox: *audience*.
2685   *contrairie, or*. B: *contra and*.
2690   *law*. B: *way*.
        wys. Bs: *gyis*. C: *use*. Fox: *wyis*.
2693   *Ha*. Bs, C: *Na*.
2697   *Goddis*. Bs, C: *his*. Here is a characteristic expurgation by the Protestant printers.
2701   *heidit*. Bs, C: *deid*.
2703   *syne*. Bs, C: *and*.
2713   *sutelté*. Bs, C: *facultie*. Fox: *suteltie*.
2716   *poleit*. Bs, C: *poete*.
2721–41   B provides these lines in the following order: 2728–41, 2721–27.
2729   *aneuch*. Bs: *full grit*.
2731   *in peax ane pureman*. Bs, C: *the pure in pece to*.
2738   *crufe*. B: *cruse*. Bs: *caff*. C: *calf*.
2750   *cairt*. Bs, C: *court*.
        and cariage. Bs, C: *or in cariage*.
2760   *be rad*. Bs, C: *dreid*.
2771   *and men*. B: *I mene*. Bs: *and fell*.

THE PADDOCK AND THE MOUSE: B, Bs, C [H, Ht]; FOX
title   B [in a later hand]: *The Mous and the Paddock*. Bs: *The Taill of the Paddok and the Mous*.
2789   *rauk*. Bs: *rank*.

2800   *your*. Bs: *thy*. In B, the Paddock uses the respectful second-person plural pronoun, at least at the outset of the dialogue; compare lines 2854–58.

2802   *Withoutin*. Bs: *Without*.

2803   *yow*. Bs: *the*.

2804   *your*. Bs: *thy*.

2805   *mervell than*. Bs: *grit wounder*.

2806   *thow can*. Bs: *can thow*.

2808   *drowin to wed*. Bs: *drounit be*.

2815   *swyme*. Bs: *row*.

2869   *O*. B, Fox: *How*.

2873   *crappald*. B: *crabit*. Bs: *carpand*. C: *trappald*. Noting that the phrase *crappald pad* appears redundant, Fox defends this emendation (a word otherwise unrecorded in Scots) in terms scribal error — the reading in C can thus be explained in terms of the easy confusion in Scots script between the letters *c* and *t*, and the reading *carpand* in Bs makes sense in relation to *crapaud* (recorded in Middle English), with inversion of *ra* and a minim error of *n* for *u* (ed., p. 331).

2877   *to fleit and*. Bs: *for to*.

2887   Bs: *With all hir mycht scho forsit hir to swym*.

2893   *this plungit in*. Bs: *plungit into*.

2898   *owthir*. Bs: *ony*.

2904   *fettislie thame*. So Fox. B: *fetly he thame*. Bs: *fettillie thame*. B's *fetly* and Fox's emendation are legitimate synonyms in Scots; B's *he* "looks suspiciously like a scribal insertion" (ed., p. 332).

2915   Bs: *To thee wer better beir the stane barrow*.

2916   *Or sweitand dig and*. B: *Of sweitand ding and*. Bs: *For all thy dayis to*. "[W]ithout conviction," Fox follows W. A. Craigie's emendation reported in G. Gregory Smith's edition (Fox, ed., p. 333).

2930   *at*. Bs: *of*.

2942   *wardit*. Bs: *wrappit*.

2946   *fysche*. Bs: *fitche*.

2947   *wappit*. Bs: *wrappit*.

2950   *twin*. Bs: *wyn*.

2957   *ay waverand*. Bs, Fox: *wer steirrand*.

2958   *Standis distinyt*. Bs: *Standand rycht different*.

2959   *spreit*. Bs: *saull*.

2960   B: *The natur of the saule wald our be borne*. The rhyme in B is imperfect. Fox records G. Gregory Smith's observation "that both versions are the results of Protestantizing emendations" (*Specimens*, p. 280, qtd. Fox, ed., p. 336).

2961   *hevinnis blis*. B: *hevinly trone*.

2967   *gud deidis*. Bs: *faith in Christ*; again, Bs has put in an acceptable Protestant emphasis in place of a now-objectionable medieval Catholic doctrine.

2972 *a sample or.* Bs: *exempill and ane.* The aphetic form *sample* is amply attested in fifteenth-century Scots (*DOST sampil*).

THE TESTAMENT OF CRESSEID: T, CH (BASE TEXT), R (LINES 1–21 ONLY), AN; FOX

6 *gart.* T, Ch, An: *can. Can* "does not have the causative sense" (Br, p. 367).

48 *Esperus.* T: *esperous.* An, Fox: *esperance.* Although Bawcutt and Riddy argue that "the context seems to require an opposition with *wanhope*" (*Br*, p. 367; compare *Garmont*, line 29), there is a thematic neatness to the astronomical Venus (as the evening star Hesperus) inspiring Troilus to hope once more; this is the influence the poet has sought at the outset of the work (lines 11–26).

89 *quhilk.* Ch: *quhik.* T, An: *whiche.*

94 *on fute.* T, Fox: *or refute.* Bawcutt and Riddy note that "*Refute*, although recorded in Scots as late as 1535, was obsolescent and hence likely to be misread by the later printers (Br, p. 367); on the other hand, the reading in Charteris reflects a strongly Henrysonian idiom (e.g., *Fables*, lines 734, 953, 2376, 2476; compare the table of contents of the Asloan Manuscript, where the title of a no longer extant poem is given as "Master Robert Hendersonnis Dreme on Fut by Forth").

95 *Disagysit.* T: *Disshevelde.* H. A. Kelly notes the precision and evocativeness of Thynne's reading (*Chaucerian Tragedy*, p. 228).

109 *was thame.* T, An, Fox: *was.* Despite its greater clarity of reference to the gods near whom Calchas resides, C's reading appears hypermetrical; this problem is resolved by reading *honourit* without treating the suffix as a distinct syllable, an option in Henryson's Scots.

151 *made apparence.* Ch, T, An, Fox: *gave his sentence.* Kelly posits that the apparent anticipation in all the witnesses of an action Saturn will not perform for some stanzas yet (compare line 315) is a textual error; Kelly proposes *presence* for *sentence* but notes that in Scots to *make apparence* "is attested to signify 'Appearance in sight or view'" (*DOST apperance*; Kelly, *Chaucerian Tragedy*, p. 234n44); this emendation is made slightly less persuasive by the use of *apperance* above, at line 143.

155 *fronsit.* Ch: *frosnit.* T: *frounsed.* An: *frozned.* The scribal error of inverting two letters produces a new, adventitiously relevant word, "frozen" for "wrinkled."

164 *gyte.* T: *gate.* Ch: *gyis.* An: *guise.* As Fox notes (ed., pp. 352–53), the corrupt reading in T points the way to a word for "robe" that was obsolete by the late sixteenth century and hence unfamiliar to Charteris; see also lines 178, 260.

178 *gyte full gay.* Ch: *gyis full.* An: *guise full gay.*

205 *upricht.* T, Fox: *unricht.* The variant in the Scottish printers' texts can be explained as a blandly ironic reference to the course of the chariot guided by Phaeton: upwards but not aright. If that explanation is

valid and *upricht* can be posited to be the earlier reading, then Thynne can be argued to have sought to clarify the implication with an explicitly pejorative adverb.

216   *and*. T, Ch omit.

        Philogie. T, Ch: *Philologie*.

218   *gay*. Ch omits.

222   *Quhyte*. T: *White*. An, Fox: *With*.

260   *gyte*. Ch, An: *gyse*.

267   *liken*. T: *lykyng*. An: *listned*. *Liken* is best explained a a rare variant of T's *lyking* (Br, p. 372).

275   *or*. Ch: *in*.

286   *returne on*. T, Fox: *retorte in*. Bawcutt and Riddy acknowledge the difficulty of choosing which of the variants is superior (Br, p. 372); in her review of Fox's edition, Ridley notes that *returne* "in the sense appropriate here, 'to send a thing back again,' is first recorded in the *OED* in 1459, 'retorte' not until 1557" (Review of Fox, *Poems of Henryson*, p. 627; compare *DOST retort*; *return* III.10).

290   *injure*. Ch: *injurie*. C uses the form of the noun more regular in English, while T and An preserve a regular Scots one.

328   *throw*. T, Fox: *through*. Ch, An: *thow*. Rather than using the English spelling *through* from T, it makes sense to treat Ch's *thow* as a typographical error and reinsert the missing *r*.

334   *I thee now*. T, Fox: *here I the*. An: *I do thee here*. The line is metrically regular in Ch, if at cost of easy colloquial pace — but, given the formality of this proclamation, the wrench is not inappropriate.

337   *mingit*. T: *menged*. Ch: *minglit*. An: *mingled*. T points to the error in the insertion of an *l* in the reading in Ch.

363   *beedes*. Ch, An: *prayers*. The Scottish printers have expurgated the offensively Catholic term.

374   *oftymes he*. T: *oftymes*. An: *he oft-times*.

382   *Unto*. T, An: *To*. The disyllabic beginning to the line in Ch is hypermetrical unless an ellipsis of the first or second syllable in *hospitall* occurs.

401   *overheled*. Ch, An: *ovirquhelmit*. T preserves a word no longer familiar to the later Scottish printers.

title   T: *Here foloweth the complaynt of Creseyde*.

408   *now*. T: *nowe*. Ch, An: *for now*.

411   *saif or sound*. T: *helpe*. Ch: *saif the of*. An: *save or sound*.

420   Ch: *The*. T, An, Fox: *Thy*. Ridley observes that the agreement between An (which Fox admits is "suspect here"; ed., p. 372) and T is not a good basis for preferring *Thy* (Review of Fox, *Poems of Henryson*, p. 627).

432   *ray*. Arguably, the aphetic form preserved in T is metrically appropriate but was obsolete by the later sixteenth century and hence unfamiliar

to the later Scottish printers (*DOST ray* n1.2); still, *array* is current in Scots throughout the fifteenth century (*DOST array, aray,* n.).

433–37   T omits.

444   T omits.

446–47   T omits.

453   T omits.

456   T places after 460.

468   *the.* T, An, Fox: *your.*

469   T omits.

479   *To.* T, An, Fox: *Go.* The variant preferred by Fox is attractive in its rhetorical emphasis on the imperative; the alternative preferred here has the advantage of cohesiveness.

480   *leif.* T: *lerne.* Ch, An: *leir.* Fox emends a mistake (compare *leir* in line 479) that "indicates that Ch, T, and An all go back to a faulty archetype" (ed., p. 376).

491   *that companie.* T: *that company come.* Ch: *that companie thai come.* An: *the troup they came.* Fox bases this emendation on the conjectural reduplication of the syllable *com-* (*companie . . . come*; ed., p. 377).

493   *Said, "Worthie.* T: *Worthy.* Fox: *Worthie.* Fox's emendation produces a metrically headless line; he defends this departure from Henryson's metrical practice as "harder, and so slightly preferable" (ed., p. 377); in the present edition, the poet's common practice is taken as the deciding factor.

523   *he.* Ch omits.

544   *swounit scho.* T, An, Fox: *fel in swoun.* The agreement of T and An is not taken to be decisive here.

            full oft or ever scho fane. T: *ful ofte or she wolde fone.* Ch: *oft or scho culd refrane.* An: *full oft ere she would fane.* Fox conjectures that Ch reflects a misunderstanding of *fane,* and that the auxiliary verbs were "introduced erroneously" in each of the witnesses (ed., p. 379).

549   *elevait.* T: *effated.* Fox: *efflated.* Pace Fox, the reading in Ch is possible for Henryson (*DOST elevat* p.p.).

583   *drowrie.* T, An: *dowry.* Ch feasibly refers to a marriage gift and need not be a corruption: "*drowry,* which properly in this context should mean only 'love-token,' had come to mean 'dowry' before the end of the fifteenth century" (Kelly, *Chaucerian Tragedy,* p. 248; *DOST drowry* n.2).

607   *Troyis.* T, An, Fox: *Troy the.*

614   *sore.* Ch, An: *schort.* T appears to preserve a reading obscured in the other witnesses by the repetition of the rhyme word from line 610.

615a   T: *Thus endeth the pyteful and dolorous testament of fayre Creseyde, and here foloweth the Legende of Good Women.* Ch, An: *Finis.*

ORPHEUS AND EURYDICE: CM, A, B (BASE TEXT); FOX

title	Cm: *Heire begynnis the traitie of Orpheus kyng and how he yeid to hevyn and to hel to seik his quene And ane othir ballad in the lattir end.* A: *Heir followis the tale of orpheus and Erudices his quene.* B: *Fable, VI. Orpheus and Eurydice* (the script is later than that of the main scribe). In a new line underneath the title in Cm, the following appears in an early six-teenth-century Scottish hand: "Memento homo quod cinis es et in cinerem Reverteris"; this verse ("Remember man that you are ashes and to ashes you shall revert"; from the liturgy for Ash Wednesday) frames the first stanza and contributes the refrain to a moral poem by William Dunbar (Bawcutt, *Poems of William Dunbar*, poem 32, line 1, etc.). In the table of contents of A, the poem is referred to as *The buke of Schir Orpheus and Erudices.*
2	*or*. B: *and*.
14	*foule*. B: *full*.
19	*ancient*. B: *anseane*.
20	*to the*. B: *to*.
22	*of a*. Cm, A, Fox: *or a*.
23	*of the*. Cm, A, Fox: *of his*.
25	*tarage*. B: *knawlege*.
29	*mountane*. B: *mount*.
	Elicone. B: *electone*. As emended, the word is trisyllabic in order to fulfill the meter.
31	*in*. Cm, A, Fox: *of*.
33	*god*. B: *goddes*. The reading in B makes grammatical sense but creates a metrical disturbance, adding an extra syllable to the fourth foot.
34	*And*. Cm, A, Fox: *Quhilk*.
38	*clippit*. Cm, A, Fox: *namyt*.
40	*is*. Cm, A, Fox: *quhilk is*.
50	*was*. B: *is*. The change in tense in B is not rhetorically justified and seems in error.
55	*In*. Cm, A, Fox: *To*.
58	*oure*. B: *Greik*. The variant in B is attractively precise but slightly illogical: the expounding will be done, not in Greek, but Scots.
59–175	Cm omits. The third and fourth leaves of the first gathering, on which these lines would have appeared, are lost.
64	*is*. B: *wes*.
65	*and*. B: *and gud*.
71	*Incressand*. A: *Quhen he was auld*.
	up. A omits.
72	*frely*. A, Fox: *farly*. The collocation in B, *frely fair*, is typical of Scots and Middle English verse style (*DOST frely*).
73	*His*. B: *Is*.
75	*Excellent*. B: *Excelland*. See the Textual Note to *Fables*, line 1625.

76	*this.* B: *that.*
78	*that.* B: *this.*
79	*And quhene.* A, Fox: *Quhen.*
84	*thay can.* A, Fox: *war at.*
88	A, Fox: *With myrth, blythnes, gret plesans and gret play.*
89	*I.* A: *we.*
94	*Bot.* A: *And.*
	in. B: *untill.*
95	*dewe.* B: *air.*
102	*till hir can he.* B: *to his cave hir.*
103	*scaith.* B: *evill.*
112	*Ontill.* A, Fox: *And till.*
116	*Quhill.* A, Fox: *Till.*
	king. A, Fox: *schir.*
117	*sone.* A, Fox: *than.*
119	*the.* A omits.
123	*Sperid.* A, Fox: *Speris.*
125	*on.* A, Fox: *in.*
130	*to the.* B: *on to.*
133	*he.* B omits.
140	*mony.* A, Fox: *thi.* The reading in B scans metrically if *pynnis*, earlier in the line, is pronounced disyllabically.
141	*pane foll.* B: *paine fell.*
147	*devoid.* B: *devod.*
	from. A, Fox: *of.*
148	*that vailyeit him.* A, Fox: *thai comfort him.* B: *that vailyeit.*
158	*and.* A, Fox: *of.*
166	*barne.* B: *sone.*
167	*panefull.* B: *pelfull.*
170	*be.* B: *to be.*
172	*that.* A, Fox: *the.*
	nevir was. A, Fox: *never was.* B: *was nevir.*
177	*I.* B omits.
178	*Till.* Cm, A, Fox: *Quhill.*
	for seke hir suth. B: *forsuth seik hir.*
179	*na.* Cm, Fox: *no.* A: *nor.*
180	*gyde.* B: *grant.*
182	*King Orpheus thus.* Cm, A, Fox: *Thus king Orpheus.*
183	*weipand.* Cm, A, Fox: *wepit.*
184	*wer thir.* Cm, A, Fox: *was the.*
190	*to all the.* Cm, A, Fox: *of all thir.*
	stormis. Cm, A: *sternis.*
195	*and.* Cm, A, Fox: *Than.*
198	*Than.* Cm, A, Fox: *Syne.*

200	*Bot.* A omits.
	he. Cm, A: *that he.*
	awin. Cm, A omit.
201	*that.* Cm, A, Fox: *it.*
202	*And.* Cm, A, Fox: *He.*
203	*his.* Cm, A, Fox: *that.*
204	*He.* Cm, A, Fox: *Than.*
	his. Cm, A, Fox: *he.*
210	*Forsuth.* B: *sur.* The idiom *for sure* is not recorded in Scots until the mid-sixteenth century (*DOST sure* adj).
214	*knawlege gat he.* B: *gat he knawlege.*
215	*he passit.* Cm, A, Fox: *than passit he.* The reading in the other witnesses produces a hypermetrical line.
217	*on to.* Cm, A, Fox: *doun to.*
223	*throu.* B: *of.*
225	*Plato.* Cm, A, B: *Pluto.*
227	*emetricus.* Fox: *epetritus.*
228	*Emolius.* Cm, A, B: *Enolius.* Fox: *Emoleus.*
229	*Epogdeus.* Cm, A: *Epodyus.* B: *Epoddeus*, altered from *Epogdeus* in the same hand.
230	*Of all.* Cm, A, Fox: *And of.*
234	*dowplait.* Cm: *duplycate.*
235	*dyapente.* B: *dyapenty.*
	the. Cm, A, Fox: *a.*
236	*Thir.* Cm, A, Fox: *This.*
	makis. Cm: *mak.*
238	*of.* Cm, A, Fox: *with.*
241	*of.* Cm, A, Fox: *at.*
245	*our.* B: *with.*
	wone. Cm, A, Fox: *wane.*
246	*allone.* Cm, A, Fox: *allane.*
248	*and ful fer and.* Cm, A: *and ful.*
258	*This.* Cm, A, Fox: *The.*
	doun on. Cm, A, Fox: *unto.*
259	*Than.* Cm, A, Fox: *And.*
261	*He passit furth ontill.* Cm, A, Fox: *Than come he till.*
	ryvir deip. Cm, A, Fox: *ryvir wonder depe.*
264	*Megera.* B: *mygra.*
265	*Turnit.* Cm, A, Fox: *Turnand.*
273	*away and.* Cm, A, Fox: *away than.*
275	Cm, A, Fox: *Syne come he till a wonder grisely flude.*
276	*that rathly.* B: *and rythly.*
279	*Quhen.* Cm: *Touch.* A: *Thocht.* Fox: *Thouch.*
281	*to slake.* B omits.

	no. A: *nor.*
283	*tolter threde.* B: *twynid.*
284	*rokkit.* B: *rollit.*
286	B: *Quhen Orpheus thus saw him sufir neid.*
287	*He tuk.* Cm, A, Fox: *Tuke out.*
288	*gat drink.* A, B: *gat a drink.*
292	*fell.* Cm, A, Fox: *scharp.*
293	*As.* Cm, A, Fox: *And as.*
	blenkit. Cm, A, Fox: *blent.*
294	*saw.* B: *saw lyand.*
	wonder. B omits.
295	*Ticius.* Cm, A: *Theseus.*
	hicht. B: *hecht.*
296	*grisly.* B: *gasly.*
299	*war.* B: *was.*
300	*thus saw him.* Cm, Fox: *saw hym this.* A: *saw him thus.*
301	*He tuke.* Cm, A, Fox: *Has tane.*
302	*fled and.* Cm, A, Fox: *fled.*
	Ticius. Cm, A: *Theseus.*
307	*That.* A: *Thai.*
309	*and.* Cm, A, Fox omit.
310	*place and.* B: *place.*
311	*with.* B: *and.*
314	*to.* B: *and to.*
316	*may.* B: *sall.*
318	*of.* B: *with.*
	hate. B omits.
319	*rycht.* B: *full.*
320	*And.* Cm, A omit.
	conquerouris. Cm, A: *Conquerour.*
	land. Cm, A: *of land.*
323	*als.* Cm, A, Fox: *thare.*
324	*And.* Cm, A: *Thare fand he.*
	his. B: *his foull.*
328	*undir.* A: *efter.*
329	*that.* Cm, A, Fox: *the.*
331	*saw.* Cm, A, Fox: *fand.*
	for. B: *for the.*
333	*eke.* B omits.
334	*Of.* B: *Was.*
336	*that.* Cm omits.
337	*mercy.* Cm, A, Fox: *pitee.*
338	*saw.* Cm, A, Fox: *fand.*

339	*dois.* B: *did.* From the perspective of a reformed Scotland, Bannatyne writes as if ecclesiastical abuses are a thing of the past.
340	*archbischopis.* Cm, A, B: *bischopis.* "With some hesitation," Fox emends this word to fulfill the demands of the meter and in line with Sir David Lyndsay's echo of the line in his *Dreme*, "And Archebischopis in thare pontificall" (line 175; ed., p. 408).
341	*and.* Cm, A: *for.*
	intrusioun. Cm, A: *ministration.*
342	*men of all.* B: *all men of.*
343	*placis.* B: *place and.*
346	*hiddirwart.* Cm, A, Fox: *thider-ward.*
347	*quhair.* Cm, A, Fox: *as.*
349	*peteous and.* Cm, A, Fox: *pitouse and.* B: *and peteous.*
350	*the.* Cm, A: *a.*
354	*your.* Cm, A, Fox: *thy.* In B, Orpheus consistently uses the formal second-person plural pronoun when addressing Eurydice; see lines 355–56.
355	*Your.* Cm, A, Fox: *Thy.*
356	*Your.* Cm, A, Fox: *Thi.*
360	*Scho hes.* Cm, A, Fox: *Thare is.*
365	*refete.* B: *revert.* The reading in the earlier witnesses is well attested in Middle English and Scots (*DOST refete*) and is semantically more precise and apposite.
	fax. B leaves an empty space in place of this word.
369	*ypodorica.* B: *ypotdorica.*
370	*gemilling.* Cm, A: *gemynyng.*
371	*Quhill.* Cm, A, Fox: *Till.*
372	*and.* A, B: *or.*
378	*without.* Cm, A, Fox: *bot wyth.*
383	*to hell forevir.* Cm, A, Fox: *forevir till hell.*
386	*Till.* Cm, A, Fox: *Quhill.*
	outwart. Cm, A, Fox: *utter.*
388	*with.* Cm, A, Fox: *in.*
389	*in hart apone his.* Cm, A, Fox: *apon his wyf and.*
394	*grete hartsare for.* Cm, A: *rycht grete hartsare.* B: *grit pety for.*
396	*How his lady that.* Cm, A, Fox: *Quhen that his wyf quhilk.*
397	*tane.* Cm, A, Fox: *hynt.*
400	*thus out on lufe can.* A: *thus out of lufe can.* B: *this out of lufe gan.*
406	*thay.* Cm, A, Fox: *he.*
407	*thay.* Cm, A, Fox: *he.*
409	*Hart on.* Cm, A: *Hert is.* Fox: *Hert.*
	handis. Cm, A, Fox: *hand is.*
410	*mone turne.* Cm, A, Fox: *turnis.*
411	*wo is.* B: *wois.*
414a	B: *Moralitas* Cm, A, Fox: *Moralitas fabule sequitur.*

415   *Now*. Cm, A, Fox: *Lo*.
420   *poesie*. B: *poetre*.
421   *Trivat*. Cm: *trowit*. A, Fox: *Trevit*.
428   *intellective*. B: *intelletyfe*.
429   *and*. Cm, A: *in*.
434   *it settis*. Cm, A, Fox: *settis*.
435   *herd*. B omits.
437   *That*. Cm, A, Fox: *Quhilk*.
             is to. Cm, A, Fox: *is ay to*.
441   *serpent stangis*. B: *serpentis stang*.
             the. Cm, A, Fox omit.
443   *is*. A: *is it*.
444   *all*. B: *and all*.
445   *reson*. B: *wisdome*.
446   *thusgait our appetyte*. Cm, A, Fox: *oure appetite thusgate*.
447   Cm, A, Fox: *And passis up to the hevyn belyve*. B: *And to the hevin he passit*
             up belyfe.
449   *will*. B: *wit*.
             eik. Cm, A, Fox: *als*.
451   *fundin*. Cm, A, Fox: *found*.
452   *within*. Cm, A, Fox: *in to*.
             bundin. Cm, A, Fox: *bound*.
456   *in thir warldly*. Cm, A, Fox: *on this warldis*.
458   *small*. B: *full small*.
461   *pas*. B *omits*.
             the. Cm, A, Fox: *yone*.
469   *our mynd is myngit with sapience*. Cm, A: *that resoun and intelligence*.
470   *And*. Cm, A omit.
484   *quhilk*. Cm, A, B omit. Fox's emendation provides an initial syllable for
             the third foot of the line.
485   *Bot*. Cm, A: *That*.
489   *on*. Cm, A, Fox: *in*.
490   *yow*. Cm, A, Fox: *the*.
             tell. B: *tell of*.
491   *of*. Cm, A, Fox: *on*.
493   *wald*. Cm, A, Fox: *wald noucht*.
             into. Cm, A, Fox: *in*.
495   *on*. Cm, A, Fox: *in*.
496   *And socht*. Cm, A, Fox: *Sekand*.
497   *foull*. Cm, A, Fox: *full*.
498   *doun*. B: *one*.
506   *a*. Cm, A, Fox: *thair*.
507   *quhen*. Cm, A: *quhen that*.
             perfyte sapience. Cm, A: *intelligence*.

508	*eloquens*. Cm, A: *conscience*.
509–14	Cm, A omit.
517	*affectioun*. Cm, A, Fox: *complexion*. Though he selects *complexion*, Fox notes that *affectioun* "is the easier reading, but may be the right one" (ed., p. 419).
523	*till his*. Cm, A, Fox: *to the*.
525–26	Cm, A, B put these lines in the opposite order. Noting the illogicality of the variant readings in Cm and A and positing that in B the variants can be accounted for as an attempt to impose a logical order, Fox transposes these lines.
525	*And*. B: *He*.
526	*Intill*. B: *Syne in*.
534	*tak*. Cm, A, Fox: *call*.
535	*him*. Cm, A: *thame*.
	thair. B: *his*.
536	*thair*. B: *the*.
537	*fill*. B: *full*.
	fynd. B: *fund*.
541	*on bed*. Cm, Fox: *and bed*. A: *bed*.
542	*othir*. B: *wyn*.
543	*thay may*. Cm, A, Fox: *may thai*.
545	*that*. B omits.
546	*conscience*. Cm, A, Fox: *eloquence*.
547–50	Cm, A omit. Noting the resemblance of line 550 to *Fables*, line 120, Fox considers that the lines "seem genuine" (ed., p. 421).
552	*tynt with grit*. Cm, A, Fox: *tynt is with*. The repetition of *grit* from the previous line and again in the one subsequent makes the reading in B suspect; arguably, the repetition has rhetorical value.
553	*avaris*. Cm, A: *avarice*. B: *grit avaris*.
555	*Of*. Cm, A, Fox: *And*.
	he. Cm, A, Fox: *thair*.
556	*To*. Cm: *Go*.
557	Cm, A, Fox: *Bot he suld drink ineuch quhenevir hym list*.
558	*to*. Cm, A: *and*.
559	*Ticius*. Cm, A: *Theseus*.
560	*wyth*. B omits.
563	*lerit it unto the spamen*. B: *lyrit it unto the spyne*.
566	*to*. B: *unto*.
569	*in*. B: *of*.
571–615	Cm, A omit. Noting G. Gregory Smith's hypothesis, followed by H. Harvey Wood, that this passage, like lines 509–14 and 547–50, are not by Henryson and may have been added by Bannatyne, Fox remarks on the contrast in style between these passages and Bannatyne's own verse (quoted, e.g., in the Explanatory Notes, p. 156). Fox adds

that omission of the present passage damages the structure of the poem: a moralization about "the effect of Orpheus's harp on Titius is needed here" (ed., p. 422).

575	*causis.* B: *caus.*
588	An incomplete rhyme indicates the omission of a line or lines in B.
607	*hell.* B: *hale.*
616	*Than.* Cm, A: *Bot.*
620	*wyse and warly.* Cm, A, Fox: *war and wisely.*
623	*fleschly.* Cm, A, Fox: *wardly.*
624	*syn.* B: *sone.*
626	*vane prosperite.* Cm, A, Fox: *sensualitee.*
630	*undirput.* Cm, A: *help us wyth.*
	hand. Cm: *land.*
631	*mantenans.* Cm: *mane temance.* Fox: *manetemance.*
633a	Cm omits. A: *Explicit the Buke of Orpheus.* B: *Finis quod Mr. R. H.*

SHORTER POEMS: STRONGER ATTRIBUTIONS

In this edition, the shorter poems are arranged in two groups, each organized alphabetically by the first line. The first of these groups, for which the textual notes follow immediately here, consists of nine poems for which Henryson's authorship is attested in the Bannatyne Manuscript or (in the case of *The Annunciation*) the Gray Manuscript. Of these nine, the case is weakest for *The Ressoning betwix Aige and Yowth*, the Maitland Folio's text of which lacks an ascription to Henryson. Many of these poems (*The Bludy Serk, The Garmont of Gud Ladeis, Robene and Makyne, Sum Practysis of Medecyne*) are preserved only in the Bannatyne Manuscript; some appear there twice, in both the manuscript proper and the so-called Draft Manuscript (*The Abbey Walk, The Praise of Age, The Ressoning betwix Aige and Yowth*; see also *The Ressoning betwix Deth and Man* and *Ane Prayer for the Pest*, in the next section).

AGAINST HASTY CREDENCE: B (BASE TEXT), MF; FOX

title	B, Mf *omit.*
5	*and.* B: *I.*
12	*weill avow it.* B: *abyd at it he.*
15	*Thus.* B: *Than.*
17–32	These stanzas are transposed in Mf.
18	*fals.* B: *the fals.*
23	*thairin.* B: *thair.*
28	*withowtin.* B: *without.*
33	*that.* B: *cumis.*
46	*thair eirris.* B: *his eir.*
50	*planlie curst.* B: *excommunicat.*
	everie. B: *all.*
56a	B: *Finis quod Mr Robert Hendersone.* Mf: *Quod Mr Robert Henryson.*

THE ANNUNCIATION: G (BASE TEXT); FOX

title	G omits.
2	*swet is*. G: *suetis*.
12	*decret is*. G: *decretis*.
24	*cround is*. G: *croundis*.
28	*applid is*. G: *applidis*.
40	*brinnis*. G: *birnis*.
72a	G: *Finis quod R. Henrisoun*.

SUM PRACTYSIS OF MEDECYNE: B (BASE TEXT); FOX

36	*sett in*. B: *sottin*.
45	*sleiffull*. B: *sleis full* (?).
64	*fon*. B: *son* (?).
70	*gufe*. B: *guse* (?).
72	*Annoynt it*. B, Fox: *Annoyntit*.
91a	*Quod Mr. Robert Henrysone*.

THE RESSONING BETWIX AIGE AND YOWTH: MK (LINES 1–40 ONLY), BD (LINES 1–24, 33–40, 25–32, 41–72), B (BASE TEXT), MF (LINES 1–32, 49–52, 54–64, 33–48, 65–72); FOX

title	Bd, Mk, Mf omit.
headings	Mk, Bd, Mf omit.
7	*this*. Bd, B: *the*.
	richt sweitly. Bd: *sweitly*. Mf, Fox: *suttellie*. "Fox prefers the reading of the Maitland Folio (Mf), which as he says is 'distinctly the most erratic witness,' to that of the Bannatyne Draft (Bd), his copy text. 'Singing this song that *sweetly* was set' (Bd) seems as appropriate as '*suttelie* was set' (Mf), if not more so, and it is supported by the Bannatyne Manuscript (B) and the Makculloch manuscript (MK)" (Ridley, Review of Fox, *Poems of Henryson*, p. 627).
10	*I*. Mk, B: *And*.
11	*lene*. B: *clene*.
13	*richt wan*. Bd, Mf, Fox: *and wan*.
16	*fellone*. Mf, Fox: *ferly*.
18	*misdome*. Mk: *misdum*. Bd, B, Mf: *makdome*.
22	*of wirth*. Bd: *half wirth*. Mk, Mf, Fox: *wirth half*.
28	*als frak, forsy, and fre*. Mf, Fox: *bayth frak, forsy, and*. Mk: *als fair frech als*. Bd: *als fors and*. B: *als fors and als*.
29	*ye*. B: *yie*.
31	*laithly luking*. Bd: *laikly lykyne*. B: *laikly luking*. Mk, Mf, Fox: *laythly lycome*.
32	*fadis fellone sone*. Bd: *etc*. Mk, Mf, Fox: *fadis ferly sone*.
33	*yit this*. Mk, Mf, Fox: *this*.
	cowth. Mk, Bd, Mf, Fox: *yit cowth*.
37	*mowis*. Bd, B: *mouthis*. Mf: *our mouthis*.
38	*secreit place*. Mk, Fox: *secretnes*. Bd: *secreit nes*. Mf: *sacreit wyse*.

40	B: *O youth be glaid etc.* Bd: *O youth etc.* Mk, Mf: *O yowth be glaid etc.*
41	*awstrene man gaif answer.* Bd, B: *awstrene greif answerit.* Mf: *anciant man gaif answer.* Fox: *This austryne man gaif answer.*
42	*cramping.* Bd, Mf, Fox: *crampyn.*
	baith. Mf omits.
43	*Thy.* Bd, Fox: *And thy.* Mf: *And all.*
	salt also. Bd, Mf, Fox: *sall.*
44	Mf: *Quhen pane sall the depryve for paramouris.*
45	*be blyth of thee.* Mf: *of the be blyth.*
46	*mynnis.* Bd: *move.* B: *wendin.*
47	*Thow.* Mf: *Than.*
	assay. Mf: *thow say.*
	be soure. Mf: *before.*
48	B: *fedis fellone sone.* Bd: *etc.* Mf, Fox: *fadis farlie sone.*
51	*sound but.* Mf: *sauf fra.*
	or but. Mf: *and fra.* Fox: *and but.*
55	*ressoun.* Bd, B: *no ressoun.*
56	*be glaid into thy flowris grene.* Bd: *be glaid etc.* B: *etc.*
58	*obey.* Mf: *abyd.*
59	*stait, thy strenth.* Mf: *strenth thy stait.*
	it be stark and. Mf: *Johne be never so.*
62	*helth.* Bd, Mf, Fox: *heill.*
	bot. B: *but.*
63	*wane.* Bd, B: *vanes.*
64	*flowris.* Mf: *yeiris.*
	fedis fellone sone. Bd: *fadis fellone sone.* B: *etc.*
65	*galyart grutchit and.* Bd, B: *gowand grathit.*
	began to. B: *with sic greit.*
66	*He.* Bd, Mf, Fox: *And.*
	wrethly went. Bd: *wrechitly he went.* Mf: *he went his wayis.* Fox: *wrethly he went.*
67	*awld.* Bd, Mf, Fox omit.
	B: *luche not.* Bd, Mf, Fox: *leuch na thing.*
69	*Of the sedullis, the suthe.* Mf: *That takkin suthlie.*
	quhen. Bd omits. Mf: *fra that.*
70	*On.* B: *Of.* Mf: *In.*
	trevist. Bd: *tremesit.* B: *triumphit.*
72	*fellone.* Mf, Fox: *ferlie.*
72a	Bd: *Finis quod Mr. Robert Henrysone.* B: *Finis quod Mr. Robert Hendersone.* Mf: *Finis.*

ROBENE AND MAKYNE: B (BASE TEXT); FOX

title	B omits. "The title comes from Allan Ramsay's *The Ever Green* (1724)" (Gray, p. 363).
27	*in certane.* B: *incertane.*

75	*ful fair.* B: *fulfair.*
125	*wewche.* B: *wrewche.*
128a	B: *Quod Mr. Robert Henrysone.*

THE BLUDY SERK: B (BASE TEXT); FOX

title	B, in the margin, in a later hand.
24	*wane.* B: *wame* [or *waine*].
73–74	B: the line break comes between *I* and *de.*
96	*And.* B: *With.*
108	*breist is.* B: *breistis.*
120a	B: *Finis quod Mr R. Henrici.*

THE GARMONT OF GUD LADEIS: B (BASE TEXT); FOX

title	B omits, but see the colophon at line 40a.
19	*Purfillit.* B may read *Furfillit* or *Pursillit.*
28	*ribbane.* B may read *ribband.*
40a	B: *Finis of the Garmont of Gud Ladeis. Quod Mr. Robert Henrysoun.*

THE PRAISE OF AGE: CM (BASE TEXT), MK, BD, B; FOX

| title | Cm, Mk, Bd, B omit. |
| 32a | Cm, Mk omit. Bd: *Finis quod Mr. R. Henrisoune.* B: *Finis quod Hendersone.* |

SHORTER POEMS: WEAKER ATTRIBUTIONS

The following four poems have been deemed to be more weakly attributed than those included in the previous group: for each of these, the evidence for Henryson's authorship in the manuscript witnesses is late or in dispute. For *The Abbey Walk*, *Ane Prayer for the Pest*, and *The Ressoning betwix Deth and Man*, the Bannatyne Draft does not confirm the mention of Henryson in the colophons in the manuscript proper; in the case of *Ane Prayer for the Pest*, the ascription appears to have been added later than the inscription of the poem, a detail which has been taken to weaken further its credibility. In the case of *The Thre Deid Pollis*, Bannatyne's ascription to Patrick Johnston seems a fairly decisive stroke against Henryson's authorship, despite his being named as the author in the Maitland Folio. As if in a neat reversal of that disagreement, it is the Maitland Folio that beclouds the authorship of *The Abbey Walk* by appending to it the note *authore incerto* (author unknown). Admittedly, any attempt to determine authorship by means of the evidence of the Bannatyne Manuscript rests on shaky ground: Fox concludes that "the attributions in B, while not worthless, are not completely trustworthy" (ed., pp. cxvii–cxxi). Some significance may be attachable to discrepancies between the draft and the manuscript proper: with regard to *The Ressoning betwix Deth and Man*, for instance, "It is perhaps suspicious that [this poem] lacks an ascription in Bd, unlike the poems which immediately precede and follow it, and it is possible that in B the scribe took the poem to be a companion piece to *The Ressoning betwix Aige and Yowth* (which it follows), and so gave it a similar title and ascription" (Fox, ed., p. 467).

THE ABBEY WALK: Bd (BASE TEXT), B, Mf; FOX
title	Bd, B, Mf omit.
7	*estait.* Bd: *stait.*
	that. Bd: *that evir.*
10	*Thy.* Bd: *In.*
	nor. Bd: *nor in.*
15	Bd: *Sen thow sic examplis seyis ilk day.* Mf: *Sen thir but dout thow man assay.*
43	*Cumis nocht throw casualtie and chance.* Mf: *Cumis nowdir throw fortoun nor chance.*
51	*warldlie.* Bd, B: *warldis.*
53	*on the.* Bd, B: *deit on.*
54	*gustit.* Bd, B: *taistit the.*
56a	Bd: *Finis.* B: *Quod Mr Robert Henrysone.* Mf: *Finis authore incerto.*

ANE PRAYER FOR THE PEST: Bd (BASE TEXT), B; FOX
title	Bd omits.
6	*Thow.* Bd: *That.*
10	*regrait.* Bd: *degrait.*
27	*perreist.* Bd: *preist.*
64a	Bd: *Finis.* According to Fox, this marginal notation is "probably in a later hand" (ed., p. 169).
76	*and thame.* Bd: *falsly and.*
77	*mend this.* Bd: *win us fra that.*
87	*be.* Bd: *be our.*
88a	Bd: *Finis.* B: *Finis quod Henrysone* (the latter two words in a later hand).

THE RESSONING BETWIX DETH AND MAN: Bd (BASE TEXT), B; FOX
title	Bd omits.
Mors	B: *Deth* (and so forth for the remainder of the poem).
Homo	B: *Man* (and so forth for the remainder of the poem).
30	*ay youtheid wald with me.* Bd: *youtheid wald with me ay.*
43	*the deid to lurk.* Bd: *deid to luke.*
48a	Bd: *Finis.* B: *Finis quod Hendersone.*

THE THRE DEID POLLIS: B (BASE TEXT), Mf; FOX
10	*thole the.* B: *suffer.*
24	*Example.* B: *Thy example.*
27	*so.* B omits.
33	*wilfull.* B: *wofull.*
45	*expert.* B: *excellent.*
47	*still.* B omits.
	ly. B: *be.*
49	*ay.* B omits.
52	*and.* B omits.

55	*And.* B: *Now.*
56	*to rew and glorife.* B: *quhen he sall call and cry.*
59	*mercy cry and.* B: *our saulis to.*
64a	B: *Finis quod Patrik Johnistoun.* Mf: *Quod Mr. Robert Henrysoun.*

 APPENDIX

Sɪʀ Fʀᴀɴᴄɪs Kʏɴᴀsᴛᴏɴ's Aɴᴇᴄᴅᴏᴛᴇ ᴀʙᴏᴜᴛ ᴛʜᴇ Dᴇᴀᴛʜ ᴏꜰ Rᴏʙᴇʀᴛ Hᴇɴʀʏsᴏɴ

In an introductory note to his Latin translation of Henryson's *Testament of Cresseid*, Sir Francis Kynaston (or Kinaston) preserved an anecdote about Henryson's death. Memorable for its coarse, circumstantial detail, this anecdote adds a piquant note to Kynaston's scholarship: this English writer of the reign of Charles I undertook his Latin translation of Chaucer's *Troilus* and Henryson's *Testament* at about the same time as he instituted an academy of learning in London, the *Musaeum Minervae*, for the sons of noblemen and gentlemen (R. Malcolm Smuts, "Kynaston, Sir Francis (1586/7–1642)," *ODNB*). In 1635, the year the *Musaeum* was founded, Kynaston's translation of the first two books of *Troilus* appeared in print: *Amorum Troili et Creseidae libri duo priores Anglico-Latini* (Oxford: Lichfield); Kynaston's Latin rhyme royal stanzas appear in italic on the verso pages with Chaucer's in gothic on the rectos, in a text derived from Thomas Speght's edition of Chaucer (1598). Dated 1639 on its title page, a manuscript survives of Kynaston's complete Latin *Troilus*, including the *Testament* (Oxford, Bodleian Library, MS. Additional C.287; see the Introduction to this edition, p. 10); this manuscript is rife with errors, corrections, and alterations (Smith, ed., 1.xcix; Dana F. Sutton, ed., Sir Francis Kynaston, *Amorum Troili et Creseidae Libri Quinque* [1639], The Philological Museum, University of Birmingham. 5 Oct. 1999 <http://www.philological.bham.ac.uk/>). Having translated *Troilus and Criseyde* into Latin, Kynaston embarked on the *Testament*, as he indicates, to show how the Scottish poet had completed Chaucer's poem; indeed, Kynaston entitles the *Testament* "The Sixt and last booke of Troilus and Creseid written by Mr Robert Henderson and called by him The Testament of Creseide" (Bodleian Library, MS. Add. C.287, p. 477). Clearly, Kynaston recognized Henryson's authorship and was interested in learning what he could about the life and work of this poet whom he esteemed as witty and learned; fortunately, he had access at court to such Scottish notables as Thomas Erskine, first earl of Kellie, who had been educated with the young King James by none other than the celebrated, irascible Reformer and humanist George Buchanan. The scribe makes a mistake with Erskine's given name, calling him "James"; the interlined correction "Thomas" appears to be in another hand.

    Denton Fox considers that the anecdote that follows may attest to "a tradition of flippant last words" (ed., p. xv). In its coarseness, the tale recalls the scatological deathbed jests of Til Eulenspiegel, an archetypal prankster known to sixteenth-century readers in England and Scotland as Howleglas (*A Hundred Merry Tales and Other English Jestbooks of the Fifteenth and Sixteenth Centuries*, ed. P. M. Zall [Lincoln: University of Nebraska Press, 1963], pp. 233–34). In its emphasis on witchcraft, however, this tale recalls the dying earl of Angus' celebratedly godly rebuff of a seemingly helpful wizard (John Spottiswood, *The History of the Church of Scotland* [London: Flesher, 1655], p. 372; *David Hume of Godscroft's History of the*

House of Angus, ed. David Reid, STS fifth series 4–5, vol. 2, pp. 397–98). Merry tales also accumulate around the last words of George Buchanan; a late, extreme instance of the blending of admonition and jest in such last words can be found in *The Witty and Entertaining Exploits of George Buchanan, Who Was Commonly Called, The King's Fool* (Glasgow: J. and J. Robertson, 1777), p. 37. None of these parallels are especially close, and none of them prove that Kynaston's anecdote is completely arbitrary in its association with Henryson.

Thus Kynaston makes memorable his salvaging of Henryson's *Testament* for classically educated British gentlemen. His contribution to a British canon of Latin works accords with his vision, shortly before the outbreak of civil war made it obsolete, of a durable, retrospectively Stuart, British culture.

For the Author of this supplement called the Testament of Creseid, which may passe for the sixt and last booke of this story I have very sufficiently bin informed by Sir Thomas Eriskin late earle of Kelly[1] and divers aged schollers of the Scottish nation, that it was made and written by one Mr Robert Henderson sometimes cheife schoolemaster in Dumfermling[2] much about the time that Chaucer was first printed and dedicated to King Henry the Eighth by Mr Thinne[3] which was neere the end of his raigne. This Mr Henderson, wittily observing that Chaucer in his fifth booke had related the death of Troilus but made no mention what became of Creseid, he learnedly takes uppon him in a fine poeticall way to expres the punishment and end due to a false unconstant whore, which commonly terminates in extreme misery. About or a litle after his time the most famous of the Scottish poets[4] Gawen Douglas[5] made his learned and excellent translation of Virgil's Aeneids, who was bishop of Dunkeld, and made excellent prefaces to every one of the twelve bookes. For this Mr Robert Henderson, he was questionles a learned and a witty man, and it is pitty we have no more of his works.

Being very old he dyed of a diarrhea or fluxe, of whom there goes this merry though somewhat unsavory tale, that all the phisitians having given him over and he lying drawing his last breath, there came an old woman unto him, who was held a witch, and asked him whether he would be cured, to whom he sayed, "Very willingly." Then quod she, "There is a whikey tree[6] in the lower end of your orchard, and if you will goe and walke but thrice about it, and thrice repeate theis wordes, 'Whikey tree, whikey tree, take away this fluxe from me,' you shall be presently cured." He told her that beside he was extreme faint and weake, it was extreme frost and snow, and that it was impossible for him to go. She told him

---

[1] See David Stevenson, "Erskine, Thomas, first earl of Kellie (1566–1639)," *ODNB* for a biography of this courtier of James VI and I.

[2] On the associations between Henryson and this royal burgh on the north shore of the Firth of Forth, see Fox, ed., p. xvi; also the Introduction to this edition, p. 14.

[3] William Thynne's *The Workes of Geffray Chaucer* appeared in 1532; in the present edition, it is cited as T. See the Introduction, p. 6. To judge from the evidence of Dunbar's *Timor mortis conturbat me* (cited above, p. 1), Henryson was dead by 1505.

[4] *Scottish poets*: after this, the phrase "in English" has been cancelled.

[5] Douglas dated the completion of his translation of the *Aeneid* 22 July 1513 (Priscilla Bawcutt, "Douglas, Gavin (c. 1476–1522)," *ODNB*); his works having been printed in London (*STC* 7073, 24797), Douglas was the Middle Scots poet most familiar to English readers.

[6] The quicken tree is the mountain ash, a tree traditionally reputed to avert evil spirits (*OED* quicken, quickbeam).

that unles he did so, it was impossible he should recover. Mr Henderson then lifting upp himselfe and pointing to an oken table that was in the roome, asked her and seied, "Gude dame, I pray ye tell me if it would not do as well if I repeated thrice theis words, 'Oken burd, oken burd, garre[7] me shit a hard turd'?" The woman, seing herselfe derided and scorned, ran out of the house in a great passion; and Mr Henderson within halfe a quarter of an houre departed this life. There is a like tale told of Mr George Buchanan,[8] who, lying at the point of death [was] proposed such a question and made such an answer to some ladies and women that came unto him perswading him to dy a Romane Catholicke; but it is so uncivell and unmannerly that it is better to suppres it in silence then relate it.

[The text of this note is derived from Smith, *Specimens*, 1.ciii–civ; see also Fox, ed., p. xiv, and Wood, *Poems and Fables*, pp. xii–xiii; the original text is Bodleian Library, MS. Add. C.287, p. 475 (476). The original abbreviations and contractions have been expanded without comment; i and j, u and v are redistributed according to modern convention; words are distributed according to modern orthography; the punctuation is lightly modernized; and paragraphing is added.]

---

[7] *garre*: "make," "cause" (*OED*, *gar*, v.)

[8] Among the many witticisms ascribed to Buchanan on his deathbed, the most apocryphal have to do with his rejection of his physicians' advice to cease drinking wine ("I had rather live three weeks, and get drunk every day, than five or six years without drinking wine") and of the godly invitation to recite the Lord's Prayer (at which he recited verses from Propertius; Pierre Bayle, *Dictionnaire historique et critique* [Rotterdam: Leers, 1697; repr. Gallica <http://gallica.bnf.fr>] 1.686nD). For a more sober account of Buchanan's deathbed pronouncements, see David Calderwood, *History of the Kirk of Scotland*, ed. T. Thomson, 8 vols. [Edinburgh: Wodrow Society, 1842–49] 1:131–32.

✤ BIBLIOGRAPHY

ABBREVIATIONS: **EETS**: Early English Text Society; **STS**: Scottish Text Society

Aitken, Adam J. "How to Pronounce Older Scots." In *Bards and Makars: Scottish Language and Literature: Medieval and Renaissance*. Ed. Adam J. Aitken, Matthew P. McDiarmid, and Derick S. Thomson. Glasgow: University of Glasgow Press, 1977. Pp. 1–21.

Aitken, Adam J., and Caroline Macafee. "A History of Scots to 1700." In *Dictionary of the Older Scottish Tongue*. Vol. 12. Oxford: Oxford University Press, 2002. Pp. xxi–clvi.

Allen, Elizabeth. *False Fables and Exemplary Truth in Later Middle English Literature*. New York: Palgrave Macmillan, 2005.

Archibald, Elizabeth. "The Incestuous Kings in Henryson's Hades." *Scottish Studies* 4 (1984): 281–89.

Aronstein, Susan. "Cresseid Reading Cresseid: Redemption and Translation in Henryson's *Testament*." *Scottish Literary Journal* 21.2 (1994): 5–22.

Barron, W. J. R., ed. *Robert Henryson: Selected Poems*. Manchester: Carcanet, 1981.

Bawcutt, Priscilla, ed. *The Poems of William Dunbar*. 2 vols. Glasgow: Association for Scottish Literary Studies, 1998.

———. *The Shorter Poems of Gavin Douglas*. Second ed. STS fifth series 2. Edinburgh: Scottish Text Society, 2003.

Bawcutt, Priscilla, and Felicity Riddy, eds. *Longer Scottish Poems*. Vol. 1: *1375–1650*. Edinburgh: Scottish Academic Press, 1987.

———. *Selected Poems of Henryson and Dunbar*. Edinburgh: Scottish Academic Press, 1992.

Bellamy, J. G. *The Law of Treason in England in the Later Middle Ages*. Cambridge: Cambridge University Press, 1970.

Bennett, J. A. W. "Henryson's *Testament*: A Flawed Masterpiece." *Scottish Literary Journal* 1.1 (1974): 5–16.

Benson, C. David. "Critic and Poet: What Lydgate and Henryson Did to Chaucer's *Troilus and Criseyde*." *Modern Language Quarterly* 53 (1992): 23–40.

Bishop, Ian. "Lapidary Formulas as Topics of Invention — From Thomas of Hales to Henryson." *Review of English Studies*, n.s. 37 (1986): 469–77.

Bitterling, Klaus. "Robert Henryson, *The Fables*, Line 428." *Notes and Queries* n.s. 40 (1993): 25–26.

Bloomfield, Morton W. "The Magic of *In Principio*." *Modern Language Notes* 70 (1955): 559–65.

Boas, Marcus, and Hendrik Johan Botschuyver, eds. *Disticha Catonis*. Amsterdam: North-Holland, 1952.

Boffey, Julia. "Lydgate, Henryson, and the Literary Testament." *Modern Language Quarterly* 53 (1992): 41–56.

———. "The Maitland Folio Manuscript as a Verse Anthology." In *William Dunbar, "The Nobill Poyet": Essays in Honour of Priscilla Bawcutt*. Ed. Sally Mapstone. East Linton: Tuckwell Press, 2001. Pp. 40–50.

Boffey, Julia, and A. S. G. Edwards. *A New Index of Middle English Verse*. London: British Library, 2005.

Borland, Catherine R. *A Descriptive Catalogue of the Western Mediæval Manuscripts in Edinburgh University Library*. Edinburgh: Constable for the University of Edinburgh, 1916.

Bower, Calvin. "Boethius." *Grove Music Online*. 14 August 2007 <http://www.grovemusic.com>. 1 February 2008.

Breeze, Andrew. "Henryson's Lowrence the Fox." *Notes and Queries* 53 (2006): 300.

Brown, Keith M. *Bloodfeud in Scotland, 1573–1625: Violence, Justice and Politics in an Early Modern Society*. Edinburgh: John Donald, 1986.

Burrow, J. A. "Dunbar, Henryson, and Other Makars." *Review* 4 (1982): 113–27.

———. "Henryson: *The Preaching of the Swallow*." In *Essays on Medieval Literature*. Oxford: Clarendon Press, 1984. Pp. 148–60. [Reprint from *Essays in Criticism* 25 (1975): 25–37.]

Burrow, J. A., and Thorlac Turville-Petre. *A Book of Middle English*. Third ed. Oxford: Blackwell, 2005.

Burrow, John A., ed. *English Verse 1300–1500*. London: Longman, 1977.

Caldwell, John. "Robert Henryson's Harp of Eloquence." In *The Well Enchanting Skill: Music, Poetry, and Drama in the Culture of the Renaissance*. Ed. John Caldwell, Edward Olleson, and Susan Wollenberg. Oxford: Clarendon Press, 1990. Pp. 145–52.

Carter, Harry, and H. D. L. Vervliet. *Civilité Types*. Oxford Bibliographical Society Publications, n. s. 14. Oxford: Oxford University Press, 1966.

Chance, Jane, ed. *The Assembly of Gods: Le Assemble de Dyeus, or Banquet of Gods and Goddesses, with the Discourse of Reason and Sensuality*. Kalamazoo, MI: Medieval Institute Publications, 1999.

Chaucer, Geoffrey. *The Riverside Chaucer*. Gen. ed. Larry D. Benson. Third ed. Boston: Houghton Mifflin Company, 1987.

Child, Francis James, ed. *English and Scottish Popular Ballads*. 5 vols. Boston: Houghton Mifflin, 1882–88.

Conlee, John W., ed. *Middle English Debate Poetry: A Critical Anthology*. East Lansing, MI: Colleague's Press, 1991.

Copeland, Rita. *Rhetoric, Hermeneutics, and Translation in the Middle Ages: Academic Traditions and Vernacular Texts*. Cambridge: Cambridge University Press, 1991.

Corbett, John. "Aureation Revisited: The Latinate Vocabulary of Dunbar's High and Plain Styles." In *William Dunbar, "The Nobill Poyet": Essays in Honour of Priscilla Bawcutt*. Ed. Sally Mapstone. East Linton: Tuckwell Press, 2001. Pp. 183–97.

Cornelius, Michael G. "Robert Henryson's Pastoral Burlesque 'Robene and Makyne' (*c*. 1470)." *Fifteenth-Century Studies* 28 (2003): 80–96.

Craigie, W. A., ed. *The Maitland Folio Manuscript*. 2 vols. STS second series 7, 20. Edinburgh: William Blackwood and Sons, 1919–27.

———. *The Asloan Manuscript*. 2 vols. STS second series 14, 16. Edinburgh: William Blackwood and Sons, 1923–25.

Craik, T. W. "An Emendation in Henryson's 'Fables.'" *Notes and Queries* 114 (1969): 88–89.

Cunningham, I. C. "The Asloan Manuscript." In *The Renaissance in Scotland: Studies in Literature, Religion and Culture Offered to John Durkan*. Ed. A. A. MacDonald, Michael Lynch, and Ian B. Cowan. Leiden: Brill, 1994. Pp. 107–35.

Davenport, Tony. *Medieval Narrative: An Introduction*. Oxford: Oxford University Press, 2004.

Davies, Martin. "A Tale of Two Aesops." *The Library* 7 (2006): 257–88.

Dictionary of the Older Scottish Tongue. Ed. W. A. Craigie et al. 12 vols. Chicago, Aberdeen, and Oxford: University of Chicago Press, Aberdeen University Press, and Oxford University Press, 1937–2004.

Dictionary of the Scots Language. Ed. Victor Skretkowicz and Susan Rennie. University of Dundee, 2001– <http://www.dsl.ac.uk/dsl/>. 28 July 2007. [This free online resource includes *DOST*.]

Diebler, Arthur Richard. *Henrisone's Fabeldichtungen*. Halle: Karras, 1885.

Douglas, Gavin. *Virgil's Aeneid Translated by Gavin Douglas*. Ed. David F. C. Coldwell. 4 vols. STS third series 25, 27, 28, 30. Edinburgh: William Blackwood and Sons, 1957–64.

———. *The Palis of Honoure*. Ed. David J. Parkinson. Kalamazoo, MI: Medieval Institute Publications, 1992.

Drexler, Robert Daniel. "Henryson's 'Ane Prayer for the Pest.'" *Forum for Modern Language Studies* 16 (1980): 368–70.

Duffell, Martin J. "The Italian Line in English after Chaucer." *Language and Literature* 11 (2002): 291–306.

Duffell, Martin J., and Dominique Billy. "From Decasyllable to Pentameter: Gower's Contribution to English Metrics." *Chaucer Review* 38 (2004): 383–400.

Dunnigan, Sarah M. "Feminizing the Text, Feminizing the Reader? The Mirror of 'Feminitie' in *The Testament of Cresseid.*" *Studies in Scottish Literature* 33–34 (2004): 107–23.

Durkan, John. "Education in the Century of the Reformation." In *Essays on the Scottish Reformation 1513–1625.* Ed. David McRoberts. Glasgow: Burns, 1962. Pp. 145–68.

Edwards, A. S. G., and Julia Boffey. "Introduction." In *The Works of Geoffrey Chaucer and The Kingis Quair: A Facsimile of Bodleian Library, Oxford, MS. Arch. Selden. B. 24.* Cambridge: Brewer, 1997. Pp. 1–28.

Ellenberger, Bengt. *The Latin Element in the Vocabulary of the Earlier Makars: Henryson and Dunbar.* Lund Studies in English 51. Lund: CWK Gleerup, 1977.

Elliott, Charles. *Robert Henryson: Poems.* Oxford: Clarendon, 1963.

Ewan, Elizabeth. "'Many Injurious Words': Defamation and Gender in Late Medieval Scotland." In *History, Literature, and Music in Scotland, 700–1560.* Ed. R. Andrew McDonald. Toronto: University of Toronto Press, 2002. Pp. 163–86.

Fein, Susanna Greer. "Twelve-Line Stanza Forms in Middle English and the Date of *Pearl.*" *Speculum* 72 (1997): 367–98.

———, ed. *Moral Love Songs and Laments.* Kalamazoo, MI: Medieval Institute Publications, 1998.

Findlay, L. M. "Reading and Teaching Troilus Otherwise: St Maure, Chaucer, Henryson." *Florilegium* 16 (1999): 61–75.

Forni, Kathleen. *The Chaucerian Apocrypha: A Counterfeit Canon.* Gainesville: University Press of Florida, 2001.

Fox, Denton. "Henryson's *Fables.*" *ELH* 29 (1962): 337–56.

———, ed. *The Poems of Robert Henryson.* Oxford: Clarendon, 1981.

Fox, Denton, and William A. Ringler, eds. *The Bannatyne Manuscript: National Library of Scotland, Advocates' MS. 1.1.6.* London: Scolar and the National Library of Scotland, 1980.

Fradenburg, Louise O. "Henryson Scholarship: The Recent Decades." In *Fifteenth-Century Studies: Recent Essays.* Ed. R. F. Yeager. Hamden, CT: Archon, 1984. Pp. 65–92.

Friedman, John Block. *Orpheus in the Middle Ages.* Syracuse, NY: Syracuse University Press, 2000.

Furnivall, Frederick J., ed. *Supplementary Parallel-Texts of Chaucer's Minor Poems.* Part One. Chaucer Society, first series 22. London: Trübner, 1871.

Geddie, William. *A Bibliography of Middle Scots Poets.* STS first series 61. Edinburgh: William Blackwood and Sons, 1912. [Henryson is cataloged on pp. 166–86.]

Giaccherini, Enrico. "From *Sir Orfeo* to 'Schir Orpheus': Exile, and the Waning of the Middle Ages." In *Displaced Persons: Conditions of Exile in European Culture.* Ed. Sharon Ouditt. Aldershot: Ashgate, 2002. Pp. 1–10.

Godman, Peter. "Henryson's Masterpiece." *Review of English Studies* 35 (1984): 291–300.

Gopen, George D., ed. and trans. *The Moral Fables of Aesop.* Notre Dame, IN: University of Notre Dame Press, 1987.

Gower, John. *Confessio Amantis.* Ed. Russell A. Peck. 3 vols. Kalamazoo, MI: Medieval Institute Publications, 2003–06.

Gray, Douglas. *Themes and Images in the Medieval English Religious Lyric.* London: Routledge, 1972.

———. *Robert Henryson.* Medieval and Renaissance Authors. Leiden: E. J. Brill, 1979.

———, ed. *Selected Poems of Robert Henryson and William Dunbar.* London: Penguin, 1998.

Green, Richard Firth. *A Crisis of Truth: Literature and Law in Ricardian England.* Philadelphia: University of Pennsylvania Press, 1999.

Greentree, Rosemary. *Reader, Teller and Teacher: The Narrator of Robert Henryson's Moral Fables.* Frankfurt: Peter Lang, 1993.

———. "Literate in Love: Makyne's Lesson for Robene." In *Older Scots Literature.* Ed. Sally Mapstone. Edinburgh: John Donald, 2005. Pp. 61–69.

Grigsby, Bryon Lee. *Pestilence in Medieval and Early Modern English Literature.* New York: Routledge, 2004.

Gros Louis, Kenneth R. R. "Robert Henryson's *Orpheus and Eurydice* and the Orpheus Traditions of the Middle Ages." *Speculum* 41 (1966): 643–55.

Haar, James. "Music of the Spheres." *Grove Music Online*. 14 August 2007 <http://www.grovemusic
.com>. 5 September 2008.

Hanham, Alison, and J. C. Eade. "Foxy Astrology in Henryson." *Parergon* 24 (1979): 25–29.

Hay, Sir Gilbert. *The Prose Works of Sir Gilbert Hay*. Vol. 3: *The Buke of the Ordre of Knychthede and The
Buke of the Gouernaunce of Princis*. Ed. Jonathan A. Glenn. STS fourth series 21. Edinburgh:
Scottish Text Society, 1993.

Heaney, Seamus, trans. *The Testament of Cresseid: A Retelling of Robert Henryson's Poem*. London:
Enitharmon, 2004.

———, trans. "*The Toad and the Mouse* by Seamus Heaney, Translated from the Scots of Robert
Henryson (c. 1420–1490)." *Guardian Unlimited Books*. *The Guardian*. 27 May 2006 <http://books
.guardian.co.uk/departments/poetry/story/0,,1783972,00.html>. 5 September 2008.

Henryson, Robert. *The Morall Fabillis of Esope the Phrygian*. Amsterdam: Theatrum Orbis Terrarum,
1970. [Facsimile of the 1570 Charteris print of *The Morall Fabillis* (C).]

Heron, Robert. *Observations Made in a Journey Through the Western Counties of Scotland*. 2 vols. Perth:
R. Morison and Son, 1793.

Hill, Thomas. "*Stet Verbum Regis*: Why Henryson's Husbandman Is Not a King." *English Studies* 86
(2005): 127–32.

Hill, Thomas D. "*Hirundines Habent Quidem Prescium*: Why Henryson's 'Preaching of a Swallow' Is
Preached by a Swallow." *Scottish Literary Journal Supplement* 26 (Spring 1987): 30–31.

Hodges, Laura F. "Sartorial Signs in *Troilus and Criseyde*." *Chaucer Review* 35 (2001): 223–59.

Holland, Richard. *Buke of the Howlat*. In F. J. Amours, ed., *Scottish Alliterative Poems in Riming Stanzas*.
STS first series 27 and 28. Edinburgh: William Blackwood and Sons, 1897. Pp. 47–81, 287–317.

Horstmann, Carl, and Frederick J. Furnivall, eds. *Minor Poems of the Vernon Manuscript*. 2 vols. EETS
original series 98, 117. London: Kegan Paul, Trench, Trübner, and Co., 1892–1901.

Huppé, Bernard, and D. W. Robertson, Jr. *Fruyt and Chaf: Studies in Chaucer's Allegories*. Princeton, NJ:
Princeton University Press, 1963.

Isidore of Seville. *Etymologies*. Trans. Stephen A. Barney, W. J. Lewis, J. A. Beach, and Oliver Berghof.
Cambridge: Cambridge University Press, 2006.

Jacobs, John C., trans. *The Fables of Odo of Cheriton*. Syracuse, NY: Syracuse University Press, 1985.

Jamieson, Ian W. A. "The Poetry of Robert Henryson: A Study of the Use of Source Material." Ph.D.
dissertation, Edinburgh, 1964.

———. "The Minor Poems of Robert Henryson." *Studies in Scottish Literature* 9 (1971–72): 125–47.

———. "'To Preue Thare Prechyng be a Poesye': Some Thoughts on Henryson's Poetics." *Parergon*
8 (1974): 24–36.

Johnson, Ian. "Hellish Complexity in Henryson's *Orpheus*." *Forum for Modern Language Studies* 38
(2002): 412–19.

Keller, Wolfram R. *Robert Henryson: A Bibliography*. University of Marburg. 14 September 2000
<http://www.staff.uni-marburg.de/~kellerw/bibliographies/Henryson.bib.html>. 1 February 2008.

Kelly, Henry Ansgar. *Chaucerian Tragedy*. Chaucer Studies 24. Cambridge: D. S. Brewer, 1997.

Kindrick, Robert L. *Robert Henryson*. Boston: G. K. Hall, 1979.

———. *Henryson and the Medieval Arts of Rhetoric*. New York: Garland, 1993.

———. "Henryson's 'Uther Quair' Again: A Possible Candidate and the Nature of the Tradition."
Chaucer Review 33 (1998): 190–220.

Kindrick, Robert L., with Kristie A. Bixby, eds. *The Poems of Robert Henryson*. Kalamazoo, MI: Medieval
Institute Publications, 1997.

Klibansky, Raymond, Erwin Panofsky, and Fritz Saxl. *Saturn and Melancholy: Studies in the History of
Natural Philosophy, Religion, and Art*. London: Nelson, 1964.

Knighton, C. S. *Catalogue of the Pepys Library at Magdalene College, Cambridge*. Vol. 5: *Manuscripts*, Part
ii: *Modern*. Cambridge: Brewer, 1981.

Kratzmann, Gregory. "Henryson's *Fables*: 'The Subtell Dyte of Poetry.'" *Studies in Scottish Literature* 20
(1985): 49–70.

Kruger, Steven F. *Dreaming in the Middle Ages*. Cambridge: Cambridge University Press, 1992.

Laing, David, ed. *The Poems and Fables of Robert Henryson*. Edinburgh: Paterson, 1865.

Langland, William. *The Vision of Piers Plowman*. Ed. A. V. C. Schmidt. New York: Dutton, 1978.

Lenaghan, R. T. *Caxton's Aesop*. Cambridge, MA: Harvard University Press, 1967.

Lyall, Roderick J. "Henryson's *Moral Fabillis* and the Steinhöwel Tradition." *Forum for Modern Language Studies* 38 (2002): 362–81.

———. "Henryson's *Morall Fabillis*: Structure and Meaning." In *A Companion to Medieval Scottish Poetry*. Ed. Priscilla Bawcutt and Janet Hadley Williams. Cambridge: D. S. Brewer, 2006. Pp. 89–104.

Lydgate, John. *The Minor Poems of John Lydgate*. Ed. Henry Noble MacCracken. 2 vols. EETS extra series 107, original series 192. London: Oxford University Press, 1911–34.

———. *The Fall of Princes*. Ed. Henry Bergen. 4 vols. EETS extra series 121–24. London: Oxford University Press, 1924–27.

———. *Troy Book: Selections*. Ed. Robert R. Edwards. Kalamazoo, MI: Medieval Institute Publications, 1998.

Lynch, Michael. *Scotland: A New History*. London: Pimlico, 1992.

Lyndsay, David. *Sir David Lyndsay, Selected Poems*. Ed. Janet Hadley-Williams. Glasgow: Association for Scottish Literary Studies, 2000.

MacDonald, A. A. "Robert Henryson, Orpheus, and the *Puer Senex* Topos." In *In Other Words: Transcultural Studies in Philology, Translation, and Lexicology Presented to Hans Heinrich Meier on the Occasion of His Sixty-Fifth Birthday*. Ed. J. Lachlan Mackenzie and Richard Todd. Dordrecht: Foris, 1989. Pp. 117–20.

———. "The Latin Original of Robert Henryson's Annunciation Lyric." In *The Renaissance in Scotland: Studies in Literature, Religion, History and Culture Offered to John Durkan*. Ed. A. A. MacDonald, Michael Lynch, and Ian B. Cowan. Leiden: E. J. Brill, 1994. Pp. 45–65.

———. "Lyrics in Middle Scots." In *A Companion to the Middle English Lyric*. Ed. Thomas G. Duncan. Cambridge: D. S. Brewer, 2005. Pp. 242–61.

MacDonald, Alasdair A. "The Cultural Repertory of Middle Scots Lyric Verse." In *Cultural Repertoires: Structure, Function and Dynamics*. Ed. Gillis J. Dorleijn and Herman L. J. Vanstiphout. Louvain: Peeters, 2003. Pp. 59–86.

Macdougall, Norman. *James III: A Political Study*. Edinburgh: John Donald, 1982.

Machan, Tim William. *Textual Criticism and Middle English Texts*. Charlottesville: University Press of Virginia, 1994.

MacQueen, John. *Robert Henryson: A Study of the Major Narrative Poems*. Oxford: Clarendon, 1967.

———. "Neoplatonism and Orphism in Fifteenth-Century Scotland: The Evidence of Henryson's 'New Orpheus.'" *Scottish Studies* 20 (1976): 69–89.

———. "Lent and Henryson's 'The Fox, the Wolf, and the Cadger.'" In *Older Scots Literature*. Ed. Sally Mapstone. Edinburgh: John Donald, 2005. Pp. 109–17.

———. *Complete and Full with Numbers: The Narrative Poetry of Robert Henryson*. Amsterdam: Rodopi, 2006.

Macrobius. *Commentary on the Dream of Scipio*. Trans. William Harris Stahl. New York: Columbia University Press, 1952.

Mann, Jill. "The Planetary Gods in Chaucer and Henryson." In *Chaucer Traditions: Studies in Honour of Derek Brewer*. Ed. Ruth Morse and Barry Windeatt. Cambridge: Cambridge University Press, 1990. Pp. 91–106.

———, ed. *Geoffrey Chaucer: The Canterbury Tales*. London: Penguin, 2005.

Mapstone, Sally. "*The Testament of Cresseid*, Lines 561–7: A New Manuscript Witness." *Notes and Queries* 32 (1985): 307–10.

———. "The Origins of Criseyde." In *Medieval Women: Texts and Contexts in Late Medieval Britain: Essays for Felicity Riddy*. Ed. Jocelyn Wogan-Browne et al. Turnhout: Brepols, 2000. Pp. 131–47.

———. "Older Scots and the Fifteenth Century." In *Older Scots Literature*. Ed. Sally Mapstone. Edinburgh: John Donald, 2005. Pp. 3–13.

———, ed. *The Chepman and Myllar Prints: Digitised Facsimiles with Introduction, Headnote and Transcription*. STS. Cambridge: Boydell and Brewer, 2008.

Marie de France. *Fables*. Ed. and trans. Harriet Spiegel. Toronto: University of Toronto Press, 1994.

Marlin, John. "'Arestyus is Noucht bot Gude Vertewe': The Perplexing *Moralitas* to Henryson's *Orpheus and Erudices.*" *Fifteenth-Century Studies* 25 (2000): 137–53.

Mathews, Jana. "Land, Lepers, and the Law in *The Testament of Cresseid.*" In *The Letter of the Law: Legal Practice and Literary Production in Medieval England.* Ed. Emily Steiner and Candace Barrington. Ithaca, NY: Cornell University Press, 2002. Pp. 40–66.

McGinley, Kevin J. "The 'Fenʒeit' and the Feminine: Robert Henryson's *Orpheus and Eurydice* and the Gendering of Poetry." In *Woman and the Feminine in Medieval and Early Modern Scottish Writing.* Ed. Sarah M. Dunnigan, C. Marie Harker, and Evelyn S. Newlyn. New York: Palgrave Macmillan, 2004. Pp. 74–85.

McKenna, Steven R. "Legends of James III and the Problem of Henryson's Topicality." *Scottish Literary Journal* 17.1 (1990): 5–20.

———. *Robert Henryson's Tragic Vision.* New York: Peter Lang, 1994.

McKim, Anne. "Tracing the Ring: Henryson, Fowler, and Chaucer's *Troilus.*" *Notes and Queries* 40 (1993): 449.

———, ed. "The Laste Epistle of Creseyd to Troyalus." In Kindrick, *The Poems of Robert Henryson*, pp. 277–300.

———, ed. *The Wallace: Selections.* Kalamazoo, MI: Medieval Institute Publications, 2003.

Mehl, Dieter. "Robert Henryson's *Moral Fables* as Experiments in Didactic Narrative." In *Functions of Literature: Essays Presented to Erwin Wolff on His Sixtieth Birthday.* Ed. Ulrich Broich, Theo Stemmler, and Gerd Stratmann. Tübingen: Niemeyer, 1984. Pp. 81–99.

Mieszkowski, Gretchen. "The Reputation of Criseyde 1155–1500." *Transactions of the Connecticut Academy of Arts and Sciences* 43 (1971): 71–153.

Mooney, Linne R., and Mary-Jo Arn, eds. *The Kingis Quair and Other Prison Poems.* Kalamazoo, MI: Medieval Institute Publications, 2005.

National Library of Scotland. *First Scottish Books.* National Library of Scotland Digital Library. 2006. <http://www.nls.uk/firstscottishbooks/>. 7 August 2007. [The Chepman and Myllar Prints]

Neilson, William Allan. *The Origins and Sources of the "Court of Love."* 1899. Rpt. New York: Russell, 1967.

Nicholson, Ranald. *Scotland: The Later Middle Ages.* Edinburgh: Oliver and Boyd, 1974.

O'Donnell, James J., ed. *Boethius' Consolatio Philosophiae.* Second ed. Bryn Mawr Latin Commentaries 1–2. Bryn Mawr, PA: Bryn Mawr College, 1990.

Offord, M. Y., ed. *The Parlement of the Thre Ages.* EETS original series 246. London: Oxford University Press, 1967.

Olson, Glending. *Literature as Recreation in the Later Middle Ages.* Ithaca, NY: Cornell University Press, 1982.

Patterson, Annabel. *Fables of Power: Aesopian Writing and Political History.* Durham, NC: Duke University Press, 1991.

Pearsall, Derek, ed. *The Floure and the Leafe, The Assembly of Ladies, The Isle of Ladies.* Kalamazoo, MI: Medieval Institute Publications, 1990.

———, ed. *Chaucer to Spenser: An Anthology of Writings in English, 1375–1575.* Oxford: Blackwell, 1999.

Perry, Ben Edwin, ed. and trans. *Babrius and Phaedrus.* Loeb Classical Library 436. Cambridge, MA: Harvard University Press, 1965.

Petrina, Alessandra. "Deviations from Genre in Robert Henryson's 'Robene and Makyne.'" *Studies in Scottish Literature* 31 (1999): 107–20.

———. "Aristeus Pastor Adamans: The Human Setting in Henryson's *Orpheus and Eurydice* and Its Kinship with Poliziano's *Fabula di Orpheo.*" *Forum for Modern Language Studies* 38 (2002): 382–96.

Poole, Russell G. "Henryson, *Fables* 2193." *Review of English Studies* 35 (1984): 508–10.

The Pricke of Conscience (Stimulus Conscientiæ): A Northumbrian Poem by Richard Rolle de Hampole. Ed. Richard Morris. Berlin: A. Asher, 1863.

Raby, F. J. E. *A History of Christian-Latin Poetry from the Beginnings to the Close of the Middle Ages.* Oxford: Clarendon Press, 1927.

Ramson, W. S. "'Lettres of Gold Writtin I Fand': A Defence of Moral Verse." *Parergon* 23 (1979): 37–46.

Riddy, Felicity. "The Alliterative Revival." In *The History of Scottish Literature*, Vol. 1: *Origins to 1660 (Medieval and Renaissance)*. Ed. R. D. S. Jack. Aberdeen: Aberdeen University Press, 1988. Pp. 39–54.

———. "'Abject Odious': Feminine and Masculine in Henryson's *Testament of Cresseid*." In *The Long Fifteenth Century: Essays for Douglas Gray*. Ed. Helen Cooper and Sally Mapstone. Oxford: Clarendon, 1997. Pp. 229–48.

Ridley, Florence H. "Middle Scots Writers: Henryson." In *A Manual of the Writings in Middle English, 1051–1500*. Ed. Albert E. Hartung. Vol. 4. Hamden: Connecticut Academy of Arts and Sciences, 1973. Pp. 965–88, 1137–80.

———. Review of Denton Fox, ed., *The Poems of Robert Henryson. Speculum* 57 (1982): 626–31.

Ritchie, W. Tod, ed. *The Bannatyne Manuscript*. 4 vols. STS second series 22, 23, 26; third series 5. Edinburgh: William Blackwood and Sons, 1928–34.

Roerecke, Howard. "The Integrity and Symmetry of Robert Henryson's *Moral Fables*." Ph.D. dissertation, Pennsylvania State, 1969.

Rollins, Hyder E. "The Troilus-Cressida Story from Chaucer to Shakespeare." *PMLA* 32 (1917): 383–429.

Rudd, Gillian. "Making Mention of Aesop: Henryson's Fable of the Two Mice." *Yearbook of English Studies* 36 (2006): 39–49.

Rutledge, Thomas. "Robert Henryson's *Orpheus and Eurydice*: A Northern Humanism?" *Forum for Modern Language Studies* 38 (2002): 396–411.

Saintsbury, George. *A History of English Prosody from the Twelfth Century to the Present Day*. 3 vols. Second ed. London: Macmillan, 1923.

Salisbury, Eve. *The Trials and Joys of Marriage*. Kalamazoo, MI: Medieval Institute Publications, 2002.

Sandison, Helen Estabrook. *The "Chanson d'Aventure" in Middle English*. Bryn Mawr, PA: Bryn Mawr College, 1913.

Scheps, Walter, and J. Anna Looney. "Writings about Robert Henryson." In *Middle Scots Poets: A Reference Guide to James I of Scotland, Robert Henryson, William Dunbar, and Gavin Douglas*. Boston: G. K. Hall, 1986. Pp. 54–117.

Schrader, Richard J. "Henryson and Nominalism." *Journal of Medieval and Renaissance Studies* 8 (1978): 1–15.

Seymour-Smith, M. C., et al., eds. *On the Properties of Things: John Trevisa's Translation of Bartholomæus Anglicus, De Proprietatibus Rerum*. 3 vols. Oxford: Clarendon Press, 1975–88.

Sheridan, Christian. "The Early Prints of the *Testament of Cresseid* and the Presentation of Lines 577–91." *ANQ* 20 (2007): 23–27.

Simpson, James. "Faith and Hermeneutics: Pragmatism versus Pragmatism." *Journal of Medieval and Early Modern Studies* 33 (2003): 215–39.

Sir Gawain and the Green Knight. Ed. J. R. R. Tolkien and E. V. Gordon. Second ed. rev. Norman Davis. Oxford: Clarendon Press, 1967.

Smith, G. Gregory, ed. *Specimens of Middle Scots*. Edinburgh: William Blackwood and Sons, 1902.

———, ed. *The Poems of Robert Henryson*. 3 vols. STS first series 55, 58, 64. Edinburgh: William Blackwood and Sons, 1906–14.

Smith, Jeremy J. "The Language of Older Scots Poetry." In *The Edinburgh Companion to Scots*. Ed. John Corbett, J. Derrick McClure, and Jane Stuart-Smith. Edinburgh: Edinburgh University Press, 2003. Pp. 197–209.

Spearing, A. C. *Medieval to Renaissance in English Poetry*. Cambridge: Cambridge University Press, 1985.

———. *Textual Subjectivity: The Encoding of Subjectivity in Medieval Narratives and Lyrics*. Oxford: Oxford University Press, 2005.

Stearns, Marshall. *Robert Henryson*. New York: Columbia University Press, 1949.

Stephenson, William. "The Acrostic 'Fictio' in Robert Henryson's *The Testament of Cresseid* (Lines 58–63)." *Chaucer Review* 29 (1994): 163–65.

Stevenson, George, ed. *Pieces from the Makculloch and the Gray MSS: Together with the Chepman and Myllar Prints*. STS first series 65. Edinburgh: William Blackwood and Sons, 1918.

Strauss, Dietrich. "Some Comments on the Moralitas of Robert Henryson's 'Orpheus and Eurydice.'" *Studies in Scottish Literature* 32 (2001): 1–12.

Strauss, Jennifer. "To Speak Once More of Cresseid: Henryson's *Testament* Re-considered." *Scottish Literary Journal* 4.2 (1977): 5–13.

Strohm, Paul. "Fourteenth- and Fifteenth-Century Writers as Readers of Chaucer." In *Genres, Themes, and Images in English Literature from the Fourteenth to the Fifteenth Century.* Ed. Piero Boitani and Anna Torti. Tübingen: Gunter Narr, 1988. Pp. 90–104.

Symons, Dana M., ed. *Chaucerian Dream Visions and Complaints.* Kalamazoo, MI: Medieval Institute Publications, 2004.

Torti, Anna. "From 'History' to 'Tragedy': The Story of Troilus and Criseyde in Lydgate's *Troy Book* and Henryson's *Testament of Cresseid.*" In *The European Tragedy of Troilus.* Ed. Piero Boitani. Oxford: Clarendon Press, 1989. Pp. 171–97.

———. "Henryson's *Testament of Cresseid*: Deconstructing the *Auctoritas.*" *Textus* 5 (1992): 3–12.

Walker, David M. *A Legal History of Scotland.* Vol. 2: *The Later Middle Ages.* Edinburgh: Green, 1996.

Walther, Hans. *Proverbia Sententiaeque Latinitatis Medii Aevi.* 6 vols. Göttingen: Vandenhoeck and Ruprecht, 1963–69.

Watson, Nicholas. "Outdoing Chaucer: Lydgate's *Troy Book* and Henryson's *Testament of Cresseid* as Competitive Imitations of *Troilus and Criseyde.*" In *Shifts and Transpositions in Medieval Narrative: A Festschrift for Dr. Elspeth Kennedy.* Ed. Karen Pratt. Cambridge: D. S. Brewer, 1994. Pp. 89–108.

Wheatley, Edward. *Mastering Aesop: Medieval Education, Chaucer, and His Followers.* Gainesville: University Press of Florida, 2000.

Whiting, Bartlett Jere. "Proverbs and Proverbial Sayings from Scottish Writers before 1600." *Mediaeval Studies* 11 (1949): 123–205; 13 (1951): 87–164.

Whiting, Bartlett Jere, and Helen Prescott Whiting. *Proverbs, Sentences, and Proverbial Phrases from English Writings Mainly before 1500.* Cambridge, MA: The Belknap Press of Harvard University Press, 1968.

Whyte, Ian D. *Scotland before the Industrial Revolution: An Economic and Social History c. 1050–c. 1750.* Harlow: Longman, 1995.

Windeatt, Barry, ed. *Chaucer: Troilus and Criseyde.* London: Penguin, 2003.

Wittig, Kurt. *The Scottish Tradition in Literature.* Edinburgh: Oliver and Boyd, 1958.

Wogan-Browne, Jocelyn, Nicholas Watson, Andrew Taylor, and Ruth Evans, eds. *The Idea of the Vernacular: An Anthology of Middle English Literary Theory, 1280–1520.* University Park: Pennsylvania State University Press, 1999.

Wood, H. Harvey, ed. *The Poems and Fables of Robert Henryson.* Second ed. Edinburgh: Oliver and Boyd, 1958.

Woolf, Rosemary. "The Theme of Christ the Lover-Knight in Medieval English Literature." *Review of English Studies* n.s. 13 (1962): 1–16.

Wormald, Jenny. *Court, Kirk, and Community: Scotland 1470–1625.* Toronto: University of Toronto Press, 1981.

———. *Lords and Men in Scotland: Bonds of Manrent, 1442–1603.* Edinburgh: J. Donald, 1985.

Wright, Aaron E., ed. *The Fables of "Walter of England."* Toronto: Pontifical Institute for Medieval Studies, 1997.

Wright, Dorena Allen. "Henryson's *Orpheus and Eurydice* and the Tradition of the Muses." *Medium Aevum* 40 (1971): 41–47.

Wright, Thomas, ed. *Songs and Carols Now First Printed From a Manuscript of the Fifteenth Century.* Percy Society 23. London: Richards, 1847.

🌿 GLOSSARY

As well as all the obviously hard words that send readers to the marginal glosses provided by the editor or to dictionaries such as *DOST*, *MED*, and the *OED*, Henryson's word-stock contains some "false friends" — words that look like each other or like common words in modern English — that for their apparent straightforwardness pose particular difficulties. The following list, which is by no means exhaustive, is provided to help the reader avoid making mistaken assumptions about the meaning of recurrent, often apparently familiar words in Henryson's poems: only words that occur more than once are included; words used only once are glossed marginally in the text proper and often discussed in the Explanatory Notes. The citations provided here are taken from the *Fables* unless indicated otherwise by title. In the alphabetical order, *y* used as a vowel appears with *i*.

abak *backwards* (437, 1138, 2823; *Testament* 222)

aganis *in opposition to* (792, 934, etc.); *against* (*Testament* 21, 475); *facing* (759); *in readiness for* (2034, 2692)

air *heir* (470, 815, 834, etc.)

air *air* (1661, 1667; *Testament* 17)

air *circuit court* (1274)

air, aire *previously* (1784; *Orpheus* 519); *early* (2233, 2486, 2937, etc.)

and *and* (5, 10, 11, etc.); *if* (528, 707, 961, etc.)

ane *a, one* (12, 17, 18, etc.)

aneuch, anew, annewche *enough* (17, 101, 265, etc.)

anis *once* (187, 325, 682, etc.)

as *as* (8, 22, 57, etc.)

as, ase *ask* (1461)

attour, atour, attoure, attouir *over* (496, 966; *Testament* 162; *Orpheus* 244); *above* (2022)

baill *misery* (521, 2478; *Robene* 37, etc.)

bair *boar* (401, 901; *Testament* 193; *Orpheus* 160)

bair *bare* (679, 1257, 1290, etc.)

baith, bayth, bath *both* (182, 214, 227, etc.)

bald *bold* (306, 2110, 2632, etc.)

bandis *fetters* (1536, 1540; *Orpheus* 405)

banis *bones* (830, 2177, 2579)

be *by* (7, 34, 59, etc.)

be *be* (21, 72, 83, etc.)

beir *bear* (901, 1209)

beir *bier* (2943)

beir *noise* (486, 1544)

beir *carry* (1402, 2125, 2148, etc.)

beit *beat, strike* (489, 1875); *heal, relieve* (*Ressoning Aige* 39)

belyve, belyif *quickly* (1090, 1731; *Orpheus* 447, etc.)

bene *pleasant* (1346, 1701, 1727, etc.; cf. **be** *be*)

bent *field* (551, 688, 1038, etc.)

bent *bent* (22, 765)

bid *ask, command* (157; *Orpheus* 611, 613, etc.); *desire* (*Robene* 56)

bla *livid* (577; *Testament* 159)

blakinnit, blaiknit *made pale* (973; *Testament* 410)

blenk, blenkis *glance; glances* (*Orpheus* 81, 355; *Testament* 226, 499)

blythe *merry, willing, glad* (1339, 1714, 2941; *Ressoning Aige* 45; *Robene* 121)

blythnes *happiness* (*Orpheus* 88)

bot *except* (107, 108, 149, etc.); *only* (65, 88; *Testament* 477); *but* (34, 53, 115, etc.)

but *free from, without* (173, 201, 481, etc.)

but weir *without doubt* (1207)

cabok *cheese* (2353, 2358, 2365, 2369, 2448)

can, could *did* (171, 183, 257); *is/was able* (52, 135, 136, etc.); *know/knew* (144, 2041, 2212, etc.)

carie, cary *go* (638, 893, 1774, etc.)

cautelous *cunning, deceptive* (402, 420, 1812, etc.)

chide, chyde *quarrel* (*Testament* 185, 357, 470, etc.)

cluke *claw* (2515, 2899; *Annunciation* 69)

compeir *appear* (864, 1057, 1158, etc.)

cop *cup* (*Testament* 343, 387, 442, etc.)

corne *cereal grain (wheat, rye, barley); peas; grain field or granary (metonym)* (10, 91, 94, 99, etc.)

corps *body* (724, 828, 1633, etc.)

craft *skill* (658, 708, 2203, etc.)

crag *neck* (1879, 1936, 2482)

craig *crag* (664, 838)

craw *crow* (465, 473, 478)

cumpas *circuit* (2049, 2133, 2159)

cunning *knowledge* (128, 148, 407, etc.); cf. **cunning** *rabbit* (913)

cuntré (cuntrie) *country* (379, 1513, 1617; *Testament* 364; *Orpheus* 375; *Bludy Serk* 16; *Ressoning Deth* 15)

curage *spirit, desire* (*Testament* 32; *Orpheus* 16; *Ressoning Aige* 53)

cure *care* (67, 1260, 2485); *remedy* (*Sum Practysis* 34, 74)

de *die* (1126, 1815, 1876, etc.)

declyne *reject* (1187, 1194); *avert* (*Prayer* 67)

decreit *decision* (2304, 2311, *Annunciation* 12, etc.)

deid, dede, deith, deth *death* (541, 653, 775, etc.)

deid, dede *deed* (*Testament* 275 328; *Orpheus* 478, etc.)

deid, dede *dead* (301, 449, 752, etc.)

deir *injury* (2150; *Robene* 21)

deir *injure* (*Garmont* 8; *Sum Practysis* 3)

deir, dere *dear* (89, 163, 186, etc.)

dern *hiding place* (755, 1712; *Robene* 7, etc.)

diseis *distress* (322; *Testament* 320)

dite, dyte *writing, style* (13, 119; *Testament* 1)

doctrine, doctryne *teaching* (17, 1219, 2594, etc.)

doolie, dolly, dully *dismal* (*Testament* 344; *Orpheus* 134, 310, etc.)

dout *fear* (482, 925, 2051, etc.); *uncertainty* (472)

dressit, drest *proceeded* (426, 917; *Testament* 404)

drug *pull* (2750, 2954)

dude, duid *do it* (676, 699, 730, etc.)

e, ee, eye *eye* (384, 626, 664, etc.)

effeird, aferit *suited* (951, 986, 1168, etc.)

effeiris, efferis *befits* (695, 2710, 2773, etc.)

efferit, effeird, effeirit, afeird *afraid* (928, 1412, 2561, etc.)

eik *also* (46, 631, 649, etc.; *Testament* 314; *Orpheus* 228, 443, 449, etc.); *augment, increase* (281, *Robene* 94)

eir *ear* (4, 1357, 1393, etc.)

eir *before* (2300)

estait, estate *status* (60, 932; *Testament* 510, etc.)

exclude *remove* (*Testament* 75, 133, 315)

extasy, extasie *trance* (490; *Testament* 141; *Orpheus* 399)

fabill, fable *fiction, fable, lie* (18, 63, 118, etc.)

fay *faithfulness* (1618; *Testament* 571)

fair, faire *attractive* (84, 323, 335, etc.)

fair, fare *entertainment* (271; *Testament* 403)

fair, fare *go* (308, 511, 583, etc.)

fang *catch* (735, 2119)

fantasie, fantesy *delusion* (1641, 2451; *Orpheus* 432, etc.)

farie, fary, phary *the fairies* (*Orpheus* 119, 125); *an act of magic* (1775); *illusion* (*Sum Practysis* 86)

feid *feud* (450, 538, 583, etc.)

feid, fede *feed* (101, 381, 1855, etc.)

feir *companion* (1456, 2235; *Bludy Serk* 54)

feir *fear* (noun: 1453; *Sum Practysis* 10; verb: 789)

feir *posture* (657; *Robene* 19)

feird, ferd, ferde *fourth* (1948; *Testament* 216; *Orpheus* 44, etc.)

feist *feast, dinner* (244, 322, 343, etc.)

ferlie, farlie, farly, ferly *marvelous* (*Orpheus* 502); *amazingly* (1581, 1770, etc.)

fervent *burning hot* (*Testament* 4, 215; *Orpheus* 449)

figure, figour *likeness* (7, 59, 1258, etc.)

fyle *defile* (971, 1491, 2632, etc.)

flane *arrow* (765, 772; *Testament* 167)

flude *river, sea* (621, 734, 2866, etc.)

frawart, fraward *ill-willed* (2661; *Testament* 323, 352, etc.)

fre *free* (355, 369, 2352, etc.); *noble, generous* (*Bludy Serk* 79; *Robene* 20, etc.); *privileged* (172)

ga, go *go* (161, 881, 1000, etc.)

gang *go* (259, 1474, 2361, etc.)

gar, ger *cause, make* (21, 1593, 2852, etc.)

gay *excellent, attractive* (58, 64, 515, etc.)

gay *go* (*to gay*, "went": 2158)

geir, gere *belongings* (1109, 1360, 2612, etc.)

gentrice *courtesy* (1312, 1461, 1895)

gif, giff, gife, geif, geve *give* (444, 507, 606, etc.)

gif, giff, gife, gyf, geve *if* (40, 103, 207, etc.)

gled *kite* (1175, 1280, 2896, etc.)

greit *weep* (314, 780)

grit, greit, grete, gret *great* (9, 86, 89, etc.)

gude, gud *good* (144, 1040, 1599, etc.)

haill, hale *whole, unharmed* (603, 1605, 1030, etc.)

haill *hail* (*Testament* 6)

haill, heill *completely* (2290; *Robene* 85, etc.); *health, well-being* (*Robene* 113)

hair *hare* (903, 1778, 2242)

hair, hoir, hore *white, frosty* (1292, 1700; *Testament* 163, etc.)

hair, haire *hair* (489, 954; *Orpheus* 159, etc.)

happie *lucky* (132, 302, 1065)

hecht *promise* (noun: 2248, 2342, 2343, etc.; verb: 527, 2250, 2275, etc.)

hecht, hicht *be named* (1375; *Testament* 213; *Orpheus* 295, etc.)

heill *heel, hoof* (1019, 1060, 2065, etc.)

hes *has, have* (75, 99, 120, etc.; *Testament* 60, 89, etc.)

heuch *crag, ravine, glen* (745)

hie, he, hye *high* (60, 200, 1156, etc.)

hie *raise* (938)

hy *haste* (noun: 1017, 1551, 2075, etc.)

hy *hasten* (verb: 747, 846, 2417, etc.)

hint *grab, grabbed* (329, 480, 2145, etc.)

ilk *each, every* (667, 1675, 2432, etc.; *Orpheus* 24, 525, etc.)

incontinent *immediately* (860, 1424, *Hasty* 36)

influence *celestial downflow* (645; *Testament* 149, 201)

intill *in, into* (411, 820, 1545, etc.)

iwis *indeed* (27, 1662, 2690, etc.)

jolie, joly *pleasing* (62, 69, 120, etc.)

keip, kepe *protect, keep* (215, 350, etc.)
kyith *show* (191, 2479)
kynd, kynde *variety* (885, 899, 920, etc.)

laif *remainder* (1054, 1419, 2090, etc.)
lair, lare *lore; school, learning* (648; *Robene* 17)
law *law* (731, 1189, 1204, etc.)
law *hill* (842)
law *low* (adjective: 2725; *Orpheus* 488; adverb: 113, 921, 1021, etc.)
law *bring down* (942; *Abbey* 55)
leid *person* (2283; *Testament* 449)
leid *people* (2022; *Testament* 451, 480)
leid *lead, govern* (502, 540, 821, etc.)
leid *lead* (the metal: 1098, 1308; *Orpheus* 351, etc.)
leif, lef *beloved* (89; *Orpheus* 524)
leif *leaf* (1580; *Testament* 238; *Robene* 66, etc.)
leif *permission, departure* (29, 353, 726, etc.)
leif, leve *leave, relinquish* (614, 2328; *Orpheus* 510, etc.)
leif *allow* (1964)
leif, leve, lyve *live* (104, 393, 508, etc.)
let, lat, lett *allow* (332, 522, 714, etc.); *stop* (246, 1005, 1388, etc.); *hinder* (341)

ma, mo *more* (1716, 1891, *Praise* 10)
may, ma *may, can* (87, 88, 98, etc.)
mair, mar, mare, moir, more *greater, more* (adjective: 173, 1107, 1251, etc.; adverb: 130, 141, etc.)
man *man* (4, 7, 50, etc.)
man, mon, mone *must* (594, 740, 787, etc.)
mane, mone *lament* (1530, 1555; *Testament* 406, etc.)
mane *manè* (*Testament* 211)
mane *strength* (2890)

markit *proceeded* (356, 1822)
marrow *companion, adversary* (2917, 2925, 2933)
mater *topic* (159, 1103; *Orpheus* 241); *case* (1209; *Testament* 303)
mavis, maveis *song-thrush* (871, 1338, 1710, etc.)
mede, meid *reward* (1241, 1306, 2720, etc.)
meir *mare* (1002, 1022, 1026, etc.)
meit, mete *food* (62, 95, 103, etc.)
meit *suitable* (2481; *Garmont* 22, etc.); *suitably* (760; *Sum Practysis* 7)
meit *meet* (1043, 1959, 2091, etc.)
mekill, mekle *much, great* (84, 96, 1733, etc.)
mend *amend, remedy, heal* (652; *Testament* 476; *Orpheus* 176, etc.)
merle, merll *blackbird* (871, 1338, 1710, etc.)
micht, mycht *power* (468, 918, 929, etc.)
micht, mycht, mocht *might, could* (103, 152, 288, etc.)
mis, mys *crime* (1309, 2670; *Praise* 30, etc.)
mis *fail to get* (1813)
moralitie, moralitee *moral, lesson* (366, 1381, 1387, etc.)

nice *haughty* (591); *extravagant* (*Testament* 220); *intricate* (2722; *Sum Practysis* 72)
nicht *night* (257, 403, 417, etc.)

of, off *off* (1091, 2480, 2493, etc.)
of, off *of, out of, about, for* (1, 3, 4, etc.)
or *before* (222, 258, 549, etc.)
or *or* (41, 81, 91, etc.)
over, our *too* (1428, 1644, 2551, etc.)
over, our *across* (152, 2784, 2803, etc.)

pane, payne, paine *suffering* (334, 833, 1142, etc.); *punishment* (865, 2670, 2768, etc.)
pece, peis, pes *peace* (1800, 2731; *Orpheus* 181, etc.)

pecis, peisis *pieces* (1695; *Orpheus* 108, 535)

pley *legal action* (1177, 1190, 1227, etc.)

pleid *dispute* (582, 1236, 2661)

ply *condition, plight* (313, 2005; *Testament* 501, etc.)

pray *prey* (582, 1813, 2259)

pray *pray* (39, 668, 1319, etc.)

preif, pruf *test* (31, 2305, 2577, etc.)

preis, pres *try, strive, push* (156, 1114, 2207, etc.)

pretend *volunteer, profess, make an excuse* (711, 1457, 2691, etc.)

provyde *predict* (1607); *prepare* (1739, 1758, etc.)

pure, peur, peure *poverty-stricken* (65, 181, 659, etc.)

quhile, quhyle, quhyll *a little while* (1213, 2219; *Orpheus* 399, etc.)

quhile, quhyle, quhilis, quhylis *at one time* (166, 193, 194, etc.)

quhill *until* (195, 258, 288, etc.)

quit, quyte *repay, repaid* (1548, 1557, 1599)

quyte *free* (527, 2085, 2352, etc.)

quyte *completely* (2167; *Robene* 106)

raith *quickly* (1001, 2248)

rax *grow strong* (539, 820, 1108, etc.)

rede, reid *advise* (983, 1748, 1857, etc.)

reheirs, rehers *repeat* (119, 1283; *Orpheus* 7, etc.)

reid *advice* (300, 1883)

reid, rede *red* (1034, 1061; *Testament* 464, etc.)

reif *robbery* (686, 822, 2430, etc.)

reif *rob, seize* (2279; *Orpheus* 584; *Robene* 49)

remove, remufe *depart* (1857, 1945; *Garmont* 16, etc.)

rent *property, revenue* (832, 2763; *Orpheus* 343)

rent *torn* (*Testament* 578; *Orpheus* 560; *Prayer* 39)

reson, ressone, ressoun *reason, statement* (394, 1123, 2692, etc.)

rew *repent, pity* (2552; *Orpheus* 407; *Robene* 4, etc.)

ring *ring* (*Testament* 582, 592, 594, etc.)

ring, regne *reign* (131, 820, 1108, etc.)

ron, rone *underbrush* (897, 1001, 1335, etc.)

roun *whisper* (2031; *Testament* 529; *Hasty* 21)

rude *cross* (1817, 2346, 2582, etc.)

rude *complexion* (*Orpheus* 354)

rude *rough* (36, 119, 2013, etc.)

sa, so, swa *so, as* (9, 12, 17, etc.)

sad *serious, steadfast* (26, 1100; *Testament* 567)

saikles, sakeles *guiltless* (2664, *Annunciation* 48; *Hasty* 52)

sair, soir, sore *disease, sore spot* (*Testament* 411; *Orpheus* 409); *painful* (346, 495, 1137, etc.); *grievously* (310, 319, 426, etc.)

sall *shall, will, ought to* (63, 119, etc.)

sang *song* (515, 1581, 1877, etc.)

sarie, sorie, sory *miserable, vile* (277, 1493, 1938, etc.)

saull, saul, saule, sawll *soul* (140, 158, 211, etc.)

saw *sow, plant* (147, 1913, etc.)

scaith, skaith *damage* (167, 2178, 2864, etc.)

schaw *thicket* (419, 1347, 1621, etc.)

schaw *show* (247, 681, 1173, etc.)

schent *damaged, punished* (960, 1983, 2191, etc.)

schir *sir* (436, 455, 686, etc.)

scho *she* (174, 176, 177, etc.)

science *knowledge* (137, 143, 148, etc.)

seill *happiness* (*Garmont* 38)

seill *seal* (696, 1707, 2395, etc.)

selie, sely, silie, sillie *pitiful* (204, 299, 334, etc.)

sen *since* (520, 527, 705, etc.)

sic, sik *such* (203, 226, 245, etc.)

syis *times* (192, 1882; *Testament* 525)

sin, syn *sin* (537, 653, 793, etc.)

syne *then* (55, 196, 315, etc.)

sis *assize, jury* (1087)

slaik, slak, slake *mitigate, satisfy* (526, 2619; *Orpheus* 281, etc.)

slaik *little valley* (1835)

sle *subtle* (667, 2913)

sleuth, slewth *sloth* (1326, 1579; *Prayer* 68)

slicht *technique, deceit* (471, 1297)

slidder, slidderie *slippery* (1835, 2608)

slide *move quietly* (908, 2511); *slip* (*Garmont* 34)

solace *pleasure, comfort* (*Orpheus* 88, 151)

sone *soon* (2255)

speid *succeed, hasten* (125, 895, 2438, etc.)

speir *ask* (1051, 2909, 2969, etc.)

speir *spear* (517; *Testament* 161, 181)

spheir, spere *sphere* (631, 1659; *Testament* 254, etc.)

spreit *spirit* (21, 698, 971, etc.)

stait, state *status, circumstances* (369, 711, 986, etc.)

stane, stone *stone* (199, 1393, 1611, etc.)

stark *strong* (123, 132; *Ressoning Aige* 59, etc.)

steid *place* (2141, 2181; *Orpheus* 142, etc.)

steid *steed* (898; *Testament* 213)

steir *govern* (1578; *Testament* 149)

steir *movement* (2066)

still, styll *motionless* (620, 737, 1412, etc.)

straitlie, straitly *strictly* (863, 1158; *Bludy Serk* 112, etc.)

suld, sowld *had to* (82, 85, 106, etc.)

suppois, suppose *believe* (295, 1573); *even if* (359, 586, 784, etc.)

sweit *sweet, gentle* (3, 12, 16, 186, etc.)

ta, tak *take, receive* (53, 60, 1008, etc.)

taill, tale *story, talk* (1063, 1146, 1389, etc.)

tais *toes* (465, 467, 2061, etc.)

tene, teyne *anger* (2098, 2475; *Testament* 194); *angry* (2103; *Annunciation* 68)

thift *theft* (822, 978, 1089, etc.)

thig *beg* (710, 2741); *ask* (2037)

thir *these* (191, 204, 1670, etc.)

thocht, thoucht *thought* (1125, 1818, 1864, etc.)

thocht, thouch *though* (1, 15, 80, etc.)

thoill, thole, tholl *suffer, endure, allow* (969, 1306, 1313, etc.)

throw, throu, throuch, throwch *through* (840, 54, etc.)

tyke *mongrel* (1045, 1082, 2065, etc.)

tyne *lose* (2190, 2269, 2320, etc.)

tod *fox* (425, 543, 565, etc.)

toun, town, towne *farm* (426, 2473); *town* (181, 259, 1253, etc.)

trew, trewe *true, faithful* (826, 1276; *Bludy Serk* 48, etc.)

twa, tway, two *two* (163, 191, 450, etc.)

untill *to* (723, 1352, 1494)

use *custom, habit* (786, 1153, 1909, etc.)

use *be accustomed* (381; *Testament* 111); *consume* (1490)

wait *knows* (525, 649, 710, etc.)

wait, wate, watt *knew* (525, 649, 710, etc.)

wait *watch out* (763, 1610)

walk *wake, guard* (1296, 1925, 2458)

walk *walk* (183; *Testament* 429; *Robene* 100, etc.)

walterand, welterand *rolling* (736, 1524, 2955, etc.)

wame *belly* (101, 223, 382, etc.); *womb* (214, *Annunciation* 17)

wand *staff* (1269; *Testament* 311, *Annunciation* 43); *branch* (179, *Ressoning Aige* 13)

wane *dwelling* (197, 260; *Bludy Serk* 24, etc.)

wane *hope* (2081; *Testament* 543)

wane *decrease* (*Ressoning Aige* 63)

want *lack* (471, 712, 2099, etc.)

war *worse* (805, 2650, 2736, etc.)

war *alert* (480, 789, 1859, etc.)

war, wair, wer, were *were* (191; *Orpheus* 20, 84)

way *path* (424, 677, 722, etc.)

weir *war* (1316, 1478, 1946, etc.)

weit, wete *wet weather* (1584, 1833; *Garmont* 24, etc.)

well *well, spring, stream* (2392, 2423, 2450, etc.)

wend *go* (709, 794, 1264, etc.)

wene *suppose* (2007, 2010, 2218, etc.)

wicht *strong* (1689, 2108, 2183, etc.)

wicht *creature* (*Testament* 435; *Orpheus* 294; *Bludy Serk* 63)

wilsum, wilsome *lonely* (183; *Orpheus* 155, 245, 290)

wirschip, worschip *honor* (109, 476, 981, etc.)

wit *understanding* (1623, 2490; *Orpheus* 55, etc.)

wit *know* (860, 929, 1613, etc.)

wo, wa *woe* (352, 1930, 2465, etc.)

wod, wode, woid, wood *forest* (481, 553; *Robene* 11, etc.)

woid, wod, woude *insane* (488, 591, 736, etc.)

wraith *anger* (1463, 2007; *Testament* 182); *angry* (2023, 2168, 2179, etc.)

wrangous, wrangus, wrangwis unjust (806, 979, 1250, etc.)

wyse, wyis *way, manner* (1352, 2690; *Testament* 92, etc.)

yede, yeid, yude *went* (196, 252, 364, etc.)

yone *that* (348, 349, 2853, etc.)

Stanzaic Guy of Warwick, edited by Alison Wiggins (2004)

Saints' Lives in Middle English Collections, edited by E. Gordon Whatley, with Anne B. Thompson and
Robert K. Upchurch (2004)

Siege of Jerusalem, edited by Michael Livingston (2004)

The Kingis Quair and Other Prison Poems, edited by Linne R. Mooney and Mary-Jo Arn (2005)

The Chaucerian Apocrypha: A Selection, edited by Kathleen Forni (2005)

John Gower, *The Minor Latin Works*, edited and translated by R. F. Yeager, with *In Praise of Peace*, edited
by Michael Livingston (2005)

*Sentimental and Humorous Romances: Floris and Blancheflour, Sir Degrevant, The Squire of Low Degree,
The Tournament of Tottenham, and The Feast of Tottenham*, edited by Erik Kooper (2006)

The Dicts and Sayings of the Philosophers, edited by John William Sutton (2006)

Everyman and Its Dutch Original, Elckerlijc, edited by Clifford Davidson, Martin W. Walsh, and Ton
J. Broos (2007)

The N-Town Plays, edited by Douglas Sugano, with assistance by Victor I. Scherb (2007)

The Book of John Mandeville, edited by Tamarah Kohanski and C. David Benson (2007)

John Lydgate, *The Temple of Glas*, edited by J. Allan Mitchell (2007)

The Northern Homily Cycle, edited by Anne B. Thompson (2008)

Codex Ashmole 61: A Compilation of Popular Middle English Verse, edited by George Shuffelton (2008)

Chaucer and the Poems of "Ch," edited by James I. Wimsatt (revised edition 2009)

William Caxton, *The Game and Playe of the Chesse*, edited by Jenny Adams (2009)

John the Blind Audelay, *Poems and Carols*, edited by Susanna Fein (2009)

Two Moral Interludes: The Pride of Life and Wisdom, edited by David Klausner (2009)

John Lydgate, *Mummings and Entertainments*, edited by Claire Sponsler (2010)

Mankind, edited by Kathleen M. Ashley and Gerard NeCastro (2010)

The Castle of Perseverance, edited by David N. Klausner (2010)

COMMENTARY SERIES

Haimo of Auxerre, *Commentary on the Book of Jonah*, translated with an introduction and notes by
Deborah Everhart (1993)

Medieval Exegesis in Translation: Commentaries on the Book of Ruth, translated with an introduction and
notes by Lesley Smith (1996)

Nicholas of Lyra's Apocalypse Commentary, translated with an introduction and notes by Philip D. W.
Krey (1997)

Rabbi Ezra Ben Solomon of Gerona, *Commentary on the Song of Songs and Other Kabbalistic Commentaries*, selected, translated, and annotated by Seth Brody (1999)

John Wyclif, *On the Truth of Holy Scripture*, translated with an introduction and notes by Ian Christopher Levy (2001)

Second Thessalonians: Two Early Medieval Apocalyptic Commentaries, introduced and translated by Steven
R. Cartwright and Kevin L. Hughes (2001)

The "Glossa Ordinaria" on the Song of Songs, translated with an introduction and notes by Mary Dove
(2004)

The Seven Seals of the Apocalypse: Medieval Texts in Translation, translated with an introduction and notes
by Francis X. Gumerlock (2009)

DOCUMENTS OF PRACTICE SERIES

Love and Marriage in Late Medieval London, selected, translated, and introduced by Shannon McSheffrey (1995)

Sources for the History of Medicine in Late Medieval England, selected, introduced, and translated by
Carole Rawcliffe (1995)

A Slice of Life: Selected Documents of Medieval English Peasant Experience, edited, translated, and with an
introduction by Edwin Brezette DeWindt (1996)

Regular Life: Monastic, Canonical, and Mendicant "Rules," selected and introduced by Douglas J.
McMillan and Kathryn Smith Fladenmuller (1997); second edition, selected and introduced by
Daniel Marcel La Corte and Douglas J. McMillan (2004)

Women and Monasticism in Medieval Europe: Sisters and Patrons of the Cistercian Reform, selected, translated, and with an introduction by Constance H. Berman (2002)

Medieval Notaries and Their Acts: The 1327–1328 Register of Jean Holanie, introduced, edited, and translated by Kathryn L. Reyerson and Debra A. Salata (2004)

🖋 MEDIEVAL GERMAN TEXTS IN BILINGUAL EDITIONS SERIES

Sovereignty and Salvation in the Vernacular, 1050–1150, introduction, translations, and notes by James A. Schultz (2000)

Ava's New Testament Narratives: "When the Old Law Passed Away," introduction, translation, and notes by James A. Rushing, Jr. (2003)

History as Literature: German World Chronicles of the Thirteenth Century in Verse, introduction, translation, and notes by R. Graeme Dunphy (2003)

Thomasin von Zirclaria, *Der Welsche Gast (The Italian Guest)*, translated by Marion Gibbs and Winder McConnell (2009)

🖋 VARIA

The Study of Chivalry: Resources and Approaches, edited by Howell Chickering and Thomas H. Seiler (1988)

Studies in the Harley Manuscript: The Scribes, Contents, and Social Contexts of British Library MS Harley 2253, edited by Susanna Fein (2000)

The Liturgy of the Medieval Church, edited by Thomas J. Heffernan and E. Ann Matter (2001; second edition 2005)

🖋 TO ORDER PLEASE CONTACT:

Medieval Institute Publications
Western Michigan University
Kalamazoo, MI 49008-5432
Phone (269) 387-8755
FAX (269) 387-8750
http://www.wmich.edu/medieval/mip/index.html

Typeset in 10/13 New Baskerville
and Golden Cockerel Ornaments display
Designed by Linda K. Judy
Manufactured by Cushing-Malloy, Inc.

Medieval Institute Publications
College of Arts and Sciences
Western Michigan University
1903 W. Michigan Avenue
Kalamazoo, MI 49008-5432
http:/ /www.wmich.edu/medieval/mip

 WESTERN MICHIGAN UNIVERSITY